每天聊点英国文化

一本书读懂英国

金利 主编

范芙蓉 杨云云 副主编

化学工业出版社

·北京·

我们从小受到东方文化的熏陶，即使学了很多年英语，一般只是应试性的"背单词、学语法"。当我们读国外文章或看英文电影，甚至是去英国留学时，有时会无法理解老外的思考方式，觉得他们的笑话很"冷"，行为也非常"怪诞"。英国文化对我们来说仿佛是罩着一层神秘的面纱，其实我们并不了解英国文化。

学习英语很多年，对老外的口头禅、特色俚语表达只是懂其"中文意思"，却不知道它们真正的来源以及地道准确的用法；很多时候背诵的单词都缺乏语言环境，导致大家记忆都不够深刻。不用担心！本书将填补各位读者在学习英语过程中的缺憾，带你追根溯源，让你在一边欣赏英国风光景色、品读趣味文化的同时，一边记下难以消化的单词和特色表达，"夸夸其谈"英国文化！

【近距离看英国】

通过这本书，最具英国特色的爱丁堡艺术节、伦敦的大本钟、圣保罗大教堂等英国文化标志在你面前通通"现身"，让你近距离了解它们。此外，我们还会带大家走进英国各大高校、了解英国国旗的由来、一睹建筑历史文化遗产"巨石阵"的奇特，为你"捅破"英国文化这层窗纸，让你对英国文化有更深入的了解。

【地毯式涵盖英国文化】

本书围绕10大分类，80个主题，涵盖了英国的多元文化、教育制度、优美风光、风土人情、民间习俗等方方面面，此外还会在每个主题里就相关内容进行延展，形式丰富，增强本书的可读性和趣味性；拓展形式有相关的名人轶事、特色景点、特色表达、历史事件的讲解。

【边品英国文化边学英语】

针对每个主题，我们从国外网站选取地道的英文素材，语言地道，且附有中文翻译和生词讲解，让你在品读英国文化的同时也学到英语知识。在对英国文化背景进行中英双讲之后，对主题相关的特色俚语和与特色表达进行深度讲解，让你知道它们的"来源"。此外，我们还会拓展与主题相关的特色英语句子，最后会与你一起用地道的英语侃谈英国文化。

这本书精心制作给对英国文化有浓厚兴趣的爱好者以及想提高口语能力的英语学习者。衷心希望此书能给你带来更精彩、更美好的生活！

编者

目录

Part 1 英国为何不可复制

Part 2 这些culture shock,有没有

Part 3 感受英伦风情的英国游

Part 4 特色英国节日"来头"大

Part 5 那些年我们追过的影视作品

Part 6 品读英国的教育

Part 7 不可不去的英国特色地标

Part 8 不可不知的英国名人

Part 9 英国人生活面面观

Part 10 穿越回去看看英国历史

Part 1

英国为何不可复制

England就是英国的全称吗

英国全称是这样的

The United Kingdom of Great Britain and Northern Ireland, commonly known as the United Kingdom (UK) or Britain, is a *sovereign* state located off the north-western coast of *continental* Europe. The country includes the island of Great Britain (a term sometimes *loosely* applied to the whole state), the north-eastern part of the island of Ireland, and many smaller islands.

So here is the difference between the United Kingdom, Great Britain, and England. Great Britain is the name of the island northwest of France and east of Ireland which *consists of* three somewhat *autonomous* regions: England, Wales and Scotland. Therefore, England is part of Great Britain, which is part of the United Kingdom. The U.K. includes Great Britain and Northern Ireland. England, Wales, Scotland, and Northern Ireland are not independent countries but the United Kingdom is.

ENGLAND

大不列颠及北爱尔兰联合王国，又称为联合王国或英国，是一个主权独立国，位于欧洲大陆西北部。它由大不列颠岛（在不严谨的情况下，有时也用来指整个国家）、爱尔兰岛的东北部和许多较小的岛屿构成。

英国、大不列颠以及英格兰所指的地区是有区别的。大不列颠指的是法国以西以北的岛屿以及爱尔兰岛的东部，它包括3个自治区：英格兰、威尔士以及苏格兰。因此，英格兰是大不列颠的一部分，而大不列颠是英国的一部分。英国由英格兰、威尔士、苏格兰以及北爱尔兰组成。英格兰、威尔士、苏格兰以及北爱尔兰不是独立的国家，英国才是。

单词释义

sovereign 有主权的	continental 大陆的	loosely 不严谨的
consist of 由……构成	autonomous 自治的	

"England" 名字的由来

The name "England" is *derived from* the Old English name Englaland, which means "land of the Angles". The Angles were one of the Germanic *tribes* that settled in Great Britain during the Early Middle Ages. The Angles came from the Angeln *peninsula* in the Bay of Kiel area of the Baltic Sea. According to the *Oxford English Dictionary*, the first known use of "England" to refer to the southern part of the island of Great Britain occurs in 897, and its modern spelling was first used in 1538.

The area now called England was first *inhabited* by modern humans during the Upper Palaeolithic period, but it takes its name from the Angles. England became a *unified* state in 927 AD, and since the Age of Discovery, which began during the 15th century, has had a *significant* cultural and legal impact on the wider world. The English language, the Anglican Church, and English law—the basis for the common law legal systems of many other countries around the world—developed in England, and the country's *parliamentary* system of government has been widely *adopted* by other nations.

英格兰（England）这个名字来源于古英语Englaland，它表示"盎格鲁人的土地"。盎格鲁人来自波罗的海基尔湾地区的安格尔恩半岛。盎格鲁人为日耳曼部落中的分支，最早于中世纪早期定居于大不列颠岛。根据《牛津英语词典》，首次用"英格兰（England）"来指大不列颠岛南部地区的时间是公元897年，而其现代拼写首次出现在1538年。

在旧石器时代后期，现代人最早开始居住于现在被称为英格兰的地区，但是它的得名源于盎格鲁人。公元927年，英格兰成为了一个统一的国家，且自15世纪的大发现时代开始，它在文化上以及司法上对越来越广阔的世界有着重要的影响。源于英格兰的英语、英国国教、英国司法体制（它是世界上许多国家司法体系的基础）以及英国的议会制已经被其他国家广泛采用。

单词释义

derive from 起源于　　tribe 部落　　　　peninsula 半岛
inhabit 居住　　　　unified 统一的　　significant 重大的
parliamentary 议会的　adopt 采用

"品" 英国特色文化

特色表达One

英格兰（England）这个名字来源于古英语Englaland，而并非英国人sleep on it思考出来的，这里的sleep on it可并不是说"睡在上面"，而是指人"彻夜思考；再三权衡"，相当于think it over。

实景链接

A：Mark, the sales manager position is available in England, and we'd like you to take it. 马克，英格兰的销售经理一职还空着，我们希望你能坐上这个位置。

B：Thank you, but I can't decide right now. **Can I sleep on it**? 谢谢，但我现在定不下来。能让我考虑一下吗？

A：Can you give me an answer tomorrow? 明天能给我答复吗？

B：Of course. 当然可以。

特色表达Two

如果有人要问你英国的全称为何是U.K.，你只需要说it's a long story，这可不是说名字的由来是一个很长的故事，而是说当你想讲一件事情却又不知道从何说起时，可以用到此句，引申为"一言难尽；说来话长"。

实景链接

A：Why do you pretend to be Jenny's boyfriend? 你为什么要冒充珍妮的男朋友？

B：**It's a long story**. I'll tell you some other time. 一言难尽。我改天再告诉你。

A：Then just make it short. I really want to know the truth. 那就简而言

之，我真的很想知道真相。

B: Well, Jenny can't find a good reason to break up with David, so... 好吧，珍妮找不到和大卫分手的正当理由，所以……

拓展特色句

1. England is not an independent country. 英格兰不是一个独立的国家。

2. Three divisions on the island of Great Britain: England, Scotland and Wales. 大不列颠岛分为三块区域：英格兰、苏格兰和威尔士。

3. I'm Daniel in Scotland, UK. 我叫丹尼尔，来自英联合王国的苏格兰。

"聊" 英国特色文化

A: Hey, Tom, could you help me?

B: Sure, what's up?

A: I'm so confused. Why are there so many names referring to the U.K.? You see, there are the United Kingdom of Great Britain and Northern Ireland, England, the United Kingdom, and Great Britain.

B: Oh, it's not so difficult. The United Kingdom of Great Britain and Northern Ireland, for short, is the United Kingdom. And Great Britain is part of the U.K., 'cause the United Kingdom consists of Great Britain and Northern Ireland.

A: I'm still kind of confused. What about England? Is it the nickname of the United Kingdom?

B: No. As I just mentioned, the United Kingdom consists of Great Britain and Northern Ireland; and Great Britain includes England, Wales, and Scotland.

A: Oh, I got it. So the United Kingdom consists of England, Wales, Scotland,

A: 嘿，汤姆，能帮我个忙吗？

B: 当然，怎么了？

A: 我很困惑，英国怎么有这么多名字？你看，我们既可以用大不列颠及北爱尔兰联合王国、英格兰，又可以用联合王国以及大不列颠来指英国。

B: 哦，这没有什么难的。大不列颠及北爱尔兰联合王国的简称就是联合王国。英国由大不列颠以及北爱尔兰组成，所以大不列颠是英国的一部分。

A: 我还是有点儿疑惑，那英格兰呢？它是英国的昵称吗？

B: 不，正如我刚才所说的，英国由大不列颠以及北爱尔兰组成，而大不列颠则由英格兰、威尔士以及苏格兰组成。

A: 哦，我明白了。所以说英国是由英格兰、威尔士、苏格兰以及北爱尔

and Northern Ireland, right?

B：Yeah, you're right.

兰组成，对吗？

B：是的，你说得没错。

"问" 英国特色文化

英国国名和英伦三岛是什么关系？

英国这个国家由许多大大小小的岛屿组成，它是一个多岛的国家，但是这个国家主要分为三个部分，即所谓的"英伦三岛"：中部与南部是英格兰，北部是苏格兰，西南部是威尔士。其中英格兰面积最大，拥有全国80％的人口，是全国政治、经济、文化的中心，这也是为什么大家习惯上用英格兰泛指"英国"。此外，英国在海外殖民地的总称是大英帝国（The British Empire）。

阅读笔记

"英国绅士"代名词从何而来

"绅士"一词从这里来

In modern speech the term gentleman refers to any man of good, *courteous* conduct. It may also refer to all men *collectively*, as in *indications* of gender-separated facilities, or as a sign of the speaker's own courtesy when addressing others.

In its original meaning, the term *denoted* a man of the lowest rank of the English *gentry*, standing below an *esquire* and above a *yeoman*. By definition, this category included the younger sons of the younger sons of peers and the younger sons of *baronets*, knights, and esquires in *perpetual* succession, and thus the term captures the common denominator of gentility shared by both constituents of the English aristocracy: the peerage and the gentry. In this sense, the word equates with the French gentilhomme ("nobleman"), which latter term has been, in Great Britain, long confined to the peerage.

现在来说，"绅士"这一词常用来指行为优雅有礼的男士。"绅士"还可在表示性别时或者演讲者开始演讲前礼貌称呼别人时用来指全体男士。

"绅士"这一词原意是指英国上流社会中最低的一个等级，低于骑士但高于自由民。根据定义，这个阶层的人包括公、侯、伯、子、男爵的孙辈，以及男爵、爵士以及骑士的儿子，且绅士采取的是永久世袭制。因此，"绅士"拥有英国广大的上流阶层人士的共同特性：贵族头衔与绅士身份。从这个意义上来，"gentleman（绅士）"这一词相当于法语中的gentilhomme(即"nobleman")，后来这个表达在大不列颠常用来指贵族。

单词释义

courteous 有礼貌的　　collectively 全体地　　indication 标志
denote 表示　　　　　gentry 上流人士　　　yeoman 自由民
baronet 男爵　　　　　perpetual 永久的

学着做英国绅士

Traditional British *etiquette* is hard to find in today's modern society. As Sir Patrick Moore once said, the *height* of Englishness is "good manners". Many of us would like to think that we are quite polite. Yet, it seems the ushering in of the modern era has long *deteriorated* the British etiquette we find in films such as *Brief Encounter* and *Breakfast at Tiffany's*.

How to be a perfect English Gentleman then? Step one: Dress *appropriately* for special occasions and outings. That doesn't mean wearing *tuxedos* everywhere. Unless it's required for an occasion of course. Just wear some nice pants with a belt, a clean shirt (tucked in), and good-looking shoes. Step two: Use high quality *hygienic* products. Also consider a nice cologne and possibly some hair gel occasionally. Step three: Be courteous to everyone. Especially women. Open doors for people, shake hands. Step four: Have good table manners. Nobody likes eating with a *slob*! Wipe your mouth with a napkin, don't *belch*, etc. Step five: Have intelligent conversations with people. It adds charm. Just don't talk about personal subjects like money.

在当今这个现代社会，传统的英国礼仪很难被发现。帕特里克·摩尔爵士曾经说过，英国风格的高贵在于"优良的举止"。我们中的许多人会觉得我们非常有礼貌，但是，现代社会的到来毁坏了我们在电影《相见恨晚》以及《蒂凡尼早餐》中看到的英国礼仪。

那怎样才能成为一个完美的英国绅士呢？第一步，出席特殊场合的时候，着装得体。这并不是要求你在任何地方都穿着小礼服，除非是特殊场合。穿一些漂亮的配有腰带的裤子、干净的衬衫（塞在裤子里）以及漂亮的鞋。第二步，使用高端卫生用品，还应考虑使用好闻的古龙香水。如果可能的话，还可以偶尔使用一些发胶。第三步，对所有人都应该非常有礼貌，特别是对女士。帮别人开门，跟别人握手。第四步，要有良好的餐桌礼仪。没人喜欢与粗俗的人一块吃饭！注意用餐巾擦嘴，不要打嗝等。第五步，聪明地与人交谈。这会增加你的个人魅力。不要把话题局限于诸如金钱类的比较隐私的内容。

单词释义

etiquette 礼仪　　　　　height 高贵　　　　　appropriately 合适地

tuxedo 小礼服　　　　　hygienic 卫生的　　　　slob 粗俗的人

belch 打嗝　　　　　　　deteriorate 使……恶化

"品"英国特色文化

特色表达One

英国的绅士一直备受大家尊重，但是其实他们并非来源于blue blood，blue blood并不是其字面意思"蓝色血液"，而是用来代指"贵族血统"。古代西班牙北部有一个王国名叫卡斯提尔，其最古老的家族都以拥有纯正血统为荣，他们相信自己的血统从未被摩尔人、犹太人等"异族"血统"扰乱"过，证据就是他们白皙的皮肤上凸显的微微发蓝的静脉血管。后来西班牙语sangre azul就被直译为blue blood，表示"贵族血统"。

实景链接

A: He has a fair bit of **blue blood** coursing through his veins. 他的血管里真的流淌着贵族的血液。

B: Actually by nature all men are alike. 事实上每个人生下来都是一样的。

A: That being said, however, he is really a gentleman. 话虽如此，但是他真的很绅士。

B: That's two things. 那又是另一码事。

特色表达Two

一提到英国绅士，就会联想起西装笔挺、外形俊俏的帅哥，用beefcake这个词来形容他们再适合不过了。beefcake可不是牛肉饼，作俚语时是"英俊男子"的意思，与其对应的是cheesecake，用来形容"漂亮的美女"。

实景链接

A: Hi! What are you talking about? 嗨！你们在聊什么呢？

B: Oh, we are talking about Hollywood **beefcake**. Who do you like? 噢，我们在讨论好莱坞的大帅哥。你喜欢谁？

A: I think Bred Pitt is a beefcake guy! 我觉得布拉德·皮特很帅！

B: Well no duh! 谁说不是呢！

拓展特色句

1. Tom behaved as a typical English gentleman. 汤姆的行为像是一个典型的英国绅士。

2. Typical English gentleman always brings an umbrella with him in my impression. 在我的印象中，典型的英国绅士总是带着一把雨伞。

3. It seems that the English gentry is next below the nobility. 英国绅士的地位好像仅次于贵族。

"聊" 英国特色文化

A: He's really a gentleman. Do you think so?

B: Yes. You know there is a course to train you to be a gentleman.

A: It sounds interesting. Why does everyone want to be a gentleman?

B: Because they are charming and attractive. Women like them of this sort.

A: Then how to be a gentleman?

B: First of all, you should pay attention to your dressing. You should dress appropriately according to different occasions.

A: OK. I got it. Then what?

B: Use high quality hygienic products and perfume.

A: What kind of perfume should I choose?

B: It's up to you. But I think nice cologne is a good choice.

A: Anything else?

B: Remember to be courteous to everyone especially women.

A: OK. Thank you.

A: 他真是一个绅士。你觉得呢？

B: 是啊。你知道现在有训练绅士的课程。

A: 听起来很有趣。为什么人人都想成为绅士呢？

B: 因为他们有魅力和吸引力。女士喜欢这种类型的。

A: 那么如何成为一名绅士呢？

B: 首先，你得注意着装。你应该根据不同的场合选择合适的着装。

A: 好的。我明白了。那么然后呢？

B: 使用高品质的卫生用品和香水。

A: 我应该选择什么样的香水呢？

B: 这取决于你。但是我认为好闻的古龙香水是一个不错的选择。

A: 还有其他的吗？

B: 记得对所有人都应该礼貌，尤其是女士。

A: 好的。谢谢。

"问"英国特色文化

英国男人真的很"绅士"吗？

但凡提到英国男人，似乎全世界的人都会联想到"绅士"这个词，这种印象来自英国悠久的历史和传统，即便在泰坦尼克号即将沉没的时刻，也是women and children first，英国男人的绅士风度可见一斑。但是为什么也有很多人会质疑英国男人在二次见面时会变得冷漠？大体分为两种原因，一种是因为他们真的把你当朋友而觉得不需要像第一面那样特别客气；还有一种则是因为英国男人属于慢热型，需要时间来慢慢了解。

阅读笔记

黑暗料理王国

英国食物基本是这样的

In the Early Modern Period, the food of England was *historically* characterized by its *simplicity* of *approach* and a *reliance* on the high quality of natural produce. It is possible that the effects of this can still be seen in traditional *cuisine*.

Traditional meals have ancient *origins*, such as bread and cheese, roasted and stewed meats, meat and game pies, boiled vegetables and *broths*, and freshwater and saltwater fish. Other meals, such as fish and chips, which were once urban street food eaten from newspaper with salt and malt vinegar, and pies and sausages with mashed potatoes, onions, and gravy, are now matched in popularity by curries from India and Bangladesh, and stir-fries based on Chinese and Thai cuisine. Italian cuisine and French cuisine are also now widely adapted. Britain was also quick to adopt the innovation of fast food from the United States, and continues to absorb *culinary* ideas from all over the world while at the same time rediscovering its roots in sustainable rural agriculture.

在近代早期，英国的食物以制作方法简单、高度依赖高质量的自然产品为主要特点。现在，在传统的饮食中仍能看到这些特点的身影。

传统的食物历史悠久，这些食物有面包与奶酪、烤肉与炖肉、肉馅饼、水煮青菜与肉汤以及淡水鱼与咸水鱼。其他的食物的流行程度不亚于来自印度与孟加拉国的咖喱以及中式或泰式食物中的炒制方法，如撒上盐与麦芽醋用报纸一包的街头小吃炸鱼薯条，以及配有土豆泥、洋葱、肉汁

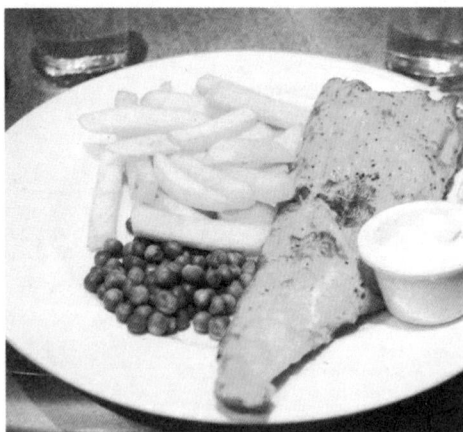

的馅饼与香肠。在英国还能找到很多改良后的意大利与法国食物。此外，英国还很好地引进了美国的快餐文化，并在不断地从世界各地饮食中吸取精华的过程中再开发其依托的可持续发展农业。

单词释义

historically 以往，过去   simplicity 简易   approach 方法
reliance 依赖   cuisine 菜肴   origin 起源
broth 肉汤   culinary 烹饪的

英国美食的独到之处

English cuisine may suffer from a relatively poor international *reputation* when compared to that of French cuisine or Italian cuisine. British eat the most ready meals in Europe. They are unhealthy and rarely taste as good as the *alternative* of cooking food fresh. People often complain that they are too busy to cook from scratch. However, more and more people are choosing to eat healthy, fresh food, *inspired* by *celebrity* chefs who are showing us that cooking doesn't have to be difficult, or even *time-consuming*.

Yet Britain still has a bad reputation for cooking. The author of 'A Fondness for Food' even wrote about "the bland, standard UK diet". Even some people may ask what food came from Britain apart from 'fish and chips'. While with many different cultures and nationalities from all over the world meeting in the UK, some of the most exciting new flavours and ideas in cooking now come from London. Today the UK seems to be

英国美食享有的国际名气也许没有法国料理或意大利美食那么高。英国是欧洲吃快餐最多的国家。这些食物既不健康，也没有现成烹饪的新鲜食物来得美味。英国人总是在抱怨他们没有时间从零开始学习烹饪。然而，受一些名厨的影响，越来越多的人选择新鲜健康的食物，因为这些名厨的烹饪方法让大家看起来既简单又没那么费时。

尽管如此，不列颠人的厨艺依然是出了名的差。《狂爱美食》一书作者甚至还写道"英国菜的标准就是淡而无味"。甚至还会有人问英国除了"炸鱼薯条"之外还有没有其他的美食。然而，来自世界各地的不同民

one of the most exciting places for creative and talented chefs. There are some of the most *renowned* restaurants and some of the most famous international chefs run them.

族、不同文化相聚在这里，许多新奇美味和创意烹调现在源自伦敦。现在的英国或许是创意天才厨师们的宝地之一，这里有不少的最著名餐厅和国际名厨。

单词释义

reputation 声誉　　　　alternative 供选择的　　　　inspire 影响
celebrity 名人　　　　time-consuming 耗时的　　　　renowned 著名的

"品" 英国特色文化

特色表达One

去英国旅行或者留学，我想英国本土的食物对他们而言一定是wet blanket，该短语出自苏格兰小说家约翰·高尔特（John Galt）的小说中，书中说："I have never felt such a wet blanket before or since."也许是由于潮湿的气候，湿毯子会让人感觉不舒服，后人就用a wet blanket指"让人扫兴的人或事"。

☆ 实景链接

A：Have you met Sandra, Jason's new girlfriend? 你见过詹森的新女友桑德拉吗？

B：Yeah, she's really a bit of **wet blanket**. 是的，她让人有些扫兴。

A：What do you mean by that? 这话怎么说？

B：She stayed for a long time, hardly talking to anybody except Jason. 她出现后待了很长时间，除了詹森没和任何人说话。

特色表达Two

英国为何经典的食物就是炸鱼薯条这类的东西，你要让我回答这个问题，可是beat me了，beat me不是"打倒我"的意思，而是"不知道"的意思。我们在表示这个意思的时候，还可以说search me，I don't have a clue，I have no idea或是you got me on that one。

⭐ **实景链接**

A: What time is the party? I am afraid we are late for it. 聚会几点开始? 我担心我们会迟到。

B: **Beats me**! I'd better call Tommy to figure it out. 不知道! 我还是问问汤米把时间搞清楚吧。

A: Go ahead. I have to refine the make-up as soon as possible. 抓紧呀,我也再尽快补补妆。

B: Okay, I will inform you of the time when I know it. 好的,时间定下来我就告诉你。

拓展特色句

1. This meat is too fatty. 这肉太肥了。

2. This food is too heavy on my stomach. 这种食物太难消化了。

3. What do you say about the British cuisine? 对英国食物你怎么看?

"聊" 英国特色文化

A: Have you ever tried authentic English food?

B: No. I heard that English people are not good at cooking.

A: That's true. British eat the most ready meals in Europe. But nowadays they pay more and more attention to their food.

B: What do they usually eat?

A: They have plentiful food for breakfast, including bacon, pudding, omelets, bread, tomatoes and tea.

B: How about lunch?

A: During lunch time most Englishmen choose to eat sandwich and roast potato. In England, people like to have afternoon tea. They have muffins or

A: 你尝试过正宗的英国食物吗?

B: 没有。我听说英国人不擅长烹饪。

A: 是的。英国是欧洲吃快餐最多的国家。但是,现在他们越来越多地关注自己的食物了。

B: 他们通常吃什么?

A: 他们早餐很丰富,包括熏肉、布丁、煎蛋、面包、番茄和茶饮。

B: 午饭呢?

A: 在午餐期间,大部分的英国人吃三明治和烤土豆。在英国,人们喜欢喝下午茶。他们吃松饼和三明治。茶对于英国人而言是很重要的。他们喜欢喝加奶和糖的茶。

sandwiches. Tea is quite important for English people. They would like to have tea with milk and sugar.

B: What about supper?

A: Supper is their main dinner. They prefer to talk when they eat. They usually spend hours on supper. They like to teach children dining etiquette at that time.

B: 晚餐呢?

A: 晚餐是英国人的主餐。他们喜欢边吃边聊。他们通常花费几个小时进餐。喜欢在进餐期间教授孩子进餐礼仪。

"问" 英国特色文化

英国真的是美食荒漠吗?

有一则笑话描述地狱是：德国警察、法国技师和英国厨师，似乎英国食物难吃已经成了世人的共识之一。但是让人意想不到的是英国人却以自己的美食为傲，任何一个英国老人，都能一板一眼地跟你讲述吃炸鱼薯条的讲究。那么英国美食真的难吃吗？其实想要了解一个地方的人文，最好的办法莫过于观察当地的食材。在英国市场上会发现它们的食材和欧洲市场的几乎一样。所以与其说英国菜是难吃，还不如说是传统和古典。

阅读笔记

你知道米字旗的由来吗

米字旗的历史由来

The United Kingdom of Great Britain and Northern Ireland uses as its national flag the royal banner known as the Union Flag or Union Jack. It consists of the red cross of Saint George (*patron* saint of England), *edged* in white, *superimposed* on the Cross of St. Patrick (patron saint of Ireland), which are superimposed on the Saltire of Saint Andrew (patron saint of Scotland). Wales, however, is not represented in the Union Flag by Wales's patron saint, Saint David, as at the time the flag was designed Wales was part of the Kingdom of England.

The earlier flag of Great Britain was established in 1606 by a proclamation of King James VI and I of Scotland and England. The new flag of the United Kingdom was officially created by an Order in Council of 1801, reading as follows: The Union Flag shall be azure, the Crosses saltire of Saint Andrew and Saint Patrick quarterly per saltire, counter-changed, argent and *gules*, the latter *fimbriated* of the second, *surmounted* by the Cross of Saint George of the third fimbriated as the saltire.

大不列颠及北爱尔兰联合王国使用的国旗被称之为联合旗帜或联合杰克。它由代表神圣乔治（英格兰的守护神）的红色正十字、代表圣帕特里克（爱尔兰的守护神）的红色白边交叉十字以及叠加在上边代表圣安德鲁（苏格兰守护神）的白色十字组成。而威尔士的守护神圣戴维并没有在英国国旗上体现，因为国旗被设计时，威尔士是英格兰王国的一部分。

早期的大不列颠国旗的诞生可追溯至1606年，由苏格兰的詹姆士六世，即英格兰和苏格兰的詹姆士一世，宣告诞生。新版的英国国旗正式诞生于1801年，主要构成如下：底色为蓝色，代表圣安德鲁白色十字与代表圣帕特里克的红色十字交叉叠加，且后者以前者为边，最上边则为代表圣乔治的正十字，以圣安德鲁的银白色为边。

单词释义

patron 守护神	edge 给……加上边	superimpose 叠加
gules 红色的	fimbriate 使……有边缘	surmount 覆在……的顶上

风靡的米字旗style

The Union Jack, the flag of the United Kingdom, is used a lot in fashion. The design crops up time and again in menswear, particularly with brands and looks that want to *anchor* themselves to British heritage. The name 'Jack' was probably adopted from naval/maritime usage. Ships of the age would run a small bow flag at the head of the vessel on ceremonial occasions. This was often called a 'Jack', hence the name 'Union Jack'. 'Union Flag' is probably the correct name for the flag, but common *usage* is the 'Union Jack'.

The bright colors and *eye-catching* design of the flag has made it a popular choice for making a statement. Many *notable* front men and women in musical and popular culture have used the flag to great effect. As a design, it's featured in many UK clothing companies and has come to play an important role in the identity of many UK brands. It's possible that the adoration for this design is because it's a good combination of colors and shapes,

联合杰克，即英国国旗，含有很多时尚的元素。男装设计尤其是大牌男装以及定位为英国遗产的品牌中屡次出现英国国旗元素。"杰克"这一名字很可能来自海上。古代，遇到嫁娶丧葬仪式，英国的船只都会在船头悬挂一面小旗帜。这面小旗帜通常被称为"杰克"，后被称之为"联合杰克"。英国国旗的准确名字很可能为"联合国旗"，但通常又称之为"联合杰克"。

英国国旗明亮的颜色以及引人注目的设计使其成为在发表声明时深受大众欢迎的选择。许多音乐界或流行文化中的著名人士都曾用过英国旗帜来造势。作为一种设计元素，英国国旗已成为许多英国服饰公司的特征，并在使许多英国品牌确立其特色时发挥重大影响。人们喜欢这种设计的原

rather than a pledge to queen and country. Youth culture has established that wearing a Jack is a *semi-ironic* nod to the Empire, rather than a celebration of conquest. There's also no *copyright* on the design, so it's open to use by anyone.

因可能在于其颜色以及形状很好地搭配在一起了，而不是在于其象征着女王与国家。在青年文化中，身穿旗帜更像是对帝国的半嘲讽，而非庆祝它征服其他国家这一举动。英国国旗的设计没有版权，所以任何人都可以将其作为设计元素。

单词释义

anchor 扎根于　　　usage 用法　　　　eye-catching 引人注目的

notable 著名的　　　semi-ironic 半嘲讽的　copyright 版权

品 英国特色文化

特色表达One

　　Jack可是英国的红人，很多地方都可以见到这个名字，就连英国的国旗都含有它的名字，即the union Jack，此外大家熟悉的句子还有：All work and no play makes Jack a dull boy. 这句话说的是"只工作不玩，聪明孩子也会变傻"。

☆ 实景链接

A：John, let's play football together. 约翰，我们一起去踢足球吧!

B：I have to learn math and later English grammar. 我还得学习数学和英语语法。

A：You have to learn to relax. **All work and no play makes Jack a dull boy.** 你要学会放松。只工作不玩，聪明孩子也会变傻。

B：It's your theory. I don't buy it. 这是你的说法，我才不吃这一套。

特色表达Two

　　如果有人跟你胡说八道米字旗的由来，这个时候就可以直接说come off it，come off多用于祈使句，意为"别瞎说！"常用在父母对孩子或平辈的朋友之间，说这句话时一般对对方说的话持有怀疑态度。

☆ 实景链接

A: Michael, it is your fault. You jinxed me before the test! 迈克尔，都是你的错，你考试前诅咒我了。

B: **Come off it**, Sam. You didn't review at all. 别胡诌了，山姆。你根本就没有复习。

A: It's one aspect. But I may have passed the examination if you said something lucky. 这是一方面，但是如果你说点好话的话，我可能就通过考试了。

B: I have never thought you are so naïve. 我真没想到你这么天真。

拓展特色句

1. Today's Union jack flag was born in January 1, 1801. 如今的米字旗诞生于1801年1月1日。

2. In 1908 the British Parliament declared that the "British Union Jack flag should be considered." 1908年英国议会宣布"米字旗应该被认为是英国的国旗"。

3. The small cake inserted with the Union Jack. 这块小蛋糕上插着英国国旗。

"聊" 英国特色文化

A: Look, you wear a new shirt. It's so nice.

B: Thank you.

A: When did you buy it?

B: I bought it in England last month when I was on business. It's made in England. There is also a flag of the United Kingdom. I think it's cool.

A: Yes. We can see the flag is used a lot in fashion.

B: There's also no copyright on the design, so it's open to use by anyone.

A: 看，你穿了一件新衬衫。真好看。

B: 谢谢。

A: 什么时候买的？

B: 我上个月出差时在英国买的。是英国制造的。这上面还有英国国旗呢。我觉得挺酷的。

A: 是啊。我们能看到英国国旗有很多时尚的元素。

B: 英国国旗的设计没有版权，所以任何人都可以将其作为设计元素。

A: 你知道它的意思吗？

A：Do you know the meaning of it?

B：Sure. I've looked it up on the internet. I think it's interesting. It is also called the Union Flag or Union Jack.

A：What does the red cross represent?

B：It represents Saint George, which is the patron saint of England.

B：当然。我在网上查过。很有趣。它也叫做联合旗帜或联合杰克。

A：红色十字代表什么？

B：它代表神圣乔治，也就是英格兰的守护神。

"问" 英国特色文化

为何有的国家的国旗上能看到英国国旗的影子？

英联邦各国的国旗都是由自己决定的，英国并未强求它们在国旗上加入米字旗，但是很多国家的国旗上还是会出现米字旗，通常是在国旗的左上角，这些国家现在或曾经都是英国的殖民地或者现在是英联邦成员国，但是也有的国家，如加拿大没有米字旗，因为英联邦只是由英国和已经独立的前英国殖民地或附属国组成的联合体，并非统一的主权国家，所有英联邦的成员地位平等，在内政和外交方面互不隶属。

阅读笔记

依旧存在的社会等级

社会等级现象

The UK has been *uncharitably* described as a society based on *privilege*, *inherited* wealth and contacts. Class is also what divides the bosses from the workers in the UK and the class struggle is at the root of many industrial disputes. It has certainly *re-ignited* over the past couple of years. Many Britons are obsessed with class and for some, maintaining or improving their position on the social ladder is a full-time occupation.

A blue-collar worker must never accept a position that *elevates* him to the ranks of the lower middle class (a white-collar job), otherwise his workmates will no longer speak to him and he will be banned from the local working men's club. Similarly, middle-class management must never *concede* an inch to the workers and, most importantly, must never have direct discussions with them about anything, particularly pay rises or a reduction in working hours.

英国一直以来都被刻画成一个坐享特权、遗产以及社会关系的社会。在英国，老板与员工也处在不同的社会阶级，而社会阶级斗争的根源是劳资纠纷。而在过去的几年，这种斗争又被重新点燃。许多英国人都非常关注自身的社会地位，且对于其中的部分人来说，保持或提高自己社会地位的重要影响因素就是其职业。

蓝领工人不能接受一份使其跻身于中产阶级下层的工作（白领），否则他的同事将不再与其交谈，而且他也会被当地工人俱乐部驱逐。类似地，中产阶级的管理层也不能向工人退让一分一毫，更不能引导他们讨论一些事情，特别是关于涨薪以及减少工作时间的话题。

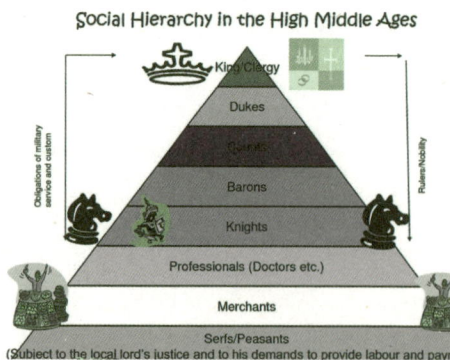

Social Hierarchy in the High Middle Ages

King/Clergy
Dukes
Counts
Barons
Knights
Professionals (Doctors etc.)
Merchants
Serfs/Peasants
(Subject to the local lord's justice and to his demands to provide labour and pay)

Obligations of military service and custom

Rulers/Nobility

单词释义

- uncharitably 无情的
- re-ignite 重新点燃
- privilege 特权
- elevate 提升……的职位
- inherited 遗传的
- concede 退让

7个阶层的社会

According to a new study, the UK population is split into no less than seven different social classes, from the "elite" to the lowly "precariat".

Precariat: This is the most *deprived* class of all with low levels of economic, cultural and social capital. The every day lives of members of this class are *precarious*.

Traditional Working Class: This class scores low on all forms of the three capitals although they are not the poorest group. The average age of this class is older than the others.

Emergent Service Workers: This new class has low economic capital but has high levels of 'emerging' cultural capital and high social capital. This group is young and often found in urban areas.

Technical Middle Class: This is a new, small class with high economic capital but seem less culturally *engaged*. They have relatively few social contacts and so are less socially engaged.

New *Affluent* Workers: This class has medium levels of economic capital and higher levels of cultural and social capital. They are a young and active group.

Established Middle Class: Members of this class have high

据一项最新研究显示，英国人分为从"精英阶层"到最底层的"匮乏者"不等的7个不同阶层。

匮乏者：这是最贫困的阶级，拥有的经济、文化以及社会资本水平非常低。这个阶层的人们颠沛流离，每天的生活都非常不稳定。

传统的工人阶级：这个阶层的人们尽管不是社会上最穷的人，但是他们享受的三种资本水平是最低的。这个阶层的人们平均年龄要比其他阶层大。

应急服务工人阶层：这一阶层的人拥有较低的经济资本，但掌握着较高的社会、文化资本。这个阶层的人比较年轻，多活跃于城市地区。

技术中产阶层：这是一个新近诞生的、人数较少的阶层，拥有较高经济资本，但在文化资本上有所欠缺。由于他们拥有的社会关系较少，所以社会资本也较低。

新贵工人阶层：这一阶层的人掌握着适中的经济资本和相对较高的社会、文化资本，构成人员普遍年轻、活跃。

levels of all three capitals although not as high as the Elite. They are a *gregarious* and culturally engaged class.

Elite: This is the most privileged class in Great Britain who have high levels of all three capitals. Their high amount of economic capital sets them apart from everyone else.

成熟的中产阶层：该阶层英国人的特点是拥有较多的经济、社会、文化资本，虽然不及精英阶层，但该阶层的英国人乐于社交，喜欢参与文化活动。

精英阶层：归属于该阶层的英国人是拥有特权最多的阶级、社会、文化资本，过高的经济资本将这一阶层的英国人与其他阶层的英国人严格划分开来。

单词释义

deprived 贫困的
engaged 参与的

precarious 不确定的
affluent 富裕的

emergent 紧急的
gregarious 爱好交际的

"品" 英国特色文化

特色表达One

在英国这个拥有7个社会阶级的国家，处在社会最高级别的elite经常需要at the wheel，这个短语可不是与方向盘有关，而是指"负责或控制一个大的组织"，这个短语最开始是用在航海，现在也可用来指开车。

实景链接

A: I always feel perfectly safe when Richard's **at the wheel**. 理查德开车，我完全放心。

B: He is absolutely a good driver. By the way, why do you have the chance to go with him? 他绝对是个好司机。顺便问一下，你怎么会有机会坐他的车呢？

A: Last Friday, we ended a meeting very late. And I found he is going on my way. so … 上周五，我们开会到很晚才结束，我发现正好顺路，所以……

B: What a coincidence. 真巧啊！

💬 特色表达Two

即使身处社会阶层的最底层，我想也不会有人喜欢to be led by the nose，to be led by the nose是指一个人在别人的控制之下，就像一头牲口被人用绳子牵着走一样。

☆ 实景链接

A：Do you have something to talk with me, dad? 老爸，你有什么话要对我说吗？

B：Remember, son, don't let other people **lead you by the nose**. 记住，儿子，别让人家牵着你的鼻子走。

A：I will keep it in my mind. I will hear the true voice in my heart. 我记住了，我会听从我心里最真实的声音。

B：That's just what I want to say. 这也正是我想说的。

拓展特色句

1. Where a person is in the social hierarchy affects many aspects in his life. 一个人在社会等级制度中所处的位置会影响他生活的很多方面。

2. Don looked more like a blue collar than the rest of us. 唐比我们几个都更像蓝领。

3. There is a huge gap between the rich and poor. 贫富之间的差距很大。

💬 "聊"英国特色文化

A：What are you doing?

B：I'm reading today's newspaper.

A：Is there anything new? Say something to me.

B：There is a strike in England. How do they like strikes?

A：U.K. is a society based on privilege, inherited wealth and contacts. Class

A：你在干什么呢？

B：我在看今天的报纸呢。

A：有什么新闻吗？跟我说说。

B：英国有一场罢工。他们到底有多喜欢罢工啊？

A：那没什么特别的。英国是一个基于特权、遗产以及社会关系的社会。在英国，老板与员工也处在不同的

is also what divides the bosses from the workers in the UK and the class struggle is at the root of many industrial disputes.

B: How many social classes are there in England, then?

A: It is said seven.

B: Are you kidding? So many classes?

A: I'm serious. I read it last week. From the "elite" to the lowly "precariat", I can't remember them precisely. We can look up later.

B: What a complicated society!

A: Yes. It's different from our country.

社会阶级，而社会阶级斗争的焦点则为劳资纠纷。

B：那么，英国有多少个社会阶层？

A：据说有7个。

B：你开玩笑呢吧？这么多阶层？

A：我是认真的。上周我从报纸上看到的。从"精英阶层"到最下层的"匮乏者"，我记得不是很准确。一会儿我们可以查查。

B：真是一个复杂的社会啊！

A：是啊。和我们国家不一样。

"问" 英国特色文化

如何给英国人划分社会等级？

没有什么像社会阶级这个事情更加困扰着英国。有段时间英国人是根据他们的工作、教育、口音以及某种程度上的消费来进行社会分层的，现在更多的是根据他们的收入、房产市值以及储蓄来衡量他们的"经济资本"；根据他们的文化兴趣和活动来衡量他们的"文化资本"；根据他们认识人的数量和地位，来衡量他们的"社会资本"。

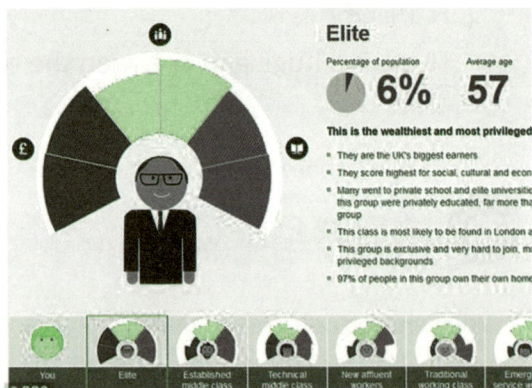

阅读笔记

英国的多元文化

多元文化是怎样形成的

People from all cultures and *ethnicities* can be found in every corner of Britain. If you walk down a street in Britain, especially in the bigger cities, you will usually see people with different hair, skin and eye colours. They may have white, brown or black skin and *blonde*, brown, black, or red hair, with blue, black, brown or green eyes.

Britain is and has always been a mixed race society. Early in the history they were *invaded* by Romans, Saxons, Vikings and Normans armies and later Africans were brought to Britain. Over the years, thousands of people have arrived in Britain as refugees from France, Ireland, Russia, and other countries, escaping from *persecution* or *famine* in their own countries. People moving to Britain have brought their own cultures and try to keep two cultures alive. An excellent example of this is the Notting Hill *Carnival* which *celebrates* the Caribbean Culture and is now a very big part of the British life today.

来自不同文化和种族的人遍布英国的各个角落。走在英国的大街上，特别是大城市的大街上，你会看到各种发色、肤色以及各种眼睛颜色的人。他们可能是白种人、黄种人，也可能是黑种人；他们可能有着金发、棕发、黑发或者红发；他们可能是蓝色的眼睛、黑色的眼睛，也可能是棕色或者绿色的眼睛。

英国一直以来都是混杂着各种种族的社会。在历史的早期，英国曾被罗马人、撒克逊人、维京人以及诺曼人侵略过，稍后，非洲人也来到了英国。随着时间的推移，为了逃离国内的迫害或者饥荒，成千上万的来自法国、爱尔兰、俄罗斯以及其他国家的人也来到了英国。搬到英国的人们带来了他们的文化，并在适应英国文化的同时还保留着他们的文化传统。关于这一说法的一个很好的例子就是诺丁山狂欢节——这个曾为庆祝加勒比文化的节日已成为英国人生活的一部分。

单词释义

ethnicity 种族　　　　blonde 金色的　　　　invade 侵略

persecution 迫害　　　famine 饥荒　　　　　carnival 狂欢节

celebrate 庆祝

新加勒比文化

Knowing the history of the Caribbean region goes a long way toward understanding its people. Each island has a unique cultural identity shaped by the European *colonialists*, the African *heritage* of slaves, and the enduring legacies of the native Indian tribes. This rich history and its lasting influence is set against a *backdrop* of *crystal* clear waters and *perpetual* sunshine.

The Caribbean lifestyle is undoubtedly a product of its tropical setting. The music, *architecture*, attitudes and customs have all, in some way, been shaped by the physical landscape and climate. The cultures of the Caribbean countries are a blend of *colonial mainstays* and *pervasive* influences by major ethnic groups of the region such as East Indians and Africans. Old African culture and customs influence much of the religious worship, artistic expression, rhythmic dancing, singing and even ways of thinking in the Caribbean.

Music has been central to Caribbean culture since the days of

了解加勒比地区的历史很大程度上在于了解加勒比地区的人们。受欧洲殖民主义者、非洲奴隶传统、本土印第安部落的影响，每个岛屿都有不同的文化身份。与清澈透明的海水和永恒的阳光相对应地就是加勒比地区的悠久历史以及其深远的影响。

加勒比地区是典型的热带生活方式。该地区的音乐、建筑、态度以及习俗在一定程度上都深受其自然景观以及气候的影响。加勒比国家的文化同时受着殖民文化以及本地主要种族如东印第安人以及非洲人影响。古老的非洲文化以及习俗影响着加勒比人的信仰、艺术表现形式、节奏感强烈的舞蹈方式、唱歌方式，甚至思考方式。

slavery, when it was a mode of mental survival and a form of recreation. Today there is a ubiquitous Caribbean soundtrack; it plays on city streets, in natives' homes and at special festivals—at Carnival people tirelessly dance for days. It is characterized by a natural, easy rhythm and multiple ethnic influences, particularly the African drum beat.

自奴隶制度存在的时代开始，音乐就作为一种精神生存以及娱乐方式对加勒比文化有着至关重要的作用。现在，加勒比独特的音乐声带无处不在——大街上、家里以及特殊的节日庆典上，如在狂欢节上成为人们不知疲倦舞蹈的背景乐。它的特点是，节奏自然、轻松，并深受多个民族的影响，尤其是非洲鼓。

单词释义

colonialist 殖民主义者	heritage 传统	backdrop 背景
crystal 清澈的	perpetual 永恒的	architecture 建筑
colonial 殖民的	mainstay 最基本组成部分	pervasive 无处不在的

"品" 英国特色文化

特色表达One

英国是有着多元化文化的国家，当别人无法理解你的想法或者行为时，试着让别人从你的角度想想，即Try to see it my way. 同时，我们也得"替别人着想"，即put oneself in sb.'s shoes。

☆ 实景链接

A: How can you say something like that to your parents? You are to blame. 你怎么可以对你父母说出那样的话？你应该受到责备。

B: Why? Have you tried to **see it my way**? 为什么？你有站在我的立场想一想吗？

A: How dare you say that. It seems you don't realize you are wrong. 你怎么敢说出这样的话来！看来你根本就没有意识到自己错了。

B: It's not my fault. 那不是我的错。

💬 特色表达Two

当你遇到令你感到惊讶的事情的时候，可以说fancy that，表示"真想不到"。fancy作动词的意思是"想象、幻想"，这句话还可以表示为just fancy!

⭐ 实景链接

A: That company went bankrupt in a single day. 这家公司在一天之内就破产了。

B: **Fancy that**! 真想不到!

A: In such financial crisis, it's very normal. 在金融危机的环境下，这是很正常的。

B: It seems I have to adapt to this change. 看来我真得适应这种变化了。

拓展特色句

1. Notting Hill Carnival is one of the Caribbean's known cultural treasures. 诺丁山文化节是加勒比文化知名的文化珍宝之一。

2. Britain is really a multi-cultural country. 英国的确是一个多元文化的国家。

3. London is a multi-cultural and open-minded city. 伦敦是一个多元文化且思想开放的城市。

"聊"英国特色文化

A: Do you know the Notting Hill Carnival?

B: Yes. I learned something about it when I was at school.

A: Can you tell me something about it?

B: Certainly. It is led by members of the West Indian community. The carnival has attracted around one million people in the past years, making it one of the largest street festivals in the world.

A: 你知道诺丁山狂欢节吗?

B: 是的。我上学的时候学过。

A: 能给我讲讲吗?

B: 当然可以。这个节日由西印第安社区的成员领导。诺丁山文化节在过去几年吸引了大约100万人参加，这使得它成为世界上最大的街道节日之一。

A: 哇。但是我听说它是来自加勒比文化的。

A: Wow. But I heard that it was from the Caribbean Culture.

B: Yes. So England is a multicultural country. And the Notting Hill Carnival is now a very big part of the British life today.

A: Britain is and has always been a mixed race society.

B: Yeah, and the races there mixed very well.

B: 是的。所以英国是一个多元文化国家。并且诺丁山文化节已成为英国人生活的一部分。

A: 英国一直以来都是混杂着各种种族的社会。

B: 是啊，而且那儿的种族融合得很好。

"问" 英国特色文化

英国的"多元文化"对英国有什么影响？

很多政治评论员和媒体担心英国的"多元文化主义已经失败了"，他们认为尊重民族文化容易导致少数人数的群落孤立，让不同的种族在同一个地区过着平行的生活，这阻碍了社会的和谐性，从而导致社会分化。但是在过去几十年里，一些地方政府鼓励少数民族保持自己的文化，并传给下一代，而多种文化传统的共存也被视为英国社会的有利财富。

阅读笔记

英式幽默，
你笑得起来吗

什么是"英式幽默"

Although some believe the words "British Humor" to be an *oxymoron*, most informed people understand that the British are well known for their *sophisticated* senses of humor. Humor is such an important part of British life that it has even *pervaded* their very language.

British humor is a somewhat general term applied to certain comedic *motifs* that are often *prevalent* in humor in the United Kingdom and the British Commonwealth. A strong theme of sarcasm and self-deprecation, often with *deadpan* delivery, runs throughout British humor. Emotion is often buried under humor in a way that seems *insensitive* to other cultures. Jokes are told about everything and almost no subject is taboo, though often a lack of *subtlety* when discussing controversial issues is considered *crass*. Many UK comedy TV shows typical of British humor have been internationally popular, and have been an important channel for the export and representation of British culture to the international audience.

尽管有些人认为"英式幽默"本身就是个矛盾所在，但是见识多广的人都知道英国人以其复杂的幽默感而闻名。幽默是英国人的生活中非常重要的一部分，以至于其在英语中都普遍存在。

英式幽默在某种程度上，常用来指在英国或者英联邦流行的某些戏剧效果。讽刺以及自嘲，且含蓄是英式幽默的主要特点。英式幽默看起来没有涉及其他文化，正是用这种方式将真正要表达的情感隐藏在幽默之中。尽管很多人认为无所顾忌讨论有争议的话题是愚蠢的，但是在英国，幽默随处可见，且主题没有任何禁忌。典型的英式幽默电视剧在全球非常流行，且这些英剧成为全球观众了解英国文化的重要途径。

单词释义

oxymoron 矛盾修饰法　　sophisticated 复杂的　　pervade 遍及
motif 主题　　　　　　　prevalent 普遍的　　　 deadpan 面无表情的
insensitive 对……没有感觉的　subtlety 敏锐　　　 crass 愚蠢的

如何辨别英国人是否在开玩笑

How do you know when a British person is joking? Or why they're joking, for that matter? Here are the *categories* you need to know to survive:

1. *Sarcasm* and *irony*

Sarcasm is the use of irony to say one thing while meaning the opposite. For example saying "At least you don't have to worry about fixing that *puncture* now" to a friend whose bike has just fallen into a pond.

2. Understatement

It's when someone *deliberately* makes out that something is less significant than it is. For instance, by saying "It's a little bit windy, isn't it?" when there's a *raging* hurricane outside is an understatement. "Deadpan humour" is also one element of understatement.

3. *Satire*

Satire involves using humour to criticize people and institutions with power, like politicians. Satire is popular in the UK because taking people "*down a peg or two*" is part

怎么辨别英国人是否在跟你开玩笑？或者他们为什么要开玩笑，开什么玩笑？要了解这些，你需要知道以下几种幽默类别。

1. 反讽与挖苦

反讽是指用挖苦的语气说一件事，其真正想表达的意思正好相反。例如跟自行车刚刚掉入池塘的朋友说"至少你现在不用再为修好轮胎上的刺孔而担忧了。"

2. 轻描淡写

轻描淡写是指使某人故意让某件事看起来不那么重要。例如：当外边狂风大作时，别人却说"外边有微风，不是吗？"这就是轻描淡写。冷面幽默也是轻描淡写的一种。

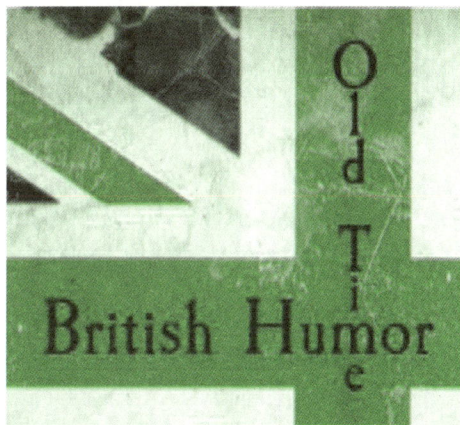
Old Time British Humor

of this culture.

4. The absurd

Absurd humour focuses on the silly, ridiculous or *surreal*. Much of British comedy is about noticing the absurd things in everyday life. Like the way everyone *squishes* onto the train even though there is another one in just one minute.

5. Banter

Banter is basically a jokey conversation between friends that involves good-natured teasing. Along with crisps and quizzes, it's a big part of pub culture in the UK. So while you're studying here, make a point of socialising with some locals—that way you can perfect your bantering skills.

3. 讽刺

讽刺是指用幽默来谴责像政客这种有权人士或机构。讽刺在英国很流行，因为用其来"灭某人的威风"是英国文化传统。

4. 荒谬之事

荒谬幽默常常讲一些愚蠢、荒诞或者离奇的事情。很多英式喜剧都非常关注日常生活中的荒谬事情，如尽管一分钟后就有另一趟列车过来，但是所有人还是拥挤上本趟列车。

5. 戏谑

戏谑通常是指朋友间谈话中出现的善意的逗弄或者玩笑话。其与薯片、恶作剧并成为英国酒吧三大文化组成部分。所以，当你在英国学习时，别忘记与当地人多多交流，那样肯定能提高你的戏谑技巧。

单词释义

category 种类	sarcasm 反讽	irony 挖苦
puncture 轮胎上的刺孔	deliberately 故意地	raging 狂暴的
satire 讽刺	down a peg or two 杀杀某人的威风	
surreal 离奇的	squish 把……挤扁	

"品"英国特色文化

特色表达One

很多人不了解英国的英式幽默，误解说话人的意思，觉得自己被误解而 bend out of shape，设想一下什么东西弯曲到已经没有了最初的形状，就像一个人发脾气得表情扭曲，也就是"大发雷霆"的意思。

☆ 实景链接

A：Are you prepared for the interview? 你做好面试的准备了吗？

B：Not yet, my mind is totally a mess. I'm dying of boredom! 还没，我现在心里一团乱，快烦死了！

A：I know you're worried about your job interview, but don't **get bent out of shape**. You'll do just fine. 我知道你在为面试担心，但别生气，保持好心情，你会表现得很好的。

B：Oh, thanks. I hope so. 噢，谢谢。希望如此吧。

💬 特色表达Two

　　有的英式幽默笑点十足，猛地一听哈哈大笑，细想一下才发现自己被人挖苦或者讽刺了，所以各位在和英国人说笑的时候，don't count your chickens before they're hatched，这可不是说不要在小鸡孵出来之前计算，而是解释为"别高兴得太早！"

☆ 实景链接

A：I want to buy a new car and a house when I win the lottery next week. 下个星期我要是买彩票中了大奖的话，就去买辆新车，买栋新房。

B：**Don't count your chickens until they hatch!** 你还没中呢，高兴得那么早干嘛!

A：It's the motivation in my life. 这是我生活中的动力。

B：You are just exaggerated. 你太夸张了吧。

拓展特色句

1. The differences between British humor and the American humor are very big. 英式幽默和美式幽默之间的差距很大。

2. One of the main forms of English humor is sarcasm. 讽刺是英式幽默的主要形式之一。

3. His English humor is unique and indigenous. 他的英式幽默是很独特的，土生土长的。

"聊" 英国特色文化

A: How did he say that? I can't understand.

B: You know what, it's British humor. We all know that the British are well known for their sophisticated senses of humor. This time you felt it by yourself.

A: How do you know when a British person is joking? Or why are they joking, for that matter?

B: It's hard. Because there are sarcasm and irony, understatement, satire, the absurd and banter. You'd better know the differences.

A: I don't think I can handle it.

B: Don't give up. It's good for you to know English culture better.

A: Maybe I should know more English people and talk with them. I think it would be helpful.

B: That's a good idea. But pay attention to your method of communication.

"问" 英国特色文化

A: 他怎么能那样说呢？我理解不了。

B: 你知道吗，那是英式幽默。我们都知道英国人以其复杂的幽默感而闻名。这次你自己亲身体验了一次。

A: 你怎么辨别英国人是否在跟你开玩笑？或者他们为什么要开玩笑，开什么玩笑？

B: 很难。因为他们有反讽与挖苦、轻描淡写、讽刺、荒谬之事和戏谑。你最好知道它们的区别。

A: 我想我做不到。

B: 别放弃啊。这有利于你了解英国文化。

A: 也许我应该多认识些英国人和他们聊聊天。我想这会有帮助的。

B: 是个好主意。但是要注意你的交流方式哦。

MONTY PYTHON and the Holy Grail

英式幽默让你笑得起来吗？

一提到英国人的性格，你脑海里可能会浮现这么几个词：拘谨、内敛，这让人们很难将幽默和他们联系起来。但是事实上，英国人是很喜欢开玩笑的，他们的喜剧行业特别发达。当然，英式幽默也有自己的一套风格，他们不太喜欢拿别人做笑料，但是特别喜欢拿自己逗乐，嘲笑自己的优缺点，甚至理想。

英国特色pub

什么叫pub

The word pub is short for public house. There are over 60,000 pubs in the UK (53,000 in England and Wales, 5,200 in Scotland and 1,600 in Northern Ireland). One of the oldest pubs, Fighting Cocks in St. Albans, Herts, is *located* in a building that dates back to the eleventh century.

Pubs are an important part of British life. People talk, eat, drink, meet their friends and *relax* there. Pubs often have two bars, one usually quieter than the other, many have a garden where people can sit in the summer. Children can go in pub gardens with their parents. Groups of friends normally buy 'rounds' of drinks, where the person whose turn it is will buy drinks for all the members of the group. And customs in British pubs differ from those in American bars. In Britain, you must go to the bar to order drinks and food and pay for your *purchase* immediately, there is no table service.

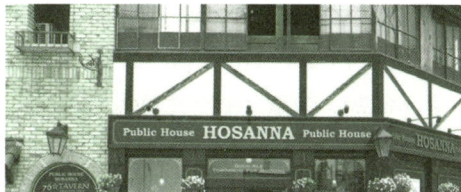

酒馆（pub）这个词是公共小屋（public house）的简称。英国有6万多个酒馆（英格兰和威尔士有大概53000个，苏格兰有5200个，北爱尔兰有1600个）。斗鸡酒馆是最古老的酒馆之一，它坐落于赫特福德郡圣奥尔本斯的一所11世纪的老房子里。

酒馆是英国人生活中很重要的一部分。人们在酒馆中交谈、吃东西、喝饮料、与朋友相聚、放松自己。酒馆里往往有两个吧台，其中一个相对较安静。很多酒馆有一个院子，在夏天人们可以待在院子里。孩子们也可以跟父母一起去酒馆的院子里。一群朋友往往一买就是"一圈"饮料，就是轮到谁谁就给这整群人买饮料。英国酒馆的习俗跟美国不同。在英国你需要去吧台点餐然后当场付款，没有餐桌服务。

单词释义

locate 位于，坐落于　　　　relax 放松　　　　purchase 购买

pub小常识

British pubs are required to have a licence, which is difficult to *obtain*, and allows the pub to operate for up to 24 hours. Most pubs are open from 11 to 11. It is sometimes difficult to get served when pubs are busy: people do not queue, but the bar staff will usually try and serve those who have been waiting the longest at the bar first. If you *spill* a stranger's drink by accident, it is good manners (and *prudent*) to offer to buy another drink.

Most pubs belong to a *brewery* but sell many different kinds of beer, some on *tap* and some in bottles. The most popular kind of British beer is bitter, which is dark and served at room temperature (not hot, not cold). British beer is brewed from malt and *hops*. More popular today though is lager, which is lighter in color and served cold. Guinness, a very dark, creamy kind of beer called a stout, is made in Ireland and is popular all over Britain. And in the West of England, *cider* made from apples, is very popular. Like wine, it is described as sweet or dry, but is drunk in beer glasses and can be stronger than beer. Beers are served in "pints" for a large glass and "halves" for a smaller one.

在英国，经营酒馆需要先获取营业许可证。这个证件非常难获得，也只有拥有这个证件，酒馆才能24小时不间断营业。大部分酒馆都从上午11点开到晚上11点。有时酒馆里客人非常多的时候，酒保一般都很忙碌，无法照顾到每个人：人们不会排队，但酒保总会设法先服务那些等得久的人。如果你不小心碰洒了别人的饮料，那么出于礼貌你最好给他再买一杯。

大多数酒馆都是隶属于某个啤酒厂，但会出售各种不同种类的啤酒。既有桶装的，也有瓶装的。英国最流行的啤酒是苦啤酒，它颜色较深，接近黑色，且往往是常温的。英国的啤酒一般由麦芽和啤酒花发酵而成。现在比较流行的是窖藏啤酒，一般是冰的而且颜色较淡。爱尔兰产的黑啤在英国也很流行。由苹果制成的苹果酒在英国西部很流行。苹果酒装在啤酒杯里，比啤酒劲大，比较甜而且干。啤酒可以按"品脱"叫一次一大杯的，也可叫一半的小量啤酒。

单词释义

obtain 获得

brewery 啤酒厂

cider 苹果酒

spill 洒

tap 桶装的酒

prudent 谨慎的

hops 啤酒花

"品"英国特色文化

特色表达One

去酒吧喝酒很有可能喝得烂醉，醉酒后的男性可能会容易come on to女孩子，这时的女孩子一定要保护好自己哦。come on to是很危险的动作吗，为什么要保护自己呢？原来，come on to在俚语中有"对……轻薄，吃……豆腐"的意思。

实景链接

A: Jack has been hit in the pub last night. 杰克昨晚被人打了。

B: What? How come? 什么，为什么？

A: It is said that he was drunk too much and came on to a girl. Then her boyfriend saw that, so... 据说他喝多了，吃一个女孩的豆腐，然后被那女孩的男朋友看到了，所以……

B: Well, he really deserved it. 那他真是活该。

特色表达Two

在英国酒吧，很多时候都得先pick up the tab，然后才能喝到酒，tab在口语中，就是"账单"的意思，pick up the tab即指代"付账"，此外，我们还可用foot the bill来表示这一意思。

实景链接

A: Rock, you **picked up the tab** last time—Let me pay this time. 罗克，上次是你买的单，这次我来付账。

B: It doesn't matter. Don't put in heart. Let's go Dutch. 没关系，别把这放在心上，我们AA制吧！

A: No way this time. 这次不行。

B: Okay, it should be on me next time. 好吧，那下次我再请。

拓展特色句

1. I felt comfortable alone in that pub. 我觉得一个人待在那家酒吧很舒服。

2. He ogled a lady in the pub. 他在酒吧里向一位女士抛媚眼。

3. This is for your service. 这是给你的小费，谢谢你的服务。

"聊" 英国特色文化

A： Would you like to have a drink after work?

B： Good idea. Let's forget about work and have some fun.

A： Do you always have a drink in the pub?

B： Yes. I think it's a good way to relax. And I like to go barhopping.

A： I heard that there are over 60,000 pubs in the UK. Is it true?

B： It's true. Pubs are an important part of British life.

A： What do they usually do in the pub?

B： People talk, eat, drink, meet their friends and relax there.

A： Are there any differences between American pubs and British pubs?

B： Yes. In Britain, you must go to the bar to order drinks and food and pay for your purchase immediately, there is no table service.

A： 下班以后去喝一杯怎么样？

B： 好主意。让我们忘了工作，痛快一会儿吧。

A： 你总是在酒馆里喝酒吗？

B： 是的。我认为这是一种放松的好方法。并且我喜欢换酒馆喝。

A： 我听说英国有6万多个酒馆。是真的吗？

B： 是真的。酒馆是英国人生活中很重要的一部分。

A： 他们通常在酒馆里做什么呢？

B： 人们在酒馆中交谈、吃东西、喝饮料、与朋友相聚、放松自己。

A： 美国酒馆和英国酒馆有什么不同的吗？

B： 是的。在英国你需要去吧台点餐然后当场付款，没有餐桌服务。

"问" 英国特色文化

Pub在英国人心中到底占什么地位?

在英国有句很有名的话：If you haven't been to a pub, you haven't been to Britain. 事实上pub对于英国人而言，是生活中不可或缺的一部分，pub是娱乐放松、释放自我的地方。每一家pub里都会保持刚刚建立时的格局，几乎看不到现代的元素。英国人就是这样珍视自己的传统，他们不会试图改变历史的遗留，而是把它们当作生活的一部分。

阅读笔记

英国的格子情节

格子呢的由来

The origins of *tartan* are *inextricably* linked with the origins of the Scottish nation. Evidence suggests that striped and *checked* materials were used for hundreds of years by the Celtic peoples who lived in what would become modern Scotland. But tartan really emerges from the shadows with the arrival on these shores from Ireland of the Scoti tribe in the fifth century. Not only would they give Scotland its name, but they would also *bequeath* tartan as an everyday garment and as a symbol of identity. The check used by the Scoti was very basic. But as time evolved, so did the *intricacies* of clan tartan. The number of stripes on the cloth came to indicate rank and the weave became associated with different clans in different parts of the country, especially the Highlands and Islands. *Variations* of pattern, even within the same clan, continued until the beginning of the seventeenth century when these patterns or setts became standardised.

格子呢的起源不可避免地与苏格兰民族的起源密切相关。有证据显示，几百年来，现代苏格兰人的祖先凯尔特人就一直使用着条纹与格子花纹的材料。事实上，格子呢真正出现在人们面前是公元5世纪，由来自爱尔兰的斯科蒂部落带来。他们不仅命名了苏格兰，还将格子呢作为日常服装以及民族的象征一代一代传下来。方格图案是斯科蒂人生活中最基础的一部分。但随着时代的进步，部落花纹格子呢也在不断变化中。衣服面料上的条纹数量来显示级别，不同的织法暗示不同区域里的不同部落，尤其是苏格兰高地和岛屿地区。即使在同一个部落里，格子呢样式也不尽相同，直到17世纪初，这些样式才逐渐统一。

单词释义

tartan 格子呢　　inextricably 逃不掉地　　checked 格子花纹的
bequeath 把……流传下去　　intricacies 错综复杂的事物　　variation 变更

苏格兰方格裙

Tartan is recognized the world over as being associated with Scotland. Though people across the globe have *woven* material with a striped pattern running *warp* and *weft*, only in Scotland has it taken on such a strong cultural *significance*, to the point where a system has developed of wearing tartans to *represent* one's clan, family, or place of origin.

The Scottish dress is called kilt in Scottish. The kilt is a knee-length *garment* with *pleats* at the rear, mostly often made of woolen cloth in a tartan pattern, originating in the traditional dress of men and boys in the Scottish Highlands of the 16th century. Since the 19th century it has become associated with the wider culture of Scotland in general, or with Celtic heritage even more broadly.

The kilt first appeared as the great kilt, a full-length garment whose upper half could be worn as a cloak draped over the shoulder, or brought up over the head. The small kilt, also known as the walking kilt was invented by Thomas Rawlinson from Lancashire sometime in the 1720s for the use of the Highlanders he employed in logging, *charcoal*

格子呢被全世界公认为苏格兰的代表物。尽管全世界的人们都在使用横竖交叉的条纹编织面料，但是只在苏格兰，这种面料才具有重大的文化意义。在苏格兰，格子呢服装可以展现出一个人的宗族、家族或是起源地。

苏格兰裙在苏格兰当地被称之为"基尔特"。"基尔特"由带有格子的呢子制成，长度及膝，后部有褶皱。它是16世纪苏格兰高地男性的传统服饰。自19世纪以来，人们将它与广泛的苏格兰文化，甚至更广义上的凯尔特文化遗产联系起来。

基尔特最早是以大基尔特形式出现的，即长裙，裙子的上半部分可以作为斗篷披在肩上或盖在头上。小基尔特，也叫行走基尔特，由兰开夏郡的托马斯·罗林森在18世纪20年代发明，供他雇用的苏格兰高地人使用，他们从事伐

manufacture and iron smelting, for which the **belted** plaid was "**cumbersome** and unwieldy".

木、煤矿生产、生铁冶炼工作。因为工人们穿着带束带的大基尔特工作起来非常的"笨重与不便"。

单词释义

woven 编织物

significance 意义

pleat 褶

cumbersome 笨重的

warp 把(纱、线)排列成经

represent 代表

charcoal 木炭

weft 纬线

garment 服装

belted 束带的

"品" 英国特色文化

特色表达One

在苏格兰，不仅是女士，就连男士也身穿格子裙，这在他们眼里可是Sunday best，Sunday best是指西方人周日去做礼拜时穿的衣服，通常都是最漂亮、最正式的衣服，以此来显示对耶稣基督的敬重，所以Sunday best就成了一个比喻，只要是最好的衣服都可以用它来表达。

☆ 实景链接

A: You've got to put on your **Sunday best** if you want to impress the girl. 要是你想给那个女孩子留下好印象的话，你一定得穿得非常漂亮。

B: As a matter of fact, I don't have any decent clothes. 事实上，我根本没有什么像样的衣服。

A: I happen to have time this afternoon. Let me select some clothes for you. 我这个下午正好有空，我去给你挑选一些衣服吧！

B: That couldn't be better. Thank you so much. 那太好了，非常感谢！

特色表达Two

苏格兰的格子裙并非只有苏格兰人可以穿，我们也可以换一下风格，试一下，给人一种a breath of fresh air的感觉，如果能让人时时刻刻体会到新鲜空气的感觉，那真是太美好了，这句话即引申为"耳目一新、如沐春风"。

☆ **实景链接**

A：What's your impression of the new colleague? 你对新来的同事印象怎么样？

B：Having her around the office is **a breath of fresh air**—she's so nice. 她的到来让办公室耳目一新——她人很好。

A：I have a different opinion. She just put on air, which makes me disgusted. 我不这么认为，她装腔作势，让我感到很恶心。

B：Is it? I haven't realized it. 是吗？我还没有发觉。

拓展特色句

1. Both my sister and I are big fans of the tartan. 我和我的姐姐都非常喜欢格子呢。

2. Susan wore a traditional Scottish dress today. 苏珊今天穿了一件传统的苏格兰裙。

3. What Scots wear are not skirts; they are called kilts. 苏格兰人穿的不是普通的裙子，它们叫苏格兰裙。

"聊" 英国特色文化

A：You bought a new dress. Can I have a look at it?

B：OK. Here you are.

A：It's a tartan dress. Is it made in Scotland?

B：Yes. How do you know?

A：It's easy. Tartan is recognized the world over as being associated with Scotland.

B：Do you know the origin of it?

A：It emerges from Ireland of the Scoti tribe in the fifth century.

B：I also heard the word "kilt"; do you know what it is?

A：你买了条新裙子。我能看看吗？

B：好的。给你。

A：是格子呢连衣裙。苏格兰制造的吗？

B：是的。你怎么知道的？

A：很简单。格子呢被全世界公认为苏格兰的代表物。

B：你知道它的由来吗？

A：它是公元5世纪由来自爱尔兰的斯科蒂部落带来的。

B：我还听说过"基尔特"这个词，你知道是什么意思吗？

A：它是苏格兰的苏格兰裙。它是16世纪苏格兰高地男性的传统服饰。

B：真有意思。也许下次我也可以买一条。

A： It's the Scottish dress in Scotland. It's the traditional dress of men and boys in the Scottish Highlands of the 16th century.

B： It sounds interesting. Maybe I can buy one next time.

"问" 英国特色文化

格子有什么值得讲究的吗？

在欧美纺织业盛传着这样一句话：苏格兰格子，等于一部大英帝国的历史。到今天为止，英国"知名格子注册中心"已注册的格子有2500多种。与人一样，格子也有贵贱之分：维多利亚女王的丈夫是苏格兰格子的爱好者，由他设计的图案被称为皇家格子；在不同场合，不同的格子也有不同的功能，在正式场合穿正装格子，在娱乐场合穿打猎格子，出席葬礼穿葬礼格子；有的公司甚至会为员工设计独特的格子，称为团体格子。

阅读笔记

Part 2

这些culture shock，有没有

英国的汽车竟是左侧行驶

为什么会左侧行驶

About a quarter of the world drives on the left side of the road in right-hand drive cars. The countries that do are mostly old British colonies. It would be almost impossible for Britain to change to right-hand drive. And this strange *quirk* of driving on the left really puzzles the rest of world but there are a few, perfectly good, reasons why.

In the *violent feudal* past, just like today, the majorities of people were right-handed and carried their swords in their right hands. As we walked around, general thinking was that when two people passed each other, they did so with their sword arms between each other. Sometime later in 1773, the UK Government was forced to introduce the General Highways Act which included a *recommendation* to keep to the left. This went on to be included in the Highways Bill of 1835.

世界上大约有1/4的国家车辆靠左行驶，而驾驶员坐在车辆的右前方，因为这些国家大多都曾为英国的殖民地。让英国人改变靠左驾驶这一习惯基本上是不可能的。靠左驾驶这一怪癖让世界上其他的人感到很疑惑，而且大家也说不出来为什么要靠左驾驶。

在暴力的封建时代，绝大多数人都跟现在一样都是右撇子，他们用右手持剑。当两个人迎面走过来时，很容易会不小心刺伤对方。1773年的晚些时候，英国政府被迫采用了公路总法案，这个法案建议人们靠左行驶。1835年的高速公路法案也囊括了这一条。

单词释义

quirk 怪癖　　　　　　violent 暴力的　　　　　　feudal 封建制度的
recommendation 推荐

英国开车的规则

Below is a summary of the basic rules of the road in Britain.

Drive on the left-hand side of the road.

Always pass (*overtake*) on the outside (right) lane.

Do not block the middle lane if the inside lane is clear.

When *approaching* a *roundabout*, give priority to traffic approaching from the right, unless otherwise indicated.

You must always stop at a red traffic light.

At a *junction* there's no general priority rule—priority is marked at most junctions.

All traffic signals and road signs must be obeyed.

All vehicles must give way to *emergency* services vehicles.

The use of a car horn is not permitted in built-up areas from 23:30 to 07:00 hours.

Do not drive in bus lanes during restricted hours. See signs by the side of the road for times.

It's *illegal* to use a mobile phone when driving. If you need to make a call, find a safe place to stop first.

Seat belts must be worn by the driver and front seat passenger. Where rear seat belts have been

以下为英国交通规则的简介。

靠左驾驶。

从外道（即右侧）超车。

当内道是通畅的时候不能阻塞在中间车道上。

开往环状交叉路口时，应让来自右侧的车先行，另有说明的情况除外。

遇红灯必须停车。

在三岔路口行车没有优先级别——大多数这样的路口已经表明了哪些车先走哪些车后走。

驾驶员必须遵守所有的交通信号灯以及路标。

所有的车辆都应该让紧急服务的车辆先行。

从晚上11点半到早上7点，禁止在有建筑的区域按喇叭。

在规定的时段，私家车不能在公交车道上行驶。具体时间请参考路边的标志。

驾驶时使用手机是非法的。如果想打电话，需找个安全的位置先停车。

驾驶员以及前排乘客必须系安全带。若后排位置上也有安全带时，也

fitted, they must also be worn.

The minimum driving age is 17.

需要系上。

最小驾驶年龄为17岁。

单词释义

- overtake 超车
- junction 三岔路口
- approach 接近
- emergency 紧急情况
- roundabout 环状交叉路口
- illegal 非法的

"品" 英国特色文化

特色表达One

说到在公路上开车难免会出事故，如果碰上有钱人撞了你的车，态度恶劣而且甩给你一句don't have a cow，估计你一定气得想痛扁他一顿。这里的don't have a cow不是指"没有奶牛"，而是"别大惊小怪"的意思。

☆ 实景链接

A: You don't look very happy today. 你今天看起来不怎么高兴啊。

B: Yeah, because of a guy. He hit my car and didn't apologize to me. He even told me **don't have a cow** and he will pay for the damages immediately. 是，因为一个家伙。他撞了我的车，不跟我道歉。还告诉我说别大惊小怪的，说他会立马赔钱给我。

A: Such a jerk. 真是过分。

B: Yeah, so I went haywire and had a fight with him. 是啊，我当时真是气极了，完全无法控制自己，跟他吵了一架。

特色表达Two

如果遇到乘坐的出租车司机或者你的朋友开车太猛，完全不顾及副驾驶的感受，是不是很想大喊一句"You drive me up the wall"。我们熟知的drive是"开车"的意思，但是这里表示的是促使，drive sb. up the wall就是指某种情况促使某人非常紧张或者使某人很烦躁。

☆ 实景链接

A: You've got here so soon. 你们这么快就到了啊。

B: It owed to John. He was driving so fast. 这都"归功于"约翰。他开得

太快了！

A: You should tell him don't go too fast. 你应该和他说别开太快了。

B: I screamed for him to slow down all the time. **He drove me up the wall.** 我一直喊着让他慢点。真是快把我逼疯了。

拓展特色句

1. There's a slope ahead; slow down! 前面有个斜坡，开慢一点。

2. The driver should turn on the left-turn signal in advance if he needs to change to the left lane. 司机在需要驶入左侧车道的时候应该提前打开左转向灯。

3. Don't occupy the emergency lane! 不要占用应急车道！

"聊" 英国特色文化

A: Look! My new driving license.

B: Cool. How about going for a ride?

A: No problem.

B: Can you drive aboard?

A: No. I have to take International Driver's License.

B: What is International Driver's License?

A: Precisely speaking, we should call it International Driving Permit. It is an identity document that allows the holder to drive a prlvate motor vehicle in any country that recognizes IDPs.

B: What does it look like?

A: It is slightly larger than a passport, is a multi-language translation of the driver's license from the issuing nation, complete with photograph and vital statistics.

A: 看！我的新驾照。

B: 酷！去兜风怎么样？

A: 没问题。

B: 能在国外开车吗？

A: 不能。得有国际驾照才行。

B: 什么是国际驾照？

A: 准确地说应该叫国际驾驶执照。它是一个允许持有者在承认国际驾驶执照的国家境内驾车的身份证件。

B: 它是什么样的？

A: 比护照稍微大点，由签发国家发放的多语言的证件，上面有照片和重要信息。

B: 我知道在不同的国家有不同的交通规则。

A: 是的。比如，在英国人们靠左行驶。世界上大约有1/4的国家车辆靠左行驶，而驾驶员坐在车辆的右前方。

B：I know there are different traffic rules in different countries.

A：Yes. For example, in Britain people drive on the left side of the road. About a quarter of the world drives on the left side of the road in right-hand drive cars.

"问" 英国特色文化

英国汽车工业为什么会盛极而衰？

英国汽车工业为什么会盛极而衰，评论普遍将原因归为英国政府。主要因为英国政府的经济政策造成了本国的汽车产业无利可图，所以英国的汽车厂在应该大规模提高产量并出口海外扩张的时候，却看不到那样做的任何好处，因而只是想在较小的产能下把车卖个好价钱。为了应对严峻的形势，英国的汽车厂开始走向联合。这一剂补药令已经过了壮年的英国汽车企业无福消受，却让外来的竞争者大受其益。衰落的英国汽车满足不了消费者猛增的消费需求，价廉物美的日本车趁机蜂拥而入，从此，英国的汽车工业就再也没有了还手之力。

阅读笔记

英国女王姓"温莎"吗

英国皇家姓氏

People often ask whether members of the Royal Family have a surname, and, if so, what it is. Members of the Royal Family can be known both by the name of the Royal house, and by a surname, which are not always the same. And often they do not use a surname at all.

Before 1917, members of the British Royal Family had no surname, but only the name of the house or dynasty to which they belonged. Kings and princes were historically known by the names of the countries over which they and their families ruled. Kings and queens therefore signed themselves by their first names only, a tradition in the United Kingdom which has continued to the present day. The names of dynasties tended to change when the line of *succession* was taken by a *rival faction* within the family, or when succession passed to a different family branch through females. Just as children can take their surnames from their father, so *sovereigns* normally take the name of their "House" from their father.

人们经常会问英国王室成员有没有姓氏，如果有的话，他们姓什么。王室成员以成员名称和姓氏为人所知，但姓氏不都相同。通常情况下，他们根本不用姓氏。

在1917年之前，英国王室成员是没有姓氏的，只有家族名称或朝代名称。在历史上，国王和亲王以他们家族统治的国家而为人所知。所以国王和女王签名只需要签他们的名字，这是英国一直以来的传统。当王位的继承权被敌对派系获得或其通过女性传到家族的不同分支时，王朝的名字也可能会发生改变。就像孩子从父亲那获得姓氏一样，君主也会采用其父亲所在家族的名称。

单词释义

- succession 继位
- sovereign 君主
- rival 对手
- faction 帮派

"温莎"姓氏的由来

In 1917 George V *adopted* Windsor, not only as the name of the 'House' or dynasty, but also as the surname of his family. The family name was changed as a result of anti-German feeling during the First World War, and the name Windsor was adopted after the Castle of the same name.

At a meeting of the Privy Council on 17 July 1917, George V *declared* that all *descendants* in the male line of Queen Victoria, who are subjects of these *realms*, other than female descendants who marry or who have married, shall bear the name of Windsor'.

The Royal Family name of Windsor was confirmed by The Queen after her *accession* in 1952. However, in 1960, The Queen and The Duke of Edinburgh decided that they would like their own direct descendants to be *distinguished* from the rest of the Royal Family, as Windsor is the surname used by all the male and unmarried female descendants of George V. It was therefore declared in the Privy Council that The Queen's descendants, other than those with the

1917年，乔治五世采用了温莎这一词，不仅将其用作"家族"和朝代的名称，也用作自己的姓氏。这个姓氏的由来源于第一次世界大战期间的反德情绪，而温莎这一名称取自同名城堡。

在1917年7月17日英国枢密院的会议上，乔治五世当众宣布所有除了将要结婚或已经结婚的女性，其他身为王储的维多利亚女王后裔，都要以温莎为姓。

女王伊丽莎白二世在1952年即位后，皇家姓氏温莎地位更加得以巩固。然而，1960年，女王和她的丈夫爱丁堡公爵想让自己的直系后裔的姓氏与其他王室成员有所区别。由于温

style of Royal Highness and the title of Prince/Princess, or female descendants who marry, would carry the name of Mountbatten-Windsor. The effect of the declaration was that all The Queen's children, on occasions when they needed a surname, would have the surname Mountbatten - Windsor.

莎是所有乔治五世的男性后裔和未婚女性后裔的姓氏，所以枢密院宣布女王的后代，除了王室殿下和有王子或公主头衔的人，或已婚女性后裔都将以蒙巴顿-温莎为姓。有了这个声明，之后当女王的子嗣需要姓氏时，就会有蒙巴顿-温莎这个姓氏。

单词释义

adopt 采用　　　　　declare 宣布　　　　　descendant 后代
realm 王国　　　　　accession 就职　　　　distinguish 区别

"品" 英国特色文化

特色表达One

英国王室里的每一个女王都是值得尊重的和让人难以忘怀的，并不像现在的某些明星只是轰动一时就被人遗忘了，这里的轰动一时即被遗忘的人或物就是a nine days' wonder。wonder作名字讲意思指"奇迹"或"奇观"，俚语a nine days' wonder表面意思是"一个只持续了9天的奇迹"，引申为"轰动一时即被遗忘的人或物"，有时和a flash in the pan表示相同的意思。

实景链接

A：Kevin seems to become famous. He has been built up into a big star. 凯文出名了，他已经被捧成大明星了。

B：I bet he's no more than **a nine days' wonder.** 我敢打赌他只不过是昙花一现。

A：What's your idea? 那你怎么想？

B：He is a poor singer, can't carry a tune. 他五音不全，唱歌总是跑调。

特色表达Two

英国女王的高贵大方，端庄典雅，相信所有人都铭记在心，他们都dressed

to the nines。这里的nine大家都知道是九，它是个数中最高的一位，所以dressed to the nines引申为穿着达到了最高级的程度，即打扮得精美而令人倾倒。需要注意的是dressed是过去分词，因为这个俚语是用来描绘穿着打扮处于什么状态的。同时注意nines是复数形式。

☆ 实景链接

A：What about Jorden's wedding? 乔登的婚礼怎么样？

B：All his friends assisted at the wedding ceremony. Everyone was **dressed to the nines**. 他的朋友们都参加了他的婚礼，大家都做了精心的打扮。

A：He is very handsome and his wife is very beautiful. It's so admiring. 他那么英俊，妻子又那么漂亮，真让人羡慕啊。

B：Yes, I believe he is. 是呀，我想也是的。

拓展特色句

1. Royal family changes their surname to Windsor in 1917. 英国王室在1917年将他们的姓氏改为温莎。

2. William and Kate are generations of the House of Windsor. 威廉王子与凯特王妃是温莎王朝的后继人。

3. George VI called his brother Duke of Windsor. 乔治六世称他哥哥为温莎公爵。

"聊" 英国特色文化

A：I'm studying the names in different countries recently.

B：An interesting issue.

A：I find that foreigners' names are so complicated.

B：Why did you say that?

A：Take British names for instance, there are two or three parts of their names.

B：What are they?

A：最近，我正在研究不同国家的人名。

B：是个有趣的课题。

A：我发现外国人的名字真复杂。

B：为什么这么说？

A：以英国人的名字为例，他们的名字有两到三部分组成。

B：都是什么？

A：第一个名字、中间名字和最后一个名字。第一个名字和中间名字是取

A: First name, middle name and last name. First name and middle name are given names, the last name is surname.

B: What's the Royal Family's surname?

A: And often they do not use a surname at all. Before 1917, members of the British Royal Family had no surname, but only the name of the house or dynasty to which they belonged.

B: Really?

A: Yes. In 1917, George V adopted Windsor as the surname of his family.

的名字,最后一个名字是姓。

B: 英国王室成员姓什么?

A: 通常情况下,他们根本不用姓氏。在1917年之前,英国王室成员是没有姓氏的,只有家族名称或朝代名称。

B: 真的吗?

A: 是的。1917年,乔治五世采用了温莎这一词用作自己的姓氏。

"问" 英国特色文化

为什么英国有女王?

传统意义上讲,英国女性的地位比男性的低一些,但差别不大。英国《王位继承法》规定了王位继承原则。君主的王位世代相袭,儿子优先于女儿,而女儿又优先于侄子或者侄女。也就是说,如果国王有儿子,那么儿子按年龄大小的顺序来排定继承顺序,接下来才是国王女儿。所以如果国王没有儿子,那么国王的女儿继承顺序最靠前,就会出现女王。比如说现在的英国女王伊丽莎白的父亲乔治六世只有两个女儿,伊丽莎白是长女,所以伊丽莎白继承王位。维多利亚女王也是由于同样的原因。

英国人为何总是在谈论天气

常谈论天气的原因

Talk to a **Briton** and, unless you know him very well, chances are that you'll be talking about the weather within the first 10 minutes or so. Even if you do know her very well, chances are that the weather will *come up*. It's a pure British *trait*, and there are countless theories about why this might be. Here are the two main ones.

Reason one: Weather is safe. In a country where people are *overwhelmingly* uncomfortable about showing their emotions in a way that, say, the Italians aren't, weather gives the Brit something to *latch* onto that's safe to talk about. There are few Brits who'll give you their life story during an elevator ride; however, you might find out how much it's been raining, shining, or snowing, and where.

Reason two: There is just so much of it. In his 1990s mini-series about Scotland, comedian Billy Connolly once *proclaimed* that the reason there were so few trees on the Shetland Isles is that they'd all blown away to Norway. Britain is a country which only a few years ago topped

跟英国人聊天时，除非你跟他很熟，不然前10分钟，你们的话题很可能是天气。即使你跟她关系很好，也可能会聊聊天气。这是纯英国式的特点，而且有非常多的理由来说明他们为什么会这样。以下就是两大理由。

理由一：聊天气是个很安全的话题。在一个大家都不喜欢随便展现自己情绪的国家，当然意大利人除外，谈论天气对英国人来说是非常安全的话题。很少有英国人会在电梯里就开始谈论他们的生活经历，相反，你会听到一些哪里在下雨、天晴或下雪的字眼。

理由二：英国人就是这么喜欢谈论天气。喜剧演员比利·康诺利曾出演20世纪90年代的有关苏格兰的迷你剧，他曾说道设德兰群岛的树之所以这么少是因为他们都被吹到挪威去了。英国是一个温度超过华氏100度（约摄氏37.8度）都要上报纸头条的国

100 degrees F for the first time, a fact that made headline news. Britain is green, green, and green... and that's because it rains, rains, and rains. And then it *coughs up* rainbows.

家，几年前，英国的温度首次突破华氏100度便上了报纸头条。英国一直绿意盎然，因为它总是下雨，有时候还会出现彩虹。

为什么对天气着迷

A study has found that for more than half of us, conversation turns to our climate at least once every six hours. A quarter of us deem the topic of such interest that we use it as an icebreaker. Our *obsession* with the weather runs so deep that almost 70 per cent of British people check the weather forecast at least once a day. And the fascination appears to increase with age, as more than 80 per cent of over-55s seek out a daily forecast, compared to 42 per cent of 18 to 24-year-olds.

Foreign observers are often quick to *gloat* that Britain's unpredictable and often wet weather is the cause of our *fixation*, however, only 44 per cent of those polled agreed. One in five claimed that weather-talk is an easy way of appearing friendly to strangers,

一项研究显示，我们中一半以上的人每6小时就会谈论一次天气。1/4的人认为我们喜欢谈论这个话题因为我们用天气来缓和拘谨的气氛，打破僵局。我们对天气的热衷是如此之深，以至于70%的英国人每天至少会看一次天气预报。而且英国人对天气的热衷度会随着年龄的增长而提高，55岁的老人中，有80%以上的人会每天看天气预报，而在18岁到24岁的人群中，这个比例只有42%。

外国人总会幸灾乐祸地说我们之所以这么执着于天气的话题是因为英国的天气总是变化多端且总是下雨，然而据调查，只有44%的人赞成这一说法。有1/5的人宣称跟陌生人谈论天气会显得英国人很友好，而另外有12%的人则认为谈论天气可以让交谈不涉及个人隐私，比较安全。社会人类学家凯特·福克斯是英国社会问题研究中

while 12 per cent said it helps keep conversations safe and *impersonal*. Social *anthropologist* Kate Fox, who is director of the Social Issues Research Centre think tank, said: "Britons need weather-talk to help us overcome our social *inhibitions* and *handicaps*." "The *variability* of the British weather makes it an ideal medium for our social messages." "We certainly talk about it a lot but this is not because it is an *intrinsically* interesting topic. Over half of the people we spoke to admitted that they used weather-talk to *facilitate* social interaction.

心智囊团的主任，她表示："谈论天气能帮我们克服社交的感情阻力与障碍。""英国天气的变化多端使其成为了社交信息的理想媒介。""我们之所以会这么痴迷于天气的话题并不是因为这个话题很有趣。我们访问过的一半以上的人都承认他们谈论天气是为了促进社交。"

单词释义

obsession 痴迷

impersonal 非个人的

handicap 障碍

facilitate 帮助

gloat 幸灾乐祸

anthropologist 人类学家

variability 变化无常

fixation 着迷

inhibition 感情阻力

intrinsically 本质的

"品" 英国特色文化

特色表达 One

英国人喜欢谈论天气，那他们真的很在乎天气变化吗？有的人可能会说 "idgaf"。乍一看，"idgaf" 跟乱码似的，其实这个 "idgaf" 是 "I don't give a fuck" 的缩写，意思等同于 "I don't care"，都可以表示不在乎的意思。

⭐ 实景链接

A： It's a beautiful day, isn't it? 今天天气不错，不是吗？

B： Yeah, nice day. 是啊，天气很好。

A: I think it will continue to be fine. 我觉得天气会一直晴朗的。

B: Idgaf. 谁管它呢。

💬 特色表达Two

英国人喜欢在社交场合以天气为话题打开话匣子，这样交谈的双方都能 bring somebody up to speed on something。这里可不是说"给某人在某些事物上加把劲"，指的是"给某人带来关于某事的最新消息"。

☆ 实景链接

A: Fairly warm this morning, isn't? 今天早上可真暖和，不是吗？

B: The sun is shining! 阳光灿烂啊！

A: But, I want to **bring you up to speed on the typhoon**. 但是，我要告诉你一些关于台风的事。

B: I've heard about it. 我也听说了。

拓展特色句

1. What do you think of the weather today? 你觉得今天的天气怎么样？

2. It probably clears up this afternoon. 今天下午可能会转晴。

3. It looks like we are going to have a thunder shower. 看样子快下雷阵雨了。

💬 英国特色文化

A: I find out an interesting phenomenon.

B: What is it? Talk to me.

A: In different countries people talk about different Topics. For example, Chinese people like to talk about food.

B: Yes. I think it must because of their different culture backgrounds.

A: I can't agree more.

B: Chinese people usually talk about

A: 我发现了一个很有趣的现象。

B: 是什么？跟我说说。

A: 不同国家的人们讨论不同的话题。比如，中国人喜欢谈论食物。

B: 是的。我想这一定是因为他们不同的文化背景。

A: 我同意。

B: 中国人见面的时候经常会谈论食物。

A: 那么英国人呢？

B: 他们认为天气是一个安全的话题，

food when they greet each other.

A: What about British, then?

B: They think weather is a safe Topic and Britain's weather is unpredictable and it often rains.

A: It's really a good way to use as an icebreaker.

并且英国的天气总是变幻莫测，还经常下雨。

A: 真是打破僵局的好办法。

"问" 英国特色文化

与英国人聊天时要注意哪些？

英国人聊天时，若是谈正事或工作，他们更喜欢单刀直入，拐弯抹角会被看成浪费时间。英国人很有幽默感，他们纯正的英式发音或许让人觉得很严肃，其实谈话中会穿插一些轻松的笑话，拉近彼此的距离。英国人不喜欢与别人聊天时过于亲热，他们认为这样太虚伪且缺少真诚，而且过于热情与过度关注会让英国人感到奇怪和不自在。在与英国人聊天时切勿谈论个人问题，婚姻、恋爱关系、财政、健康等话题最好不要涉及，除非对方是很要好的朋友。

阅读笔记

TOP 4 英国人开口闭口都是love，你受得了吗

叫昵称是为了展示友好

In Britain there we have a funny habit that will either make you wonder what *on earth* is going on, or make you feel right at home! 'Pet names' have developed across each part of each of the countries. You'll hear the little old man in the local shop say "There you go love" as they hand you your biscuits, though you've never been to their shop before. Hairdressers and waitresses will greet you with "Hello my love" or "Hi hon'". Strangers will say "Cheers sweetie!" if you do something to help; boys will call to each other "Alright mate!". These words are used so often in fact, that in some parts of the country, you might notice more if they are not used than when they are! Many foreigners to Britain find these terms of *endearment* to strangers really *eccentric* when they first arrive, but grow to realize that they are simply ways of showing friendliness; and many of us miss these little terms a lot when we move elsewhere!

I ❤ YOU

英国有一个非常有趣的习俗，会让人们有两种极端的反应——这究竟是怎么回事或是宾至如归的感觉。英国的各个地方的人都会使用昵称，如在本地商店的老人递给你饼干时，可能会说"给你，亲爱的。"虽然事实上这是你第一次光临这个商店。美发师与女招待跟你打招呼的时候也会说"你好，我的爱人"或"嗨，亲爱的。"如果你帮助了陌生人，他们会跟你说"谢谢，甜心！"而男孩们则会互称为"好伙计！"这些昵称的使用是如此频繁，以至于在一些地方，你已经习惯了这些称呼，而当别人没有使用时，你马上就会再注意到。许多来到英国的外国人刚来时觉得对陌生人使用这种爱称是非常奇怪的，但渐渐地，他们就会发现这些爱称只是为了显示他们的友好之情；当你搬到别的地方时，还会怀念这种昵称呢！

单词释义

on earth 究竟　　endearment 亲爱的表示　　eccentric 怪异的

063

该什么时候用昵称呢

These little terms of endearment can be used in public, by anyone, at almost any time. Usually people who deal with a lot of *general public* will use pet names just as a natural part of speech: waitresses, shop keepers, hairdressers, car mechanics, builders, workmen. People in professional environments tend not to use them so much! It's a kind of *casual* language, but people who work in environments where there's no need to be formal, will just use them in every part of life, with friends, family and probably with you, if you are ever in Britain!

So the rules on using these words are, only when you feel comfortable! How you use them and how often are really just a *reflection* of personal taste. Some people use them all the time (e.g. shop keepers/waitresses), others, just when they feel like it, or around friends. Avoid using them in professional environments, such as at business meetings, although, even here, you may not always be safe from hearing them!

任何人几乎任何时候都可以在公开场合使用昵称。一般情况下，昵称会成为服务行业人员的口头禅，这些行业的人有女招待、店主、美发师、汽车修理师、施工人员以及工人等。在一些比较职业的场合，人们使用昵称的频率会低很多！昵称不是一种正式的语言，但是如果人们的工作环境没有那么正式，他们也常常会对朋友、家人甚至身在英国的你使用昵称。

所以只要你愿意，你就可以使用这些昵称！你怎么使用或使用的频率通常反映你的个人品位。有些人会一直将其挂在嘴边（如店主或者女招待），而有些人只在愿意的时候或者与朋友之间才会使用。在商务会议这种商务环境中最好避免使用这些昵称，尽管有时在这种场合你也避免不了会听到这样的称呼！

单词释义

general public 公众 casual 非正式的 reflection 反应

"品" 英国特色文化

特色表达One

通常，英国人喜欢称呼别人"亲爱的"，若是遇上帅哥或辣妹，他们会如何打招呼呢？在英国俚语里，人们一般用hottie来形容帅哥或美女。但这个称呼有些轻佻和不雅，最好不要当面称一位女士为"hottie"，否则你可能惹上麻烦哦。

☆ 实景链接

A: Did you see that hottie over there? 你看到那边那个帅哥没有？

B: He is such a **hottie**! 他好性感啊！

A: Yeah, he is so charming. 是的，他太迷人了。

B: I wanna know everything about him. 我想知道他的一切。

特色表达Two

有的留学生初次来到英国不能适应这里"火热"的昵称叫法，常常被drive somebody up the wall。这里的wall是"墙"，那么up the wall就是"上墙"，而上墙可不是什么容易活儿，所以在俚语里它的意思是"把某人逼疯了"。

☆ 实景链接

A: I cannot endure his rudeness any longer. 我再也不能忍受他的无礼了。

B: If he has offended you, he does not mean it. 如果他得罪了你，那他是有口无心。

A: But, he always calls me "love", and this **drives me up the wall**. 但是他总是叫我"亲爱的"，这快把我逼疯了。

B: Well, don't care for what he said. 好吧，不要太在意他说的。

拓展特色句

1. I love my family very much. 我很爱我的家人。

2. Do you believe in love at first sight? 你相信有一见钟情这种事吗？

3. I love you too much to see you get hurt. 我那么爱你，不想让你受伤害。

"聊" 英国特色文化

A: What's wrong? It seems that you are unhappy.

B: His frivolity annoyed me. This is our first time meet each other. He called me "love". It made me uncomfortable.

A: Where does he come from?

B: Britain. What's up?

A: It's nothing strange then. 'Pet names' have developed across each part of each of the countries. You will get used to it sooner or later.

B: How can they do that?

A: I think it must due to their culture. But how you use them and how often are really just a reflection of personal taste.

B: Can you give me an example?

A: Sure. Shop keepers or waitresses use them all the time.

B: When can't we use them?

A: Avoid using them in professional environments, such as at business meetings.

A: 你怎么了？看起来不太高兴啊。

B: 他的轻浮惹恼了我。这是我们第一次见面。他叫我"亲爱的"。这让我很不舒服。

A: 他是哪里人？

B: 英国。怎么了？

A: 那就没什么奇怪的了。英国的各个地方的人都会使用昵称。你迟早会适应的。

B: 他们怎么这样呢？

A: 我认为这取决于他们的文化。但是你怎么使用和使用频率通常反映你的个人品位。

B: 能给我举个例子吗？

A: 当然可以。如店主或者女招待会一直将其挂在嘴边。

B: 什么时候不能用呢？

A: 在商务会议这种商务环境中最好避免使用这些昵称。

"问" 英国特色文化

Sir Madam

英国人一般如何称呼别人？

　　英国人一般对刚认识的人，根据不同的情况采取不同的称呼方式。首先，对地位高或年龄较长的男女，英国人通常称他们为Sir(先生)或Madam(夫人)，而不带姓，要么则用Mr.和Mrs.带上姓。这些称呼都比较正式，如果双方关系好或经常往来，就会自然改为用个人的名字，如John, Mary, Sam等。随着时间推移，许多英国人也常常用名字称呼别人(如Tom, Linda, John等)，而不用某某先生、某某太太或某某小姐，甚至初次见面就直呼名字。

英式英语的潜规则，你能读懂吗

遭受潜规则

Ever been told by a new neighbour 'You must come for dinner' then spent weeks waiting for a *follow-up* invitation that never arrives? Or been *thrilled* when the boss said he'd bear your 'very interesting' idea in mind and been surprised when it was never mentioned again. Then you've been *victim* of the uniquely British trait of being too *prim* and polite to say what we really mean. And if it can be *baffling* for us, imagine what it must be like for foreigners who take our every word at face value.

When a British person begins a sentence 'With the greatest respect...', they're really saying 'I think you are an idiot.' 'I hear what you say' means 'I disagree and do not want to discuss it further' while 'That is a very brave proposal' translates as 'You are *insane*'.

是否曾遇到过新邻居对你说"你得过来吃个晚饭"，可几个礼拜后邀请却迟迟没来？或是激动地听到上司说他会记住你"非常有趣"的想法，却惊讶他再也没提过这件事？如果你真的经历过，那你已经沦为了英式英语的受害者了，英式英语有一个特征，即对于表达真实所想太过于拘谨，也太过于礼貌了。其实对于我们英国人来说，想想外国人可能会把我们说过的每句话都信以为真，也挺令人困扰的。

当一个英国人说话时，以"怀着最高的敬意"开头，他们实际想表达的却是"我认为你是一个白痴"。"我听到你所说的什么"代表"我不同意也不想再继续讨论下去了"，"这是一个勇敢的提议"代表"你疯了"。

单词释义

follow-up 后续的
prim 拘谨的

thrilled 极为激动的
baffling 令人困惑的

victim 受害人
insane 疯狂的

英国人的社交距离法则

Among the English, *gossip* about one's own private doings is *reserved* for *intimates*; gossip about the private lives of friends and family is shared with a slightly wider social circle; gossip about the personal affairs of *acquaintances*, colleagues and neighbours with a larger group; and gossip about the intimate details of public figures' or celebrities' lives with almost anyone. This is the distance rule. The more 'distant' from you the subject of gossip, the wider the circle of people with whom you may gossip about that person.

If, for example, you want to find out about an English person's attitudes and feelings on a sensitive subject, such as, say, marriage, you do not ask about his or her own marriage – you talk about someone else's marriage, *preferably* that of a *remote* public figure not personally known to either of you. When you are better acquainted with the person, you can discuss the domestic difficulties of a colleague or neighbour, or perhaps even a friend or relative. (If you do not happen to have colleagues or relatives with suitably *dysfunctional* marriages, you can always invent these people.)

英国人的个人隐私一般只限于在亲密朋友之间讨论；关于朋友及其家人的一些琐事也只会在稍微宽一点的社交圈子里讨论；熟人、同事或邻居等话题可以在更广的社交圈子里谈论；如果是某位名人的个人隐私，那么绝对是街知巷闻。这就是社交距离的规则。当你和谈论对象的距离越远时，你就会和更大的社交圈子的人谈论他们的事。

但是，如果你想了解英国人对于某个敏感话题的态度或感觉，比如说婚姻，那么你就不能直接询问他自己的婚姻，而应该尝试谈论其他人的婚姻，最好是那些彼此都认识的名人的婚姻。当你和此人的距离拉近以后，你就可以和他谈论一些身边同事或者邻居的家事，乃至是亲友的问题也无妨（如果你的同事或亲友没有不正常的婚姻，你可以编造一些人）。

单词释义

gossip 闲聊　　　　　reserve 保留，留给　　　intimate 密友

acquaintance 熟人　　preferably 更适宜　　　remote 关系疏远的

dysfunctional 不正常的

"品" 英国特色文化

特色表达One

与英国人谈论时一定要注意保持距离，可以谈一些发生在熟人身上的事情拉近距离，这样才能和他们亲切地交谈，享受bed of roses的谈话气氛。据说300年来，英国人常用bed of roses来形容称心如意的境遇，如今bed of roses常和not或者no连用来表达"忙得焦头烂额"。

☆ 实景链接

A: Do you hear that Lily does double duty? 你听说了吗，莉莉做了两份工？

B: What happened to her? 她怎么了？

A: She has to take care of her two children, while her husband lost his job. 她得照顾两个孩子，她丈夫还失业了。

B: Her life these days is no **bed of roses**. 她这些天过得可真惨。

特色表达Two

人人都有得意时，当你得意时尽量别到处炫耀，小心laugh out of the other side of his mouth。这个短语可不是说"笑声从嘴的另一边出来"，在俚语里，它指的是"意外打击使人哭笑不得、转喜为忧"。

☆ 实景链接

A: Do you know Mary thought she got a real bargain? 你知道吗，玛丽觉得她自己占了大便宜？

B: Why does she think so? 为什么她这样认为？

A: Because she bought a car at half price of the normal one. 因为她半价买下了新车。

B: But, I heard that car was stolen by someone, so she may **laugh out**

of the other side of his mouth later. 但据我所知，那辆车是赃车，估计等会她会笑不出来了。

拓展特色句

1. This Chinglish sign can be quite misleading for foreign guests. 这种中国式英语的标志会误导外国游客的。

2. He can understand fairly complex English expression. 他能使用相当复杂的英语表达。

3. She perhaps misunderstood what you said. 她可能误解你说的话了。

"聊" 英国特色文化

A：What are you busy with?

B：My new neighbor invited me to her home. I'm just preparing for it.

A：When is it? Have you fixed the time?

B：Not yet. She probably forgot it.

A：I think I'd better inform you that your neighbor didn't really invite you. She said that just out of politeness.

B：I can't quite understand you. What do you mean?

A：You've been victim of the uniquely British trait of being too prim and polite to say what we really mean.

B：Really? How foolish I am!

A：It's not your fault.

A：你在忙什么呢？

B：我的新邻居说要邀请我到她家。我正做准备呢。

A：什么时候？你们确定好时间了吗？

B：还没。也许是她忘了。

A：我想我最好还是告诉你。你的邻居并不是真的要邀请你。她那么说只是出于礼貌。

B：我没太明白。你什么意思？

A：你已经沦为了英式英语的受害者了，英式英语有一个特征，即对于表达真实所想太过于拘谨，也太过于礼貌了。

B：真的吗？我真傻！

A：这不是你的错。

"问" 英国特色文化

英国人都说标准的英式英语吗？

很多中国留学生接触到的是标准的英式英语，其实在英国，真正讲标准英音的人非常少。在英国很多城镇，尤其是英格兰、苏格兰和威尔士大部分地区的人们讲的英语都不一样。比如，英格兰中部以伯明翰为中心的地区的英语鼻音很重，这种口音叫作brummie；而英格兰西北部的利物浦地区发音比较粗糙生硬，这种口音叫作scouse等。由于地域的差别，各地的英式发音融合了当地的发音习惯，就像中国的普通话，各省的人们说的也不是标准普通话。

If I had a
ritish Accen
I'd

阅读笔记

银行也有假期

什么是银行假期

A bank holiday is a public holiday in the United Kingdom, Commonwealth countries, other European countries such as Switzerland, and a *colloquialism* for a public holiday in Ireland. There is no *automatic right* to *time off* on these days, although banks close and the majority of the working population is granted time off work or extra pay for working on these days, depending on their contract.

Bank holidays are often *assumed* to be so called because they are days upon which banks are shut, but days that banks are shut aren't always bank holidays. For example: Good Friday and Christmas Day are not bank holidays, they are common law holidays. The dates for bank holidays are set out in *statute* or are proclaimed by *royal decree*. In England and Wales a bank holiday tends automatically to be a public holiday, so the day is generally observed as a holiday.

在英国、英联邦国家或其他如瑞士这样的欧洲国家，银行假期是公众假期，而银行假期也是爱尔兰对于公共假期的口头表达。在银行假期期间，法律并没有规定所有的人都可以休假，但是由于银行关门，绝大部分工人都会休假，如果他们在这几天仍在工作的话，他们会根据他们的劳动合同获得一笔额外的收入。

之所以会采用"银行假期"这个称呼是因为在这些天中，银行都会休业，但不是所有银行休业的日子都被称之为银行假期。例如，银行在耶稣受难日以及圣诞节也会关门，但这两个节日并不是银行假期，而是一般的法定假期。银行假期的具体放假时间都在英国法规或者皇家法令里有注明。在英格兰与威尔士，银行假期通常都会成为公众假期，所以这天一般都被称之为假期。

单词释义

colloquialism 口语　　automatic right 理所应当享有的权利　　time off 休假

assume 采用　　statute 法规　　royal decree 皇家法令

银行假期怎么来的

Prior to 1834, the Bank of England observed about 33 saints' days and **religious** festivals as holidays, but in 1834 this was reduced to four: 1 May (May Day), 1 November (All Saints Day), Good Friday, and Christmas Day. In 1871, the first **legislation** relating to bank holidays was passed when Liberal **politician** and banker Sir John Lubbock introduced the Bank Holidays Act 1871. The English people were so thankful that some called the first Bank Holidays St Lubbock's Days for a while. Scotland was treated separately because of its separate traditions: for example, New Year is a more important holiday there.

The Act did not **specify** Good Friday and Christmas Day as bank holidays in England, Wales, or Ireland because they were already recognised as common law holidays: they had been **customary** holidays since before records began. In 1903, the Bank Holiday (Ireland) Act added 17 March, Saint Patrick's Day, as a bank holiday for Ireland only. New Year's Day did not become a bank holiday in England until 1 January 1974.

1834年之前，英国央行通常将33个圣人节与宗教节日作为假期。但在1834年，这些假期减至4个，分别为5月1日的五一国际劳动节、11月1日的万圣节、耶稣受难日以及圣诞节。1871年，自由党的政客与银行家约翰·卢布克爵士提出了《银行假期法案》，首部关于银行假期的法规得以通过。英国人对他是如此感激，以至于有一段时间银行假期被称之为圣卢布克节。苏格兰跟英格兰的情况有所区别，因为苏格兰有其自己的传统，如新年对于苏格兰人来说是一个更为重要的假期。

这个法案没有规定耶稣受难日与圣诞节在英格兰、威尔士或爱尔兰也是银行假期，因为这几个节日已是法定假日——自有记录以来，这就已经是传统的假期了。1903年，《银行假期法案》单独给爱尔兰将3月17日的圣帕特里克节也定为银行假期。直到1974年1月1日，新年在英格兰才成为银行假期。

2013		
1 January	Tuesday	New Year's Day
29 March	Friday	Good Friday
1 April	Monday	Easter Monday
6 May	Monday	Early May bank holiday

单词释义

prior 在前的　　　　　religious 宗教的　　　　　legislation 法规
politician 政治家　　　specify 规定　　　　　　customary 惯例的

"品" 英国特色文化

特色表达One

很多英国人在银行假期都能休假与家人小聚，但也有特殊行业的人因不能放假而go haywire。据说以前欧美地区的农民常用一根细的铁丝把干草一捆捆地捆起来，于是做成了haywire。要是在捆干草时不够小心，铁丝的尖端就会刮破农民的皮肤和衣服，农民们就会生气，即go haywire。所以，在俚语里，go haywire表示"生气"的意思。

☆ 实景链接

A：Have you saw Jam? 你看到吉姆了吗？

B：What's wrong with him? 他怎么了？

A：Today is Bank Holiday, but he has to go to work, so he really **goes haywire**. 今天是银行假期，但他不得不去上班，所以他很生气。

B：Well, he might be used to it. 好吧，他应该要适应的。

特色表达Two

在英国，即使大部分公司都在银行假期放假，但对那些bed of nails的公司来说，这天可不能松懈。bed of nails这个短语难道指的是铺满了尖针的床吗？其实，在俚语里，这个短语的意思是"处境艰难，苦不堪言"。

☆ 实景链接

A：Do you know Mike's looking for another job? 你知道吗，麦克在找别的工作？

B：Well, it has come to my knowledge that he resigned. 我听说他辞职了。

A：Why did he do so? 他为什么这样做？

B：He told me that his job is a real **bed of nails** for him. 他说他的工作处境极其艰难。

拓展特色句

1. I had to work on Bank Holiday Friday. 星期五公休，可是我还得上班。

2. London markets closed on Tuesday for a bank holiday. 伦敦股市因银行假期周二休市。

3. The name Bank Holiday comes from the time when Banks were shut and so no trading could take place. "银行假期"这个名字起源于银行关闭以至所有交易停止的时期。

"聊" 英国特色文化

A: Look at these photos. We took them last Christmas. We really had a good time that day.

B: Yes. Christmas can be the most important festival for British, like the Spring Festival for Chinese people.

A: What holidays are there in Britain?

B: New Year's Day in January, Valentine's Day in February, Women's Day in March, Easter in April, Mother's Day in May, Father's Day in June, Thanksgiving Day in October, Halloween in November, Christmas in December and so on.

A: I heard that there is a bank holiday. What is it?

B: It is a public holiday in the United Kingdom.

A: It sounds interesting.

B: Yes. Bank holidays are often assumed to be so called because they are days upon which banks are shut.

A: 看这些照片。我们去年圣诞节的时候拍的。那天我们玩得真开心啊。

B: 是啊。圣诞节对于英国人而言是最重要的节日了，就像春节对于中国人而言。

A: 英国都有什么假日？

B: 一月的新年，二月的情人节，三月的妇女节，四月的复活节，五月的母亲节，六月的父亲节，十月的感恩节，十一月的万圣节，十二月的圣诞节，等等。

A: 我听说有一个银行假期。那是什么？

B: 它是英联邦国家的一个公共假期。

A: 听起来真有意思。

B: 是啊。之所以采用"银行假期"这个称呼是因为在这些天中，银行都会休业。

"问" 英国特色文化

银行假期对英国人来说意味着什么？

首先，银行假期是英国的法定公众假日，即Bank Holiday，由于在这天银行放假不营业，其他一些行业也无法正常营业，所以很多商店会在这天停业休整，除了那些特殊行业(如水电、消防、救护、警务、卫生保健)等，幸运的是他们会在这天得到双倍报酬。几乎英国全民都特别喜欢这个Bank Holiday，因为是法定假期，所以放假的员工们可以跟家人一起休息或出门度假。如果"银行假期"恰逢周末，就会与邻近的日子连在一起休假，方便公众利用假期远游。总之，银行假期在英国人心中就如我们的"十一黄金周"。

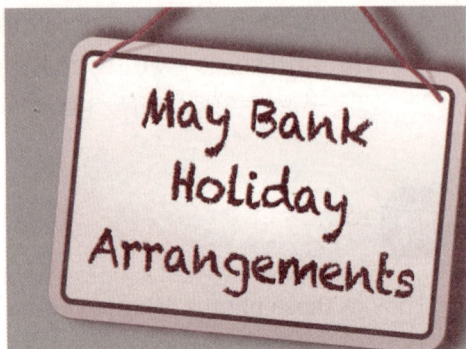

阅读笔记

Part 3

感受英伦风情的英国游

伦敦

首府简介

London, the capital of England and the United Kingdom, standing on the River Thames, was founded 2000 years ago by the Romans as Londinium. The city has been Western Europe's largest city for centuries. Today London is not only the largest city but also one of the most visited thanks to its *numerous* famous *attractions* such as the Tower Bridge and the Big Ben.

London is the most *populous* region, urban zone and *metropolitan* area in the United Kingdom. It is a leading global city, with strengths in the arts, *commerce*, education, entertainment, fashion, finance, healthcare, media, professional services, research and development, tourism and transport all contributing to its *prominence*. It is one of the world's leading financial centres and has the fifth-or sixth-largest metropolitan area GDP in the world depending on measurement. In 2012, London became the first city to host the modern Summer Olympic Games three times.

伦敦是英格兰以及英国的首府，横跨泰晤士。2000多年前，罗马人建立了这座都市，命名为伦底纽姆。几个世纪以来，伦敦一直都是欧洲最大的城市。如今，伦敦不仅是欧洲最大的城市，得益于其诸如塔桥和大本钟这样的无数著名景点，而且它还成为了欧洲最受欢迎的旅游城市之一。

伦敦是英国人口最稠密的地区、城市带以及大都会。伦敦在艺术、商业、教育、娱乐、时尚、金融、卫生保健、传媒、专业服务、研发、旅游以及交通上卓越成就，奠定了它在世界上的领先地位。它还是世界上名列前茅的金融中心，拥有世界上城市地区GDP的1/5~1/6。2012年，伦敦成为唯一举办了三次现代夏季奥运会的城市。

单词释义

numerous 无数的　　　　attraction 游览胜地　　　　populous 人口稠密的
metropolitan 大都市的　　commerce 商业　　　　　　prominence 突出

伦敦旅游

London has a *diverse* range of peoples and cultures, and more than 300 languages are spoken within its *boundaries*. It contains four World Heritage Sites: the Tower of London; Kew Gardens; the site comprising the Palace of Westminster, Westminster Abbey, and St Margaret's Church; and the historic settlement of Greenwich. Other famous landmarks include Buckingham Palace, the London Eye, Piccadilly Circus, St Paul's Cathedral, Tower Bridge, Trafalgar Square, and The Shard. London is home to numerous museums, galleries, libraries, sporting events and other cultural institutions, including the British Museum, National Gallery, Tate Modern, British Library and 40 West End theatres.

London is a *cosmopolitan* mixture of the Third and First Worlds, of *chauffeurs* and beggars, the *avowedly* working class and the *avant-garde*. Unlike comparable European cities, much of London looks unplanned and *grubby*, but that is part of its appeal. Visiting London is like being let loose on a giant-sized Monopoly board clogged with traffic. Even though you probably won't know where you are exactly, the names will at least look reassuringly

伦敦是一个非常多元化的大都市，其居民来自世界各地，具有多元的文化；城市中使用的语言超过300种。伦敦有四处世界遗产景点：伦敦塔、英国皇家植物园、包括威斯敏斯特宫、威斯敏斯特大教堂和圣玛格丽特教堂在内的地区以及格林威治遗址。伦敦的其他地标性建筑还有白金汉宫、伦敦眼、皮卡迪利广场、圣保罗大教堂、塔桥、特拉法加广场以及碎片大厦。

伦敦市是一个第三世界与第一世界的结合体，这里充斥着司机、乞丐、工人以及前卫人士。与其他欧洲大都市不同，伦敦的许多地方看起来都是脏乱的，但这也正是它魅力的一部分。参观伦敦就像是在玩交通拥挤的大富翁游戏。尽管你可能不知道自己究竟身在何处，但是各种地名看起

familiar. The city is so enormous, visitors will need to make maximum use of the underground train system: unfortunately, this *dislocates* the city's geography and makes it hard to get your *bearings.*

来至少会觉得很熟悉。这座城市是如此之大，所以作为游客，你一定要物尽其用，好好利用伦敦畅通的地铁体系。不幸的是，它错综复杂，以至于你常常会弄不清楚方位。

单词释义

diverse 多种多样的

boundary 边界

cosmopolitan 世界性的

chauffeur 司机

avowedly 明确的

avant-garde 前卫派

grubby 肮脏的

dislocate 使……混乱

bearing 方位

"品" 英国特色文化

特色表达One

来到伦敦，看到梦想中的繁华大都市，相信对于初来乍到的游客们已经眼花缭乱了，但是还是要尽量keep your eyes peeled，这句话的意思是"要用心看，仔细观察"的意思。

实景链接

A: London is so beautiful tonight. 伦敦今晚看起来太美了。

B: Yeah, and I heard there's a concert in the park. 是啊，而且我听说在公园还有演唱会呢。

A: What! Is that true? 啊！是真的吗？

B: Yes, **keep your eyes peeled**. You may be seeing your favourite star. 是真的，所以你要仔细观察，没准儿会遇到你最喜欢的那个明星哦。

特色表达Two

伦敦这么大，你有没有计划好自己的行程安排呢？千万不要只给自己一天的时间来欣赏这座城市，否则肯定会累到让自己want to crash，什么？让自己被撞或者是崩溃吗？当然不是，这里的crash是"睡觉"的意思。

☆**实景链接**

A：Are you tired, Ali? 阿里，你累了吗？

B：Yes, I need to **crash** for a while. 是呢，我需要睡一会儿。

A：Go on, and I'll wake you up later. 去睡吧，待会儿我叫你。

B：It's very kind of you. 你真是太好了。

拓展特色句

1. He grew up in the foggy city London. 他在雾都伦敦市长大。

2. Would you book a ticket to London for me? 能为我订一张到伦敦的机票吗？

3. During the visit to London I enjoyed walking and looking at the old buildings. 在伦敦旅游时，我非常享受于踱步在古老建筑群中的感觉。

🗨 **英国特色文化**

A：What makes you so happy?

B：We will travel in London next month. Have you ever been there before?

A：Yes. I've been there several times.

B：Cool. I just know it's the capital of Britain. Can you tell me something else?

A：Sure. The city is Western Europe's largest city and it's one of the most visited cities.

B：What should I see when I arrive in London? Do you have any recommendation?

A：It contains four World Heritage Sites: the Tower of London; Kew Gardens; the site comprising the Palace of Westminster, Westminster Abbey, and St Margaret's Church; and the

A：你怎么这么高兴？

B：下个月我们要去伦敦旅游。你以前去过那儿吗？

A：是的。我去过几次。

B：真酷。我只知道它是英国的首都。能告诉我些别的吗？

A：当然可以。它是欧洲最大的城市。它是最受欢迎的旅游城市之一。

B：到了伦敦我应该看什么呢？你有什么建议吗？

A：伦敦有四处世界遗产景点：伦敦塔、英国皇家植物园、包括威斯敏斯特宫、威斯敏斯特大教堂和圣玛格丽特教堂在内的地区以及格林威治遗址。

B：还有吗？

A：伦敦的其他地标性建筑还有白金汉

historic settlement of Greenwich.

B: Anything else?

A: Other famous landmarks include Buckingham Palace, the London Eye, Piccadilly Circus, St Paul's Cathedral, Tower Bridge, Trafalgar Square, and The Shard.

宫、伦敦眼、皮卡迪利广场、圣保罗大教堂、塔桥、特拉法加广场以及碎片大厦。

"问" 英国特色文化

伦敦为什么被称为雾都?

这主要有两方面的原因：一是自然因素，每到秋冬季节，北大西洋较暖的水流与大不列颠群岛区域较冷的水流汇合，同时从海上吹来大量暖空气与岛屿上空较冷的气团相遇，形成浓浓的海雾和陆雾；二是人为因素，伦敦为英国工业革命的主要发源地之一，工厂众多，烟囱林立，加上城市人口密集，伦敦人大部分都使用煤作为家居燃料。于是，烟与雾交集混杂在一起，造成了伦敦的烟霞，英语称为London Fog(伦敦雾)。因此，伦敦由此得名"雾都"。1952年12月5日至9日期间，伦敦烟雾事件令4000人死亡，政府因而于1956年推行了《空气清净法案》，于伦敦部分地区禁止使用产生浓烟的燃料。时至今日，伦敦的空气质量已经得到明显的改观。

阅读笔记

爱丁堡简介

Edinburgh is the capital of Scotland, *situated* in Lothian on the southern shore of the Firth of Forth. It is the second most populous city in Scotland and the seventh large city in the United Kingdom. The city is also home to many national *institutions* such as the National Museum of Scotland, the National Library of Scotland and the Scottish National Gallery. Edinburgh's the biggest financial centre in the UK after London. Many Scottish companies have their head offices there.

The city is rich in historical associations and has many surviving historic buildings. Edinburgh's Old Town and New Town are listed as a UNESCO World Heritage Site. The city's historical and cultural attractions, together with an annual calendar of events aimed *primarily* at the tourist market, have made it the second most popular tourist destination in the United Kingdom, attracting over one million overseas visitors each year. The city is also famous for the Edinburgh International Festival, which is the biggest annual international arts festival in the world.

爱丁堡是苏格兰的首府，位于福斯湾南岸的洛锡安区。它是苏格兰第二大、英国第七大城市。这座城市也是许多国家机构如苏格兰国家博物馆、国家图书馆以及苏格兰国家美术馆的所在地。爱丁堡是英国继伦敦后最大的金融中心。许多苏格兰公司的总部都设在这里。

这座城市历史悠久，保留了很多古建筑。爱丁堡老城和新城均被联合国教科文组织列为世界遗产。这座城市的历史文化景点，同主要针对旅游市场的年度活动一起，每年都会吸引100多万海外游客来此参观，因此，爱丁堡也成了英国第二大最受欢迎的旅游城市。这个城市还以世界上最大的国家艺术节——爱丁堡国际艺术节而出名。

单词释义

situate 位于   institution 机构   primarily 主要地

爱丁堡的美丽春季游

Edinburgh in spring is a *riot* of colour and charm-from the fresh green of Princes Street Gardens to the lines of daffodils that spring up around the city, to the collective happiness of the locals as Edinburgh *unfurls* in the gentle sunlight. Edinburgh has 12 major festivals across the year, and in spring the themes of re-growth and development are the strongest with the Science and Imagination festivals, both of which have a strong focus on robust children's programmes of exploration and *innovation*.

Spring in Edinburgh is leisurely in pace, and as such is a perfect time for families to get *involved* in the spirit of the festivals. The year *kicks off* with the Edinburgh International Science Festival, which runs from the 5-20th April 2014. The festival programme has not yet been announced, but some returning favourites include the five floors of festival fun in the City Arts Centre which in the past has contained everything from the popular Dig up a Dinosaur to explorations of *creepy crawlies* and

爱丁堡的春天颜色缤纷，魅力非凡，从王子街花园的绿意盎然到随处可见的水仙，再到沐浴在春日温暖阳光下的爱丁堡人们的喜气洋洋。爱丁堡每年主要有12个节日，而在春天，这些节日的主题主要是重生与发育，其中以爱丁堡国际科学艺术节和爱丁堡国际想象艺术节为主，这两个节日都非常关注孩子们对事物的探索与创新。

爱丁堡的春天非常悠闲，这也让各个家庭专心于各个节日的精神。2014年的4月5日至20日是爱丁堡国际科学艺术节，这是爱丁堡的第一个节

beginners experiments.

In addition to a variety of **exhibitions** and lectures, there are a range of family friendly activities around the city that can **complement** a spring festival experience. Many museums and historical spaces are traditionally free in Scotland, and the National Museum of Scotland is a good place to start. Other family friendly spaces include Edinburgh Castle, the Botanic Gardens and Camera Obscura.

日。这个节日的具体计划尚未公布，但是以往深受大家喜爱的项目包括在该市艺术中心占用5层的各种项目，如从最受欢迎的挖掘恐龙到探索爬行虫以及初学者实验。

除了一系列的展览与讲座之外，还有很多能丰富春日节日氛围的亲子家庭活动。苏格兰的很多博物馆与历史遗址都不收门票，而苏格兰国家博物馆就是一个开始家庭活动的好地方。其他适合家庭一块去的地方还有爱丁堡城堡、植物园以及暗室。

单词释义

riot 丰富多样
involved 专心于……的
crawly 小爬虫

unfurl 迎风招展
kick off 开始
exhibition 展览

innovation 创新
creepy 爬行的
complement 补充

"品"英国特色文化

特色表达One

如果你能有幸在爱丁堡参加了国际科学艺术节，相信每个人都会激动得对你说：You're a lucky dog! 听到这句话不要以为别人是在嫉妒你，说你的坏话。在西方，狗被认为是人们的好朋友，所以You're a lucky dog表示"你真是个幸运儿"。如果朋友碰到了好运也可以用这句话。You lucky beggar. 这句话也有相同的意思。

☆ 实景链接

A: I had the pleasure of attending the Edinburgh International Festival. 我有幸参加了爱丁堡国际艺术节。

B：Wow, **you're a lucky dog**! 哇，你真是个幸运儿！

A：Yes, it's a place of my dream. 是啊，那一直都是我梦寐以求的地方。

B：Congratulations! Your dream has come true. 恭喜你，梦想成真了！

特色表达Two

　　来了爱丁堡，最不能忘记带的就是相机了。赶紧将爱丁堡独有的春色美景拍下来传到朋友圈吧，我想，看到照片的亲们除了狂点赞之外，也会附上一句You have an eye for beauty. 意思是"你真是有一双发现美的眼睛！"这里的have an eye for something表示"对某事(某物体)了解得非常清楚"，引申为"对某事(某物体)有眼光，有见解"。

☆ 实景链接

A：I found you uploaded lots of photos. Did you go to Edinburgh? 我发现你传了很多照片。你是去爱丁堡了吗？

B：Yes, I took all the photos. It has terrific museum, botanic garden and Edinburgh International Festival. 是呀，我都拍下来了。爱丁堡有很棒的博物馆、植物园和爱丁堡艺术节。

A：You really **have an eye for beauty**. 你真是有一双发现美的眼睛啊！

B：Thank you for your praise! 谢谢你的夸奖！

拓展特色句

1. We need to buy a guide to Edinburgh. 我们需要买一本爱丁堡旅游手册。

2. Where should I wait for the express to Edinburgh? 我应该到哪里等候开往爱丁堡的快车呢？

3. The couple met one summer at the Edinburgh Festival. 一个夏天，那对情侣在爱丁堡艺术节相遇了。

"聊" 英国特色文化

A：Do you know Edinburgh?

B：Of course. It's the capital of Scotland.

A：Last week I went there on business.

A：你知道爱丁堡吗？

B：当然知道。它是苏格兰的首府。

A：上周我去那儿出差。那儿真是一个

It's a beautiful place.

B：I heard that the city is rich in historical associations and has many surviving historic buildings.

A：You are right. Edinburgh's Old Town and New Town are listed as a UNESCO World Heritage Site.

B：How about the natural sight?

A：Edinburgh in spring is a riot of colour and charm-from the fresh green of Princes Street Gardens to the lines of daffodils that spring up around the city, to the collective happiness of the locals as Edinburgh unfurls in the gentle sunlight.

B：It's really a family friendly space. I'm wondering to have my holiday there this year.

美丽的地方。

B：我听说这座城市历史悠久，保留了很多古建筑。

A：是的。爱丁堡老城和新城均被联合国教科文组织列为世界遗产。

B：自然风光怎么样？

A：爱丁堡的春天颜色缤纷，魅力非凡，从王子街花园的绿意盎然到随处可见的水仙，再到沐浴在春日温暖阳光下的爱丁堡人们的喜气洋洋。

B：真是一个适合全家人去的好地方。我考虑今年去那儿度假。

"问" 英国特色文化

为什么爱丁堡又叫"北方的雅典"？

爱丁堡位于苏格兰中部低地的福斯湾南岸，这里依山傍水，风光秀丽。夏秋两季绿树成荫，鲜花盛开，古代宫殿、教堂和城堡点缀其间，文化遗产丰富，素有"北方雅典"之称，它的这个名称源于英国的国家纪念碑。站在爱丁堡新城东部卡尔顿山上的国家纪念碑处，远眺蓝色的福斯海湾，鸟瞰爱丁堡全景，你会觉得爱丁堡是一座有着欧洲中世纪建筑特色的美丽城市。国家纪念碑是爱丁堡的标志性建筑，它是模仿雅典帕特侬神庙，为纪念在拿破仑战争中的牺牲者而建造的。

曼彻斯特文化概况

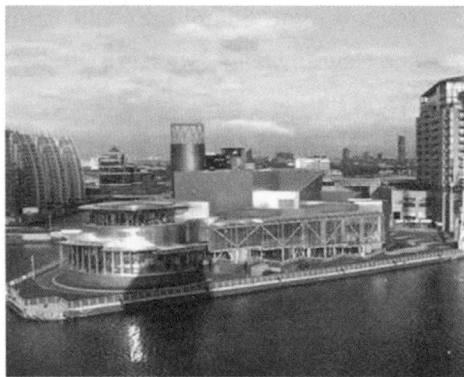

The Culture of Manchester is notable artistically, architecturally, theatrically and musically. Despite being the 9th largest city in the United Kingdom by population, and only the third largest *conurbation*, Manchester has been ranked as the second city of the United Kingdom in numerous polls since the 2000s, with an influential culture scene helping to *elevate* Manchester's importance in the national psyche.

Often cited as the world's first industrialized city, with little pre-factory history to speak of, Manchester is the third most visited city in the United Kingdom after London and Edinburgh and is a major centre of the creative industries. History and heritage make Manchester interesting, but what makes it truly special are its *distractions* of pure pleasure. You can dine, drink and dance yourself into happy *oblivion* in the *swirl* of *hedonism* that is one of Manchester's most cherished characteristics.

曼彻斯特是重要的艺术、建筑、喜剧以及音乐文化中心。尽管它是英国人口第九大城市，也是全英国第三大都市，但自21世纪来，许多民意调查都将其列为英国第二大城市，因为其文化影响力巨大，提升了其在民族精神中所占的地位。

作为世界上第一个工业化城市，曼彻斯特市是继伦敦和爱丁堡后的第三大旅游城市以及创意产业的主要中心地区。历史与文化遗产使曼彻斯特变得生动有趣，而使其真正变得特别的则是其纯粹的娱乐消遣活动。在这里，你可以享受美食与美酒，可以唱歌跳舞，让自己沉浸在欢乐的海洋里，而这也是曼彻斯特最受人珍视的一点。

单词释义

conurbation 大都市　　elevate 提升　　distraction 消遣，娱乐
oblivion 遗忘　　swirl 漩涡　　hedonism 快乐主义

曼彻斯特大学风光

About a mile South of the city, the University of Manchester is one of England's most *extraordinary* institutions, and not just because it is a top-class university with a remarkable academic *pedigree* and a great place to party. It is also home to a world-class museum and a superb art gallery. If you're into natural history and social science, this extraordinary museum is the place for you. It has galleries devoted to *archaeology*, *archery*, botany, *ethnology*, geology, *numismatics* and zoology. The real treat here, though, is the Egyptology section and its collection of mummies. One particularly interesting part is devoted to the work of Dr Richard Neave, who has rebuilt faces of people who have been dead for more than 3000 years; his pioneering techniques are now used in criminal *forensics*.

The Whitworth Art Gallery, housed in the University of Manchester, is renowned for its collections of British watercolors, drawings, prints, modern art and *sculpture*. It also is home to the largest textile and wallpaper collections outside of London. All this high art aside, you may find that the most interesting part of the gallery

曼彻斯特大学位于曼彻斯特城市以南一英里，是英国最杰出的院校之一。它不仅是一所有着深厚学术背景的顶级院校，还是一个非常适合社交聚会的地方。它还拥有世界一流的博物馆以及美术馆。如果你对自然历史以及社会科学非常感兴趣，那顶级博物馆就是你的好去处。美术馆主要是关于考古学、箭术、植物学、人种学、地理、钱币学以及动物学的。这里最负盛名的就是埃及古物学部分以及木乃伊藏品。最有趣部分莫过于理查德·尼夫博士的工作了，他致力于恢复去世超过3000年的人的面部。现在他开创性的技术已经应用于刑事取证。

位于曼彻斯特大学的惠特沃斯美术馆，以英国壁纸、图纸、印刷、现代艺术和雕塑藏品而闻名。它也是位于伦敦外最大的纺织品与壁纸收藏地。在所有的高雅艺术品之中，你会发现该美术馆中最有趣的部分是一组

is the group of rooms dedicated to wallpaper – proof that bland pastels and horrible flowery patterns are not the final word in home decoration.

关于壁纸的房间，这些关于壁纸的房间正好证明了平淡的蜡笔以及多样的花样并不是装饰家庭的唯一选择。

单词释义

extraordinary 非凡的　　　pedigree 门第　　　archaeology 考古学
archery 箭术　　　　　　　ethnology 人种学　　numismatics 钱币学
forensics 取证　　　　　　 sculpture 雕塑

"品" 英国特色文化

特色表达One

在享受美食，唱歌跳舞的同时，如果能邂逅合得来的人，那真的是太幸福的事了！这里说的"合得来"用俚语表达就是click，click常有"点击"之意，但是在口语里常表示"两个人很合拍"，它既可以用在异性之间，也可以用在同性之间。

☆ 实景链接

A：What do you think of Sophie? 你觉得苏菲怎么样？

B：I like staying with her. I think we two really **click**. 我很喜欢和她待在一起。我觉得我们两个蛮合得来的。

A：Many say she is a person with a sense of humor. 很多人都说她是个有幽默感的人。

B：I also think so. 我也这样认为。

特色表达Two

曼彻斯特大学常会举办社交聚会，在聚会中永远都会有那么一个"mack daddy"让众多女孩倾心不已，没错，mack daddy指的就是"有魅力，有事业，有女人缘的男人"。mack daddy起源于一首黑人歌曲"the great mac daddy"，daddy曾表示"皮条客"的意思，慢慢地演变成了"有影响力的男人"。

☆ **实景链接**

A：Do you have the favourite movie stars? 你有喜欢的电影明星吗？

B：Yes, he is so handsome in **The Fast and the Furious**. 有呀。他在《速度与激情》中太帅了。

A：Are you talking about Paul Walker? 你说的是保罗·沃克吗？

B：Yeah, he is a **Mack daddy**! 是啊，他简直就是个万人迷！

拓展特色句

1. The flight will arrive in Manchester in the afternoon. 那一航班会在下午到达曼彻斯特。

2. Have you guys enjoyed your time in Manchester? 你们在曼彻斯特过得还愉快吧？

3. I met your mother when she was 20 and studying at Manchester University. 我遇见你妈妈的时候，她20岁，当时正就读于曼彻斯特大学。

"聊" 英国特色文化

A：Where will you go this summer holiday?

B：I would like to choose Manchester.

A：Is there anything special?

B：It is the third largest city of United Kingdom. The Culture of Manchester is notable artistically, architecturally, theatrically and musically.

A：It sounds nice.

B：You can dine, drink and dance yourself into happy oblivion in the swirl of hedonism that is one of Manchester's most cherished characteristics.

A：There is a university called the University of Manchester.

A：今年暑假打算去哪儿啊？

B：我想选择曼彻斯特。

A：那儿有什么特别的吗？

B：它是英国第三大城市。曼彻斯特是重要的艺术、建筑、喜剧以及音乐文化中心。

A：听起来不错。

B：在那里，你可以享受美食与美酒，可以唱歌跳舞，让自己沉浸在欢乐的海洋里，而这也是曼彻斯特最受人珍视的一点。

A：那儿还有一个曼彻斯特大学。

B: Yes. It is one of England's most extraordinary institutions.

A: I hope that you will have a good time. Remember to take some photos and share with us.

B: 是的。它是英国最杰出的院校之一。

A: 希望你在那儿玩得愉快。别忘了拍些照片回来和我们分享。

"问" 英国特色文化

为什么曼彻斯特不再是"肮脏的老城"？

曼彻斯特是英国传统的工业重镇，其工业化和城市化水平在领先于全球的同时，也率先面临着工业化进入成熟期之后的一系列经济社会矛盾。当时，被称为英国民歌之父伊万·麦考创作了一首歌曲，名为《肮脏的老城》，这首歌就深刻地控诉了工业化对曼彻斯特城市和人民健康的破坏。后来，由于政府监管有力的法律制度和完善的职业病防治举措，如今的曼彻斯特早已告别"肮脏的老城"，成为了一个职业病发病率低、充满生机和活力的城市。

阅读笔记

利物浦

不可取代的利物浦

Few English cities are as *shackled* by reputation as Liverpool, and none has worked so hard to outgrow the *cliches* that for so long have been used to define it. Yes, the city has had a *hardscrabble* history *beset* by *chronic* misfortune and a myriad of social ills. Yes, those tough times have helped *forge* the city's famous sense of humour, which is really just a coping mechanism for getting through difficulty. Yes, they love football here. And yes, the Beatles occupy a huge chunk of the city's cultural heritage.

All these things are true. Liverpool has *transformed* its centre via a breathtaking programme of urban regeneration and is home to some of the best museums and galleries north of the Watford Gap. The main attractions are Albert Dock, and the trendy Ropewalks area. Lime St station, the bus station and the Cavern Quarter – a mecca for Beatles fans—lie just to the north.

几乎没有英国的城市像利物浦这样被其声誉桎梏着，也没城市像利物浦这样一直努力发展以摆脱以前人们对它的印象。是的，由于长期的不幸与被无数的社会弊病所困扰，这座城市有着不堪回首的历史。是的，正是这些艰苦的日子培养了该城市最负盛名的幽默感，而这幽默感成为了人们面对困难时的应对机制。是的，他们喜欢足球。此外，披头士也是这里的文化遗产的重要部分。

这些都是真的。通过令人惊叹的城市重建项目，这座城市改造了其中心城区，成为了沃特弗德峡北部最棒的博物馆以及画廊的所在地。这里最著名的景点有阿尔伯特码头以及时髦的绳索工场。而莱姆街火车站、公交车站以及披头士粉丝的圣地卡文街区就在它的北边。

单词释义

shackle 桎梏　　　　cliches 陈词滥调　　　　hardscrabble 贫瘠的
beset 困扰　　　　　chronic 长期的　　　　　forge 塑造
transform 改造

披头士纪念馆

The Beatles Story is dedicated to the 1960s pop group The Beatles, located in the Fab Four's hometown of Liverpool. It is an *atmospheric* journey into the lives, times, culture and music of The Beatles. You can see how four young lads from Liverpool were *propelled* to the *dizzy* heights of worldwide fame and fortune to become the greatest band of all time – from their childhoods in Liverpool, to the early days of the band, to world *domination* and on to their solo careers.

Liverpool's most popular museum won't *illuminate* any dark, juicy corners in the *turbulent* history of the world's most famous *foursome* – there's ne'er a mention of internal *discord*, drugs or Yoko Ono – but there's plenty of genuine *memorabilia* to keep a Beatles fan happy. Particularly impressive is the full-size replica Cavern Club (which was actually tiny) and the Abbey Rd studio where the lads recorded their first singles, while George Harrison's crappy first guitar (now worth half a million quid) should inspire budding, penniless musicians to keep the faith. The museum is also the departure point for the Yellow Duckmarine Tour. You can also get a combo ticket

披头士纪念馆是为纪念20世纪60年代流行乐队披头士而建，位于披头士的家乡利物浦。这是领略披头士生活、时代、文化以及音乐独特氛围的旅程。在这里，你能看到这四个人从出道到声名鹊起，再到成为世界上最伟大乐队的星路历程——从利物浦的童年时期，到乐队出道早期，到统治世界，再到自己的独唱生涯。

利物浦最受欢迎的博物馆并没有将披头士乐队中著名的四人纷争历史这一黑暗面展现出来，里边没有提及任何关于四人纷争、毒品或小野洋子的事情，相反，博物馆展出了很多有纪念意义的展品，以让披头士的粉丝们保持愉悦的心情。除了能激励刚出道身、无分文的音乐家保持信仰的乔治·哈里森的第一把做工粗糙吉他（现在价值50万英镑）在展出外，其中最令人印象深刻的是与卡文俱乐部(实际上非常小)以及披头士第一首单曲录制地艾比路工作室尺寸一样的复印品。该博物馆还是利物浦著名的水陆两用观光船旅程的起始点。你还能

for the *Elvis & Us* exhibit at the new Beatles Story extension on Pier Head.

在码头顶的披头士新纪念馆中购买到《猫王与我们》展览的套票。

单词释义

atmospheric 有独特氛围的
domination 统治
foursome 四人对抗赛

propel 鼓励，推进
illuminate 照亮
discord 纷争

dizzy 嫉妒的
turbulent 混乱的
memorabilia 纪念展品

"品"英国特色文化

特色表达One

利物浦足球俱乐部是欧洲乃至世界最成功的足球俱乐部之一。能有这样的成绩除了队员的不懈努力外，也一定离不开他们在球场上的walk on eggshells。eggshell是"鸡蛋壳"的意思。鸡蛋壳是很脆弱的，如果想在鸡蛋壳上走，就需要非常小心谨慎，所以这句俚语表示"谨慎行事，小心谨慎"。

☆ 实景链接

A: Which team are you in now? 你现在为哪个球队效力？

B: An unknown one. 一个不太出名的球队。

A: What's you boss like? 你的老板怎么样？

B: He was a very religious man and we need to **walk on eggshells**. 他是个非常严谨的人，所以我们都会谨慎行事。

特色表达Two

一说到披头士，让我们印象深刻的一定有他们早期的马桶盖发型，而这个发型就是贝司手斯图尔特的女友阿斯特丽德·科尔什赫设计的。当时乐队在汉堡演出期间，斯图尔特对阿斯特丽德一见钟情，顿时take a shine to her，这是一句日常很常用的俚语，表示"喜欢某人，对……有好感"。

☆ 实景链接

A: I met a glamorous girl today! She was really so pretty! 我今天看到了一个迷人的女孩，她真的太美了！

B：You mean you **took a shine to that girl**? 你的意思是你对那个女孩动心了是吗？

A：Yes, but I don't know her name and her address! 是啊，但是我不知道她的名字和地址。

B：What a pity! 太可惜了！

拓展特色句

1. Welcome to Liverpool Football Club. 欢迎来到利物浦足球俱乐部。

2. I am now a Liverpool player; it is perfect. 我现在是一名利物浦队的运动员了，太棒了。

3. The government says it will not tolerate any violence on the streets of Liverpool. 政府表示不会容忍任何在利物浦街头发生的暴力事件。

"聊"英国特色文化

A：I'd like to travel with my wife next month. How about Liverpool?

B：Have you ever been there before?

A：Not yet.

B：In my opinion you can have a try. It is a famous port city in northwest of England, it is also the fourth largest city in United Kingdom.

A：How about the climate there?

B：It is marine climate. The average temperature is between 10 and 32 centigrade.

A：What should I visit there?

B：The Beatles Story is a good choice.

A：Is it dedicated to the 1960s pop group The Beatles?

B：Yes. You can see how four young lads

A：下个月我想和妻子去旅行。去利物浦怎么样？

B：你以前去过那儿吗？

A：还没。

B：我觉得你们可以试试。它是位于英格兰西北部的一个重要港口城市，也是英国第四大城市。

A：那儿的气候怎么样？

B：那儿是海洋性气候。平均气温在10~32℃。

A：我们在那儿应该参观什么呢？

B：披头士纪念馆是一个不错的选择。

A：是为纪念20世纪60年代流行乐队披头士而建立的吗？

B：是的。在这里，你能看到这四个人从出道到声名鹊起，再到成为世界上最伟大乐队的星路历程。

from Liverpool were propelled to the dizzy heights of worldwide fame and fortune to become the greatest band of all time.

"问" 英国特色文化

利物浦足球俱乐部有多厉害?

利物浦足球俱乐部是英格兰足球超级联赛的球队之一，位于英格兰西北港口城市利物浦，于1892年成立，是英格兰的一支足球俱乐部。利物浦是英格兰足球历史上最成功的俱乐部之一，也是欧洲乃至世界最成功的足球俱乐部之一。共获得了18次英格兰足球超级联赛冠军，7次英格兰足总杯冠军，8次英格兰联赛杯冠军。在欧洲赛场上，利物浦是英格兰最成功的俱乐部，5次欧洲冠军杯冠军，3次欧洲联盟杯冠军，创造了英格兰纪录。值得一提的是除了足球超级联赛和英格兰足总杯外，其他的均是英格兰联赛的最高纪录。俱乐部的精神格言是"你永远不会独行"(You'll never walk alone)。

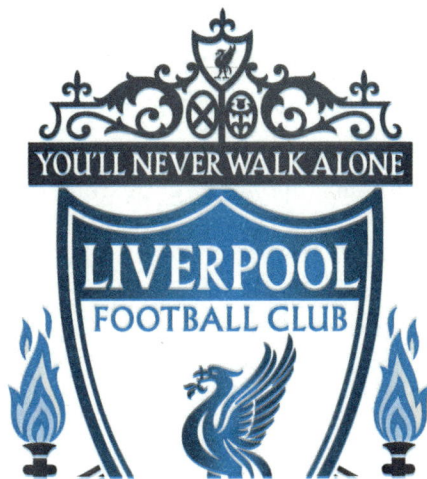

阅读笔记

伯明翰

伯明翰简介

Birmingham, in the West Midlands, is Britain's second largest city (by local authority district). Known in the Victorian era, as "the City of a 1000 Trades"and the "Workshop of the World", Brum as locals call the city, is enjoying a 21st century *resurgence* as a great shopping and cultural destination. Birmingham was at the heart of the UK's industrial revolution, and its wealth was built upon the *multitude* of trades that were *spawned*.

The city's notable associations are as diverse as HP Sauce, Tony Hancock, Cadbury's chocolate, The Lunar Society, Black Sabbath, UB40, the Spitfire and the Mini (car, not skirt). Birmingham has many of its own tourist attractions, has an extremely lively night life, and the shopping is arguably one of the best outside of London.

伯明翰位于西米德兰兹区域，是英国第二大城市(按照管辖区域来划分)。伯明翰在维多利亚时代被称之为"千业之城"与"世界工厂"。当地人称为Brum的伯明翰正在复兴，以成为重要的购物以及文化中心。伯明翰是英国工业革命的核心，它的财富来源于大量的生产贸易。

这座城市拥有各种各样著名的人和物，如HP沙司、托尼·汉考克、吉百利巧克力、月光社、黑色安息日乐队、UB40乐队、喷火式战斗机和宝马的Mini汽车。伯明翰有许多旅游胜地，有多项风采多姿的夜生活，此外，它也是除伦敦外最好的购物天堂。

单词释义

resurgence 复活　　　　multitude 众多　　　　spawn 大量生产

伯明翰风光

Birmingham has been a major player on the British jewellery scene ever since Charles II brought back a taste for fancy buckles and *sparkly brocade* from France in the 17th century. Stretching north from the last Georgian square in Birmingham, the Jewellery Quarter still produces 40% of the jewellery manufactured in the UK, and dozens of workshops are open to the public. In the Museum of the Jewellery Quarter, the Smith & Pepper jewellery factory is *preserved* as it was on its closing day in 1981, after 80 years of operation. You can explore the long history of the trade in Birmingham and watch master jewellers at work.

Cadbury World, about 4 miles south of Birmingham in the village of Bournville, sets out to educate visitors about the history of cocoa and the Cadbury family, but sweetens the deal with free samples, displays of chocolate-making machines, and chocolate-themed rides. Surrounding the chocolate works, pretty Bournville Village was built by the *philanthropic* Cadbury family to *accommodate* early-20th-century factory workers. In the centre of the village, Selly Manor is a *bona fide* 14th-century manor house, shifted brick and *mortar*

自17世纪查理二世从法国带回来了对装饰性的带扣以及闪亮的锦缎之后，伯明翰就成为了英国珠宝界的主要生产商。伯明翰的珠宝区为格鲁吉亚广场以北地区，全英国有40%的珠宝产自这里，这里还有几十个对公众开放的珠宝工作坊。珠宝区的博物馆保存了生产了80年后于1981年关闭的史密斯佩伯珠宝工厂。你可以探索伯明翰悠久贸易史，观看珠宝大师的工作。

吉百利世界位于伯明翰南部4英里处的伯恩维勒，旨在让游客了解可可与吉百利家族的历史，通过给游客发送免费样品来笼络感情，展示制作巧克力的机器，还设有以巧克力为主题的游乐设施。围绕巧克力作坊的是伯恩维勒村，这是乐善好施的吉百利家族建的给20世纪早期的工人们住宿的。村子的中心是塞利庄园，它是一座真正的14世纪的庄园，乔治·吉百

from its original location by George Cadbury to save it from destruction.

Birmingham's grandest civic buildings *cluster* around pedestrianized Victoria Sq, at the western end of New St, dominated by the stately facade of Council House, erected in 1874–1879. A *facelift* in the 1990s gave the square modernist sphinxes and a fountain topped by a naked female figure, nicknamed "the floozie in the Jacuzzi" by locals.

利通过给其增加砖块以及灰浆而将其从毁灭中拯救了出来。

伯明翰最宏伟的建筑聚集在维多利亚广场周围的步行区域，它位于新街的西部，具有英地方当局营造的房屋的庄严外观，建于1874年至1879年。20世纪90年代，政府对这些房屋进行了翻新，这个广场新增了具体现代特色的狮身人面像以及以被当地人称之为"the floozie in the Jacuzzi"的裸体女性为顶点的喷泉。

单词释义

sparkly 耀眼的	brocade 锦缎	preserve 保存，保护
philanthropic 乐善好施的	accommodate 供……住宿	bona fide 真实的
mortar 灰浆	cluster 聚集	facelift 翻新

"品" 英国特色文化

特色表达One

伯明翰绝对算得上是购物天堂，仿古商业街、现代购物中心、精品店和品牌商铺云集于此，很少会让购物者遇到a dime a dozen的东西。这里的a dime a dozen，字面意思看来就是一角钱可以买一打，所以引申为"不太值钱"的意思。

☆ 实景链接

A: Hey, Danny! Look what I've find! Some crystal stones! 嘿，丹尼，快看我找到了什么！水晶般的石头！

B: STop fussing. Those are **a dime a dozen**. 别大惊小怪了。那种石头到处都是。

A: Oh no! 啊！不是吧！

B: You have rejoiced too soon. 你就是空欢喜一场。

特色表达Two

如果想chasing the skirt，那么就把她带到巧克力梦工厂——伯明翰吉百利世界吧。chasing the skirt里的chase有"追逐"的意思，而skirt又是女孩子穿的裙子，所以通过字面意思追逐裙子，引申为"追求女孩子"。

☆实景链接

A：What's John up to these days? 约翰最近忙什么呢？

B：He is always out drinking beer and **chasing the skirt**. 他每天只知道出去喝酒泡妞儿。

A：Is his girlfriend not upset? 他女朋友不生气吗？

B：They broke up last month. 他们上个月就分手了。

拓展特色句

1. Birmingham was originally a remote and marginal area. 伯明翰起初只是一个偏远的边区。

2. Birmingham suffered heavy bomb damage during World War II. 伯明翰曾在第二次世界大战时期遭到严重轰炸。

3. Birmingham is located in the centre of the West Midlands region of England. 伯明翰坐落在英格兰西米德兰地区的中心。

"聊" 英国特色文化

A：Do you know Birmingham?

B：The second biggest city in Britain?

A：Yes. My colleague went there last Sunday. The photos show that they had a good time.

B：I heard that Birmingham was at the heart of the UK's industrial revolution, and Cadbury's chocolate is one of the notable associations.

A：I love the taste of it. I will prepare a

A：你知道伯明翰吗？

B：英国第二大城市？

A：是的。我的同事上周日去那儿了。从照片上看他们玩得很愉快。

B：我听说伯明翰是英国工业革命的核心，它的财富来源于大量的贸易生产，而吉百利巧克力就是其中一个著名机构。

A：我喜欢它的味道。每次开派对我都会准备很多和朋友分享。

lot of it to share with friends when I have a party.

B： Cadbury World sets out to educate visitors about the history of cocoa and the Cadbury family. The displays of chocolate-making machines and chocolate-themed rides are to attract customers.

A： It's a suitable place for me.

B： You can enjoy yourself there.

A： I'd better take my wife and children. This will be my next destination.

B： Of course. May you have a nice trip.

B： 吉百利世界旨在让游客了解可可与吉百利家族的历史。在那里展示制作巧克力的机器，开设以巧克力为主题的游乐设施都是为了吸引顾客。

A： 这个地方很适合我。

B： 你能在那儿玩得愉快。

A： 我会带上妻子和孩子们一起去。它就是我的下一个目的地了。

B： 当然。祝你旅途愉快。

"问" 英国特色文化

为什么伯明翰是体育之城?

体育是伯明翰人生活中的重要组成部分，在伯明翰市中心的阿克斯运动中心有很多运动场地，如射箭、滑雪、攀岩等。伯明翰市内分布很多足球、网球和板球场，如著名的三个职业足球俱乐部——阿斯顿维拉、伯明翰城和西布罗姆维奇以及埃格卑斯顿国际板球比赛的主赛场。此外，这座城市还有众多可以随时使用的游泳池和健身中心供市民和游客选择。1990年，伯明翰被正式命名为"欧洲体育之城"。

剑桥

感受剑桥的学术氛围

Abounding with *exquisite* architecture, *steeped* in history and tradition and renowned for its *quirky rituals*, Cambridge is a university town *extraordinaire*. It lies in East Anglia, on the River Cam, about 50 miles north from London. The tightly packed core of ancient colleges, the *picturesque* 'Backs' (college gardens) leading on to the river, and the leafy green meadows that seem to surround the city give it a far more *tranquil* appeal than its historic rival Oxford.

Like "the Other Place", as Oxford is known, the buildings here seem unchanged for centuries, and it's possible to wander the college buildings and experience them as countless prime ministers, poets, writers and scientists have done. The sheer academic achievement seems to *permeate* the very walls, with cyclists loaded down with books negotiating narrow cobbled passageways, earnest students relaxing on manicured lawns and great minds debating life-changing research in historic pubs.

剑桥是座令人神往的传统大学城，它富于优美的建筑，沉浸在历史与传统中，以奇特的礼制闻名于世。剑桥郡位于伦敦以北50英里处的东安格利亚，横跨剑河。剑桥郡的核心——古老的大学，河边如图画般美丽的风景、看似将剑桥郡围绕起来的碧绿草地都使剑桥郡看起来比它一直以来的对手牛津郡要宁静得多。

就像牛津闻名于世的"the Other Place"一样，这里的建筑几个世纪以来一直都没有任何改变，所以你可以像无数的首相、诗人、作家、科学家那样漫游在大学的各个建筑之中，感受它们。纯粹的学术成就似乎弥漫在整个剑桥，骑自行车的人推着载有一摞书的自行车沿着铺有鹅卵石的人行道交谈，认真的学生躺在修建整齐的草坪上休息，伟大的思想家在具有历史意义的酒吧里辩论着生活的改变。

单词释义

abound 富于   exquisite 优美的   steep 沉浸

quirky 奇怪的   ritual 礼制   extraordinaire 非凡的

picturesque 风景如画的   tranquil 宁静的   permeate 渗透，弥漫

剑桥的荣耀——国王学院礼拜堂

In a city crammed with show-stopping architecture, this is the show stealer. Chances are you will already have seen it on a thousand postcards, tea towels and choral CDs before you catch your first glimpse of the *grandiose* King's College Chapel, but still it inspires awe. It's one of the most extraordinary examples of Gothic architecture in England, begun in 1446 as an act of piety by Henry VI and finished by Henry VIII around 1516. Its *steeples* have long been a *magnet* for night climbers.

While you can enjoy stunning front and back views of the chapel from King's Pde and the river, the real drama is within. Mouths drop open upon first glimpse of the inspirational *fan-vaulted* ceiling, its *intricate* tracery soaring upwards before exploding into a series of stone fireworks. This vast 80m-long canopy is the work of John Wastrel and is the largest expanse of fan vaulting in the world. The chapel is also remarkably light, its sides *flanked* by lofty stained-

在一座充满了让人留下深刻印象建筑的城市里，这是一个抢镜的地方。在见到宏伟的国王学院礼拜堂真实面目之前，你可能已经在无数明信片、茶巾或是赞诗CD上见过它，但当你真正见到它时，你仍然会感到震撼。它是英国哥特式建筑的非凡代表作之一，为亨利六世在1446年下令建造，耗时80年，于1516年亨利八世在位时完工。它的尖塔一直深深地吸引着喜欢晚上攀爬的人们。

虽然你可以在国王河旁欣赏这个礼拜堂宏伟的正面和背面，但实际上这条河也是这幅美景图中的一部分。无须深度探索国王学院礼拜堂，只需第一眼看到其带有灵感的扇形拱顶天花板、错综复杂的窗饰，你就会感到非常震撼。这个礼拜堂长达80米的天

glass windows that retain their original glass. The antechapel and the choir are divided by a superbly carved wooden screen, designed and executed by Peter Stockton for Henry VIII. The thickly carved wooden stalls just beyond the screen are a stage for the chapel's world-famous choir. You can hear them in full voice during the magnificent Evensong.

棚出自约翰·瓦斯特尔之手，是世界上最宽的扇形拱顶。该建筑能辐射出光线，其墙壁的每一面上都装有高大的窗户，窗户上仍装有原来的彩色玻璃。分隔礼拜堂前厅与唱诗班的是一个木雕屏风，它由彼得·斯托克顿为亨利三世所设计与制作。木雕屏风的后边就是这个礼拜堂闻名于世的唱诗班。在晚祷时，你能听到庄严的祷告声。

单词释义

grandiose 宏伟的　　　　steeple 尖顶　　　　magnet 有吸引力的事物
fan-vaulted 扇形的　　　intricate 错综复杂的　　flank 位于……的侧面

"品" 英国特色文化

特色表达One

能有幸在剑桥郡的大学城里读书的同学一定都是elite了，虽然只有简短一个单词，但是完全表达了一个人的优秀程度，即"精英，精华，社会名流"，如：Brown is absolutely an elite student in our school.（布朗在我们学校绝对是精英。）

☆ 实景链接

A：Have you chosen the college yet? 你选好大学了吗？

B：Not yet. What about you? 还没呢，你呢？

A：My dream school is Cambridge University. But it only admits **elite** students. 我的理想学校是剑桥大学。但是它只招收最好的学生。

B：Be confident! You are great! 自信点，你很棒的！

特色表达Two

国王学院的礼拜堂是剑桥的荣耀，也是公认的全欧最出色的哥特式建筑。当它真正呈现在你的面前时，你仍然会感到震撼，会情不自禁地说：fan-crapping-tastic！它和fantastic同意，表示"太好了，太棒了"。

☆ 实景链接

A：Where did you go? Your phone couldn't get through a few days ago. 你去哪儿了？前几天一直打不通你的电话。

B：I went to King's College Chapel. 我去国王礼拜堂了。

A：Wow, how do you feel? 哇，你感觉怎么样？

B：It's **fan-crapping-tastic**. I can't find words to express how much I like it. 太美了！我无法用语言表达我多喜欢它。

拓展特色句

1. She used to run when she was at Cambridge. 她过去在剑桥时经常跑步。

2. The Cambridge University rows against Oxford every year. 剑桥大学每年都与牛津大学进行划船比赛。

3. We decided to motor over to Cambridge to see some of my friends. 我们决定开车去剑桥看我的一些朋友。

"聊" 英国特色文化

A：Why so many people like to visit Cambridge?

B：I think it must because it is an extraordinaire university town with exquisite architecture and steeped in history and tradition.

A：It is a good place to take photos and movies.

B：Yes. The buildings here seem unchanged for centuries; the sheer academic achievement seems to permeate the very walls.

A：No wonder that I have usually seen it on a thousand postcards, tea towels and choral CDs.

A：为什么这么多人喜欢去剑桥参观？

B：我想是因为它是一座拥有优美建筑并且沉浸在历史与传统中的非凡的大学城。

A：这是一个适合摄影或者拍电影的好地方。

B：是啊。这里的建筑几个世纪以来一直都没有改变，纯粹的学术成就似乎弥漫在整个剑桥。

A：难怪我常在无数明信片、茶巾或是赞诗CD上见过它。

B：但当你真正见到它时，你仍然会感到震撼。

A：它是什么时候建造的？

B: But at the first glimpse of the grandiose King's College Chapel, it still inspires awe.

A: When was it built?

B: It was begun in 1446 as an act of piety by Henry VI and finished by Henry VIII around 1516.

A: What a grand project!

B: 它是亨利六世在1446年下令建造，于1516年亨利八世在位时完成，耗时80年。

A: 真是一项宏伟的工程。

"问" 英国特色文化

剑桥大学为什么受学生的欢迎?

在每年的世界大学排名的排行榜上我们几乎都能看到剑桥大学的身影。这样的排名，已经说明了剑桥大学在世界大学中的分量。剑桥大学历史悠久，诞生过很多伟大人物，也是培养过最多诺贝尔奖得主的高等学府。学校非常静谧，非常适合学习。这里的导师制是剑桥一直保持的一大特色。因为导师不仅在学业上给学生以指导，而且在品行、心理等方面给学生以指导，成为学生的良师益友。这种导师制对正处于世界观、价值观形成期的本科学生将是一种巨大的财富，可能会影响一个人的一生。

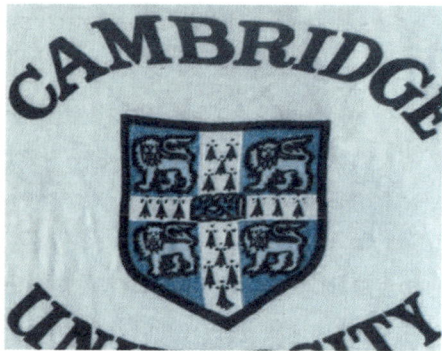

阅读笔记

TOP 7 格拉斯哥

格拉斯哥概览

Glasgow is Scotland's largest city and is *renowned* for its culture, style and the friendliness of its people. It offers a *blend* of internationally-acclaimed museums and galleries, stunning architecture, *vibrant* nightlife, fantastic shopping and *a* diverse *array of* restaurants and bars. Vibrant and *energetic*, Glasgow enjoys a year-round buzz with an arts scene that regularly produces *cutting-edge* productions and attracts *high-profile* exhibitions that led to the city being *crowned* European City of Culture in 1990. Glasgow was also the UK's City of Architecture and Design in 1999 and its architecture is an attraction in itself. The city centre has countless impressive Victorian structures and then there are the unique *masterpieces* of one of the city's most celebrated sons, the *legendary* architect and designer Charles Rennie Mackintosh. The city has a long-standing reputation for its live music scene and is very well off too in terms of city parks.

格拉斯哥是苏格兰第一大城市，以其辉煌的文化、独特的风格以及热情友好的民风而闻名于世。这里有国际知名的博物馆和画廊，绝妙的建筑，多姿多彩的夜生活，精彩的购物体验和各式各样的餐馆与酒吧。充满活力、精力充沛的格拉斯哥全年都充满着定期制作出先进影片艺术场景的繁忙景象，同时，它吸引了很多高知名度的艺术展览，由此，这座城市在1990年被加冕为欧洲文化之城。格拉斯哥在1999年还被评为英国建筑设计之城，其很多建筑已经成为了旅游景点。格拉斯哥的市中心分布着无数令人印象深刻的维多利亚时代的建筑，还有一件

非常独特的杰作，出自该城市最著名的孩子之一，即传说中的建筑师与设计师查尔斯·罗纳·麦金托什。该城市的现场音乐也久负盛名，此外，这里还因拥有许多城市公园而闻名。

单词释义

renowned 著名的
a array of 大量
high-profile 知名度高的
legendary 传奇的

blend 融合，混合
energetic 精力充沛的
crowned 王室的

vibrant 充满生命力的
cutting-edge 尖端的
masterpiece 杰作

布雷尔收藏馆

One of Glasgow's top attractions is the Burrell Collection. *Amassed* by wealthy industrialist Sir William Burrell before being donated to the city, it is housed in an *outstanding* museum, 3 miles south of the city centre. Burrell collected all manner of art from his teens to his death at 97, and this *idiosyncratic* collection of treasure includes everything from Chinese *porcelain* and *medieval* furniture to paintings by Degas and Cézanne. It's not so big as to be overwhelming, and the stamp of the collector lends an *intriguing coherence*.

Visitors will find their own favourite part of this museum, but the exquisite tapestry galleries are outstanding. Intricate stories capturing life in Europe are woven into *staggering* wall-size pieces dating from the 13th to 16th centuries.

Within the spectacular interior, carved-stone Romanesque doorways

格拉斯哥最著名的景点之一就是布雷尔收藏馆。它位于该城市市中心以南3英里外的一个著名博物馆里，由工业巨子威廉·布雷尔爵士创建并捐献给格拉斯哥市。这里展出了布雷尔从十几岁到97岁毕生收藏的特殊艺术珍品，从中国瓷器到中世纪家具，再到德加和塞尚的画作，这里藏品繁多。它并没有大到让你无法抗拒，但是收藏家布雷尔的标记会让你觉得非常吸引人。

游客在这里会有自己最喜欢的藏品，但是这里精致的挂毯展示中心非常著名。描绘着从13世纪到16世纪欧洲人们生活的有如一面墙大小的编织物着实让人惊叹。

进入博物馆令人惊叹的内部，你会发现由石头刻成的罗马风格门廊与整个建筑融为一体，你可以从它们之间穿过。从地板连至天花板的落地窗让自然光完全照进来，外面的树木和风景也更衬托出了展品的效果，让你感觉自己漫步在宁静的温室之中。

春天的时候，在这里逛上一整天是非常值得的，花一些时间徜徉在点

are *incorporated* into the structure so you actually walk through them. Floor-to-ceiling windows admit a flood of light, and enable the surrounding landscape outside to enhance the effect of the exhibits. It feels as if you're wandering in a huge tranquil greenhouse.

In springtime, it's worth making a full day of your trip here and spending some time wandering in the beautiful park, *studded* with flowers. Once part of the estates of Pollok House, which can be visited, the grounds have numerous *enticing* picnic spots; if you're not heading further north, here's the place to see *shaggy* Highland cattle, as well as heavy horses.

缀着鲜花的美丽公园。还可以去参观开放的波勒克之屋，附近有很多迷人的野餐地点；如果你不想向北走，你可以在这里欣赏到毛发粗长的高原牛与重装马。

单词释义

amass 收集，积累
porcelain 瓷器
coherence 一致性，连贯性
stud 散布

outstanding 著名的
medieval 中世纪的
staggering 令人惊愕的
enticing 迷人的

idiosyncratic 特殊的
intriguing 吸引人的
incorporate 使并入
shaggy 毛发粗长的

英国特色文化

特色表达One

很多城市都有独具特色的博物馆或收藏馆，格拉斯哥也不例外。在这个城市里，坐落着一个收藏馆收藏着a nine days'wonder，但却是收藏者心中最美的风景。a nine days'wonder字面意思是"九天的奇迹"，在俚语里指的是"昙花一现，或轰动一时的人物"。

☆实景链接

A：Let's go to the museum at the weekend. 咱们周末去博物馆吧。

B：Of course! I like visiting museums. 好啊。我喜欢参观博物馆。

A：How about the Burrell Collection? 去布雷尔收藏馆怎么样？

B：Alright, I heard that there been many art works, and some of them are **nine days' wonders**. 好啊，我听说那里有很多的艺术品，有些曾轰动一时呢。

💬 特色表达Two

格拉斯哥是英国著名的文化名城，在这里，街头歌唱的是流浪音乐家，路边吆喝的也许是曾名动一时的雕塑家，这里少有商场与政界get the drop on。get the drop on最早出自拓荒西部时期，那时很多男人携带枪支，经常不和就开枪解决，于是谁先开火，谁就占上风能先发制人了。后来人们用这个短语形容"胜过某人，比某人领先"。

☆实景链接

A：Jane, do you want the afternoon off? 简，你下午想请假，是吗？

B：Yeah, I want to ask off to relax with a cup of beer at Glasgow. 是的，我想请假去格拉斯哥小酌几杯，放松一下。

A：Tell me the reason, Lily. 告诉我理由，莉莉。

B：I have been busy **getting the drop on** our competitors, I was so tired. 我一直争取领先，比我们的竞争对手更优秀，我太累了。

拓展特色句

1. The pink mattress was picked up in a shop in Glasgow. 这个粉红色的床垫是从格拉斯哥的一家店里买来的。

2. Her father belongs to Glasgow. 她父亲是格拉斯哥人。

3. I've seen the authentic one of this painting in Burrell Collection. 我在布雷尔收藏馆看到过这幅画的真迹。

"聊" 英国特色文化

A: This book mentioned a place called Glasgow. Do you know anything about it?

B: Is it a book about travel? It is Scotland's largest city and is renowned for its culture, style and the friendliness of its people.

A: No, it's an autobiography. The author just mentioned it. I don't quite know Scotland.

B: Glasgow attracts high-profile exhibitions that led to the city being crowned European City of Culture in 1990. It was also the UK's City of Architecture and Design in 1999.

A: What's the famous tourist attraction?

B: It's the Burrell Collection.

A: What's in it?

B: Burrell collected all manner of art from his teens to his death at 97, and this idiosyncratic collection of treasure includes everything from Chinese porcelain and medieval furniture to paintings by Degas and Cézanne.

A: 这本书提到了一个叫做格拉斯哥的地方。你知道这个地方吗？

B: 是关于旅游的书吗？它是苏格兰第一大城市，以其辉煌的文化、独特的风格以及热情友好的民风而闻名于世。

A: 不是，是一本自传。作者只是提到了它。我不是很了解苏格兰。

B: 格拉斯哥吸引了很多高知名度的艺术展览，由此，这座城市在1990年被加冕为欧洲文化之城。在1999年还被评为英国建筑设计之城。

A: 著名景点有什么？

B: 布雷尔收藏馆。

A: 里面有什么？

B: 这里展出了布雷尔从十几岁到97岁毕生收藏的艺术珍品，从中国瓷器到中世纪家具，再到德加和塞尚的画作，藏品繁多。

"问" 英国特色文化

格拉斯哥城是如何形成的？

　　"格拉斯哥"这个的名字源自布利屯语中的"glas cu"，它的意思是"绿色的空地"。据说，格拉斯哥地区在公元前已有部落聚居于此。后来，古罗马人在格拉斯哥地区设立了前哨站，建筑了安多宁长城。6世纪时，越来越多的人来到此地生活，其中有位叫圣姆格的基督教传教士在此修建了教堂，为格拉斯哥日后发展奠定了基础。后来到20世纪80年代中期时，格拉斯哥的经济有了明显进步，众多金融公司的迁入加速了它的发展。于是到16世纪初，格拉斯哥已演变为重要的宗教与学术城市。如今，格拉斯哥也是苏格兰地区的主要城市之一。

阅读笔记

纽卡斯尔

曾经的港口城市——纽卡斯尔

Newcastle upon Tyne has gone through many stages in its history as a city, from Roman fortress to a shipping centre from the late 18th to the mid 20th century. Today, however, the city is mostly *reliant* on office and *retail businesses* for its economy, and has become something of a cultural *hub*. The Byker Wall is now listed by UNESCO as one of the outstanding buildings of the 20th century. The first Biotechnology Village or "Centre for Life" in the United Kingdom was also established in Newcastle upon Tyne, which has helped transform the city into a scientific centre as well as a cultural one. It is full of cultural attractions and *monuments* that will delight visitors; Earl Grey's Monument, St. Nicholas Cathedral, St. Mary's and the old Castle Keep are all historic landmarks worth visiting.

从18世纪末到20世纪中期，从罗马要塞到航运中心，位于泰恩河下游的纽卡斯尔作为一个城市数次登上了历史的大舞台。然而，现在这个城市的经济主要依靠企业和零售业，同时也成了一个文化中心。这里的拜克墙被联合国教科文组织列为20世纪最杰出的建筑之一。英国的第一个生物技术村"生命中心"也成立于纽卡斯尔，这也让这个城市转变为科技中心与文化中心。这里有很多能取悦游客的文化景点与历史遗址；格雷伯爵纪念碑、圣尼古拉斯教堂、圣玛丽和旧城堡这些具有历史意义的地标都非常值得参观。

单词释义

reliant 依赖的　　　　retail businesses 零售业　　hub 中心

monument 历史遗迹

纽卡斯尔人的特色

Newcastle's *hip* reputation is built on a set of deep-rooted traditions *embodied* by the city's greatest strength: the locals. The locals are known as Geordies, and they have a distinct character and *dialect*. Geordie is recognised as a separate dialect from standard English and it stems from a mixture of Old English, Nordic languages and Scots (having a number of words that are present in modern Swedish). Everyone speaks standard English and will use it when in the presence of a non-local. The accent is difficult to *interpret* at first, but you will be able to understand it fairly quick and easy.

Raised and *subsequently* abandoned by coal and steel, Geordies are a *fiercely* independent bunch, tied together by history, *adversity* and that *impenetrable* dialect. They are generally friendly and very sociable; nights out on 'tha Toon' are generally good fun, with a wide selection of bars and clubs dotted around the compact city centre, it was voted 7th best night out in the world by Weissman Travel correspondents. It's nearly a guarantee that you'll find yourself on the dance floor with several locals by the end of the night, having an absolute whale of a time!

纽卡斯尔的声誉来自其许多根深蒂固的传统，这些传统体现在其最具优势的地方——纽卡斯尔人的身上。纽卡斯尔人被称为泰恩赛德人，他们有着不同的性格和方言。泰恩赛德人使用的语言是标准英语的分支，为古英语、日耳曼语以及苏格兰语(现在瑞典语中能留存有很多词汇)的混合物。这里所有的人都会说标准英语，跟外地人说话时也会用标准英语。纽卡斯尔方言的口音比较重，刚开始可能会很难理解，但习惯后，你就能很快听懂。

作为一个依靠煤和钢而发展起来、到最后被煤和钢抛弃的城市，泰恩赛德人是一个非常独立自处的群体，被历史、灾祸以及那费解的方言紧紧地团结在了一起。他们通常都非常友好，也很善于交际；夜晚在图恩那通常很有趣、琳琅满目的酒吧和俱乐部遍布紧凑的市中心；它被《斯曼旅行》记者评为世界上第七大夜生活最丰富的城市。我可以保证，到深夜的时候你会发现自己正在和几个当地人在一起跳舞，共度了一段欢乐时光。

单词释义

hip赶时髦派的　　　　embody 体现　　　　dialect 方言

interpret 理解　　　　subsequently 随后　　fiercely 非常

adversity 灾祸　　　　impenetrable 费解的

"品" 英国特色文化

特色表达One

纽卡斯尔曾名列全球七大夜生活最丰富的城市之一，这里随处可见奢靡浪漫的酒吧，灯红酒绿的都市夜生活是这里永恒的基调，可也有人宁可宅在internest也不乐意外出压马路。Internest是由internet(互联网)和nest(窝，巢)组合而成，在俚语中，它指的是"在家上网"。

⭐实景链接

A：Hey where's Lily? 嘿，简在哪里？

B：Oh, she is in her **internest**. 哦，她窝在家上网呢。

A：So, she would rather be in the **internest** than hanging out in a bar. 所以她宁可在家上网也不愿去酒吧。

B：She's just one of those people! 她就是那样的人。

特色表达Two

即使外面灯红酒绿的诱惑再多，也总会有那么一群人，他们是妻子心中的好丈夫，是孩子眼中的好父亲，他们就是husbeen。这个词的词形与husband类似，其实词义也有些许相关，husbeen在俚语中指的是妻管严，就是听老婆话的丈夫。

⭐实景链接

A：Do you know Bill? 你认识比尔吗？

B：You mean Bill Robert? 你说的是比尔·罗伯特吗？

A：Yeah, you know him! 是的，你认识他呀！

B：Well, he is such a **husbeen**. 喔，他就是个妻管严。

拓展特色句

1. The Newcastle airport was already shut. 纽斯卡尔机场已经关闭了。
2. He has been in sensational form for Newcastle United this season. 这一赛季，他在纽斯卡尔联队中表现出色。
3. The "Angel of the North" is built of 200 tonnes of steel. "北方天使"是由200吨的铁铸成的。

"聊" 英国特色文化

A: Today I would like to talk about Newcastle.

B: Is there anything special about it?

A: It played an important role in the history. It has gone through a period from Roman fortress to a shipping centre from the late 18th to the mid 20th century.

B: How about the situation now?

A: Today the city is mostly reliant on office and retail businesses for its economy, and has become something of a cultural hub.

B: What's the population of it?

A: More than 500 thousand.

B: How many universities are there in Newcastle?

A: There are two. One is Newcastle University, the other is Northumbria University.

B: Is there a football club?

A: Of course. The Newcastle United Football Club owns the most fans in England.

A: 今天我想谈谈纽卡斯尔。

B: 它有什么特别的吗？

A: 它在历史中扮演了重要的角色。从18世纪末到20世纪中期，经历了从罗马要塞到航运中心的演变。

B: 现在的处境呢？

A: 现在这个城市的经济主要依靠企业和零售业，同时成为了一个文化中心。

B: 人口有多少？

A: 50多万。

B: 纽卡斯尔有几所大学？

A: 两所。一所是纽卡斯尔大学，另一所是诺桑比亚大学。

B: 那儿有足球俱乐部吗？

A: 当然。纽卡斯尔联足球俱乐部拥有全英格兰最多的球迷。

"问" 英国特色文化

纽卡斯尔有哪些著名的艺术品?

纽卡斯尔市是英格兰最受欢迎的城市之一,它具有悠久的历史与传统。纽卡斯尔有很多著名的艺术品,其中最享盛名的非"北方天使"(Angel of the North)莫属。"北方天使"其实是北英格兰地区的著名地标,也是英国境内最大的雕塑,被誉为英国最为杰出的艺术品之一。"北方天使"树立在纽卡斯尔著名的产煤区盖茨黑德(Gateshead)最高的山坡上,若你飞驰在英国的高速公路上就一定可以看到壮丽的雕塑。

阅读笔记

Part 4

特色英国节日 "来头"大

圣诞节

圣诞节英国人怎样庆祝

In the UK (or Great Britain), families often celebrate Christmas together, so they can watch each other open their presents! Most families have a Christmas Tree in their house for Christmas. The decorating of the tree is usually a family occasion, with everyone helping. Holly, Ivy and Mistletoe are also sometimes used to decorate homes or other buildings. Like a lot of countries, Nativity Plays and *Carol Services* are also very popular at Christmas time.

Children believe that Father Christmas or Santa Claus leaves presents in stockings or *pillow-cases*. These are normally hung up by the fire or by the children's beds on Christmas Eve. Children sometimes leave out *mince pies* and brandy for Father Christmas to eat and drink when he visits them. Now, some people say that a non-alcoholic drink should be left for Santa as he has to drive! And Boxing Day is a very old custom that started in the UK and is now taken as a holiday in many countries around the world.

在英国，家人们通常团聚在一起过圣诞节，因此大家能看到彼此打开圣诞节礼物的瞬间！大多数家庭都会为圣诞节准备一棵圣诞树。装饰圣诞树通常是全家人都在一起的场合。有时人们还会用冬青、常春藤或者槲寄生来装饰房屋或其他建筑。跟许多其他国家一样，基督诞生戏剧和圣诞颂歌仪式在圣诞节期间也很受欢迎。

孩子们相信圣诞老人会在袜子或枕套里留下礼物。在平安夜，袜子和枕套通常会被悬挂在火炉或者孩子的床边。有时孩子们还会给圣诞老人留下肉馅饼和白兰地，以便他来到他们家中时吃喝。现在，有些人表示由于圣诞老人是驱车前往，所以应该给他喝不含酒精的饮料！节礼日也是始于英国的一个非常古老的习俗，现已成为世界上许多国家的假期。

单词释义

Carol Service 圣诞颂歌仪式 holly冬青   ivy 常春藤
mistletoe 槲寄生   pillow-case 枕套   mince pie 肉馅饼

圣诞节大餐

In the UK, the main Christmas Meal is usually eaten at lunchtime or early afternoon on Christmas Day. It was traditionally *roast* beef or goose, although it's common to have turkey now, roast vegetables and "all the trimmings" which means *stuffing* and sometimes bacon and sausages. (In Scotland, some people might even have Haggis instead of turkey!) Dessert is often Christmas Pudding. Mince pies and lots of chocolates are often eaten as well!

Almost all British people, regardless of age, wear colored paper hats when having the Christmas dinner, the Christmas cracker. A Christmas cracker is a *cardboard* paper tube, wrapped colored paper, usually in green, red or gold, and twisted at both ends. There is a small *banger* inside the cracker and once the cracker is pulled apart, the cracker makes a bang.

Crackers are typically pulled at the Christmas dinner table or at parties. Contents inside the tube typically are a colored paper hat

在英国，人们通常在圣诞节当天的中午或下午早些时候享用圣诞大餐。传统的圣诞大餐主要包括烤牛肉或烤鹅，而现在多为火鸡，还有烤蔬菜以及香肠全餐。香肠全餐含有肉馅填料，有时也有熏肉和香肠 (在苏格兰，有些人甚至会用羊肉杂碎布丁代替火鸡作为圣诞大餐的主食)。甜点通常是圣诞布丁。此外，人们还会吃肉馅饼和巧克力！

无论老少，几乎所有的英国人在享用圣诞大餐时都会戴一顶彩色的纸帽子，即圣诞拉炮。圣诞拉炮是一个由硬纸板制成的纸筒，外面包有绿色、红色或金色等色彩鲜艳的纸，纸的两端是被拧紧的。圣诞拉炮里面有个小爆竹，当拉炮被拉开时，拉炮就会发出"嘭"的一声。

人们通常会在圣诞大餐的餐桌

or crown; a small toy, small plastic model or a *motto*, a joke, a *riddle* on a small strip of paper. In one version of the cracker tradition, the person with the larger portion of cracker empties the contents from the tube and keeps them. In another, each person will have their own cracker and will keep its contents.

旁或在圣诞聚会上拉响圣诞拉炮。拉炮里面通常会有一顶彩色的纸帽或纸王冠、一个小玩具、塑料小模型或者一张带有座右铭、笑话或谜语的小纸条。有一个传统是拿到最多的拉炮的人可以拿走纸筒里全部的东西。另一个版本则是每个人都会拿到自己的拉炮，并拥有里面的东西。

单词释义

roast 烘烤的	stuffing 填料	cardboard 硬纸板
banger 爆竹	motto 座右铭	riddle 谜语

💬 英国特色文化

💬 特色表达One

　　圣诞节是英国一年一度的大日子，这天时常会下点小雪，营造点浪漫的气氛，但若是漫天大雪导致封路或无法回家等状况，就如同fly in the ointment。这里的fly是"苍蝇"，ointment则是"油膏"，那么这个短语就是"小苍蝇掉进了油膏里"的意思，在俚语里，其引申义可以表示"美中不足的事情"。

☆ 实景链接

A：Look! It's snowing. 瞧！下雪了。

B：Great. Today is Christmas Eve. 太好了，今天是圣诞夜。

A：Listen to the news! It seems that it is going to be a heavy snow and the express way will be closed. 听听新闻！似乎要下大雪，而且高速路也要封闭了。

B：Oh, that's too bad. It's like a **fly in the ointment**. 哦，那太糟糕了。真是美中不足。

💬 特色表达Two

世界上会有永恒的职业吗？或许那个叫"圣诞老人"的职业就是如此吧。

从圣诞节诞生的那一天起，圣诞老人就成为了nevertiree。nevertiree是一个新词，表示"永不退休的人"的意思，通常是指那些到了退休年龄却仍然坚守岗位，不想退休的人。

☆ 实景链接

A：Does Santa Claus really exist? 圣诞老人真的存在吗？

B：There is no Santa Claus. 哪里有什么圣诞老人。

A：Well, I think Santa Claus is a **nevertiree** to some degree. 呃，我想在某个程度上，圣诞老人算是永不退休的人。

B：Come on, Santa Claus does not exist. 拜托，圣诞老人是不存在的。

拓展特色句

1. Let's sing some Christmas Carols. 让我们来唱圣诞赞歌吧。

2. Wish your parents merry Christmas for me. 请代我跟你父母说圣诞快乐。

3. I hope you have the best Christmas ever. 愿你有个最棒的圣诞节。

"聊" 英国特色文化

A：Christmas is coming. How do you celebrate it every year?

B：It's a western festival and I'm not quite interested in it. But I always go shopping on that day.

A：Last Christmas my friend took me to the church. There were so many people there. More and more Chinese people begin to celebrate it.

B：How do British people celebrate it?

A：In the UK, families often celebrate Christmas together.

B：How do they decorate their house?

A：Most families have a Christmas tree

A：圣诞节要来了。你每年都怎么过圣诞节？

B：它是一个西方节日。我不是很感兴趣。但那天我总是去购物。

A：去年圣诞节我的朋友带我去了教堂。那儿的人真多啊。越来越多的中国人都开始庆祝圣诞节了。

B：英国人怎么庆祝这个节日？

A：在英国，家人们通常团聚在一起过圣诞节。

B：他们怎么装饰房子呢？

A：大多数家庭都会为圣诞节准备一棵圣诞树。人们还会用冬青、常春藤

for Christmas. They also use Holly, Ivy and Mistletoe to decorate the houses.

B: What do they eat at that time?

A: It was traditionally roast beef or goose, but now, turkey is becoming very common.

或者槲寄生来装饰房屋。

B：那时他们吃什么呢？

A：传统的圣诞大餐是烤牛肉或烤鹅，而现在火鸡变得十分普遍。

"问" 英国特色文化

英国人有多喜爱圣诞树？

众所周知，圣诞树对于西方传统的圣诞节是必不可少的装饰树，是西方人过节日时必备的道具。近年来，由于人们疯狂地采购圣诞树，导致英国开始闹"树荒"。最早"树荒"归咎于德国和丹麦等地因霜冻导致冷杉受损、产量降低，于是一棵普通的进口圣诞树已达到90英镑的高价，但仍然一树难求。英国人对圣诞树的热爱到底有多深呢？据说，英国最高的圣诞树高27.5米、最大直径10米，这棵树耗费了7天的时间才被装点完好。这棵巨型圣诞树上点缀有10万个LED小彩泡，上面还装饰有1000个足球大小的红色球状装饰品，拥有浓厚的节日气氛。

阅读笔记

复活节英国人怎么庆祝

Easter Sunday in the United Kingdom is traditionally about Jesus Christ's *resurrection* from death, according to Christian belief. Many people use the day to *decorate* Easter eggs, share chocolate eggs and participate in Easter egg competitions. The Easter date depends on the *ecclesiastical approximation* of the March *equinox*. It is the first Sunday after the first full moon on or after the March equinox. People who regularly attend church often attend special services on Easter Sunday. These may be longer or more *elaborate* than on other Sundays. In churches, it is generally a festive occasion with an emphasis on the dawn of a new life. In Battersea Park in London, there is a large Easter *parade*.

On Easter Sunday nearly all non-essential businesses and organizations are closed. In England and Wales, stores are also closed. In Scotland, they are allowed to open. Public transport systems may run on a different schedule from other Sundays. In some areas there may be no public transport.

根据基督教教义，从传统上来说，在英国复活节是纪念耶稣复活的日子。人们在这天会装饰彩蛋，分享巧克力蛋并参加复活节彩蛋争抢活动。复活节的日期是教会决定的最接近春分的日子。通常是每年春分或春分后的月圆过后的第一个星期日。定期去教堂做礼拜的人们会在复活节这天参加教会的特别活动。这天的活动会比平常周日的活动长一些。在教堂，这通常是象征着重生与希望的节日。伦敦的巴特西公园会有规模盛大的复活节游行。

在复活节这天，几乎所有非必要的企业和机构都会关门。在英格兰和威尔士，商店在这天会休业。而在苏格兰，商店则可以开门。公共交通系统在复活节的时间表会和普通的周日不同。还有一些地方的公共交通会在这天停运。

单词释义

resurrection 复活　　　　decorate 装饰　　　　ecclesiastical 教会的
approximation 接近　　　equinox 春分　　　　elaborate 详尽的
parade 游行

复活节彩蛋

Many people celebrate Easter Sunday by decorating, exchanging or searching for eggs. The eggs may be fresh or *boiled* eggs laid by chickens or other birds, chocolate eggs or eggs made of other materials. Many children believe that the Easter *bunny* or rabbit comes to their house or garden to hide eggs. They may search for these eggs or find that the Easter bunny has left them in an *obvious* place.

The oldest tradition of making Easter egg is to use dyed or painted chicken eggs, but a modern custom is to *substitute* chocolate eggs, or plastic eggs filled with *confectionery* such as jelly beans for them. These eggs can be hidden for children to find on Easter morning, who may be told they were left by the Easter Bunny. They also may be put in a basket filled with real or *artificial* straw to *resemble* a bird's nest.

The egg is widely used as a symbol of the start of new life. The egg is seen by followers of Christianity

许多人会装饰、交换以及寻找彩蛋来欢度复活节。制作复活节彩蛋的可以是生的或水煮的鸡蛋或其他禽类的蛋，可以是巧克力蛋，也可以是其他材料制成的蛋。许多孩子都认为在复活节这天，会有复活节兔子来到他们的院子里藏一些彩蛋。他们会去院子搜索，或找那些复活节兔子放在明显地方的复活节彩蛋。

制作复活节彩蛋的最古老的传统是将鸡蛋染色或是在上面画画，但现在的习俗是用巧克力蛋或者塑料蛋来装满糕点糖果，比如胶质软糖。这些彩蛋通常会被藏起来，好让孩子们在复活节的早上自己寻找。家长们可能会告诉孩子这是复活节兔子留下的。彩蛋也可能放在填满稻草或假稻草的模仿鸟窝的篮子里。

as a symbol of resurrection: while being dormant it contains a new life sealed within it.

彩蛋通常象征着新生命的开始。基督教徒则认为彩蛋象征着复活：蛋中沉封着一个沉睡的新生命。

---

boiled 煮熟的   bunny 兔子   obvious 明显的

substitute 替代   confectionery 糕点糖果   artificial 仿造的

resemble 相似

"品" 英国特色文化

特色表达One

复活节在英国是个重大的日子，即使在whistle stop这样的地方也洋溢着浓厚的节日气氛。这里的whistle指"火车的汽笛"，这样的铃声通常在边远小镇响起，提醒乘客赶紧下车。后来，人们把这样的乡镇称为whistle stop。

实景链接

A：How about going to the church at the Easter? 复活节那天去教堂如何？

B：Which church do you prefer? 你想去哪个教堂？

A：Let's head for the **whistle stops** surrounding London. 我们去伦敦周边的小乡镇吧。

B：Anything you say is all right with me. 你说好就好。

特色表达Two

每当复活节来临，就有很多人cosplay复活节兔子，四处招摇，他们令大街小巷都充满了节日的欢喜气氛。但也有人喜欢dress down。dress down这个短语可指"责骂"，在俚语中，它还指"轻松随意的打扮"。

实景链接

A：I look forward to Saturday. 我期待周六快来。

B：Why? Are you planning to go out? 为什么呢？你打算出去吗？

A：No, I don't plan to go out. I just wanna **dress down** on

Saturday. 不，我不打算出去。只是想在周六时穿点轻松的衣服。

B：Yeah, I can also put on my T shirt. 是的，我也能穿T恤了。

拓展特色句

1. My family goes to church on Easter. 我家在复活节会去教堂。

2. Easter is always on Sundays. 复活节总在星期天。

3. We usually have an Easter egg hunt on Easter. 我们在复活节通常会有复活节彩蛋寻宝活动。

"聊" 英国特色文化

A：When is the Easter?

B：It's different every year. It is the first Sunday after the first full moon on or after the March equinox.

A：Why do westerners celebrate the Easter?

B：Easter Sunday is traditionally about Jesus Christ's resurrection from death, according to Christian belief.

A：Do the people go to work during Ester?

B：No. It's a holiday for them.

A：How do they celebrate it?

B：Many people celebrate Easter Sunday by decorating, exchanging or searching for eggs.

A：How to make an Easter egg?

B：The traditional Easter egg is dyed or painted chicken eggs, but a modern one can be chocolate egg, or plastic egg filled with confectionery.

A：复活节是什么时候?

B：每年都不一样。复活节通常在每年春分月圆之后的第一个星期日。

A：西方人为什么庆祝复活节?

B：根据基督教教义，复活节传统上用来纪念耶稣基督复活的日子。

A：复活节期间人们工作吗?

B：不工作。这是他们的假期。

A：他们怎么庆祝?

B：许多人同通过装饰、交换以及寻找彩蛋来欢度复活节。

A：如何制作复活节彩蛋?

B：传统的复活节彩蛋是将鸡蛋染色或者在上面画画，但现在的彩蛋可以是巧克力蛋或者装满糕点糖果的塑料蛋。

"问" 英国特色文化

为什么英国人过复活节少不了复活节兔子?

复活节兔子是英国复活节的象征之一。因为兔子繁殖能力强,所以它们象征着万物苏醒的春天,代表新生命的开始。而且兔子备受众神宠爱,它不仅是爱神阿弗洛狄特的宠物,还是日耳曼土地女神霍尔塔的持烛引路者。因此,作为引路者的兔子得到了给孩子们送复活节蛋的任务。据说全球最大的复活节兔子来自英国,它的名字是"大流士",是一只超肥的巨兔,体重达22.25千克,身长1.32米,几乎每天需要吃掉12根胡萝卜。

阅读笔记

圣帕特里克节

爱尔兰守护神圣帕特里克

St. Patrick's Day occurs on March 17. It is a national holiday in Ireland and *commemorates* one of its *patron* saints, St. Patrick. He is believed to have died on March 17 in or around the year 493. He grew up in mainland Britain, but spent time in Ireland as a young man and later as a *missionary*. According to popular legend, he is buried under Down Cathedral in Downpatrick, County Down, and *banished* all snakes from Ireland. The "snakes" may refer to *pagan* worshipers of snake gods.

Green *ribbons* and *shamrocks* were worn in celebration of St. Patrick's Day as early as the 17th century. Saint Patrick is said to have used the shamrock, a three-leaved plant, to explain the Holy Trinity to the pagan Irish, and the *ubiquitous* wearing and display of shamrocks and shamrock-inspired designs has become a feature of the day.

每年3月17日是圣帕特里克节。这个爱尔兰的全国性节日是为了纪念爱尔兰守护神圣帕特里克。人们认为圣帕特里克于3月17日去世，大约是公元493年。他成长在英国本土，但从年轻的时候就前往了爱尔兰，并成为了一名传教士。根据最普遍的说法，他去世后被葬在唐郡的唐帕特里克的大教堂，并将爱尔兰所有的蛇都驱逐了出去。"蛇"大约是指代信奉蛇神的异教徒。

从17世纪开始，人们就会佩戴绿色丝带以及三叶草来庆祝圣帕特里克节。据说圣帕特里克曾用三片叶子的三叶草向爱尔兰的异教徒阐明了圣父、圣子、圣神三位一体的教义，由此，人们普遍使用三叶草或来源于三叶草的设计来庆祝这一天，而这也成为了圣帕特里克节的特色。

单词释义

commemorate 纪念　　　patron 守护神　　　missionary 传教士
banish 驱逐　　　　　　pagan 异教的　　　ribbon 丝带
shamrock 三叶草　　　　ubiquitous 普遍存在的

英国人的庆祝活动

March 17 is a *bank holiday* in Northern Ireland. The degree to which people celebrate St. Patrick's Day varies according to their religious and political *affiliations*. Those, who believe that Northern Ireland should remain part of the United Kingdom, do not generally celebrate the day. Those, who believe that Northern Ireland should become part of a United Ireland often celebrate St. Patrick's Day. A large parade is held in Belfast but the level of public funding it receives depends on which political parties control the *local council*.

A weekend of celebrations is organized in Nottingham. These include a parade, children's *workshops*, an arts festival and performances by well-known Irish musicians. There is also a parade, attended by many thousands of people in Birmingham. An Irish festival lasting three days is held in Liverpool.

A whole week of celebrations is organized around St. Patrick's Day in London. These include a parade and a festival held close to, but not always on, March 17. The parade visits Trafalgar Square and Covent Garden and the festival are held in Trafalgar Square, Leicester Square

3月17日在北爱尔兰是一个公共假日。拥有不同信仰和政治背景的人们庆祝圣帕特里克节的方式也有所不同。认为北爱尔兰仍然应该是英国一部分的人通常都不庆祝圣帕特里克节，而认为北爱尔兰应该属于爱尔兰的人们通常会庆祝这个节日。这一天在贝尔法斯特会举行大游行，而这一天能收到多少公共资金取决于由哪个政党控制当地市政委员会。

诺丁汉有持续一周的庆祝活动。这些活动包括游行、儿童文艺汇演、艺术节以及爱尔兰著名音乐家的演出。在伯明翰也有几千人参加的游行。而在利物浦则会举办为期3天的爱尔兰节日庆典。

在伦敦则有持续整个周末的圣帕特里克节庆祝活动。这些活动包括游行和节日庆典，庆典一般在3月17日左右，并不总是在当天举行。游行队伍会经过特拉法加广场、考文特花园，而节日庆典就在特拉法加广场、莱斯

and Covent Garden. Together, the parade and festival allow people to experience many aspects of Irish culture including food, *crafts*, dance and music.

特广场和考文特花园举行。人们通过游行和节日庆典能同时体验到爱尔兰文化的方方面面，如食物、工艺品、舞蹈和音乐等。

单词释义

affiliation 从属关系　　local council 市政委员会　workshop 文艺汇演

craft 工艺品

"品"英国特色文化

特色表达One

当年，圣帕特里克为了传教，踏遍了爱尔兰的千山万水，若是他稍微blow hot and cold，就不会有今日的"圣帕特里克节"了。这里的blow hot and cold可不是"吹冷风又吹热风"，在俚语中，它的意思是"犹豫不决，意志不坚"。

☆ 实景链接

A: It's said that St. Patrick could make up his minds right away. 据说，圣帕特里克做事当机立断。

B: Yeah, if he **blew hot and cold**, he couldn't escape. 是的，若他犹豫不决，就不能逃跑了。

A: But he was caught again. 但他又被捉住了。

B: Well, his determination grows stronger with each failure. 嗯，好在他愈挫愈勇。

特色表达Two

据说圣帕特里克当年接二连三地被捕入狱，又成功越狱，就是因为当时的祭祀掌握着whip hand，他只能一直反抗。whip hand原指拿着鞭子赶车的人的手，马匹走得快慢全掌握在他手里，所以执鞭的手是掌握控制权的。后来人们用这个whip hand形容"手握大权"。

☆ 实景链接

A：Do you know why they celebrate the St. Patrick's Day? 你知道为什么他们要庆祝圣帕特里克节吗?

B：People celebrate that day in memory of St. Patrick. 人们为了纪念圣帕特里克而庆祝那天吧。

A：It's said that the priest wanted to hold the **whip hand** over him at that time. 据说当时的祭司妄想控制他。

B：But he showed great courage and determination. 但他表现得十分勇敢和果断。

拓展特色句

1. St. Patrick's died on March 17 so that day has been commemorated as St. Patrick's Day ever since. 圣帕特里克死于3月17日，所以这一天成为他的纪念日。

2. St. Patrick's Day is originally a Catholic holy day and now has evolved into a holiday. 圣帕特里克节原本只是天主教神圣的节日，但后来逐步发展成为一个假日。

3. Irish population celebrates St. Patrick's Day with big parades. 爱尔兰人以盛大的游行庆祝圣帕特里克节。

"聊" 英国特色文化

A：I heard of a festival.

B：What is it?

A：St. Patrick's Day.

B：It is a national holiday in Ireland.

A：What is it for?

B：It commemorates one of its patron saints, St. Patrick.

A：Who is he?

B：He grew up in mainland Britain, but he went to Ireland as a young man and later as a missionary.

A：我听说了一个节日。

B：是什么?

A：圣帕特里克节。

B：这是爱尔兰的一个全国性节日。

A：这个节日是干什么的?

B：它是为了纪念爱尔兰守护神圣帕特里克。

A：他是谁?

B：他成长在英国本土，但他年轻时就去了爱尔兰，并成为了一名传教士。

A：人们什么时候庆祝这个节日?

A: When will people celebrate the festival?

B: On March 17th.

A: How do people celebrate it?

B: People in different places celebrate it in different ways. For example, a weekend of celebrations is organized in Nottingham.

A: How about others places?

B: There is also a parade in Birmingham. And a celebration lasting three days is held in Liverpool.

B: 在3月17日。

A: 人们怎么庆祝?

B: 不同地方的人庆祝方式不一样。比如说,在诺丁汉有持续整个周末的庆祝活动。

A: 其他地方呢?

B: 在伯明翰会有游行。而在利物浦,则有持续3天的庆祝活动。

"问" 英国特色文化

"圣帕特里克"之名从何而来?

在英国,人们会在每年的3月17日庆祝圣帕特里克节,圣帕特里克是爱尔兰守护神。据说,他于公元385年出生在威尔士,教名是麦克斯威恩。当圣帕特里克16岁的时候,他居住的村庄遭到一伙强盗,他不幸被卖作了奴隶囚困起来。6年后,他历经艰辛逃到一所修道院,跟随一位主教学习了12年。在这段岁月里,他深刻地认识到他的使命就是让更多的人相信上

帝,成为基督徒。于是,他因为传教多次被捕入狱,但他坚强不屈,每次都成功越狱,继续传教爱尔兰,并在全国修建了许多修道院。人们以他的名字作为节日,并在圣帕特里克节纪念他。

阅读笔记

彭斯之夜

这一天用来纪念诗人

Burns Night is annually celebrated in Scotland on or around January 25 which is an *observance* but it is not a bank holiday in the United Kingdom. It commemorates the life of the *bard* (poet) Robert Burns, who was born on January 25, 1759. The day also celebrates Burns' contribution to Scottish culture.

Robert Burns was born in Alloway, Scotland, on January 25, 1759. He died in Dumfries, Scotland, on July 21, 1796. He was a bard (poet) and wrote many poems, lyrics and other pieces that *addressed* political and civil issues. Perhaps his best known work is *Auld Lang Syne*, which is sung at New Year's Eve celebrations in Scotland, parts of the United Kingdom, and other places around the world. Burns is one of Scotland's important cultural *icons* and is well known among Scottish *expats* or *descendants* around the world. He is also known as: "Rabbie Burns"; the "Bard of Ayrshire"; "Scotland's favourite son"; and in Scotland "The Bard".

在每年的1月25日或前后2天，苏格兰会庆祝彭斯之夜，在英国这只是一个惯例，而不是公共假日。这是为了纪念吟游诗人罗伯特·彭斯诞辰，因为他出生于1759年1月25日。这个节日也是为了纪念彭斯对苏格兰文化的贡献。

Celebrate Burns Night

罗伯特·彭斯于1759年1月25日出生于苏格兰阿洛韦，于1796年在苏格兰敦夫里斯去世。他是一名吟游诗人，创作了许多针对政治以及社会问题的诗歌、歌词以及其他作品。或许其最著名的作品就是《友谊地久天长》，在苏格兰、英国和世界上其他一些地区，人们在新年前夜会唱这首歌。彭斯是苏格兰重要的文化偶像之一，他在生活于世界上其他地方的苏格兰人或苏格兰后裔中也非常有名。他也被称之为"拉比·彭斯""埃尔郡诗人""苏格兰的宠儿"以及"苏格兰的吟游诗人"。

单词释义

observance 惯例　　　bard 吟游诗人　　　address 使用书面言词针对……发言
icon 具有代表性的人物　expat离乡背井者　descendant 后裔

彭斯之夜的晚餐

Many people and organizations hold a Burns' supper on or around Burns' Night. These may be informal or formal, only for men, only for women, or for both genders. Formal events include toasts and readings of pieces written by Robert Burns. *Ceremonies* during a Burns' Night supper vary according to the group organizing the event and the location.

At Burns' Night events, many men wear *kilts* and women may wear *shawls*, skirts or dresses made from their family tartan. Many types of food are associated with Burns' Night. These include: cock-a-leekie soup (chicken and *leek* soup); haggis; neeps (mashed turnips or swedes) and tatties (mashed potatoes); Cranachan (*whipped cream* mixed with raspberries and served with sweet *oat* wafers); and bannocks (a kind of bread cooked on a *griddle*). Whisky is the traditional drink. The evening centers on the entrance of the haggis (a type of sausage prepared in a sheep's stomach) on a large *platter* to the sound of a

在彭斯之夜，许多人和机构会准备彭斯晚餐。有些是正式的，也有一些是非正式的，有的专为女性准备，有的专门为男士准备，也有男女都可参加的。比较正式的庆典包括祝酒并朗诵一首罗伯特·彭斯的作品。彭斯之夜晚餐的仪式会因举办机构和所在地而有所不同。

在彭斯之夜庆典上，男士会着苏格兰短裙，女士则会系上代表其家族的格子呢制成的披巾、裙子或礼服。彭斯之夜庆典上会有许多食物，比如韭菜鸡肉汤、羊肉杂碎布丁(一种将香肠放在羊肚里的菜肴)、萝卜(捣碎的红萝卜或大头菜)与土豆(土豆泥)、Cranachan(搅拌起沫的奶油中加上覆盆子，通常搭配甜燕麦片食用)和薄饼(在浅锅里煎制成的一种面食)。在彭斯之夜喝威士忌也是一个传统。这个夜晚

piper playing *bagpipes*. When the haggis is on the table, the host reads the *Address to a Haggis*. This is an **ode** that Robert Burns wrote to the Scottish dish. At the end of the reading, the haggis is ceremonially sliced into two pieces and the meal begins.

的高潮是伴随着苏格兰的风笛声，用大浅盘端上羊肉杂碎布丁的时候。羊肉杂碎布丁上桌后，主人会朗诵《羊肚脍颂》。这是罗伯特·彭斯写给这道苏格兰佳肴的颂诗。主人朗诵完毕后，这道羊肉杂碎布丁也会一分为二，这标志着晚餐的开始。

单词释义

ceremony 仪式	kilt 苏格兰式短裙	shawl 披巾
leek 韭葱	whipped cream 生奶油	oat 燕麦
platter 大浅盘	piper 风笛手	bagpipe 风笛
ode 颂歌，颂诗		

英国特色文化

特色表达One

彭斯之夜时，男士们都会穿着苏格兰格子呢短裙。但要是在平时看到男士穿裙子，会不会觉得很可笑，有点"不太对劲"呢？如果你觉得有些事情不对头时，就可以说：I smell a rat. 这句话并不是说有老鼠来了，在俚语中，这句话的意思是"我觉得不对劲"。

☆ 实景链接

A：Where is Tom? 汤姆去哪儿了？

B：He didn't show up the whole afternoon. 整个下午他都没出现。

A：It is strange that we can't find him. 我们找不到他，这很奇怪。

B：Well, I **smell a rat**. 嗯，我觉得这不对劲。

特色表达Two

彭斯之夜的晚餐免不了要喝酒，都说一醉方休，可有的人喝酒海量，就是醉不了。而a hollow leg就可以指某人"酒量大、喝不倒"。其字面意思是"一条中空的腿"，这个比喻很形象，因为是空的，所以无论倒进多少酒都无大碍喽。

☆ **实景链接**

A: Tomorrow is the Burns' Night. Want to drink Tom under the table? 明天是彭斯之夜，想把汤姆喝倒吗？

B: Well… you can never do. He **got a hollow leg**. 呃，你不可能把他喝倒的，他是海量。

A: How do you know that? 你怎么知道的？

B: Don't you remember that? Last week we all got drunk but not him. 你不记得了吗？上周我们都喝醉了，就他没醉。

拓展特色句

1. Burns-night started 200 years ago. "彭斯之夜"始于200年前。

2. Burns-night is celebrated as a tribute to the famous Scottish poet, Robert Burns. "彭斯之夜"是向苏格兰的著名诗人罗伯特·彭斯致敬的节日。

3. We can have authentic Scottish haggis to accompany their neeps and tatties on Burns night. 我们可以在"彭斯之夜"吃到正宗的苏格兰羊肉杂碎布丁，并配有萝卜和土豆。

"聊" 英国特色文化

A: Can you say something about Burns Night?

B: It commemorates the life of the bard Robert Burns in Scotland.

A: What did he do for the country?

B: He was a bard and wrote many poems and lyrics. Perhaps his best known work is *Auld Lang* Syne.

A: I know this song but I don't know the poet. By the way, when is Burns Night?

B: Around January 25.

A: Is it a holiday?

A: 你能介绍一下彭斯之夜吗？

B: 彭斯之夜是苏格兰纪念吟游诗人罗伯特·彭斯的诞辰。

A: 他为这个国家做了什么？

B: 他是一个吟游诗人，创作了许多诗歌和歌词。或许其最著名的作品就是《友谊地久天长》。

A: 我知道这首歌，但是不了解诗人。顺便问一下，彭斯之夜是在什么时候？

B: 在1月25日前后。

A: 这是一个假期吗？

B: 它在英国只是一个惯例而不是公共

B：It is an observance but it is not a bank holiday in the United Kingdom.

A：What do people do that day?

B：Many people and organizations hold a Burns' supper on or around Burns' Night.

A：Do they wear any special costumes?

B：Many men wear kilts and women may wear shawls, skirts or dresses made from their family tartan.

假日。

A：那天人们会干什么？

B：在彭斯之夜的时候，许多人和机构会举办彭斯晚餐。

A：他们会穿一些特殊的服装吗？

B：男士会着苏格兰短裙，而女士会系上代表其家族格子呢制成的披巾、穿裙子或礼服。

"问" 英国特色文化

原来《友谊地久天长》是英国人的作品？

在中国，一曲《友谊地久天长》曾红遍了大江南北，可有多少人知道这首歌最早来自英国呢？这首歌来自英国著名诗人彭斯的诗歌《Auld Lang Syne》，这首歌曲也曾风靡英国，它唱出了人们对友谊的崇敬与期待，对美好未来的向往与追求。在英国，几乎每年新年，人们都会唱起这首歌来怀念彼此的友谊，畅快地干一杯，纪念那些携手的美好时光。

Auld Lang Syne

阅读笔记

139

威尔士艺术节

威尔士艺术节是这样来的

National Eisteddfod is the largest and oldest celebration of Welsh culture, unique throughout Europe as each year it visits a different area of Wales. Eisteddfod *literally* means a sitting (eistedd = to sit), perhaps a *reference* to the hand-carved chair traditionally awarded to the best poet in the ceremony "The Crowning of the Bard".

The National Eisteddfod of Wales dates back to 1176 when it is said that the first Eisteddfod was held. Lord Rhys invited poets and musicians from all over Wales to a grand gathering at his *castle* in Cardigan. A chair at the Lord's table was awarded to the best poet and musician, a tradition that continues today in the modern Eisteddfod.

Each year, Welsh people from all over the world return to Wales to take part in a special welcoming ceremony staged during Eisteddfod week. The ceremony is organised by Wales International, an association of ex-patriates from all over the world. The Wales International ceremony is held within the Eisteddfod Pavilion on the Thursday of Eisteddfod week.

全国诗歌音乐大会是威尔士最大最古老的庆祝威尔士文化的盛会，这个节日与欧洲的其他节日都不同，因为它每年会在威尔士境内的不同地点举行。Eisteddfod的字面意思是"坐席"，也许是参考了在加冕仪式上，最优秀的诗人会获得一把手工雕刻的椅子这一传统。

全国诗歌音乐大会的起源可以追溯到1176年，那年是首次举办这一艺术节。里斯勋爵邀请了遍及威尔士全国的诗人和音乐家前往他位于卡迪根的城堡举办盛会。在盛会上，他奖励了最优秀的诗人和音乐家一把椅子，这个传统一直持续至今。

每年，世界各地的威尔士人都会回到威尔士参加全国诗歌音乐大会开幕式。这一仪式是由来自世界各地的威尔士人创办的威尔士国际组织举办的。威尔士国际艺术节会在全国诗歌音乐大会周的周四在诗歌音乐馆举办。

单词释义

literally 字面意思地　　　　reference 参考　　　　castle 城堡

威尔士艺术节的庆祝

The National Eisteddfod is traditionally held in the first week of August and the competitions are all held in the Welsh language. The Eisteddfod Act of 1959 allowed local authorities to give financial support to the event. Hundreds of tents, *pavilions* and little *stands* are erected in an open space to create the maes (field). The space required for this means that it is rare for the Eisteddfod to be in a city or town but instead it is held somewhere with more space. Car parking for day visitors alone requires several large fields, and many people camp on the site for the whole week.

The festival has a heavy *druidic* flavour, with the crowning and chairing ceremonies for the *victorious* poets being attended by bards in flowing white costumes, dancing *maidens*, *trumpet fanfares* and a symbolic Horn of Plenty.

As well as the main pavilion with the main stage, there are other *venues* through the week. Some are *fixtures* every year, hosting *gigs* (Maes B), plays and shows (Maes C)

全国诗歌音乐大会通常于每年8月的第一周举办，所有活动的官方语言都是威尔士语。1959年的全国诗人及音乐家大会法案允许地方政府资助这一盛会。每当举办全国诗歌音乐大会的时候，人们会在空地上搭建成百上千个大大小小的场馆和看台。举办这个盛会的地点并不一定要在城市或城镇里，相反，需要在有大片空地的地方。仅仅是白天前来的游客就需要很多空地来停车，更别提还有很多要在营地待一周的人了。

这个庆祝活动有着浓浓的督伊德教意味，诗人们伴随着少女的欢乐舞蹈、喇叭声以及丰收号角入场参加加冕以及赠送椅子的仪式，他们都穿着飘逸白色衣服。

除了主场馆的主舞台外，全国诗歌音乐大会周期间还有一些其他场馆。有些活动是每年都会固定举办的，如现场演奏会(B场馆)、话剧以及

and other fixtures of the maes where groups, societies, councils, charities and shops exhibit and sell. Some eisteddfod-goers never go near the main pavilion, but spend their time wandering the maes and meeting friends.

戏剧(C场馆)等；此外，还有一些场地供各类机构、理事会、慈善机构或商店展览或售卖货物。有些去参加全国诗歌音乐大会的人们可能根本就不会去主场馆参加加冕仪式，而是去周围的场地逛逛、见见朋友等。

单词释义

pavilion 大帐篷，馆	stand 看台	druidic督伊德教的
victorious 胜利的	maiden 少女	trumpet 喇叭
fanfare 吹奏声	venue 场地，场馆	fixture 定期举办的活动
gig 现场演奏会		

"品" 英国特色文化

特色表达One

在看表演的时候，最好把你的手机调整到airplane mode。但你知道这个说法还有其他含义吗？当人们失恋或是工作失利的时候，可能会不想和外界沟通，因此不会使用手机和任何社交网络。这时就可以说某人in airplane mode，字面意思是"某人正处于飞行模式"，其实是指"想要与世隔绝"。

☆ 实景链接

A: What's wrong with Joe? 乔怎么了？

B: Joe is sad and went into **airplane mode**. 乔很伤心，他现在想与世隔绝。

A: Let's take her out to the National Eisteddfod. 我们带他一起去全国诗歌音乐大会吧。

B: That's a good idea. 这个主意不错。

特色表达Two

聪明的商家不会放弃任何赚钱的机会，比如有些商人会在威尔士艺术节为有潜力的年轻音乐家投资，他们常常在谈生意时说：Let's get down to brass tacks. 这句话可不是说"让我们一起去看看平头铜钉。"在俚语中，它指的是"让我们谈正事吧"。

☆ 实景链接

A：How about holding concerts during National Eisteddfod? 在全国诗歌音乐大会期间举办音乐会怎么样？

B：You mean hold the concert for the young singer? 你是说为那个年轻歌手举办音乐会吗？

A：In my mind, he's very talented. 在我的印象中，他很有才华。

B：**Let's get down to brass tacks**. What should we do now? 言归正传。那我们现在该做什么呢？

拓展特色句

1. The Royal National Eisteddfod is one of Europe's largest competitive annual cultural festivals. 皇家国家诗歌音乐艺术节是欧洲最大的竞赛式年度文化节之一。

2. Non-Welsh speakers are also very welcome at the National Eisteddfod. 全国诗歌音乐大会也非常欢迎不说威尔士语的人。

3. Annual Eisteddfod attracts singers and musicians from all around the world. 一年一度的音乐节吸引着世界各地的歌手和音乐家。

"聊" 英国特色文化

A：When will the National Eisteddfod be held every year?

B：It is traditionally held in the first week of August.

A：Where will it be held?

B：Each year it visits a different area of Wales.

A：What does the word "Eisteddfod" mean?

B：Eisteddfod literally means a sitting, perhaps a reference to the hand-carved chair traditionally awarded to

A：全国诗歌音乐大会每年什么时候举办？

B：一般会在每年8月的第一周举办。

A：在什么地方举办？

B：它每年都会在威尔士的一个地方举办。

A："Eisteddfod"是什么意思？

B：Eisteddfod按字面意思理解是"坐席"，也许是参考了在加冕仪式上，最优秀的诗人会获得一把手工雕刻的椅子这一传统。

the best poet in the ceremony "The Crowning of the Bard".

A： What activities will it include?

B： Some are fixtures every year. For example, there are hosting gigs, plays and shows.

A： What else do people do?

B： Some eisteddfod-goers spend their time wandering the maes and meeting friends.

A： 全国诗歌音乐大会都包括什么活动?

B： 有些活动是每年固定举办的。比如现场演奏会、话剧以及戏剧等。

A： 人们还会做什么事?

B： 有些去参加全国诗歌音乐大会的人也会在周围的场地逛逛、会见朋友等。

"问" 英国特色文化

为什么音乐节在威尔士举行?

威尔士是一个充满诗情画意的地方，在这里到处弥漫着诗歌文化。同时，威尔士在欧洲素有"音乐之乡"之称，因为它的历史上曾培养出许多享誉世界的音乐天才和音乐团体，如举世闻名的威尔士男声合唱团。所以，威尔士每年都会举办全国诗人与音乐家大会，这是全欧洲最古老、规模最大的文化节，同时将举办各种传统典礼、比赛和音乐会等，展示威尔士的悠久文化传承。

阅读笔记

万圣节

看到这些就知道万圣节来了

Halloween is a holiday annually celebrated on October 31. Some people hold Halloween parties on or around this date, where the hosts and guests often dress up as *skeletons*, ghosts or other *scary* figures. There are various symbols are associated with Halloween. The colors orange and black are very common. Other symbols include pumpkin *lanterns*, witches, *wizards*, ghosts, spirits and characters from horror films. Animals associated with the festival include bats, spiders and black cats.

Halloween has its origins in pagan festivals held in England, Wales, Scotland and Ireland. People believed that, at this time of year, the spirits of dead people could come "alive" and walk among the living. They thought that it was important to dress up in costumes when *venturing* outside, to avoid being harmed by the spirits. This may be the origin of the Halloween costumes seen today.

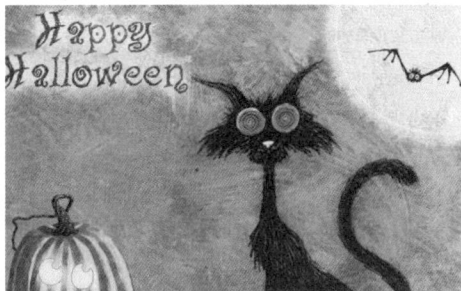

万圣节通常是在每年的10月31日庆祝。人们会在这天或者前后两天举办万圣节派对。在派对上，主人和客人会打扮成骷髅、鬼魂或其他恐怖的形象。万圣节有许多象征。万圣节最常见的颜色是橙色与黑色。其他常见的象征还有南瓜灯、女巫、男巫、鬼魂、幽灵以及其他恐怖电影中的角色。与这个节日相关的动物有蝙蝠、蜘蛛以及黑猫。

万圣节曾为英格兰、威尔士、苏格兰和爱尔兰地区的异教徒节日。人们相信每到这个时候，去世的人的灵魂会复活，游荡在人群之中。他们认为要想免受幽灵的伤害，人们走在外边时最好乔装打扮一下。这或许就是现代万圣节服装的起源。

单词释义

skeleton 骷髅   scary 恐怖的   lantern 提灯
wizard 男巫   venture 冒险行事

庆祝万圣节

Halloween celebrations in the United Kingdom include parties where guests are often expected to arrive in a costume to *reflect* the day's theme. Other people gather together to watch horror films, either at home or at a cinema.

Some children go *trick-or-treating*. This means that they dress up and go to other peoples' houses, knocking on the door for treat of sweets or a snack. Those who do not give out a treat may be *tricked* with a joke instead. The practice of dressing up in costumes and begging door to door for treats on holidays dates back to the Middle Ages and includes Christmas *wassailing*. Trick-or-treating *resembles* the late medieval *practice* of souling, when poor folk would go door to door on Hallowmas, receiving food in return for *prayers* for the dead on All Souls Day. The custom of wearing costumes and masks at Halloween goes back to Celtic traditions of attempting to copy the evil spirits or *placate* them, in Scotland for instance where the dead were *impersonated* by young men with masked, *veiled* or blackened faces, dressed in white. *Guising* at Halloween in Scotland is recorded

在英国，万圣节的庆祝活动包括各种派对，宾客们会按照当天的主题乔装打扮后前来参加。还有一些人会聚在家中或在电影院，一起观看恐怖电影。

孩子们则会进行"不给糖就捣蛋"的游戏。他们会穿着各式各样的稀奇古怪的服装、挨家挨户地索要糖果和零食。那些没有给他们糖果的人就会被他们戏弄。这种穿着奇怪的服装、挨家挨户讨要糖果的传统可以追溯到中世纪，也包括圣诞酒宴。"不给糖就捣蛋"的游戏类似于中世纪后期祭祀亡魂的仪式，穷人们会在万圣节这天挨家挨户收集食物，这些食物是为了报答在万圣节为去世的人所做的祷告。在万圣节穿着特定服装、佩戴面具的传统可追溯到苏格兰凯尔特人模仿邪灵的习俗，比如在苏格兰，年轻男子会带着黑色面具或把脸涂黑，穿着白色的衣服模仿已故的人。

in 1895, where *masqueraders* in disguise carrying lanterns made out of scooped out *turnips*, visit homes to be rewarded with cakes, fruit and money.

根据记录，苏格兰人在万圣节伪装自己的习俗出现在1895年，伪装者提着用挖空的红萝卜制成的灯笼，挨家挨户地拜访人们后会获得蛋糕、水果或金钱。

单词释义

reflect 反应
wassail 酒宴
prayer 祷告
veil 遮盖
turnip 芜菁

trick-or-treating 不给糖就捣蛋
resemble 类似，像
placate 安抚
guise 伪装

trick 戏弄
practice 仪式
impersonate 扮演，模仿
masquerader 伪装者

"品" 英国特色文化

特色表达One

万圣节是狂欢的好日子，但你若是在party上表现得cellfish可是会招人厌烦的。cellfish的读音与selfish(自私)相同，而cell的意思是"手机"，所以cellfish指的就是"在公共场所打电话，不顾他人感受"。

实景链接

A: Annie, you are **cellfish**! 安妮，你这样打电话太自私了！

B: Did I do something wrong? 我做错了什么了吗？

A: You have loud conversations on your cell phone. Don't forget that you are in restaurant. 你打电话太大声了。别忘了你是在餐厅里。

B: Who cares? 谁在乎呢？

特色表达Two

在中国，有些苛刻的家长即使在节日里也对孩子要求严格，除非小孩保证下次考个perfect ten，否则不让出去玩耍。在英国可不一样了，在万圣节这样的日子里，孩子们可尽情狂欢，才不会去管什么成绩。perfect ten在俚语中，就有"满分"的意思。

☆ 实景链接

A：Where is Lucy? 露西在哪里？

B：She's been doing her homework for hours at home. 她连续几个小时在家写作业。

A：Come on, today is Halloween, we have already planned to play with her. 拜托，今天是万圣节，我们都已经约好跟她玩了。

B：Well, she said her mother asked her to score a **perfect ten** in the exam, so you know… 呃，她说她妈妈要求她在考试中得满分，所以你知道的……

拓展特色句

1. Children will dress up as ghosts and stop by their neighbor's homes to ask for candy on Halloween. 孩子们会在万圣节装扮成鬼，到邻居家门口要糖果。

2. What are you dressing up as for Halloween? 你万圣节要扮成什么样？

3. We are going to carve a jack-o-lantern. 我们要去雕个南瓜灯。

"聊" 英国特色文化

A：I will hold a wonderful Halloween party this year.

B：When will you hold it?

A：On October 31.

B：Why do people celebrate this holiday?

A：People believed that at this time of year, the spirits of dead people could come "alive" and walk among the living.

B：People will wear different clothes that day, right?

A：Yes. They thought that it was important to dress up in costumes

A：今年我要举办一个很棒的万圣节派对。

B：你什么时候举办？

A：在10月31日。

B：人们为什么要庆祝这个节日？

A：人们相信每到这个时候，去世的人的灵魂会复活，游荡在人群之中。

B：人们在这天会穿不同的服装，对吗？

A：是的。人们认为为了免受幽灵的伤害，走在外边时最好乔装打扮一下。

B：孩子们喜欢这个节日吗？

A：是的。孩子们会去玩"不给糖就捣蛋"的游戏。他们会乔装打扮，挨

when going out, to avoid being harmed by the spirits.

B: Do children like the festival?

A: Yes. Children will go trick-or-treating. They will dress up and go to other peoples' houses, asking for sweets or a snack. Those who do not give out a treat may be tricked with a joke instead.

家挨户去别人家索要糖果和零食。如果你没有给他们糖果，他们就会戏弄你。

"问" 英国特色文化

万圣节有什么必吃食物？

万圣节是英国的重要节日，在这天有几样食品是必备的，比如南瓜派、苹果、糖果，有的地方还会准备上等的牛羊肉。大家都知道"不给糖就捣蛋"是万圣节的传统习俗，所以各色各样的糖果就不必多说了。其次就是万圣节的象征南瓜了。最后要说的是苹果，每年的11月1日不仅是万圣节，还是古罗马的波摩娜节。波摩娜是"果树之神"，掌管所有果树的生与死、丰收与歉收。后来人们便会在万圣节吃苹果。

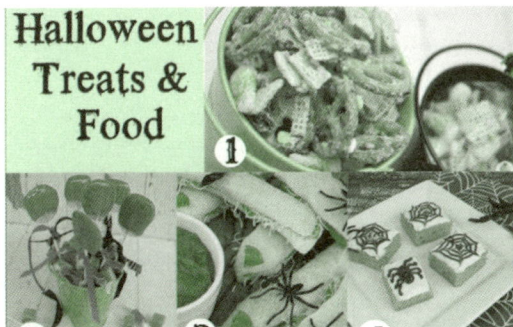

阅读笔记

阅读笔记

Part 5

那些年我们追过的 影视作品

《神探夏洛克》

剧情与文化影响

Many writers make references to Sir Arthur Conan Doyle's famous literary creation, the detective Sherlock Holmes, and these often become *embedded* within popular culture. While Holmes exists *predominately* in the context of Victorian-era London, he has been mentioned in such *outre* contexts as the 22nd century or hunting aliens or *supernatural* enemies. The versions of Holmes usually wear the deerstalker hat shown only a few in the original Strand pictures, as opposed to the far more common top hat, and frequently they say "Elementary my dear (name)" to another character. The Sherlock Holmes stories contribute one of the most enduring *paradigms* for the production and consumption of popular culture in the twentieth and the twenty-first centuries.

The stories *precipitated* a *burgeoning* fan culture including various kinds of participation, wiki and crowd-sourcing, fan-fiction, virtual realities and role-play gaming. All of these had existed before but they were *solidified*, *magnified*

许多作家都会经常提及阿瑟·柯南·道尔爵士的著名文学作品《侦探夏洛克·福尔摩斯》，且他们已深深地嵌入了流行文化之中。尽管福尔摩斯生活在维多利亚时期的伦敦，但他的生活背景一直都很奇怪，或生活在22世纪，或在抓捕外星人，或是超自然现象的敌人。在这些版本里，少数的原始图像显示福尔摩斯经常带着猎鹿帽，而非普普通通的大礼帽，且经常对别人说"我亲爱的（名字）"。在20世纪以及21世纪，福尔摩斯探案的故事成为电影以及流行文化中经久不衰的典范。

福尔摩斯探案的故事促成了一种发展迅速的粉丝文化，它包括各种各样的分享、维基网站和玩家外包、粉丝小说、虚拟世界以及角色扮演的游戏。虽然这些早已存在，但是夏洛克·福尔摩斯的崇拜者与福尔摩斯探

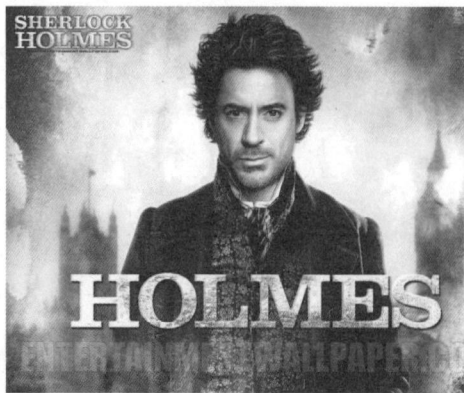

and united by Sherlockians and Holmesians in entirely new ways and on scales never seen before. All popular culture phenomena that followed shared its viral pattern.

案迷用全新的方式以及见所未见的规模将其组合团结起来，并发扬光大。所有的流行文化都以病毒传播的形式来分享开来。

单词释义

embedded 嵌入的
supernatural 超自然现象
burgeoning 迅速增长的

predominately 主要的
paradigm 典范，范例
solidify 团结，凝固

outre 奇怪的，荒诞的
precipitate 引起，促成
magnify 放大，增大

英国伦敦警察厅为什么叫"苏格兰场"

Scotland Yard is a *metonym* for the *headquarters* of the Metropolitan Police Service of the British capital, London. The Metropolitan Police Service is responsible for *law enforcement* within Greater London, excluding the square mile of the City of London, which is covered by the City of London Police. It *derives from* the location of the original Metropolitan Police headquarters at 4 Whitehall Place, which had a rear entrance on a street called Great Scotland Yard. The Scotland Yard entrance became the public entrance to the police station. Over time, the street and the Metropolitan Police became *synonymous*. The Metropolitan Police moved away from Scotland Yard in 1890, and the name "New Scotland Yard" was

苏格兰场是对英国首都伦敦警察厅总部的代称。苏格兰场负责维持除伦敦外的整个大伦敦地区的公共治安与交通秩序，因为伦敦的警务直接由伦敦市警察管辖。"苏格兰场"这个代称起源于警察厅的旧址白厅广场4号。当时警察厅的一扇后门正对着一条名为"大苏格兰场"的大街。此后，这扇门就成了警察厅的公共入口。久而久之，"苏格兰场"就成了伦敦警察厅的代名词。1890年，警察厅搬离了苏格兰场地区，现在所说的"新苏格兰场"也就是对警察厅新总部的称呼。

作为警务和侦探的代名词，苏格兰场出现在了许多犯罪小说中，由此而蜚声国际。在柯南·道尔的著名小说《夏洛克·福尔摩斯》中，苏格兰场的警察们与侦探福尔摩斯的关系也是亦敌亦友；苏格兰场也曾出现在小

adopted for the new headquarters.

Scotland Yard has become internationally famous as a symbol of policing, and detectives from Scotland Yard feature in many works of crime fiction. They were frequent allies, and sometimes *antagonists*, of Sherlock Holmes in Sir Arthur Conan Doyle's famous stories. It is also referred to in Around the World in Eighty Days. In the James Bond novels and short stories, Assistant Commissioner Sir Ronald Vallance is a recurring fictional character who works for Scotland Yard.

说《环游世界80天》中；在007系列小说中，助理局长罗尼·瓦蓝斯多次出场，他也是为苏格兰场效力的。

单词释义

metonym 转喻词	headquarter 总部	law enforcement 执法
derive from 起源于	synonymous 同义的	antagonist 对手

英国特色文化

特色表达One

不知道看过《夏洛克·福尔摩斯》的粉丝们，记不记得该剧第一季第一集里的场景，阿福的老哥麦考夫·福尔摩斯（Mycroft Holmes）悄悄地把华生"绑"来见面，却没想到华生对这突如其来的"绑架"并没有感到害怕，他那种 What will be will be 的沉着表现令大家印象深刻，这个短语其实就是中文中所说的"是福不是祸，是祸躲不过"的意思。

☆ 实景链接

A: Have you seen Sherlock Holme before? 你之前看过《夏洛克·福尔摩斯》吗？

B: Yeah, it's a very good teleplay. It taught me what will be will be.

Just be brave. 嗯，是部非常好的电视剧。他教会我是福不是祸，是祸躲不过。就勇敢面对吧。

A：That's right. 说得对啊。

B：So watch it. I strongly recommended. 所以，看看吧，我强烈推荐。

特色表达Two

男主角福尔摩斯在受伤之后总是很快就能up and running，让观众看到他的力量。这里的up and running字面意思是"起来跑跑"，引申为"恢复精神的，生龙活虎的"。

☆ 实景链接

A：Who is the man on the picture? 照片上的那个人是谁？

B：My boyfriend. 我男朋友。

A：He seems tired. What does he do? 他看起来挺累的，他是做什么工作的。

B：You observed so carefully. He works at the police station. Don't worry. He'll be up and running in a few days. 你观察得好仔细啊，他在警局工作。别担心，过几天他又会生龙活虎的。

拓展特色句

1. It is said that the second season of Sherlock has been pushed back to 2012. 据说《夏洛克·福尔摩斯》第二季首播日期被推迟到了2012年。

2. Do you like the Sherlock Holmes in movies or television series better? 你喜欢电影里的福尔摩斯多一些还是电视剧里的？

3. No detectives can match that of Arthur Conan Doyle's Sherlock Holmes. 没有哪个侦探形象能与柯南·道尔笔下的福尔摩斯相媲美。

"聊"英国特色文化

A：What are you reading?

B：Sir Arthur Conan Doyle's famous literary creation *Sherlock Holmes*.

A：Wow. It's really a classic detective

A：你在读什么书呢？

B：阿瑟·柯南·道尔爵士的著名文学作品《夏洛克·福尔摩斯》。

A：哇。那可是一部经典小说。

story.

B: Yes. The stories precipitated a burgeoning fan culture.

A: Can you tell me something about the author?

B: Sure. He was a Scottish physician and writer.

A: It's interesting. By the way, what is Scotland Yard?

B: Scotland Yard is a metonym for the headquarters of the Metropolitan Police Service of the British capital, London.

A: What a strange name! Do you know the origin of it?

B: It derives from the location of the original Metropolitan Police headquarters at 4 Whitehall Place, which had a rear entrance on a street called Great Scotland Yard. The Scotland Yard entrance became the public entrance to the police station.

A: I see. So over time, the street and the Metropolitan Police became synonymous.

B: That's right.

B: 是啊。这些故事促成了一种发展迅速的粉丝文化。

A: 你能告诉我一些关于作者的事吗？

B: 当然。他是一名苏格兰的医生和作家。

A: 真有趣。顺便问一句，苏格兰场是什么意思？

B: 苏格兰场是对英国首都伦敦警察厅总部的代称。

A: 真是一个奇怪的名字。你知道它的由来吗？

B: "苏格兰场"这个代称起源于警察厅的旧址白厅广场4号。当时警察厅的一扇后门正对着一条名为"大苏格兰场"的大街。此后，这扇门就成了警察厅的公共入口。

A: 我明白了。所以久而久之，"苏格兰场"就成了伦敦警察厅的代名词。

B: 是的。

"问" 英国特色文化

为什么杰里米·布雷特（Jeremy Brett）扮演的福尔摩斯那样深入人心？

研究起电视剧里福尔摩斯的扮演者，最受人欢迎的要属杰里米·布雷特（Jeremy Brett），这也是中国观众最为熟悉的一版福尔摩斯了。也许是因为他的形象非常符合书中对于福尔摩斯的相貌描写："有六英尺多高，身体异常瘦削，身材颀长；目光锐利；细长的鹰钩鼻显得他格外机警、果断；下颚方正而突出，说明他是个非常有毅力的人"。他贡献出了一个充满热情、幽默感强烈、有时也有点神经质的中年绅士形象。只是杰里米·布雷特于1984年接下福尔摩斯这个角色时，已年近50岁，所以他演绎的福尔摩斯已经相当成熟。

阅读笔记

《唐顿庄园》

剧情及成就

Downton Abbey is a British period drama television series created by Julian Fellowes and co-produced by Carnival Films and Masterpiece. The series, set in the fictional Yorkshire country estate of Downton Abbey, depicts the lives of the *aristocratic* Crawley family and their servants in the post-Edwardian era—with the great events in history having an effect on their lives and on the British *social hierarchy*. Such events depicted throughout the series include news of the sinking of the RMS Titanic in the first series; the outbreak of the First World War, the Spanish *influenza pandemic*, and the Marconi scandal in the second series; the Interwar period and the *formation* of the Irish Free State in the third series; and the Teapot Dome scandal in the fourth series.

Downton Abbey has received critical *acclaim* from television critics and won numerous *accolades*. By the third series, it had become one of the most widely watched television shows in the world.

英国历史连续剧《唐顿庄园》由朱利安·费罗斯主创，嘉年华电影公司与精英娱乐公司共同出品。这部电视连续剧背景设定在约克郡一个虚构的庄园——唐顿庄园，描述了后爱德华时期英国贵族克劳利家族与其仆人们生活百态，还描述了英国当时社会的重大历史事件对他们的生活以及社会等级制度的影响。这些重大事件贯穿了整部连续剧，它们包括第一部中泰坦尼克号沉船的消息，第二部中的第一次世界大战爆发、西班牙流感流行与马可尼丑闻，第三部中的内战与爱尔兰自由州的建立，第四部中的蒂波特山油田丑闻。

《唐顿庄园》收到了众多电视评论家的好评，并赢得了无数的赞誉。到第三部的时候，它已经成为世界上观看人数最多的电视剧之一了。

单词释义

aristocratic 贵族的   social hierarchy 社会等级   influenza 流感
pandemic 流行性疾病   formation 建立   acclaim 称赞
accolade 赞誉

《唐顿庄园》热风

The *LA Times* has called *Downton Abbey* a pop culture phenomenon, while Variety hailed it as '*mesmerizing*' television… old-fashioned but not unsophisticated". Such is the *appeal* stateside of the English-country-house soap opera that its second series *garnered* 16 Emmy nominations, with the *finale* attracting 5.4 million U.S. viewers double the ratings for the most recent series of *Mad Men*.

Downton's dress codes have now become something of a fashion phenomenon, not least in the U.S. Pop magazine dedicated its cover and a 20-page feature to *Downton* style. The makers of gentlemen's *requisites* in Mayfair, Piccadilly and St James's report a boom in American trade not seen since the onset of the double-dip European recession. America accounts for around 60 per cent of Savile Row bespoke-suit sales; prices start at around £3,500, though they rise dramatically when ordering formal dress in the style of Lord Grantham.

《洛杉矶时报》称《唐顿庄园》是一种流行文化现象，而一些综艺节目则称赞它为"令人着迷的电视剧……古典但不纯朴"。这部英国历史肥皂剧极具吸引力，它的第二部获得了16项艾美奖提名，大结局吸引了540万的美国观众，它的收视率是最新电视连续剧《广告狂人》的两倍。

《唐顿庄园》的着装规范现在已成为了一种流行时尚，美国流行杂志不仅将其作为封面，甚至还用20页的内文来专门介绍《唐顿庄园》的服装特色。梅费尔、皮卡迪利、圣詹姆斯等地的男士必需品生产商报告显示，自从欧洲经济二次衰退以来，美国贸易首次出现激增。起价约为3500英镑的萨维尔街高级定制套装中有60%都销往了美国，且定制格兰瑟姆伯爵风格的套装的人数骤然上升。

《唐顿庄园》与其说是唤起了人们对旧时代的记忆，不如说是给英国顶级手工艺品打的广告。梅费尔的奢侈品公司，如文具和皮具供应商斯迈森、顶级百货公司爱丝普蕾、珠宝古董经销商瓦特斯基都把其商品借给了《唐顿庄园》的演员们用作道具。

Downton Abbey is as much an advertisement for the best of British craftsmanship as it is a *reminiscence* of an age long since passed. Luxury-goods houses in Mayfair, such as stationer and leather-goods *purveyor* Smythson, high-end *emporium* Asprey and jeweller and antiques dealer Wartski, loaned pieces to dress the cast and sets of the show.

单词释义

mesmerizing 令人着迷的　　appeal 吸引力　　garner 获得
finale 结局　　requisite 必需品　　reminiscence 唤起记忆的事物
purveyor 供应商　　emporium 百货公司

"品" 英国特色文化

特色表达One

　　《唐顿庄园》之所以如此让人着迷，除了它制作精良、与历史吻合度高和情节曲折精彩之外，还有一个重要原因就是Nostalgia。没错，这部剧勾起了很多人的怀旧情结。为何怀旧如此美好，也许是因为"怀旧之情能使美好的旧时光更美好"吧，这句有深度的话的英文表达就是Nostalgia is a file that removes the rough edges from the good old days.

实景链接

A: Are you listening? You are spaced out. 你在听吗？感觉你魂不守舍的。

B: Well, I often remind her face and I've never forgotten it. 我时常想起她的样子，无法忘怀。

A: Oh, come on, man. It's in the past. 算了吧，老兄，都过去了。

B: You do not understand. **Nostalgia** is a file that removes the rough edges from the good old days. 你不会明白的，怀旧之情能使美好的旧时光更美好。

特色表达Two

从《唐顿庄园》里我们不难看出一些人的不同价值观的体现，可以把它称之为"贵族精神"，就是我们说的noble spirit，或者优雅一点叫做绅士品格。形容一个人很绅士，可以直接用gentleman或者gentlemanly来表示。

☆ 实景链接

A：Tell you some good news; I met my idol this morning. 告诉你一些好消息，我今天早上遇到我的偶像了！

B：Jimmy? 是吉米吗？

A：Yeah, he acted the **gentlemen** and went to open the door for me. 是的，而且他特别绅士地帮我开了门。

B：You're so lucky. 那你真是太幸运了！

拓展特色句

1. Where can I read the latest information about *Downton Abbey*? 我在哪儿能读到《唐顿庄园》的最新消息？

2. I recommend you watch the award-winning Downton Abbey. 我推荐你看《唐顿庄园》，名气很高的。

3. Michelle Dockery plays Lady Mary Crawley in *Downton Abbey*. 米歇尔·道克瑞在《唐顿庄园》中扮演玛丽·克劳利小姐。

"聊"英国特色文化

A：Do you know *Downton Abbey*?

B：Sure. It's a British period drama television series.

A：Are you crazy about British TV series?

B：Of course. I've watched the whole four series. I love their lordliness and elegant dressing.

A：But I think those events happened in the history in the series can help us to know the history better. It's a good

A：你知道《唐顿庄园》吗？

B：当然。它是一部英国历史连续剧。

A：你热衷于英剧吗？

B：当然。我看过整个四季。我喜欢他们的贵族气派和优雅的穿着。

A：但是我认为剧中那些历史重大事件可以帮助我们更好地了解历史。这是学习英国语言和英国历史的好方法。

B：这些都是《唐顿庄园》如此受欢迎的原因。

way to learn British language and British history.

B: All of them are the reasons why *Downton Abbey* is so popular.

A: Yes. Its second series garnered 16 Emmy nominations, with the finale attracting 5.4 million U.S. viewers— double the ratings for the most recent series of *Mad Men*.

B: When you find other good British series next time remember to share with me.

A: No problem.

A: 是的。它的第二季获得了16项艾美奖提名，大结局吸引了540万的美国观众，它的收视率是最新电视连续剧《广告狂人》的两倍。

B: 下次你发现好看的英剧时记得和我分享啊。

A: 没问题。

"问" 英国特色文化

为什么唐顿庄园没有被拆除？

《唐顿庄园》的拍摄场地海克力尔城堡(Highclere Castle)因为这部剧的热播受到了关注。这座城堡位于英格兰南部汉普郡，是典型富裕的英格兰地区，宛如中国的江南。英国乡间建筑，曾经遭遇过"拆迁潮"，20世纪英格兰大约有1/6的建筑被拆毁。唐顿庄园的原型得以保存，首先得力于卡纳冯伯爵家族，现任八世伯爵是英女王伊丽莎白二世的教子；其次，归功于他们的改变，将房子提供出来做旅游，并出让给《唐顿庄园》做拍摄场地用，两种方式都有可观的收入。

阅读笔记

《猜火车》

电影主题介绍

Trainspotting is a 1996 British black comedy/drama film directed by Danny Boyle based on the novel of the same name by Irvine Welsh.

Set in the late 1980s of Edinburgh, the movie is about the *corrupted* life of a young Scottish man named mark Renton and his so-called friends—a bunch of losers, liars, *psychos*, thieves and *junkies*. This tragic-comedy *charts* the *disintegration* of their friendship as they proceed, seemingly *inevitably* towards *self-destruction*. Mark alone has the insight and opportunity to escape his fate and live a stable and traditional life. But soon after mark quits heroin, his peaceful life is disturbed by his former friends. This time Mark finally makes a decision to get rid of them entirely.

Beyond drug addiction, other themes in the film are *exploration* of the urban poverty and *squalor* in "culturally rich" Edinburgh.

《猜火车》是1996由丹尼·博伊尔导演的一部英式黑色喜剧或剧情片，改编自欧文·威尔士的同名小说。

电影中人物所处的背景为20世纪80年代的爱丁堡。电影讲述了一位名叫马克·瑞顿以及他的朋友们的生活。他所谓的朋友们其实是一群失败者、撒谎者、精神病、小偷以及瘾君子。这部悲喜剧记录随着他们不可避免地走向自我毁灭的道路，以及他们友谊的瓦解过程。马克本有机会逃避他的命运，过着传统的稳定生活，但是他戒毒后的平静生活却被他之前的朋友们打乱了。直到这时，马克才真正下定决心改头换面，断绝与他们的关系。

除了瘾君子之外，这部电影还探究了有着深厚文化底蕴的爱丁堡的另一面——贫困与肮脏。

单词释义

corrupted 堕落的　　psycho 精神病　　junky 吸毒者
chart 记录　　disintegration 瓦解，崩溃　inevitably 不可避免地
self-destruction 自毁　exploration 探究　squalor 肮脏

《猜火车》对流行文化的影响

The film *Trainspotting* had an immediate impact on popular culture. In 1999, *Trainspotting* was ranked in the 10th spot by the British Film Institute (BFI) in its list of Top 100 British films of all time, while in 2004 the magazine *Total Film* named it the fourth greatest British film of all time. *The Observer* polled several filmmakers and film critics who voted it the best British film in the last 25 years. In 2004, the film was voted the best Scottish film of all time by the public in a poll for *The List* magazine. *Trainspotting* has since developed a *cult* following. It has also been recognised as an important piece of culture and film during the 1990s British cultural *tour de force* known as Cool Britannia. It was *featured* in the *documentary Live Forever: The Rise and Fall of Brit Pop* as well.

The *cryptic* film title is a reference to a scene (not included in the film) in the original book, where Begbie and Renton meet 'an *auld* drunkard' who turns out to be Begbie's *estranged* father, in the *disused* Leith Central railway station, which they are using as a toilet. He asks them if they are "trainspotting". Irvine Welsh himself has explained

电影《猜火车》对流行文化产生了直接影响。1999年，在英国电影协会(BFI)颁布的Top100英国电影中，《猜火车》这部电影位列第十；2004年，杂志《完全电影》将这部电影称之为英国历史上第四杰出的电影。《观察家》对投票认为《猜火车》是过去的25年里最佳电影的制片人和评论家进行了问卷调查。2004年，在杂志《榜单》的一项民意调查中，公众投票认为《猜火车》是史上最棒的苏格兰影片。从那时起，《猜火车》就有了属于它自己的忠实粉丝。这部电影被认为是20世纪90年代被称为"酷不列颠"英国文化与电影的代表作之一。它也是纪录片《永生:英国流行文化的兴衰》的重头戏。

《猜火车》这部电影的得名源自原著(电影中没有出现)中的一个情景——在由于废弃不用而沦为他们厕所的利斯中央火车站里，贝吉比与瑞顿遇到了一个老酒鬼，而这个酒鬼正是与贝吉比关系疏远的父亲。他询问他们是否是在

in a Q&A that the title is also a reference to people thinking that the hobby of trainspotting makes no sense to non-participants. Likewise, the same applies to heroin addiction: to non-addicts the act seems completely pointless whereas, to someone hooked on heroin, it makes absolute sense.

猜火车。欧文·威尔士在一个记者问答中也曾解释道，片名引用了这样一种事实，即猜火车这个游戏对于没有参与的人来说是没有任何意义的。同样的，这也可用于指代戒除毒瘾，即对于不吸毒的人来说，戒毒这一行为根本没有任何意义，而对于瘾君子来说，这一行为意义非凡。

单词释义

cult 狂热崇拜的
documentary 纪录片
estranged 疏远的

tour de force 精心杰作，代表作
cryptic 令人困惑的
disused 废弃不用的

feature 特写
auld 老的（苏格兰）

“品” 英国特色文化

特色表达One

《猜火车》这部电影就是那种要么让人喜欢到不行，要么让人看到句中的情节气得想要发疯的节奏，这里说的"快气疯了"就可以用俚语go ballistic来表达。如果一个人go ballistic，意思是他的怒火被点燃起来，像火箭一样发射出去，进入弹道飞行的状态。可想而知，他这个时候一定是怒不可遏了。

☆ 实景链接

A：I met Peter today. 我今天见到彼得了。

B：Then what? 怎么了？

A：I saw he flirted with Mia. 我竟然看到他在和米娅调情！

B： Oh, god. If Linda finds it out, she'll **go ballistic**. 哦，天哪，如果琳达知道了这事，她会气疯的。

特色表达Two

当主人公马克尝试戒毒，但最终还是succumb to temptation(抵不住诱惑)，恶习依旧，继续和丹尼尔等人抢劫游客(rob tourists)，用得来的钱买毒品时，我

想，影迷对于这一幕的情景都无法忘记，也知道这样的行为一定会face the music的，face the music不是面对音乐，而是"接受惩罚"的意思。

☆ **实景链接**

A：What's the matter with Paul? 保罗怎么了？

B：I heard he was once again taking drugs. 我听说他又开始吸毒了。

A：How is that? 怎么会这样啊？

B：I'm surprised, too. And he will **face the music**. 我也很吃惊，他肯定要接受惩罚了。

拓展特色句

1. He watched the movie *Trainspotting* over and over. 他一遍又一遍地看电影《猜火车》。

2. When a junkie would go to buy his drugs, he would say that he was going "Trainspotting". 当一个瘾君子去买毒品的时候，通常都说自己去"猜火车"。

3. *Trainspotting* is set in the late 1980s of Edinburgh. 《猜火车》背景设在20世纪80年代的爱丁堡。

"聊" 英国特色文化

A：Have you ever watched *Trainspotting*?

B：No.

A：Are you kidding? It's so famous and influential.

B：What's it about?

A：The movie is about the corrupted life of a young Scottish man named mark Renton and his so-called friends.

B：Who's the director?

A：Danny Boyle.

B：The man who directed *Slumdog Millionaire* and won Academy Award

A：你看过《猜火车》吗？

B：没有。

A：开玩笑吧？它这么有名气和影响力。

B：是关于什么的？

A：电影讲述了一位名叫马克·瑞顿以及他的朋友们的生活。

B：导演是谁？

A：丹尼·博伊尔。

B：就是执导《贫民窟的百万富翁》并且赢得奥斯卡最佳导演奖的那个人？

A：是的。这是他的早期作品。

for Best Directing?

A: Yes. This is his early works.

B: Is there anything special about this movie?

A: It had an immediate impact on popular culture. It has also been recognized as an important piece of culture and film during the 1990s British cultural tour de force known as Cool Britannia.

B: It sounds interesting. I can watch it later.

B: 这部电影有什么特别的吗？

A: 它对流行文化产生了直接影响。这部电影被认为是20世纪90年代被称为"酷不列颠"英国文化与电影的代表作之一。

B: 听起来很有趣。过会儿我去看看。

"问" 英国特色文化

为什么电影的名字是《猜火车》？

"猜火车"原指一种游戏，是无所事事的人在火车经过的地方，即兴打赌猜测下一班火车经过的时间和目的地，借此打发时间。影片以此为名意义深远，当火车狂啸过站时，不知要将主人公们的命运载往何方。影片所反映的社会现实，以及它所流露出的冷漠、非主流群落对主流社会的抵制与反抗，给了在常态社会中生活的人们强烈的冲击。《猜火车》是一部带有写实性质的电影，里面表现的青少年的生活方式是惊世骇俗的，其间所反映出的社会问题如吸毒、暴力、抢劫等都值得人们深思。

《泰坦尼克号》

电影的成就

Titanic is a 1997 American *epic* romantic disaster film directed, written, co-produced, co-edited and partly financed by James Cameron. A *fictionalized* account of the *sinking* of the RMS Titanic, it stars Leonardo DiCaprio and Kate Winslet as members of different social classes who fall in love aboard the ship during its ill-fated maiden voyage.

Upon its release on December 19, 1997, the film achieved *critical* and commercial success. Nominated for fourteen Academy Awards, it won eleven, including the awards for Best Picture and Best Director, tying *Ben Hur* for most Oscars won by a single film. With an *initial* worldwide gross of over $1.84 billion, it was the first film to reach the billion-dollar mark. It remained the highest-grossing film of all time, until Cameron's 2009 film *Avatar* surpassed its gross in 2010. A 3D version of the film, released on April 4, 2012, *commemorates* the *centenary* of the sinking of the ship.

《泰坦尼克号》是于1997年拍摄的一部史诗般的浪漫灾难电影，由詹姆斯·卡梅隆导演、创作、共同监制、编辑及赞助。这部电影以泰坦尼克号在其处女起航时触礁冰山而沉没的事件为背景，讲述了来自不同社会阶层的莱昂纳多·迪卡普里奥与凯特·温斯莱特在船上相识相爱的故事。

在1997年12月19日上映时，这部电影大受好评，票房爆满。它获得了14项奥斯卡金像奖提名，并将包括最佳影片、最佳导演奖等11项大奖收入囊中，打破了《宾虚》单部电影在奥斯卡获奖最多的纪录。这部电影全球票房高达18.4亿美元，是世界上首部票房超过10亿美元的电影。直到2010年，其票房收入才被卡梅隆2009年拍摄的电影《阿凡达》所超越，它在票房冠军的座椅坐了12年。《泰坦尼克号》在2012年4月4日以3D版形式重新发布，以纪念泰坦尼克号沉船事件100周年。

单词释义

epic 史诗般的　　　　fictionalized 小说化的　　　　sinking 沉没

critical 获好评的　　　initial 最初的　　　　　commemorate 纪念

centenary 百年纪念

为何成为当时成本最高的电影

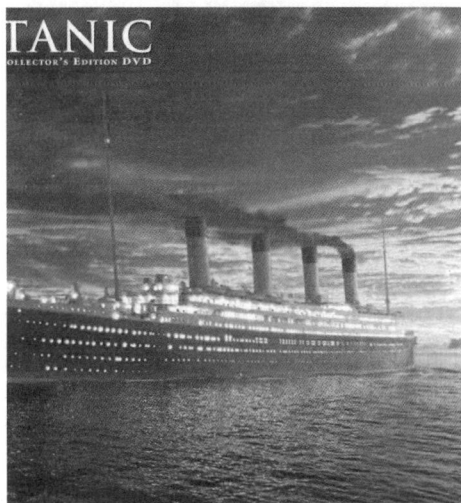

Cameron's *inspiration* for the film was predicated on his fascination with shipwrecks; he wanted to convey the emotional message of the tragedy and felt that a love story *interspersed* with the human loss would be *essential* to achieving this. Production on the film began in 1995, when Cameron shot *footage* of the actual Titanic wreck. The modern scenes were shot on board the Akademik Mstislav Keldysh, which Cameron had used as a base when filming the wreck. A *reconstruction* of the Titanic built at Playas de Rosarito in Baja California, scale models, and computer-generated imagery were used to recreate the sinking.

Cameron wanted to push the boundary of special effects with his film, and *enlisted* Digital Domain to continue the developments in digital technology. He encouraged them to shoot their 45-foot long miniature of the ship. Afterwards, digital water and smoke were added, as were *extras* captured on a motion capture stage. There was also a 65-foot long model of the ship's stern that could break in two repeatedly, the only miniature to be used in water.

An *enclosed* 5,000,000 US

卡梅隆拍摄《泰坦尼克号》这部电影的灵感源自其对海难事件的着迷。他想传达出海难这一悲剧的信息，而通过穿插人员伤亡情节的爱情故事则是实现这一目标的关键。这部电影的制作开始于1995年，卡梅隆对泰坦尼克号现实中的残骸进行了取景。电影中，人物的取景是在凯尔迪什号上，该船正是卡梅隆之前取景泰坦尼克号时的基地。泰坦尼克号的重建在是加利福尼亚半岛的罗萨里多完成的；为了重现泰坦尼克号沉船那一幕，拍电影时使用了泰坦尼克号的成比例模型与计算机合成影像。

卡梅隆想在他的电影中推动特效的发展，所以支持数字领域公司继续发展数字技术。他鼓励他们拍摄泰坦尼克号长达45英尺的模型。此后，在动作捕捉拍摄时，还加入了数字效果的水和烟雾。此外，船尾还有一个65英尺 (20

gallons tank was used for sinking *interiors*. In order to sink the Grand Staircase, 90,000 US gallons of water were dumped into the set as it was lowered into the tank. The post-sinking scenes in the freezing Atlantic were shot in a 350,000 US gallons tank, where the frozen corpses were created by applying a powder on actors that *crystallized* when exposed to water, and wax was coated on hair and clothes.

米)长、中间可以断开的泰坦尼克号模型，这是唯一可以下水的模型。

拍摄船沉没的情景时，还使用了一个可盛500万加仑水的水箱。为了呈现主楼梯沉没的情景，他们往装置中注入了9万加仑的水，因为它需要沉于水箱中。泰坦尼克号在冰冷的大西洋沉没后的场景拍摄于在35万加仑的水箱；演员们涂上一种的粉末，遇水时会结晶；他们还在衣服及头发上涂上蜡，以营造像冻死了一样的效果。

单词释义

inspiration 灵感
footage 镜头
enclosed 全封闭的

interspersed 穿插的
reconstruction 重建
interior 内景

essential 必要的
enlist 支持
crystallize 结晶

"品"英国特色文化

特色表达One

电影中有一个桥段是罗丝介绍杰克时说"a person of limited greens..."，这里说的"greens"、不是绿色，而是代表"钞票"的意思。罗丝用"a person of limited greens"委婉地暗示杰克是一个穷小子的身份；她母亲用疑问和讥讽的口气询问杰克"the means to travel"即挣钱旅行的方式；而在杰克向罗丝表白时也用"ten bucks"很无奈地道出自己几乎身无分文。

⭐实景链接

A: Do you know Abel and Angela are in love? 你知道艾贝尔和安吉拉恋爱了吗？

B: I don't know. When did this happen? 我不知道啊，什么时候发生的事？

A: But Angela told me he was **a person of limited greens**. 但是安吉拉告诉我他是个穷小子。

B：Let's pray he is a diamond in the rough. 那就让我们祈祷他是一个潜力股吧。

📝 特色表达Two

当看到杰克知道自己就要离罗丝而去，却坚持着对她说我还有一个心愿，要活下去，不能绝望，无论多么艰难，答应我一定做到时，是不是为他们的爱情而感动，并且cheeks dripped with tears？泪流满面可以用cheeks dripped with tears来表达，也可以形象地说 One's face is covered with tears.

⭐ 实景链接

A：Lily, what kind of films do you like? 莉莉，你喜欢什么样的电影？

B：Of all the movies, I like *Titanic* best. 在所有电影中，我最喜欢《泰坦尼克号》了。

A：It thrilled everyone. 它让每个人都很激动！

B：Yes, each time when I saw it, my **cheeks dripped with tears**. 是的，每次看这部电影我都会泪流满面。

拓展特色句

1. The film Titanic thrilled the audience. 电影《泰坦尼克号》令观众激动。

2. An iceberg in the Atlantic took down the Titanic. 泰坦尼克号撞上大西洋的一座冰山，沉入海底。

3. The Titanic was designed to be a passenger liner. 泰坦尼克号被设计成了一艘客轮。

💬 英国特色文化

A：I heard that Titanic will be made in Sichuan to attract more visitors. It will cost a billion yuan.

B：It's a huge project.

A：It reminds me the romantic film *Titanic*. It's really a masterpiece.

B：Yes. The love story between Jack and

A：我听说泰坦尼克号将在四川建造来吸引更多的游客。它将花费10亿人民币。

B：真是一个巨大的项目啊。

A：它使我想起了那部浪漫的电影《泰坦尼克号》。真是一部杰作啊。

B：是啊。杰克和罗丝之间的爱情故事

Rose moved a lot of people.

A： The music in it is fair-sounding and classic. Until now plenty of people still love to listen and sing it.

B： Did you watch Cameron's *Titanic*?

A： Yes. The 3D version is fantastic.

B： Cameron spent a lot on this film.

A： Yes. The post-sinking scenes in the freezing Atlantic were shot in a 350,000 US gallons tank, where the frozen corpses were created by applying a powder on actors that crystallized when exposed to water and wax was coated on hair and clothes.

感动了很多人。

A： 里面的音乐也很动听和经典。直到现在许多人仍然喜欢听并且演唱这首歌曲。

B： 你看过卡梅隆版的《泰坦尼克号》吗?

A： 看过。3D版的效果棒极了。

B： 卡梅隆为这部电影投入了很多。

A： 是啊。泰坦尼克号在冰冷的大西洋沉没后的场景拍摄于在35万加仑的水箱；演员们涂上一种粉末，遇水时会结晶；他们还在衣服及头发上涂上蜡，以营造像冻死了一样的效果。

"问" 英国特色文化

《泰坦尼克号》为何如此震撼人心?

据权威统计，1998年春天《泰坦尼克号》登陆中国市场后，总票房达3.6亿元人民币，这个记录保持了10年。据了解，当年出现过盲人观看《泰坦尼克号》的情形，一位上海的男孩还创下了连续观看14遍的纪录。许多影院门前都出现过排队买票的场面。当时在中国70元一张票，很贵，但电影院里还是坐满了观众，深受震撼的不仅仅是爱情，而且还有伟大的人性。中影集团从1994年开始引入"进口大片"，但直到《泰坦尼克号》出现，大家才真的明白了什么叫"大片"。这部电影也成了那一代观众无法抹去的记忆。

《哈利·波特》

作品简介

Harry Potter is a series of seven fantasy novels written by the British author J. K. Rowling. The series, named after the *titular* character, *chronicle* the adventures of a *wizard*, Harry Potter, and his friends Ronald Weasley and Hermione Granger, all of whom are students at Hogwarts School of Witchcraft and Wizardry. The main story arc concerns Harry's quest to overcome the Dark wizard Lord Voldemort, who aims to become *immortal*, *conquer* the wizarding world, *subjugate* non-magical people, and destroy all those who stand in his way, especially Harry Potter.

In 1998, Rowling sold the film rights of the first four *Harry Potter* books to Warner Bros. for a reported £1 million. Rowling demanded the *principal cast* be kept strictly British, nonetheless allowing for the inclusion of Irish actors such as the late Richard Harris as Dumbledore, and for casting of French and Eastern Europe actors in *Harry Potter and the Goblet of Fire* where characters from the book are specified as such.

《哈利·波特》是英国作家J.K.罗琳写的魔幻系列小说，共7部。这套书书名以小说主角哈利·波特为名，讲述了他与好友——同是霍格沃茨魔法学校学生的罗恩·韦斯莱和赫敏·格兰杰的冒险故事。故事的主线围绕着哈利与黑巫师伏地魔的斗争展开，因为伏地魔追求永生，企图占领魔法世界、征服普通民众，摧毁挡在他路上的人，特别是哈利·波特。

1998年，罗琳将《哈利·波特》前四部小说的电影拍摄权以100万英镑的高价出售给了华纳兄弟。出售时，罗琳要求《哈利·波特》里的主要演员必须由英国人来出演，尽管如此，随着剧情的需要，后续演员阵容里还加入了饰演邓布利多的爱尔兰演员理查德·哈里斯，且在《哈利·波特与火焰杯》中还加入了法国以及东欧的演员。

单词释义

titular 名称的   chronicle 记录   wizard 巫师
immortal 不死的   conquer 战胜   subjugate 征服
principal cast 主要演员

美女作家——J. K. 罗琳

J. K. Rowling, is a British novelist, beJ. K. Rowling, is a British novelist, best known as the author of the *Harry Potter* fantasy series. The Potter books have gained worldwide attention, won *multiple* awards, and sold more than 400 million copies. They have become the best-selling book series in history, and been the basis for a series of films which has become the highest-grossing film series in history. Rowling had overall approval on the *scripts* and maintained creative control by serving as a producer on the final *installment*.

Rowling has led a "*rags to riches*" life story, in which she progressed from living on state benefits to *multi-millionaire* status within five years. She is the United Kingdom's best-selling author since records began, with sales in excess of £238m. The 2008 *Sunday Times Rich List* estimated Rowling's fortune at £560 million ($798 million), ranking her as the twelfth richest woman in

J. K.罗琳是英国小说家，其最负盛名的作品便是奇幻系列小说《哈利·波特》。《哈利·波特》这套书受到全世界人们的瞩目，获得了多个奖项，销量超过4亿册。它们是史上最畅销的图书，根据其改变的电影也成为史上最卖座的电影。罗琳将电影的剧本完全授权了出去，但在拍摄最后一部时，她担任了制片人以把控电影剧本的更改。

罗琳白手起家，在5年内，完成了从靠社保度日到千万富翁的角色演变。她是英国有纪录以来最畅销图书的作家，图书收入超过2.38亿英镑。2008年

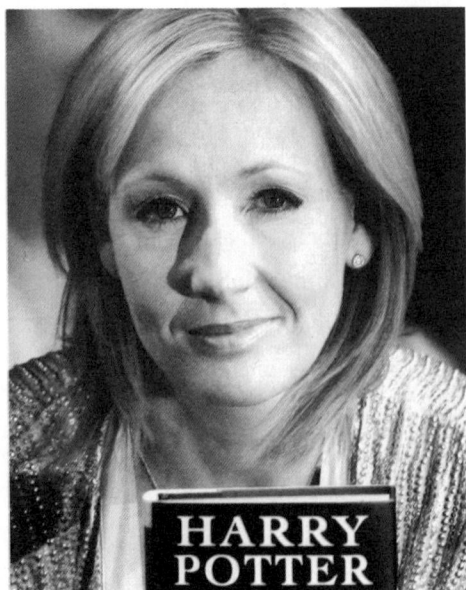

the United Kingdom. Forbes ranked Rowling as the forty-eighth most powerful celebrity of 2007, and *TIME* magazine named her as a *runner-up* for its 2007 Person of the Year, noting the social, moral, and political inspiration she has given her fans. In October 2010, Rowling was named the "Most Influential Woman in Britain" by leading magazine editors. She has become a notable *philanthropist*, supporting many charities.

的《星期日泰晤士报》富豪榜估计罗琳的财富高达5.6亿英镑（约7.98亿美元），是英国排名第12位的最富有女性。《福布斯》2007年最具影响力名人排行榜中，罗琳位列第48位。《时代》杂志根据其给粉丝带来的社会、道德以及政治启发，而将其列为2007年年度人物的亚军。2010年10月，罗琳被主流杂志编辑评为"英国最具影响力的女性"。她成为了一位著名的慈善家，支持了许多慈善事业。

单词释义

multiple 许多的
rags to riches 白手起家
philanthropist 慈善家

script 剧本
multi-millionaire 千万富翁

installment 分册
runner-up 亚军

"品" 英国特色文化

特色表达One

曾经《哈利·波特》风靡全球，里面的台词也随着主角的大红而飘红，如书中的人物常说的"attaboy"，你可别按音译理解成"邋遢男孩"，其实，这个单词在俚语里表示鼓励或赞美，最早来自20世纪初"That's the boy."，这句话的意思是"好小子！做得不错哈！"

☆实景链接

A：Have you read *Harry Potter*? 你读过《哈利·波特》吗？

B：You mean the adventures of a wizard, Harry Potter? 你说的是魔法师哈利·波特的冒险吗？

A：Of course. 当然啦。

B：I have read the book, Harry Potter is a **attaboy**! 我读过啊，哈利·波特相当棒呢！

💬 特色表达Two

畅销书《哈利·波特》的作者J. K.罗琳既聪颖睿智又坚强独立，作为一名知性女性是很多人的to be a dream boat。这里的dream boat可不能理解为"理想的小船"，在俚语里，这个短语的意思是"理想的女人"。当然，dream boat也可以指"理想的男人"。

☆ 实景链接

A：Do you know the writer of *Harry Potter*? 你知道《哈利·波特》的作者吗？

B：Of course, it's J. K. Rowling. 当然知道，是J. K.罗琳。

A：She is a great woman. 她是一个伟大的女性。

B：And she is a **dream boat** of mine. 她是我的理想型。

拓展特色句

1. We have *Harry Potter* in three languages, English, French and Russian. 我们有三种语言版本的《哈利·波特》——英语、法语和俄语。

2. *Order of the Phoenix* is the fifth book in the series. 《哈利·波特与凤凰社》是系列的第五部。

3. Have you seen *Harry Potter and the Goblet of Fire*? 你看过《哈利·波特与火焰杯》吗？

"聊" 英国特色文化

A：Why are you holding a besom? 你为什么拿个扫把？

B：I'm imitating Harry Potter. Cool? 我正在模仿哈利·波特呢。酷吧？

A：Did you watch the latest one? 你看了最新的一部吗？

B：Yes. I watched it last night. I love this film. 是的。我昨天晚上看的。我喜欢这部电影。

A：J. K. Rowling is really a genius. How can she create such a masterpiece? J. K.罗琳真是个天才。她是怎么创作出这样一部杰作的呢？

B：She had a bad time before *Harry Potter* became popular. She had to endure high pressure and felt blue. 她在《哈利·波特》成名前度过了一段很困难的时光。她忍受了巨大了压力，心情也很糟糕。

A：Thank god they are all over. She progressed from living on state benefits to multi-millionaire statuses.

B：In October 2010, Rowling was named the "Most Influential Woman in Britain" by leading magazine editors.

A：Yes, and she has become a notable philanthropist, supporting many charities. I think we women should learn from her.

A：谢天谢地，这一切都过去了。她完成了从靠社保度日到千万富翁的角色演变。

B：2010年10月，罗琳被主流杂志编辑评为"英国最具影响力的女性"。

A：是的，并且她成为了一位著名的慈善家，支持了许多慈善事业。我觉得我们女人应该向她学习。

"问" 英国特色文化

《哈利·波特》反映了英国的哪些文化？

《哈利·波特》给人的第一印象就是魔法的存在了。因为在古老的英国，人们习惯用所谓的"魔法攻击"来解释一些个人的不幸或者社会的灾祸，而使用这些"魔法攻击"的人则是魔法师或巫师。有的魔法师天赋异禀，生来就是魔法小成者，也有的巫师通过后天学习而获得各种魔法传承。在近代英国，人们还将一些神秘团体当作是巫师社团，他们属于非人类甚至反人类，若是抓住了基本要被处死，因此，很多人都无辜牺牲了。其实，好多人是无害的民间魔法师，可是世俗的偏见却让他们命丧黄泉。

阅读笔记

《英国达人秀》

节目介绍

Britain's Got Talent (often shortened to BGT) is a British television talent show competition which started in June 2007 and *originated* from the *Got Talent franchise*. It is known as one of Britain's biggest television talent competitions and has also proven popular throughout Europe.

Anyone of any age with some sort of talent can *audition* for the show. Acts compete against each other in order to gain the audience support while trying to win the title of *The winner of Britain's Got Talent*. Throughout the show, *contestants* must perform in front of the judges, and each year *initial auditions* have been held in front of a live audience.

The winner of each series is given the opportunity to perform at the Royal Variety Performance in front of members of the British Royal Family, including Queen Elizabeth II. The winner also receives a cash prize, which is £250,000 in series 7.

《英国达人秀》（简称为BGT）始于2007年6月，是一档英国电视达人选秀节目，其前身是《达人选举》。它是英国最大的电视选秀类节目，也是欧洲最流行的节目。

只要拥有某项才能，你就可以参加这个节目的试镜。不同的达人之间会相互竞争，以获得观众的支持从而赢得《英国达人秀》的总冠军。在节目录制期间，选手必须在评委前表演，而每年的海选都会现场直播。

《英国达人秀》的冠军获得者将有机会参考英国皇家文艺汇演，在包括伊丽莎白二世女王在内的英国王室面前表演。在《英国达人秀》第七季中，冠军还获得了高达25万英镑的奖金。

单词释义

originate 起源于　　　audition 视镜　　　contestant 选手
initial audition 海选

被达人秀捧红的苏珊大妈

Susan Boyle is a Scottish singer who came to international attention when she appeared as a contestant on the TV programme *Britain's Got Talent* on 11 April 2009, singing "I Dreamed a Dream" from Les Misérables. Her first album was *released* in November 2009 and *debuted* as the number one best-selling album on charts around the globe.

Susan Boyle's initial appearance on the talent show fired public imagination when her modest stage introduction and thick speaking accent left audience, viewers and judges alike unprepared for the power and expression of her *mezzo-soprano* voice. Before she had finished the song's opening phrase a standing *ovation* for Boyle had erupted. An international media and Internet response *coincided*. Within nine days of the audition, videos of Boyle—from the show, various interviews and her 1999 *rendition* of "Cry Me a River"—had been watched over 100 million times.

Boyle's debut album, *I Dreamed a Dream* (2009) instantly became the UK's best-selling debut album of all time, beating the previous

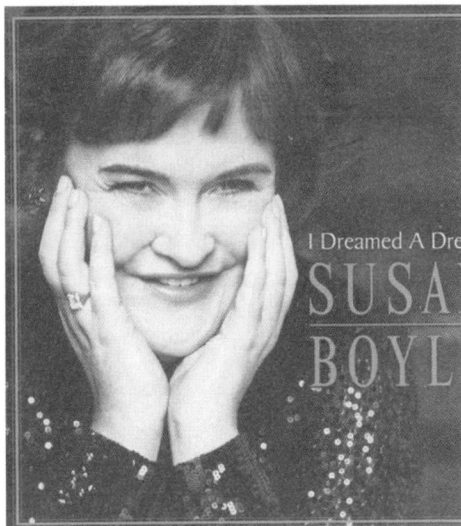

苏珊·波伊尔是一位苏格兰歌手，在2009年5月11日的电视节目《英国达人秀》上以选手的身份唱了《悲惨世界》中的《我曾有梦》而一举成名。她的首张个人专辑于2009年11月推出，并成为全球排行榜上最畅销的专辑。

苏珊·波伊尔首次出现在达人秀上时其貌不扬，带有浓重的口音，关于她的介绍也很一般，这让观众与评委以为她没有做充分的准备，但是她富有感染力的歌声却震撼了全场。她的歌还没有唱完，观众们就已经起身为她欢呼。媒体以及网络上对她表演的反应也是非常轰动。在9天的试镜时间里，波伊尔的表演、访谈以及她1999年的表演《泪流成河》的视频被人们点击次数就超过了1亿次。

波伊尔的首张专辑《我曾有梦》

record held by *Spirit* by Leona Lewis. The success was continued with her second album, and was followed by Boyle's third album. In 2013, Boyle had sold over 19 million albums worldwide and received two Grammy Awards nominations.

（2009年）替代了丽安娜·刘易斯的《精神》成为了英国史上最畅销的专辑。波伊尔的第二张与第三张专辑也非常成功。2013年，波伊尔的专辑在全球的销量超过了1900万张，她也获得了两项格莱美奖的提名。

单词释义

release 发行　　　　　debut 初次登台　　　　mezzo-soprano 女中音
ovation 热烈欢呼　　　coincide 一致　　　　　rendition 演奏

"品" 英国特色文化

特色表达One

所谓的《英国达人秀》，就是要达人们上台相互竞争，展现才艺，在英国人看来，达人们在台上需要Blah-blah-blah。这里的Blah-blah-blah可不是指气球噗噗噗地一点点变大，而是指"絮絮叨叨地说个不停"。

☆ 实景链接

A: Look that girl, I think she may lose in this round. 看那个女孩，她这个回合可能会输。

B: Why? I think she performs well. 为什么？我觉得她发挥得很好啊。

A: But all she does is go "**blah-blah-blah**" in this round. 但是她在这个回合都是絮絮叨叨。

B: Well, she should be more active. 好吧，她应该更活泼点。

特色表达Two

《英国达人秀》是达人们的秀场，也是达人们需要go whole hog的竞争舞台。go whole hog这个短语中的hog是"猪"或是"像猪一样的人"，那go whole hog的意思是"像一整猪一样行走"吗？其实，这个短语在俚语中是"全力以赴"。

✦ **实景链接**

A：Do you think it's easy to take part in the *Britain's Got Talent*? 你觉不觉得参加《英国达人秀》是件很容易的事情？

B：No, I don't think so. *The Britain's Got Talent* is pretty competitive. 我不这么认为，《英国达人秀》竞争很激烈的。

A：Really? Do the players have to compete with each other? 真的吗？选手们还得相互竞争吗？

B：Of course, everyone here must **go whole hog**. 当然啦，每个选手都必须全力以赴。

拓展特色句

1. Susan Boyle became famous overnight on Britain's popular TV show *Britain's Got Talent*. "苏珊大妈"因英国热门选秀节目《英国达人秀》一夜成名。

2. The 17-year-old singer appeared to be emulating Madonna on *Britain's Got Talent* last night. 昨晚那个17岁的女歌手在《英国达人秀》的表演上模仿了麦当娜。

3. He is now working as a judge on *Britain's Got Talent*. 他如今在《英国达人秀》担任评委。

"聊" 英国特色文化

A：Why are you laughing?

B：Susan Boyle is so cute.

A：Oh, you are watching *Britain's Got Talent* again.

B：I like this program. It can help ordinary people make their dream come true. And it's fair.

A：It's similar to *American Idol*. And I heard that it appeared before *American Idol*. But due to some reason it was postponed.

B：A lot of programs in our country

A：你笑什么呢？

B：苏珊大妈太可爱了。

A：哦，你又看《英国达人秀》呢。

B：我喜欢这档节目。它能帮助普通人实现梦想。而且很公平。

A：其实，这个节目和《美国偶像》类似。我听说它比《美国偶像》出现得早，但是由于某种原因被推迟了。

B：我们国家有好多节目模仿它。

A：许多人都有梦想。这是一个展示他

imitate it.

A： Many people have a dream. This is the best platform for them to show their talent.

B： Talent agents can look for the ones they need here.

A： Like the old saying "Kill two birds with one stone."

B： Maybe I can have a try, too. I think I do well in acting.

们天赋的最好平台。

B： 星探也可以在这儿寻找他们需要的人。

A： 就像那句老话说的"一举两得"。

B： 也许我也可以试试。我认为自己擅长表演。

"问" 英国特色文化

平民也能胜出达人秀吗？

曾经很多英国人质疑达人秀的公正性，而2010非专业杂技团体Spellbound在《英国达人》取胜后开创了平民化偶像的神话奇迹，因为Spellbound团体的各个成员大多来自社会中下阶层，他们中有的人搞清洁工作，有的在酒吧打工。当年6月5日晚，Spellbound"欢乐弹跳"不仅令现场的所有评委惊艳不已，也同样震惊了电视机前的观众，关注这场比赛的人都赞不绝口称这是他们在直播选秀节目上看到的最令人震撼的表演。

阅读笔记

....

....

....

《英国偶像》

节目介绍

The X Factor is a British television music competition to find new singing talents, *contested* by aspiring singers *drawn from* public auditions. It is the biggest television talent competition in Europe and has proved hugely popular with the public.

The show began in September 2004 and has since *aired* annually from August/September through to December. The show is broadcast on the ITV network in the United Kingdom and TV3 in Ireland, with *spin-off* behind-the-scenes show The Xtra Factor screened on ITV2. The X Factor was *devised* as a replacement for the highly successful Pop Idol, which was put on indefinite *hiatus* after its second series. The perceived similarity between the two shows later became the subject of a legal dispute. The "X Factor" of the title refers to the *undefinable* "something" that makes for star quality.

《英国偶像》是一档英国的歌唱选秀节目，旨在通过海选寻找歌唱新星。这是欧洲最大的才艺比拼类节目，深受大家的欢迎。

这档节目开始于2004年9月，于每年8、9月份至12月份播放。这档节目在英国的ITV电视台以及爱尔兰的TV3均有播出，由于大获成功更是衍生出一档在ITV2台播出的幕后花絮节目——《The Xtra Factor》。《英国偶像》的诞生是为了代替曾经大获成功的《流行偶像》，因为《流行偶像》在第二季时便无限期停歇了。由于两档节目内容太过于类似还一度引起法律纠纷。《英国偶像》节目名中的"X Factor"指要成为明星所需具备的"神秘因素"。

单词释义

contest 竞赛　　　　　drawn from 从……中得到　air 播送
spin-off 子产品　　　　devise 设计　　　　　　hiatus 中断
undefinable 无法定义的

曾经的参赛选手现在何处

Granted, there are plenty of former X Factor contestants who can be found performing in student unions and nightclubs, but the successful ones have made their fortune *maximising* their TV experience. After three months in the media *spotlight*, many contestants come out with *recognisable* faces and thousands of Twitter *followers*.

This brand-ready combination has landed several advertising deals: Leona Lewis, who won in 2006 and worth an estimated £12 million, has fronted campaigns for Superdrug and American company Cotton Incorporated. Alexandra Burke, 2008's winner, reached number one in the album charts with her debut record, promotes Sure Deodorant and has reportedly earned £5 million. Boy band and 2009 runners-up JLS are listed as having earned £6 million a piece and promoted safe sex with Durex while Little Mix, The X Factor's only winning girl band, became brand *ambassadors* for Schwarzkopf hair dye after their victory in 2011.

毫无疑问，很多前《英国偶像》参赛选手会在一些学生联谊会或酒吧里表演，但是那些一炮而红的选手则积攒了很多上电视经验与财富。在媒体的聚光灯下生活了3个月后，许多选手已经被大家熟知，且有了成千上万的推特粉丝。

这种塑造明星的节目与很多厂商签订了广告合同：身价约为1200万英镑的2006年冠军丽安娜·刘易斯就成为了超级药房与美国棉花公司的代言明星；首张专辑位列排行榜第一的2008年冠军亚历山大·波尔克为Sure除臭剂代言，获得了500万英镑的收入；男孩乐队与2009年亚军JLS据称也因为为杜蕾斯提倡安全性行为而获得了600万英镑的收入；而唯一获得《英国偶像》冠军的女子团队"小混混"在2011年获冠后成为了施华蔻染发剂的品牌大使。

单词释义

maximize 最大化	spotlight 聚光灯	recognizable 可识别的
follower 粉丝	ambassador 大使	

"品" 英国特色文化

特色表达One

《英国偶像》中偶尔也会有黑马选手出现，他们一直低调让人觉得胜利与他们不沾边，却关键时刻drop a bombshell。这里的drop a bombshell可不是指扔个炸弹，这个短语源自第一次世界大战期间形容飞机神出鬼没地就扔下了炸弹。之后，人们就用drop a bombshell指"出人意料或者轰动"。

☆ 实景链接

A：Oh, dear! The girl won the competition. 哦！天啊！这个女孩赢了比赛。

B：Yeah, she is so cool! 是的，太不可思议了！

A：I've never thought she would win before the match. 在比赛前我从不认为她能获胜。

B：I think her winning will produce **a bombshell**. 她的胜出将引起轰动。

特色表达Two

在英国，很多年轻人为了参与《英国偶像》海选不惧艰辛，即使时常flightmare也告诉自己坚持下去。我们都知道flight是飞机，mare是噩梦，那flightmare就是飞机噩梦，指的是在飞机上丢失财物，或因飞机误点而耽误毕业典礼等。

☆ 实景链接

A：How did you get here? 你怎么来的？

B：I came by air, but I prefer to travel by ship. 我坐飞机来的，但是我宁愿坐船来。

A：Why do you think so? 你为什么这么想？

B：I've lost some money in that fight, it's my **flightmare**. 我在飞机上丢了钱，真是飞行噩梦。

拓展特色句

1. Walsh appeared as one of the judges on *The X Factor tonight*. 沃尔什在今晚作为评委之一参加了《英国偶像》节目。

2. I planned to stay at home and watch *The X Factor*. 我打算在家看《英国偶像》。

3. He was kicked off last night. 他昨天晚上被淘汰了。

"聊" 英国特色文化

A: Can you tell me something about the X Factor? It seems that it's very popular.

B: The X Factor is a British television music competition to find new singing talent.

A: Like The Voice of China from Zhe Jiang Satellite TV Station?

B: Yes. We bought the copyright of The Voice.

A: Can anyone attend it?

B: Yes. But if you want to win you must have the ability to attract raters and go through fierce competition. Many contestants come out with recognizable faces and thousands of Twitter followers.

A: Maybe they can get some chances to shoot commercials.

B: Definitely. Leona Lewis, who won in 2006, has fronted campaigns for Superdrug and American company Cotton Incorporated.

A: What a sudden rise in life!

A: 能给我讲讲《英国偶像》吗？它似乎很受欢迎。

B: 《英国偶像》是一档英国的歌唱选秀节目，通过海选寻找歌唱新星。

A: 像浙江卫视的《中国好声音》？

B: 是的。我们购买了《好声音》的版权。

A: 每个人都能参加吗？

B: 是的。但是如果你想赢的话必须有吸引评委的能力，并且经历激烈的竞争。许多选手被大家熟知，且有了成千上万的推特粉丝。

A: 也许他们有拍广告的机会。

B: 毫无疑问。2006年冠军丽安娜·刘易斯就成为了超级药房与美国棉花公司的代言明星。

A: 真是一炮而红啊！

"问" 英国特色文化

《英国偶像》走出来的明星会有"生命力"吗?

曾全民关注的《英国偶像》如今也难逃指责。很多业界人士认为《英国偶像》制造出的偶像缺少"长红"的生命力,那些冠军们虽在英国本土很受欢迎,却在海外反响平平,因此很多英国观众把《英国偶像》骂得一文不值,认为该节目是音乐行业的毒瘤。但《英国偶像》依旧拥有大批粉丝,他们认为《英国偶像》给选手们提供了一个公平展示的舞台,而脱颖而出的人借由这个舞台开始崭露头角,这是一个难得的造星机会,它可以帮助平民们发现自己的特长与魅力,进而积极向上地生活。

阅读笔记

Part 6

品读英国的教育

教育体系各不相同

Education in the United Kingdom is a *devolved* matter with each of the countries of the United Kingdom having separate systems under separate governments: the UK Government is responsible for England; the Scottish Government, the Welsh Government and the Northern Ireland Executive are responsible for Scotland, Wales and Northern Ireland, *respectively*.

There are five stages of education: early years, primary, secondary, Further Education (FE) and Higher Education (HE). Education is *compulsory* for all children between the ages of 5 (4 in Northern Ireland) and 16; before this children can be educated at *nursery*. FE is non-compulsory, and covers non-advanced education which can be taken at further (including *tertiary*) education colleges and HE institutions (HEIs). The fifth stage, HE, is study beyond GCE A levels (and their equivalent) which, for most full-time students, takes place in universities and other HEIs and colleges.

英国的教育并不是由英国政府统一监管，每个地区的政府都有其独立的教育体系——英国政府管辖英格兰的教育体系，而苏格兰政府、威尔士政府与北爱尔兰行政当局则分别管辖苏格兰、威尔士以及北爱尔兰的教育体系。

英国教育体系分为五个阶段：幼儿教育、小学教育、中学教育、大学预备教育以及高等教育。5岁（北爱尔兰为4岁）至16岁为法律规定的义务教育阶段，接受义务教育前，家长可以送孩子去托儿所。大学预备教育不是强制性的，在此阶段，老师并不会教授任何在大学（包括第三级教育）或者高等教育机构会学到的课程。第五个阶段——高等教育一般在大学或其他高等教育机构对大多数全日制学生进行授课，而授课内容高于普通教育高级证书课程（A-Level）或其同等水平考试。

单词释义

devolved 权力下放的　　respectively 分别地　　compulsory 义务的
nursery 托儿所　　　　　tertiary 第三级

大不列颠四块国土的不同教育情况

The "National *Curriculum*", established in 1988, provides a *framework* for education in England and Wales between the ages of 5 and 18; in Scotland the nearest equivalent is the 5-14 programme, and in Northern Ireland there is something known as the common curriculum. The Scottish *qualifications* the Standard Grades, Highers and Advanced Highers are highly similar to the English Advanced Subsidiary (AS) and Advanced Level (A2) courses.

Traditionally a high-performing country in international rankings of education, the UK has *stagnated* in recent years in such rankings as the Programme for International Student Assessment (PISA) tests; in 2013, for reading and maths the country as a whole stood in the middle-rankings, a position that was broadly similar to three years before. Within the UK, Scotland performed *marginally* better than England; both were slightly ahead of Northern Ireland, and *markedly* ahead of Wales. And the costs for a normal education in the United Kingdom are as follows:

Primary: No Charge

Secondary: No Charge

Further Education in either a sixth form or college: No Charge if

"国民教育课程"确立于1988年，它为英格兰和威尔士年龄段在5~18岁人群的教育系统提供了一个框架；在苏格兰，类似的教育体系则是5~14岁计划，而在北爱尔兰则是共同课程。苏格兰的标准教育课程（Standard Grades）、高等教育课程（Highers）、高级高等教育课程（Advanced Highers）的证书就相当于英国普通教育高级程度证书（AS）以及高等学历（A2）。

传统上，作为全球教育高效国家，英国在最近几年的国际学生评估项目（PISA）中排名却一直停滞不前。2013年，在阅读以及数学领域评估中，英国排名中等，与3年前的排名差不多。在英国国内，苏格兰学生的表现要比英格兰的稍好，且都稍稍领先于北爱尔兰学生，而大大领先于威尔士学生。英国普通教育费用如下。

under 19 in that particular academic year or on a low income.

Higher Education (University): A tuition fee per year (varies from £1,000 to £9,000).

Primary and Secondary education can also be charged for, if a fee-paying (public) school is attended by the child in question.

小学：免费

中学：免费

中学或大学的预科：年龄小于19岁的学生免费或者仅收取一点点费用。

高等教育（大学）：每年学费从1000英镑到9000英镑不等。

如果是特殊儿童的话，去的免费（公立）小学或者中学也需要缴纳一定的学费。

单词释义

curriculum 课程　　framework 框架　　qualification 资格证书
stagnate 停滞　　marginally 稍微地　　markedly 显著地

"品" 英国特色文化

特色表达One

学生在学校学习，必须有一个冷静的大脑才能高效学习，那么"冷静的大脑"在英语中如何表达呢？难道是"a calm head"？其实在俚语中的正确表达是"a cool head"。

☆ 实景链接

A：The examinations were nearing. 要考试了。

B：So, I decided to study harder than before. 所以我决定比以前更努力学习了。

A：I always get the jitters before exams. 我考试前总是很紧张。

B：You have to **keep a cool head**. 你必须保持冷静的头脑。

特色表达Two

英国私立学校成长的孩子大多有点趾高气扬，但也不乏down-to-earth的好学生。这里的down-to-earth可不是指"摔倒地上的"，这个短语的意思是"脚踏实地，谦虚"。

⭐ 实景链接

A： Do you know that Emma comes from a wealthy family? 你知道吗，艾玛家境富裕?

B： Really? But, she is less proud. 真的吗? 但是她一点也不骄傲。

A： Yeah, she is warm and friendly and always popular at school. 是的，她平易近人，在学校很受欢迎。

B： She's truly **down-to-earth**. 她真是踏实谦虚啊。

拓展特色句

1. England, Scotland and Wales have a compulsory starting age of five. 英格兰、苏格兰和威尔士的儿童从5岁开始接受义务教育。

2. I heard that the UK Government will increase University tuition fees. 我听说英国政府要提高英国大学的学费。

3. Most of the British universities are public institutions. 大部分英国的高校是公立机构。

"聊" 英国特色文化

A： I'd like to continue my study in England. Do you have any recommendation?

B： Do you know Education in the United Kingdom?

A： A little.

B： In the United Kingdom each of the countries has separate systems.

A： I know that there are five stages of education.

B： Yes. From early years, primary, secondary, Further Education (FE) to Higher Education (HE).

A： I want to have graduate study there.

B： You must send your information to the college and apply, then wait

A： 我想去英国继续学习。你有什么建议吗?

B： 你了解英国的教育吗?

A： 一点点。

B： 在英国每个地区的政府都有其独立的教育体系。

A： 我知道那儿有五个教育阶段。

B： 是的。从幼儿教育、小学教育、中学教育、大学预备教育到高等教育。

A： 我想去那儿进行研究生学习。

B： 你必须将信息发送到大学进行申请，然后等待结果。你可以申请几个学校来提高成功的机会。

for the result. You can send your application to several colleges and enhance the chance of success.

A：How much will I spend?

B：It depends on the college. About 250 thousand a year.

A：A large amount of money.

A：我要花多少钱？

B：这取决于学校。大约一年25万。

A：一大笔钱啊。

"问" 英国特色文化

英国大学的成绩分几等分呢？

一般来说，英国大学学位成绩可以分为以下几个等级，即一等成绩(First Class)、二等成绩(Second Class)、三等成绩(Third Class)、普通成绩(Ordinary degree)。有的学位附加优异成绩(Honours)，有的没有，要看学生在学期间的平均分数而定。通常英国大学的及格线定在40分，能得到70分那就是一等成绩了。二等成绩是仅次于一等成绩的第二高成绩，大部分的毕业生都以二等成绩毕业，这个成绩也是很多公司企业的要求。而三等成绩相当于中国的平均分60至70之间。最低的普通成绩相当于40分及格，勉强能拿到学位证书。

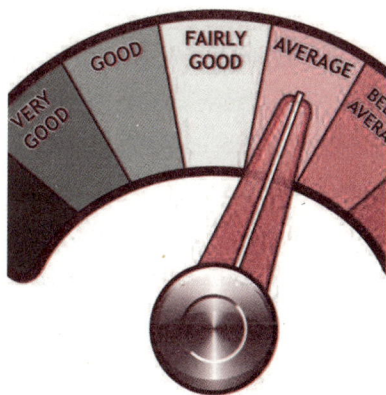

阅读笔记

夏山——英国最具争议的私立学校

夏山声名远扬的原因

Summerhill's reputation tends to *precede* it. The *progressive* boarding school in Suffolk, founded by AS Neill in the 1920s, may only have 80 pupils, but is as well known as Eton or Harrow, which it *resembles* in not the slightest detail. It *labels* itself "the school where kids have freedom to be themselves", which hardly sounds *radical*. Most, though, know it better as "the school where children don't have to go to lessons". Or, "the school with no rules".

It is how their school rules are set that makes Summerhill stand out. All have been agreed at the regular school council meetings where teachers and pupils each have one vote. Though the 14 full and part-time staff are *outnumbered*, it is this school council that makes the decisions about what goes on at Summerhill.

夏山的名声好像远远超过了其教育质量。这所改革派的寄宿学校位于萨科福马，由AS·尼尔于20世纪20年代创建。虽然只有约80名学生，但它却与名校伊顿、哈罗齐名，而风格却与它们大相径庭。它标榜自己是"让孩子们享有自由的学校"，这听起来一点都不激进，但是，对这句话正确的理解却是"不用上课的学校"，或者"毫无规章的学校"。

正是校规的通过程序让夏山与众不同。他们都经过学校日常理事会投票通过，与会的每位学生和老师各持一票。尽管学生的人数远超过了14名全职或兼职员工的数量，但就是这个学校理事会决定了夏山将如何运作。

单词释义

precede 超越	progressive 改革派的	resemble 相似
label 把……称为	radical 激进的	outnumbered 数量上超过的

夏山的教育理念及争议

Summerhill challenges almost everything that people learn about children and childhood. It lets children take emotional and physical risks. It trusts children to make decisions. It gives children the right to talk to adults in the way they want. And that, I'm afraid, is *frightening* because people know that children should be seen and not heard. There is an expectation that children will follow a certain course, learn a set number of things, and will achieve *academically* and therefore be happy.

Summerhill has been given the perfect opportunity to *nail its colours to the mast* in an *eponymous* four-part drama series for the BBC's children's channel. The film is based on the school's courtroom fight to defend its particular ethos against Ofsted, which in 1999 filed a formal "notice of complaint" against Summerhill in an apparent effort to close it down. At dispute was, inevitably, not requiring pupils to attend lessons. That was just too much for an *inspectorate* with rather more conventional views on children and childhood. The matter ended up before an independent schools' *tribunal*, which, encouraged by

夏山向人们对孩子和童年的理解发起了全面的挑战。它让孩子们承担了情感和生理上的风险。它信任孩子们，并让他们来做出决定。它赋予孩子们权力以他们想要的方式去向大人表达他们所要说的内容。而我想这正是夏山让人们恐惧的原因，因为孩子们历来都是被照看而不是被倾听的对象。人们对孩子的期望总是上一些课程，学一套东西，再获得学位，然后就皆大欢喜了。

BBC儿童频道播出了与夏山同名的四集连续剧《夏山》，这给了夏山绝佳的机会来宣扬自己的立场。该片以学校在法庭上与教育标准办公室抗争，维护自己独特风格为背景。后者在1999年正式提交对夏山的"投诉通知书"，旨在让它关门大吉。毫无疑问，令人争论不休的关键就是不要求学生上课。对于对孩子和童年有着传统理解的观察员来说，这简直是忍无

placard-waving current Summerhillians, eventually found in the school's favour.

可忍。事件后来在独立学校法庭画上了句号，受夏山人的游行潮的鼓舞，法庭最终判夏山获胜。

单词释义

frightening 令人恐惧的　　academically 学业上

nail one's colours to the mast 公开宣布并坚持自己的主张

eponymous 与作品同名的　　inspectorate 观察员　　　　tribunal 法庭

"品"英国特色文化

特色表达One

因为夏山的教育方针与教育管理部门向左，所以后者曾给夏山发出pink slip，为什么发的是"粉色的小纸条"呢？据说在100年前的美国，有位老板开始用粉红纸条写着解雇通知，然后将其夹在雇员的工资袋里，告诉他们被炒鱿鱼了。之后人们就用pink slip形容"失业、被解雇"。

实景链接

A：You look upset. What's wrong? 你看起来心情不好。怎么了？

B：I am disappointed; I have bad news. 我很失望，有个坏消息。

A：Hey, what's the matter? 拜托，到底怎么了？

B：I got a **pink slip** in my pay envelope today. 我的工资袋里加了一张解雇通知书。

特色表达Two

在夏山学习的孩子们大都遵纪守法，他们有善解人意的老师照料着，很少just for laughs。这里的just for laughs可不是指"为了笑一笑"，在俚语里的意思是"仅仅为了取笑他人，做出怀有恶意的恶作剧"。另外，just for laughs也可以表示"为了轻松一下"。

实景链接

A：Yay! I've finished my exam! 哦，我终于考完了！

B：Hey? Lucy! Come on and grab your jacket. 露西，带着你的夹克赶紧

出来。

A：What's up? 怎么了？

B：Let's go out and have a couple of beers **just for laughs**. 让我们出去喝啤酒乐一乐。

拓展特色句

1. School begins at eight and ends at three. 学校早上8点上学，下午3点放学。

2. This is worth a detention. 这样会被留校察看的。

3. The teachers there, do they check the attendance? 那里的老师会点名吗？

"聊" 英国特色文化

A：What's the difference between public schools and private schools in the United Kingdom?

B：First, the main difference between private and public schools is money.

A：Anything else?

B：The other difference is that private schools are not obliged to follow the national state governed curriculum, or even to take the state examinations. So they have a much greater degree of freedom.

A：Are the students pampered in private schools?

B：No, the students in private schools are treated just like students in public schools; they're expected to behave well.

A：Eton College and Summerhill are two famous private schools in the United

A：英国公立学校和私立学校有什么不同？

B：公立学校和私立学校最大的区别就是一个是免费的，一个是收费的。

A：还有别的吗？

B：公校和私校的另一个区别就是私立学校没有责任必须采纳国民教育课程。所以在某种程度上它们更自由。

A：那么私立学校的学生是不是娇生惯养？

B：不是的。私立学校的学生和公立学校一样，他们都得好好表现。

A：伊顿公学和夏山是英国的两所著名的私立学校。

B：是的。但是它们有所不同。不像伊顿公学，夏山标榜自己是"让孩子们享有自由的学校"，或者"不用上课的学校""毫无规章的学校"。

Kingdom.

B: Yes. But they are different. Unlike Eton College the Summerhill labels itself "the school where kids have freedom to be themselves", or "the school where children don't have to go to lessons", "the school with no rules".

"问" 英国特色文化

夏山到底是所怎样的学校?

夏山学校起初是一所实验学校,如今它是一所革新的学校,充满了自由的活力。当初尼尔与妻子一起开办学校所持的共同理念,就是创造一个以孩子为中心,全校的师资围绕孩子而行动的学校,所以这里是一所让孩子们能真正自由生活的场所,抛弃了教育管理部门对孩子的标准教育或宗教教育。尼尔主张孩子们的本性是善良的,他们还没有受到社会的污染,老师们只需让孩子们依自己喜欢的方式去做,依靠自己的能力去成长,摸索着自己的志趣,追随着自己的梦想,想成为什么人物都可以。

阅读笔记

世界贵族男校翘楚
——伊顿公学

伊顿公学校况

Eton College is a British independent boarding school located in Eton, near Windsor in England. It educates over 1,300 pupils, aged between 13 and 18 years and was founded in 1440 by King Henry VI as "The King's College of Our Lady of Eton".

Eton is one of nine English independent schools, commonly referred to as "public schools", included in the original Public Schools Act 1868. Following the public school tradition, Eton is a full *boarding* school, which means all pupils live at the school, and is one of four such remaining *single-sex* boys' public schools in the United Kingdom to continue this *practice*. It has educated nineteen British Prime Ministers and generations of *aristocracy*, and has been referred to as the chief nurse of England's *statesmen*.

伊顿公学是英国的一所私立的寄宿学校，坐落于伊顿市，紧挨着英格兰温莎。如今，它容纳了1300多名学生前来学习，这些学生的年龄在13~18岁。伊顿公学于1440年由国王亨利六世建立，被誉称"伊顿圣母国王公学"。

伊顿公学是英国9所私立学校之一，俗称"寄宿学校"，为初版《1868公立学校法案》中的学校之一。根据寄宿学校的传统，伊顿公学是一所全寄宿式学校，即所有的学生都要住校，英国1/4的公立男校继续这一传统。它培育出了19位英国首相和一代又一代的贵族，被称作是培育英国政界精英的摇篮。

单词释义

boarding 供膳的　　　　single-sex 单性别的　　　practice 习俗
aristocracy 贵族　　　　statesmen 政治家

英国的公立与私立学校

A public school, in common British usage, is a school which is usually *prestigious* and historic, which charges fees, does not *arbitrarily* restrict admissions, and is financed by bodies other than the state, commonly as a private *charitable trust*. In British usage, a government-run school (which would be called a 'public school' in other areas, such as the United States) is called "a state school".

The term "public" (first adopted by Eton) historically refers to the fact that the school was open to the paying public, as opposed to, a religious school that was only open to members of a certain church, and in contrast to private education at home (usually only practical for the very wealthy who could afford tutors).

An independent school is a school that is independent in its finances and governance; it is funded by *a combination of* tuition charges, donations, and in some cases the investment yield of an endowment. The terms independent school and private school are often *synonymous* in popular usage outside the United Kingdom.

公学，是英国常见的一种用法，指的是历史悠久的名校，这类学校收取学费，不随意限制招生，办学经费并非由政府而是由私人慈善信托基金出资。在英国，政府经营的学校(在其他地方会被称为"公学"，比如美国就这么称呼)，被称作"国立学校"。

"公学"这个术语(被伊顿公学首先采用)在历史上指的是学校公开招生的意思，不像宗教学校只招收某些教会的成员，也不像家庭私人教育(通常只适用于那些非常富有的能请得起家教的家庭)。

独立学校是指办学经费和学校管理都是独立式的，以学费和捐款为教育资金，或者有时靠的是捐赠基金的投资收益。"独立学校"和"私立学校"这两种说法在英国以外的国家一般是同义的。

单词释义

prestigious 有名望的   arbitrarily 任意地   charitable trust 慈善信托

a combination of 组合   synonymous 同义的

"品" 英国特色文化

特色表达One

很多毕业于伊顿公学的lady killer，他们不仅把女孩子们迷得团团转，还秒杀众多成年妇女。这里的lady killer字面意思是"女士杀手"，人们常用它指"师奶杀手"，尤其是长相英俊的年轻人。

☆ 实景链接

A：Which school does Bob go to? 鲍勃在哪所学校念书？

B：He studies at Eton College. So does my friend John. 他在伊顿公学学习，我的朋友约翰也在那所学校学习。

A：I know Eton College is a British independent boarding school located in Eton. 我知道伊顿公学是一所私立的寄宿学校，坐落于伊顿市。

B：Yeah, what's more, many **lady killers** graduated from it. 是的，而且很多师奶杀手都是从那里毕业的。

特色表达Two

有些父母一听说某家男孩毕业于伊顿公学就张罗着自己孩子去进行a blind date。这里的a blind date可不是"遮着眼的约会"，而是指从未见过面的两个人的约会，即"相亲"。

☆ 实景链接

A：Do you know White attend **a blind date**? 你知道吗，怀特去相亲了？

B：Well, he just graduated from Eton College. Many girls would like him. 呃，他是刚从伊顿公学毕业的，很多女孩都会喜欢他的。

A：Yeah, what will you do after graduation? 是啊，那你毕业后准备干什么呢？

B：Don't know. Maybe travelling around the world. 不知道，或许环游世界吧。

拓展特色句

1. Max won a scholarship to the elite Eton College when he was a child. 小时候，麦克思就赢得了就读于精英学校伊顿公学的奖学金。

2. The four most famous of all are Eton College, Harrow School, Winchester College and Rugby School. 英国最盛名的四所公学是伊顿公学、哈罗公学、温彻斯特公学和拉格比公学。

3. He was going to Eton in the following autumn. 秋天他就要去伊顿公学念书了。

"聊" 英国特色文化

A: What are you doing now?

B: I'm looking at the photo of the queen family. This is Prince William, this is his wife Kate Middleton and this is their baby.

A: What a happy family! Is he the son of Charles Philip Arthur George and Diana Spencer?

B: Yes. He graduated from Eton College.

A: Is that famous private school?

B: Yes. And it has educated nineteen British Prime Ministers and generations of aristocracy, and has been referred to as the chief nurse of England's statesmen.

A: The poet Byron is also graduated from a private school. Am I right?

B: Yes, you are right. That is Harrow School, another famous private school.

A: Why did they choose private schools?

B: They have enough money and want to have better education.

A: 你在干什么呢？

B: 我在看女王一家的照片呢。这是威廉王子，这是他的妻子凯特·米德尔顿，这是他们的宝宝。

A: 真是幸福的一家人啊！他是查尔斯王储和戴安娜王妃的孩子吗？

B: 是的。他是从伊顿公学毕业的。

A: 是那所著名的私立学校吗？

B: 是啊。而且它培育出了19位英国首相和一代又一代的贵族，被称作是培育英国政界精英的摇篮。

A: 诗人拜伦也是从私立学校毕业的。对吗？

B: 是的，你说的没错。那所学校叫哈罗公学，是另一所著名的私立学校。

A: 他们为什么选择私立学校呢？

B: 他们有足够的钱，并且想得到更好的教育。

"问" 英国特色文化

伊顿公学的校服有哪些特色?

伊顿公学为不同职位、不同等级、不同荣誉的获得者设计了不同着装。伊顿的校服包括类似绅士的黑色燕尾服、白色衬衫、圆领扣、黑色的马甲、长裤和皮鞋。这套行头就要700英镑,加上配套的成打衬衫、领带等。在黑色燕尾服中,有一些带披风的,那是国王奖学金获得者的标志。有些穿不同颜色马甲的,是伊顿5年级的"明日之星",他们是从所有获奖者中选出的佼佼者。如果配有银色扣子,则代表最高级别的优秀学生,他们有权参与学校政务。通过这些日常服饰上的变化,让学生充分体会优胜者的优越感、荣誉感。

阅读笔记

牛津大学校况

The University of Oxford is a collegiate research university located in Oxford, England. Although its exact date of *foundation* is unclear, there is evidence of teaching as far back as 1096, making it the oldest university in the English-speaking world, and the second-oldest surviving university in the world, after the University of Bologna.

The University is made up from a variety of *institutions*, including 38 *constituent* colleges and a full range of academic departments which are organized into four Divisions. Oxford has nurtured many prominent *alumni*, and fifty-eight Nobel Laureates have been *affiliated* with the university. Twenty-six British prime ministers, at least 30 other world leaders, 12 *saints* and 20 *archbishops* of Canterbury have been Oxonians. It regularly contends with Cambridge for the first place in the UK *league tables*.

牛津大学是一所研究型大学，坐落于英格兰的牛津市。其建校的具体日期仍是个谜，但有证据显示1096年有教学记录，所以牛津大学成为英语国家中最古老的大学，也是世界上现存的第二古老的大学，仅次于博洛尼亚大学。

牛津大学由多个院校构成，包括38所学院和一系列的学术部门，统组为4个部门。牛津培育出了很多著名校友，其中58位诺贝尔获奖者曾在牛津大学求学或工作，26位英国首相，至少30位其他国家的领导人，12位圣人，20位坎特伯雷主教来自牛津大学。如今，牛津大学常与剑桥大学角逐英国排行榜的第一位。

单词释义

foundation 建立	institution 机构，院校	constituent 构成的
alumni 男校友	be affiliated with 与……有关系	saint 圣人
archbishop 大主教	league tables 学联盟排行榜	

牛津大学的入学程序

In common with most British universities, *prospective* students apply through the UCAS application system; but, prospective applicants for the University of Oxford, along with those for medicine, dentistry, and University of Cambridge applicants, must observe an earlier *deadline* of 15 October.

Undergraduate applicants are not permitted to apply to both Oxford and Cambridge in the same year. The only exceptions are applicants for Organ Scholarships and those applying to read for a second undergraduate degree.

Students from all backgrounds are encouraged to apply. Most applicants choose to apply to one of the individual colleges, which work with each other to ensure that the best students gain a place somewhere at the University regardless of their college preferences. *Shortlisting* is based on achieved and predicted exam results and school references; and, in some subjects, written admission tests or candidate-submitted written work. Approximately 60% of applicants are shortlisted, although this varies by subject. If a large number of shortlisted applicants for a subject

与英国大部分的大学一样，预申请牛津大学的学生在大学和学院招生服务中心的申请系统上提交申请，另外，预申请牛津大学的学生，和其他医科、牙科以及剑桥大学的申请者的申请时间截止到10月15日。

本科生不允许在同年同时申请牛津和剑桥两所大学。除非是申请机构奖学金的学生和那些申请读本科第二学位的学生。

不同背景的学生们都被鼓励申请，大多数学生选择申请某个特色学院，这些学院相互协作，以保证最好的学生不论选择了哪所学院都能在牛津大学有一席之地。最终的候选人名单是以学生的考试结果、预计得分结果以及其毕业学校的推荐信为基础来进行筛选的；还有一些学科是以书面的入学考试或者候选人提交的书面作业为基础确定候选者的。尽管每个学科招收的学生人数不同，但大约60%的申请者都会被列为候选人。如果某一

choose one college, then students who named that college may be *reallocated randomly* to *under-subscribed* colleges for the subject.

学科有很多入围的申请人都报了同一所学院，那么申请该所学院的学生则可能会被任意调剂到招收人数不足的学院。

单词释义

- prospective 预申请的
- deadline 截止日期
- shortlist 决选名单
- reallocate 重新分配
- randomly 随意地
- under-subscribed 未招满的

"品" 英国特色文化

特色表达One

要想进入牛津大学深造，就得好好填写申请书，可别弄成a real dog's breakfast。这个短语字面意思是"一份切实的狗食早餐"，可它在俚语中指的是"一团糟"的场面。

实景链接

A: Could you tell me how to get into the Oxford? 你能告诉我如何进入牛津大学吗？

B: First of all, you should know how to write the applications. 首先，你要知道如何写申请书。

A: You mean apply through the UCAS application system? 你说的是在大学招生服务中心上提交申请吗？

B: Yeah, you are right, you shouldn't make it **a real dog's breakfast**. 是的，正是如此，你可别搞成一团糟。

特色表达Two

想要进入牛津大学，可不要做一个wishy-washy的人，你需要坚定信念狠狠下一番努力才可以的哦。这里的wishy-washy指的是"思想不坚定的，不清楚的"，也就是我们平时所说的"优柔寡断"。

☆ 实景链接

A：Mary wanna be a student of The University of Oxford. 玛丽想成为牛津大学的学生。

B：I've heard that. 我听说了。

A：But do you think Mary will succeed? 你觉得玛丽能成功吗？

B：Well, Mary is a **wishy-washy** girl; she had to make great efforts to achieve the goal. 玛丽是个优柔寡断的女孩，她要想考入牛津大学就得下番狠功夫了。

拓展特色句

1. She is reading for a degree of classical literature in Oxford. 她正在牛津大学攻读古典文学学位。

2. He has a doctorate from Oxford. 他拥有牛津的博士学位。

3. My brother will be up at Oxford for the next few years. 今后几年我弟弟要到牛津去上大学了。

"聊" 英国特色文化

A：Which is the most famous university in Britain?

B：It must be the University of Oxford. Besides that it is also the oldest university in the English-speaking world, and the second-oldest surviving university in the world, after the University of Bologna.

A：How about the University of Cambridge? What's the relationship between them?

B：In 1209, the students of the University of Oxford had a clash with the citizens. After that some scholars moved to Cambridge and set up the University of Cambridge.

A：哪所大学是英国最著名的大学？

B：那肯定是牛津大学。此外，它还是英语国家中最古老的大学，也是世界上现存的第二古老的大学，仅次于博洛尼亚大学。

A：那剑桥大学呢？他们是什么关系？

B：1209年，在牛津学生与镇民的冲突事件过后，一些牛津的学者迁离至剑桥镇，并成立了剑桥大学。

A: How can a student enter such a school?

B: In common with most British universities, prospective students apply through the UCAS application system.

A: Are there anything applicants should pay attention to?

B: Undergraduate applicants are not permitted to apply to both Oxford and Cambridge in the same year. The only exceptions are applicants for Organ Scholarships and those applying to read for a second undergraduate degree.

A: 学生怎么能进入到这样一所学校呢？

B: 与英国大部分的大学一样，预申请牛津大学的学生在大学入学申请办事处的申请系统上提交申请。

A: 申请者要注意哪些东西？

B: 本科生不允许在同年同时申请牛津和剑桥两所大学。除非是申请机构奖学金的学生和那些申请读本科第二学位的学生。

"问" 英国特色文化

牛津大学是一所怎样的大学？

牛津大学的学院中有许多中世纪建筑瑰宝。街两旁布满中世纪的四合院，每个四合院就是一所学院，四周往往围绕着美丽的庭园。每所学院均有其辉煌的历史、神话般的建筑遗迹，可以描画出各种有趣的史实。牛津城内有很多中世纪的塔楼，它们古色古香，是文艺复兴风格的建筑，弥漫着浪漫气息。牛津大学位于民众方庭的图书馆，是英格兰

最古老的图书馆；这里幽深绵长的皇后小巷，路边的石凳长满了青苔，周边是王尔德坐过的木凳，萧伯纳倚过的书架，都照原样没动。可想而知，这是一座充满古典文化氛围的学府。

闻名于世的剑桥大学

剑桥大学概况

The University of Cambridge is a *collegiate* research university in Cambridge, England. Originally founded in 1209, it is the second-oldest university in English-speaking areas, and the world's third-oldest surviving university. The university grew out of an *association* of scholars that was formed in 1209, early records suggest, by scholars leaving Oxford after a dispute with *townsfolk*. The two "ancient universities" have many common features and are often *jointly* referred to as Oxbridge.

Today, Cambridge is formed from a variety of institutions that include 31 constituent colleges and *comprehensive* academic departments which are organised into six Schools. It has *nurtured* many notable alumni, and 90 Nobel laureates have been affiliated with the University, which is the highest in the world. Cambridge is also a member of various academic associations and forms part of the "golden triangle" of English universities. It is regularly placed among the world's best universities in different league tables.

剑桥大学是英格兰剑桥郡的一所研究型大学。它最初建于1209年，是英语世界中历史第二悠久的大学，也是世界现存的第三古老的大学。大学的前身是一个于剑桥市成立的学者协会。早期的文献记载，有关协会的创办者原为牛津大学的成员，因为与当地居民发生冲突故移居到剑桥，牛津大学和剑桥大学这两所"古老的大学"在很多方面都很相似，经常会被合称为"牛剑"。

剑桥大学目前由很多学院组成，共包括31所成员书院及综合性学术部门，这些学术部门则被归入6个主要的学术学院里。剑桥大学培育了很多著名的校友，也是诞生诺贝尔奖得主最多的学校之一，共有90位诺贝尔奖得主曾经在剑桥大学学习或工作。它也是众多学术联盟的成员之一，并且是英国"金三角"名校之一。在各种不同的英国学联盟排行榜中，剑桥大学经常跻身于世界顶级大学之列。

单词释义

collegiate 学院的   association 协会   townsfolk 镇民
jointly 共同地   comprehensive 综合的   nurture 养育

剑桥与当地镇民的关系

The relationship between the university and the city has not always been positive. In 1381, strong *clashes* brought about attacks and *looting* of university properties while locals contested the *privileges* granted by the government to the academic staff. Following these events, the Chancellor was given special powers allowing him to *prosecute* the criminals and re-establish order in the city. Attempts to reconcile the two groups followed over time, and in the 16th century agreements were signed to improve the quality of streets and student accommodation around the city. However, this was followed by new *confrontations* when the *plague* hit Cambridge in 1630 and colleges refused to help those affected by the disease by locking their sites.

Nowadays, these conflicts have somewhat subsided and the University has become an opportunity for employment among the population, providing an increased level of wealth in the area. The enormous growth in the number of high-tech, biotech, providers of

大学与当地镇民的关系并不一直都是那么和谐。1381年，当地居民因不满大学一些处处受政府袒护的贵族教职员的行为，而破坏及抢掠大学资产。之后，大学校长获授特权去捉拿滋事者归案，重新确立镇上的秩序，并一直尝试改善学校与本地居民的关系，双方甚至在16世纪就街道质量的维护以及学生在镇上的住宿问题签署了和平协议书。但这宁静很快被1630年在剑桥爆发的鼠疫打破。当时大学书院方面拒绝为受感染的居民治病，并封锁他们的住处。这又一次引起了冲突。

如今，这样的纠纷已经平息了。大学为当地人带来了就业机会，改善

services and related firms situated near the town has been termed the Cambridge Phenomenon: the addition of 1,500 new, registered companies and as many as 40,000 jobs between 1960 and 2010 has been directly related to the presence of the educational institution.

了居民的财富水平。镇子附近高科技企业、生物技术企业、各种服务商以及相关企业的大幅增长被称为剑桥现象：1960年至2010年间，有1500家新增公司注册营业，并且增加了多达40000个工作机会，这都与剑桥这一教育机构的存在有着直接的关系。

单词释义

clash 冲突　　　　　　loot 洗劫　　　　　　privilege 特权
prosecute 起诉　　　　confrontation 对抗　　plague 瘟疫

"品" 英国特色文化

特色表达One

剑桥大学是个美丽的地方，有很多人前来赏景，也有人在这泄愤，说着"Get out of my face."拒绝别人的关心。get out of my face的字面意思是"从我面前消失"，在日常生活中，人们常用它的引申意义，即"滚开，走开，看到你就烦"。

☆ 实景链接

A：What's the matter with you? 你怎么了？

B：Just a bit of a headache, nothing serious. 没啥，有点头疼。

A：Are you OK? How about going walking at Cambridge? 你还好吗？不如去剑桥走走？

B：Just **get out of my face** and leave me alone! 别烦我了，让我一个人静静。

特色表达Two

浪漫的剑桥大学连徐志摩都难以忘怀，他在这里书写了一首首动人心弦的诗篇，美丽的风景下，很容易令人have a crush on某个人哟。have a crush on这个短语的意思是"喜欢上了……""对……有好感"。

☆ 实景链接

A：Do you still **have a crush** on Jessica? 你还喜欢着杰西卡吗？

B：I can't forget her. I still remember the first time that we met. 我不能忘记她。我仍然记得我们第一次见面的时候。

A：Where did you meet? 你们在哪儿见面的？

B：We met on a fair day at Cambridge. 在一个天清风朗的日子里，我们在剑桥邂逅。

拓展特色句

1. I was accepted by the University Cambridge! 我被剑桥大学录取了！

2. He entered school at the Top of his class. 他以全班第一名的成绩入学。

3. The headmaster made remarks at the opening ceremony. 校长在开学典礼上发表了讲话。

"聊" 英国特色文化

A：You will graduate this summer. What do you plan to do after graduation?

B：I don't want to work so early. So I will continue my further study.

A：Have you chosen the university? It's a big deal.

B：Yes. I want to go to the University of Cambridge.

A：It's a famous university but studying in Britain will cost a lot of money. Can you tell me why you choose such a university?

B：First of all, I'm crazy about British culture.

A：And then?

B：Then it is a collegiate research university. It has nurtured many notable alumni,

A：今年夏天你就要毕业了。毕业之后你打算干什么？

B：我不想这么早就工作。所以我要继续学习。

A：选好大学了吗？这是大事啊。

B：选好了。我想去剑桥大学。

A：它是一所著名的大学，但是在英国学习要花很多钱。能告诉我你选择这所学校的原因吗？

B：首先，我痴迷于英国的文化。

A：然后呢？

B：然后，它是一所研究型大学。剑桥大学培育了很多著名的校友，也是诞生诺贝尔奖得主最多的学校之一，共有90位诺贝尔奖得主曾经在剑桥大学学习或工作。我认为我在

and 90 Nobel laureates have been affiliated with the University, which is the highest in the world. I think I can learn something there.

A: It seems that you have thought carefully. I'll support you. If you have any problems don't hesitate to tell me.

B: Thank you.

那儿能学到东西。

A: 你似乎已经深思熟虑过了。我支持你。有什么问题尽管来找我。

B: 谢谢。

"问" 英国特色文化

剑桥大学有很多中国校友吗?

很多中国有为之士曾留学剑桥大学这座著名学府，比如作家萧乾、叶君健，数学家华罗庚，还有张文裕、蔡翘、王鸿祯、朱既明、王竹溪、戴文赛、伍连德、丁文江、李林等。其中最为著名的应该是文学家徐志摩了。20世纪初，徐志摩前往剑桥大学留学，他的《再别康桥》给远在东方的同胞们生动地还原了诗意的剑桥，令人遐想。

阅读笔记

Part 7

不可不去的英国特色地标

大本钟

大本钟的地标意义

Big Ben is the biggest *four-faced*, chiming clock in the world. The real name of the tower, housing the clock, is 'Clock Tower'. Big Ben is the nickname of the main bell, formally known as the Great Bell, housed within the tower. However, the nickname is more popular than the official one. A survey of 2,000 people was *conducted* in 2008 that came up with conclusion that the tower was the most popular landmark in the United Kingdom.

Clock Tower is the focus of New Year celebrations in the United Kingdom, with radio and TV stations tuning to its *chimes* to welcome the start of the year. On *Remembrance Day*, the chimes of Big Ben are broadcast to mark the 11th hour of the 11th day of the 11th month. ITN's "News at Ten" *opening sequence* features an image of the Clock Tower, with the sound of clock's chimes *punctuating* the announcement of the news headlines. It has done so, on and off, for the last 41 years. The tower has become one of the most *prominent* symbols of the United Kingdom and is often in the *establishing shot* of films set in London.

大本钟是世界上最大的四面报时钟。安置该钟的塔实际名为"钟楼"。"大本"是安置在塔内的巨钟的昵称，官方称之为"大撞钟"。但人们更喜欢叫它的昵称。2008年进行的一次访问人数为2000的调查得出结论，钟楼是英国最受人欢迎的地标建筑。

钟楼是英国人民庆祝新年的重点地方。收音机和电视都会播出它的钟声来迎接新一年的开始。在阵亡将士纪念日，大本钟钟声的传出标志着第11个月的第11天的第11个小时的默哀

开始。独立电视新闻的"十时新闻"以大本钟的图像作为开播画面，并以其钟声作新闻预告的配乐。该节目断断续续41年都是以这种形式播报的。钟楼已经成了英国最重要的象征之一，许多在伦敦拍摄的电影都是以钟楼为定场镜头的。

four-faced 四面朝向的　　　　　conduct 实施　　　　　chime 敲钟
Remembrance Day 荣军纪念日　　opening sequence 片头　　punctuate 加标点于
prominent 显著的　　　　　　　establishing shot 定场镜头，远景

大本钟的构造

The Clock Tower of the Palace of Westminster - officially named Saint Stephen's Tower - is commonly known as the Big Ben.

The clock inside the tower was the world's largest when it was installed in the middle of the nineteenth century. The name Big Ben actually refers to the clock's hour bell, the largest of the clock's five bells. The hour bell was probably named after Benjamin Hall, the First *Commissioner* of Works. The clock faces have a diameter of almost 25ft (7.5m). The hour hand is 9ft (2.7m) long and the minute hand measures 14ft (4.25m) long. The clock is known for its *reliability* and has rarely failed during its long life span. Even after the nearby House of Commons was destroyed by bombing during World War II, the clock kept on chiming. The clock's *mechanism*, designed by Edmund Beckett Denison, has a remarkable *accuracy*. The clock's rate is adjusted by simply adding small pennies on the shoulder of the *pendulum*. The tower was

威斯敏斯特宫的钟楼——其官方名称为圣斯蒂芬楼——被人们普遍称为大本钟。

安置于钟楼内的钟在19世纪中期建成时是当时世界上最大的。大本钟这个名字实际上来自于5个排钟中最大的时钟。该时钟可能是以建造工程的第一名专员本杰明·霍尔命名的。钟盘的直径大约为25英尺(7.5米)。时针长9英尺(2.7米)，分针据测长14英尺(4.25米)。大本钟一向以其准时而著名，从开始报时起很少停走过。第二次世界大战时期，尽管它旁边的众议院被炮弹击毁，它仍然没有停止报时。钟的机械装置是由埃德蒙·贝克特·丹尼森设计的，非常精准。钟的

constructed between 1843 and 1858 as the clock tower of the Palace of Westminster. It rises 316ft high (96m) and the clock faces are 180ft (55m) above ground level.

速率则仅仅是通过在钟摆上添加小的硬币来调整的。钟楼建于1843年到1858年间，当时是作为威斯敏斯特宫的塔楼建造的。楼高316英尺(96米)，钟盘则距地面180英尺(55米)。

单词释义

commissioner 理事，专员　　reliability 可靠性　　accuracy 准确度

mechanism 机械装置　　pendulum 钟摆

英国特色文化

特色表达One

　　"大笨钟"可一点都不笨，它一向是以准时闻名的。"准时"在英语中有一个很形象的表达，就是on the dot。其中，dot的意思是"点，圆点"，on the dot直译为"在点上"，引申含义就是"正点；准时"了。比如：He arrives on the dot.（他准时到了。）

实景链接

A: Is Frank here or is he late again? 弗兰克在吗，还是又迟到了？

B: He arrives **on the dot**. I thought he'd be late too. 他准时到了，我也以为他会迟到的。

A: Tell him to go to the manager's office then. 那你告诉他一声去经理办公室一趟吧。

B: Sure. 没问题。

特色表达Two

　　新年夜独自一人在伦敦吗？没关系，你可以伴着大本钟与远在异乡的朋友们telecountdown哦！telecountdown这个单词中的tele是"telephone"（电话)或者"mobile phone"(手机)，后面的count down意思是"倒数"，那么telecountdown就是通过电话一起新年倒数。

☆ 实景链接

A：Lily, you are alone in London. What's your plan for the New Year Eve? 莉莉，你自己一个人在伦敦，除夕夜打算怎么过呢？

B：I don't know. 我不知道。

A：Why don't we **telecountdown** together tonight? 不如我们今晚通过电话一起新年倒数吧。

B：That's fine. 好啊。

拓展特色句

1. The clock tower, commonly called Big Ben is among London's most iconic landmarks. 钟楼，通常被叫作大本钟，是伦敦众多标志性景观之一。

2. The name of Sir Benjamin Hall is inscribed on the bell. 本杰明·霍尔公爵的名字被刻在了钟上。

3. The clock tower was now leaning towards the north-west. 大本钟现在向西北方向倾斜了。

"聊" 英国特色文化

A：Big Ben is a lot bigger and more impressive than I thought.

B：I felt the same way when I saw it for the first time.

A：Then how tall is it?

B：316 feet.

A：That's so high. I can see a light on above the clock. What does that mean?

B：It means that the parliament is in session.

A：Well, how did Big Ben get its name?

B：Most people think that Big Ben is the name of the clock but the name Big

A：大本钟比我想的更大，更令人难忘。

B：我第一次见到它的时候也是这种感觉。

A：那它有多高呢？

B：316英尺。

A：真高啊。我看到钟上方亮着灯。那是什么意思？

B：那代表正在召开议会。

A：哦，那大本钟这个名字是怎么来的？

B：大多数人都以为"大本"是这个时钟的名字，但实际上它是以第一个负责此项工程的本杰明·霍尔爵士的名字命名的。

Ben actually was named after the first commissioner of works, Sir Benjamin Hall.

A：So, that it how it was.

A：原来如此啊。

"问" 英国特色文化

当大本钟走不动时英国人民怎么办?

1859年7月11日，大本钟首次整点报时。据负责大本钟的英国钟表师说，大本钟每3天就会失去动力，所以需要工作人员每周爬上去3次，为它上弦。同时，他们还能通过调整钟摆上方放置的小钱币，来调整大本钟走时的快慢。比如，添加1便士硬币(1英镑=100新便士)，就相当于一天把表调快了0.4秒。时间就是金钱，在大本钟上倒是体现得不错哦。

阅读笔记

伦敦塔

伦敦塔的建造

Construction of the Tower of London was initiated in 1070 by William the *Conqueror*, shortly after his victory at Hastings in 1066. It was built to enforce the power of the king over the newly conquered region. The tower was *expanded* during the 13th century into the fortified complex that we know today. The Tower's most popular attraction is its famous collection of Crown Jewels.

The *fortress*, strategically located at the Thames, was originally not more than a *temporary* wooden building which was replaced later by the White Tower. Over time the complex was expanded into a *stronghold* with about 20 towers. Today the Tower of London is best known for its Crown Jewels, but it used to be *notorious* for the many political opponents of the kings that were locked, tortured and killed in the Tower. The Tower was also a royal residence: several kings lived here, especially during *turbulent* times when the *donjon* seemed a lot safer than the palace in Westminster.

伦敦塔是在公元1070年由征服者威廉开始建造的，就在1066年威廉取得黑斯廷斯战役的胜利不久后。它的建立是为了巩固威廉在新征服区域的政权。该塔在13世纪期间被扩建成我们如今所熟知的经加固的复合体。其最具吸引力的景观要属皇家珠宝馆。

伦敦塔这一要塞，战略选址于泰晤士河岸边，起初只是一个临时性的木制建筑，不久后便被白塔所取代。随着时间的推移，该复合体被扩建为约含20座塔的大要塞。如今伦敦塔最著名的是其皇家珠宝馆藏，但它一度声名狼藉，因为这里曾经关押、拷打以及处死过很多国王的政敌。这座塔也是王室居住的地方，数名国王曾在此居住，尤其是在动乱时期，那时候城堡主楼要比威斯敏斯特大教堂安全得多。

单词释义

conqueror 征服者　　　　expand 扩建　　　　　　fortress 堡垒，要塞
temporary 临时的　　　　stronghold 要塞，大本营　notorious 声名狼藉的
turbulent 动荡的　　　　donjon 城堡主楼

伦敦塔主要景观

The main entrance of the Tower of London is at the Byward Tower, where you'll find the so-called **Beefeater**s or Yeoman Warders. Dressed in historic clothes, they not only guard the tower, but also give guided tours of the fortress. One of the about 40 Yeoman Warders is known as the Ravenmaster, responsible for the ravens that have been living here for centuries. Yeoman Warder Legend has it that the Tower and the kingdom will fall if the ravens leave. Hence King Charles II placed the birds under royal protection and the wings of the ravens are *clipped* to prevent them from flying away.

The most famous tourist attraction in the Tower of London is the collection of Crown Jewels that has been on display here since the 17th century, during the reign of Charles II. Most of the jewels were created around the year 1660, when the *monarchy* was *reinstalled*. The majority of the older crown jewels were destroyed by Oliver Cromwell.

伦敦塔的主要入口是拜弗德塔，在那里你能见到所谓的伦敦塔卫兵或皇家近卫军仪仗卫士。他们身穿古装，不仅为伦敦塔的守卫，还会向游客讲解城堡的景点。约40名伦敦塔卫兵中就有一名是乌鸦守卫，负责看守已在塔内居住几个世纪之久的乌鸦。伦敦塔卫兵信奉这样一个传说：乌鸦如果飞走，国王会落败，塔也会倒塌。因此，国王查尔斯二世令皇家军保护起这些乌鸦，并剪除这些乌鸦的翅膀以防其飞走。

伦敦塔最著名的游览景观是它的皇家珠宝馆，这些珠宝从17世纪查理二世国王在位的时候就开始展出。大部分的珠宝是在1660年左右，封建

The jewels can be found in the Jewel House, which is part of the Waterloo Barracks just north of the White Tower. Some of the *highlights* of the collection are the 530 *carat* First Star of Africa, which is set in the Imperial State Crown *Scepter* of the Cross; the Imperial State Crown with more than 2800 diamonds and the famous Koh-I-Noor, a 105 carat diamond.

王朝复辟的时候制造而成。多数较古老的皇冠珠宝被奥利弗·克伦威尔销毁了。这些珠宝可以在宝石屋看到，宝石屋是滑铁卢兵营的一部分，就在白塔的北面。这里有些非常耀眼的收藏，比如530克拉的非洲之星，镶于帝王冠的权杖上；帝王皇冠镶有2800多颗钻石，著名的重达105克拉的"光之山"巨钻也镶于其上。

单词释义

Beefeater 伦敦塔卫兵　　　　clip 修剪　　　　　　monarchy 君主政体

reinstall 重新建立　　　　　highlight 重头戏　　　　carat 克拉

scepter 节杖

"🔊" 英国特色文化

💬 特色表达One

　　白蛇曾被法海压在西湖的雷峰塔下18年，同样英国的伦敦塔也曾作为监狱，用来关押上层阶级的囚犯，并且因为这一用途还产生出一条短语sent to the Tower，字面含义是"送进塔里去"，实际指代"入狱"。比如：He was sent to the Tower by for political crimes. （他因政治罪被关押入狱。）

☆ 实景链接

A：Do you know Charles, duke of Orleans? 你听说过新奥尔良的查尔斯公爵吗？

B：No. What's his story? 没听说过，他有什么故事吗？

A：The first Valentine card was sent in 1415 by him to his wife. He was **sent to the Tower** by for political crimes at that time and he sent the card when he's imprisoned. 第一张情人节卡片就是他在1415年送给他妻子的。当时他因政治罪被关押入狱，他是在被囚禁期间把卡片送给夫人的。

B：That sounds quite moving. 听起来好感人啊。

特色表达Two

现代人几乎什么肉都吃，猫肉、兔肉、青蛙肉……但很少有人愿意吃乌鸦肉(eat crow)吧。就口味而言，乌鸦肉酸、涩、平，令人难以下咽。而俚语eat crow与吃乌鸦的现实意义是相通的，指的是"把话吞回去；忍气吞声；被迫道歉"。比如，地震局发出警报，某市将遭遇6级地震，待市民一片仓忙撤离该市后，地震局发现预测有误。这时面对公众，有关负责人只能eat crow了。

☆ 实景链接

A：The forecast of the earthquake was wrong. 那次地震预测是错误的。

B：Yeah, I heard all citizens had been evacuated from the city. 是的，我听说所有市民都从城市撤离了。

A：Then those who were responsible have to **eat crow**. 那些负责人得被迫道歉了。

B：That's right. 对啊。

拓展特色句

1. Many people were executed at the Tower of London for treason. 很多人因为叛国罪被处死在伦敦塔内。

2. Ravens at the Tower of London are quite mysterious. 伦敦塔上的乌鸦很神秘。

3. The tower of London is one of the most popular tourist attractions in London. 伦敦塔是伦敦最吸引人的旅游热点之一。

"聊" 英国特色文化

A：Hello, everyone. I am your guide Steven, a guard at the Tower. Hope you enjoy your visit today.

B：We know the Tower of London is a very old castle. But when did it found?

A：It was founded about 900 years ago.

B：Well, we heard the Tower has had a

A：大家好，我是你们的导游斯蒂文，伦敦塔的一名卫兵。希望你们今天能游览得愉快。

B：我们知道伦敦塔是一座非常古老的城堡。那它是什么时候建立的呢？

A：900多年前建立的。

B：嗯，我们听说伦敦塔有着血腥的历

bloody history. How is that to be?

A: That's because many political opponents of the kings were locked in the Tower. It has seen so many executions.

B: Horrible. What about the ravens? Why keep 7 ravens here?

A: There is a legend that says, should the ravens leave the Tower of London, the Tower of London will collapse, and the monarchy will disappear.

B: No wonder you take such a good care of them.

史。那是怎么回事？

A: 是因为很多国王的政敌曾被关押在塔内，很多人被处死在这里。

B: 太可怕了。那这些乌鸦呢，为什么要在这里养7只乌鸦呢？

A: 因为这里有一个传说，如果乌鸦飞走了，塔就会倒塌，国家也会灭亡的。

B: 怪不得你们那么悉心照料那些乌鸦。

"问" 英国特色文化

为什么黑乌鸦是伦敦塔的宠儿？

伦敦塔被视为英国王室数百年兴衰的见证，然而，如此庄严之地的形象大使竟是当地"特产"黑乌鸦。时至今日，乌鸦仍被当作关乎国运的"神鸟"，地位之重超乎想象。这种现象和一个古老传说是分不开的，黑乌鸦在伦敦塔消失之日，便是国家灭亡之时。这一传说还导致全英国最特殊的工种"乌鸦官"的产生。而要想担任这位黑乌鸦的"专属保姆"，须是在英国军队服役22年以上的退役军官才行。2006年欧洲爆发禽流感时，伦敦塔甚至为了保护这群"神鸟"，史无前例地将它们关进笼内"避难"。

阅读笔记

大英博物馆的组成

Established in 1753 with the *donation* of 71,000 objects from the collection of Sir Hans Sloane, the British Museum quickly became one of the city's top attractions. Since 1754, the museum's home has sat at the site of the Montague House in Bloomsbury. Smirke Building was originally built to house the personal library of King George III. It is the core of the building that visitors see today when they visit the museum. A domed, *circular* reading room was added in 1857, and the White Wing, designed by *architect* John Taylor, was added 30 years later. King Edward VII's Galleries, a Beaux Arts style addition, became part of the British Museum in 1914. The Parthenon *Galleries*, by American John Russell Pope, was built to house the *Parthenon sculptures* and opened in 1939. Another new wing, opened in 1980, housed public *facilities* like a restaurant and gift shop. Finally, the Queen Elizabeth II Great Court opened in 2000.

于1753年建造的大英博物馆因汉斯·斯隆爵士捐赠的71000件物品而很快成为伦敦市的著名景点之一。自1754年以来，博物馆馆址一直设在布鲁姆斯伯里的蒙塔古大楼内。斯莫克大楼起初是为了安置国王乔治三世的私人藏书室。该藏书室是如今游客游览博物馆时参观的大楼的主要地方。1857年新增了一个带有穹顶的圆形阅读室，并于30年后由约翰·泰勒设计建造了白翼馆。国王爱德华七世美术馆，一座美学建筑，在1914年新增为大英博物馆的一部分。由美国人约翰·拉塞尔·波普建造的为放置帕特农神庙雕塑的帕特农神庙馆于1939年向公众开放。另外一个1980年开放的新翼厅，提供公共设施，如餐厅及礼品店等。最后女王伊丽莎白二世大展在2000年向公众开放。

单词释义

donation 捐赠　　　circular 圆形的　　　architect 建筑师
gallery 画廊　　　Parthenon 帕特农神庙　　　sculpture 雕塑
facility 公共设施

大英博物馆馆藏

The collection found at the British Museum is enjoyed by millions each year. Because the museum is so large, many visitors take more than one day to explore. Not all of the more than 7 million artifacts are on display, but much of the collection constantly *rotates* so you'll see something new with each visit.

The Elgin Marbles, the collection of marble sculptures that were taken from the Parthenon in *Athens*, is one of the museum's most famous attractions. They are located in the purpose-built Parthenon Galleries.

Another highlight of the British Museum is the *extensive* Egyptian collection. Besides many *sarcophagi* and statues, including an enormous one of Pharaoh Ramesses II, the collection is home to the famous Rosetta stone, used by Jean-François Champollion to *decipher* the *hieroglyphic* writing. The British Museum is also known for its very large and popular collection of Egyptian *mummies* and *coffins*. You can even find animal mummies here.

And the *Assyrian* collection features relief carvings from the palaces of the Assyrian kings at Nimrud, Khorsabad and Nineveh. The enormous winged bulls from

每年在大英博物馆内展出的藏品达数百万之多。因为博物馆非常之大，很多游客要花上1天多的时间才能看完。并不是所有这700多万的器物都在出展，但大部分藏品都轮流展出，因此你每一次参观都能看到新的藏品。

埃尔金石雕，来自雅典帕特农神庙的一组大理石雕塑品，是博物馆最为著名的景观之一。它们位于专门建造的帕特农神庙馆。

大英博物馆另外一个出彩之处是拥有大量的埃及藏品。除了许多石棺和雕像以外，还包括一个巨大的法老拉美西

斯二世雕像，该藏品即由著名的罗塞塔石碑刻而成，被让-弗朗索瓦·商博良用来解读古埃及象形文字。大英博物馆还因其大量的、受人欢迎的埃及木乃伊及棺木而为人所知，你甚至可以在那里看到动物木乃伊。

而亚述人藏品以来自宁鲁德、豪尔萨巴德和尼尼微的亚述诸王宫殿的浮雕最有特点。大量来自萨尔贡二世

| the palace of Sargon II are especially impressive. | 宫殿的带翅膀的人头牛身雕像很是令人印象深刻。 |

rotate 使轮流

sarcophagi 雕花大理石石棺

mummy 木乃伊

Athens 雅典

decipher 解密

coffin 棺材

extensive 大量的

hieroglyphic 象形文字

Assyrian 亚述人；亚述人的

"品" 英国特色文化

特色表达One

你知道有一种微笑叫archaic smile吗？据说古希腊雕像的脸部往往带有一种独特的微笑，人们称之为古风式微笑。古风式微笑的研究者有两种看法：一种看法认为它反映了人们健康的情绪和幸福的生活，另一种看法则认为那是雕刻上的难度造成的结果，后人把这种archaic smile用来指"端庄、典雅的笑容"。

☆ 实景链接

A: Do you see her **archaic smile**? So charming. I'm gonna make a pass at her. 你看到她那端庄的笑容了吗？太有魅力了。我要追她。

B: I don't think you can handle a girl like her. 我觉得那样的女孩你应付不来的。

A: Come on. I need your support. 拜托，我需要你的支持。

B: Fine. What are friends for! 好吧，谁让我跟你是朋友呢!

特色表达Two

大英博物馆的馆藏中任何一件都价值连城，想买的话肯定要cost you an arm and a leg了，为什么这么说呢？难道必须要留下一只胳膊和一条大腿才能得到那里的珠宝吗？别怕，其实an arm and a leg在这里指的是"一大笔钱；昂贵的代价"，当你想表示什么东西非常昂贵时，你就可以用it costs an arm and a leg来表示。

☆ 实景链接

A: The color suits you, man. But it is a little loose. Let's see if we can find you a smaller size. 这颜色很适合你啊。但是有点儿大，我们再找

找看有没有小号的。

B：Wait, I'm reading the label. 等等，我在看价签。

A：How much is it? 多少钱？

B：Oh, it costs **an arm and a leg**. The price is 1000 dollars. 噢，这实在太贵了。要1000美元。

拓展特色句

1. I've seen that object at the British Museum in London. 我在伦敦的大英博物馆看到过那件物品。

2. The British Museum is free for visitors. 大英博物馆是免费向游客开放的。

3. He visited the British Museum pretty often when living in London. 在伦敦居住期间，他常去大英博物馆。

"聊" 英国特色文化

A：It's kind of you to show me round the British Museum, Can you tell me something about its history?

B：Well, it was founded in 1753. And was the first national public museum in the world.

A：Where did the collections come from?

B：Sir Hans Sloane had a collection of over 71, 000 Objects. He bequeathed them to the nation in return for 20, 000 pounds.

A：How many objects now?

B：Recent count shows there are approximately 7 million.

A：That's really massive. How much for the tickets then?

B：They are openly displayed free of

A：感谢你带我参观大英博物馆。能给我讲讲它的历史吗？

B：好的，它是在1753年建立的。是全世界第一家国立公共博物馆。

A：这些藏品是从哪儿来的？

B：汉斯·斯隆爵士拥有71000件收藏品，它以2万英镑的低价将藏品遗赠给了国家。

A：那现如今有多少藏品？

B：最近的数字显示大约有700万件。

A：真多啊。那门票是多少钱？

B：它是免费向公众开放的。

A：真不可思议。这肯定吸引了很多游客来这里参观吧。

B：是的，每年我们这里会有500万来自世界各地的游客。

charge.

A：Amazing! That must attract a large number of visitors here.

B：That's right. We have 5million visitors all over the world every year.

"问" 英国特色文化

建大英博物馆的钱是哪里来的?

1753年6月7日国会建立大英博物馆的决议获得国王的御准，并且通过了《大英博物馆法》。为收购斯隆爵士等人的收藏，法案决定采用发行彩票的办法筹募购买收藏的资金。彩票发行后，共募得资金95194.82英镑，托管人用这笔经费以2万英镑购买了斯隆爵士的收藏，1万英镑购买了哈利家族的图书馆，另以1万英镑买下蒙塔古府邸(Montagu House)作为博物馆的馆舍，除整修和维护蒙塔古府邸的所需费用外，其余的钱有3万英镑购买了政府债券，以备以后维持博物馆之用。经过筹备，1759年1月15日，大英博物馆终于正式开馆，对外开放。

阅读笔记

白金汉宫

白金汉宫的建造史

Buckingham Palace, one of several palaces owned by the British Royal family, is one of the major tourist attractions in London. The original building was constructed as a *country house* in 1705 by the duke of Buckingham, John Sheffield. King George III bought the house in 1761 for his wife and had it *altered* by William Chambers. In 1826, King George IV asked famed architect John Nash to expand the house - then known as Buckingham House - into a palace. King George IV as well as his younger brother and *successor* King William IV both died before the palace was completed. Queen Victoria was the first to *reside* in the palace.

The palace was expanded in 1850 with a new east wing. The *monumental facade* of the east wing was built in 1913 by Aston Webb. It is this facade, facing the Mall and St James's Park, which is now known by most people.

白金汉宫是英国王室所拥有的数座宫殿之一，也是伦敦最主要的旅游景点之一。起初该建筑是由白金汉公爵约翰·谢菲尔德于1705年建造的一个乡间别墅。国王乔治三世在1761年将其买下送给了他的妻子，并令威廉·钱伯斯对其进行了改建。1826年，国王乔治四世命建筑师约翰·纳什对该房屋进行了扩建——后称之为白金汉屋——建成了一座宫殿。国王乔治四世和他的王位继承者弟弟威廉四世在修缮工程竣工之前都相继去世。维多利亚女王是入住该宫殿的第一任君主。

该宫殿在1850年被新增了一侧东翼。东翼正面的纪念碑是由阿斯顿·韦伯在1913年建造的。这面纪念碑，正对着购物中心和圣詹姆斯公园，为大多数人所熟知。

单词释义

Country house 乡间别墅　　alter 改变，改动　　successor 继位者
reside 居住　　monumental 纪念碑的　　facade 正面；表面

王室家族的气息

A part of the Buckingham Palace is still used by the Royal family. A flag is *hoisted* each time the Queen is in the Palace. The palace has about 600 rooms, including a throne room, a ballroom, picture gallery and even a swimming pool. Some of these rooms can be visited during a couple of months in the summer - when the Royal Family is not in the palace - including the *lavishly* decorated State Rooms: the Throne Room, Green Drawing Room, Silk Tapestry Rooms, Picture Gallery, State Dining Room, Blue Drawing Room, Music Room and White Drawing Room are all part of the tour around the Buckingham Palace.

Another interesting part of the palace that is open to visitors is the Queen's Gallery, where works of art from the royal collection are on display. The palace's *stables*, the Royal Mews, can also be visited. Here you'll find a number of royal horse-drawn *carriages*. Right in front of the building is the Queen Victoria Memorial, signed by Sir Aston Webb and built in 1911 in honor of Queen Victoria, who *reigned* for almost sixty-four years.

The changing of the guard takes place daily at 11 o'clock in front of Buckingham Palace. A colorfully

白金汉宫的一部分目前仍为英国王室所用。当女王入住之时宫殿便会升起一面君主旗。该宫殿有大约600个厅室,包括王座室、舞厅、美术馆甚至还有一个游泳池。在没有王室居住的时候,一些房间在夏季的几个月可以对外开放游览,包括很多装修豪华的大厅:王座室、绿厅、丝绸织锦厅、美术馆、国宴厅、蓝厅、音乐厅和白厅,这些都是白金汉宫可供游客观赏的地方。

另外一个有意思的供游客游览的地方就是女王美术馆,馆内展有王室收藏的艺术珍品。宫殿内的皇家马厩也能被观赏。在那里你能看到很多王室马车。美术馆的正前方是一座维多利亚女王纪念碑,该纪念碑是在1911年,出于尊敬在位将近64年的维多利

dressed *detachment*, known as the New Guard, parades along the Mall towards Buckingham Palace and during a ceremony replaces the existing, Old Guard. The ceremony, which is accompanied by music played by a military band, always attracts *throngs* of *onlookers*.

亚女王由阿斯顿·韦伯署名建造的。

皇家卫队每天11点钟会在白金汉宫前交接换岗。穿着华丽的分遣队，人们称之为新卫队，会在购物中心通往白金汉宫的路上列队游行，在交接仪式中替换旧卫队。换岗仪式通常会伴着军乐进行，常常吸引游客围观。

单词释义

hoist 升起　　　　　　lavishly 浪费地　　　　　stable 马厩

carriage 四轮马车　　　reign 统治　　　　　　　detachment 分遣队

throng 人群　　　　　　onlooker 旁观者

"品" 英国特色文化

特色表达One

18世纪建造的白金汉宫可以说是as old as Adam了。这是什么意思呢？《圣经》记载，Adam是上帝创出的世上的第一个人，所以as old as Adam就是"和亚当一样老"，自然是"非常古老"了。

☆ 实景链接

A: Do you like Buckingham Palace? 你喜欢白金汉宫吗？

B: Yeah. I like ancient buildings a lot and it is just **as old as Adam.** 喜欢啊，我很喜欢古建筑，白金汉宫是非常古老的。

A: When was this palace constructed then? 这座宫殿是什么时候建造的啊？

B: In 1705 by the duke of Buckingham. 是在1705年由白金汉公爵建造的。

特色表达Two

说到白金汉宫殿内的皇家马厩，我们就来讲一个有关马和羊的故事，早年的赛马比赛中，驯马师在赛前，常把山羊置于马厩中，据说可以起到安抚烈马的功效。不过，卑劣的赌徒为了赢得"马彩"，会对末下赌注的马匹做手脚，偷偷把"安抚使者"山羊牵走。所以就有了短语to get someone's goat，原指"把山羊从马的身边牵走，惹马生怒"，随后演变成"惹人愤怒"之意。

☆ 实景链接

A：Jack has carried it too far. That really **gets my goat**! 杰克做得太过分了，真是把我给气炸了。

B：Chill out. What happened? 冷静点，怎么了？

A：He is dating someone else. How can he cheat on me again and again? 他在跟其他人交往。他怎么能一再欺骗我呢？

B：If I were you I would dump him immediately and never go back. 如果我是你我一定马上把他甩了，再也不会回头。

拓展特色句

1. Crowds gathered outside Buckingham palace. 很多人聚集在白金汉宫门口。

2. The Changing of the Guard at Buckingham Palace is worth seeing for tourists in London. 对于去伦敦的游客来说白金汉宫皇家卫队的换岗仪式很值得一看。

3. Kings and queens live in Buckingham Palace. 国王和王后住在白金汉宫。

"聊" 英国特色文化

A：British queen opens her house for the visitors to have a visit.

B：Yeah, we have to admit that it's a good way to earn money for the country because people are all curious about the place where she lives.

A：So Buckingham Palace became one of the major tourist attractions in London.

B：That's right.

A：英国女王开放了她的家给游客参观。

B：嗯，我们得承认这是个为英国赚钱的好方法，因为人们都对她的住处很好奇。

A：所以，现在白金汉宫成了伦敦最主要的旅游景点之一。

B：对的。

A：它什么样子？

B：我看报纸上说该宫殿有大约600个厅室，包括王座室、舞厅、美术馆

A : What does it look like?

B : I read it in the newspaper that the palace has about 600 rooms, including a throne room, a ballroom, picture gallery and even a swimming pool.

A : Wow! How luxurious!

B : Yes. During summer some rooms can be visited when the Royal Family is not in the palace.

甚至还有一个游泳池。

A：哇！真奢华！

B：是啊，夏天在没有王室居住的时候，一些房间是可以对外开放游览的。

"问" 英国特色文化

谁曾在白金汉宫上演"不爱江山爱美人"？

故事的主角是爱德华八世与沃利斯·辛普森。1931年，沃利斯·辛普森与还是亲王的爱德华相爱。1936年，爱德华继位，成为爱德华八世。上任不久，他便向王室宣布要和沃利斯结婚。这时沃利斯与丈夫的离婚案也被提上日程。爱德华八世的决定遭到朝野的强烈反对，他们无论如何也接受不了一个结过2次婚的女人成为王后。多次交涉未果后，爱德华八世决定逊位来完成这桩亘古未有的婚姻。1936年12月，即位不足1年的英国国王爱德华八世为了和离异2次的美国平民女子辛普森夫人结婚，毅然宣布退位。爱德华八世的弟弟乔治六世继位后，授予他温莎公爵的头衔。如今，温莎公爵的动人爱情故事仍被广为传诵。

阅读笔记

国会大厦

国会大厦的历史

The Houses of Parliament, also known as the Palace of Westminster is the seat of Britain's two *parliamentary* houses, the House of Lords and the House of Commons.

In the middle of the 11th century, King Edward the *Confessor* had moved his court to the Palace of Westminster, *situated* on a central site near the river Thames. In 1265 a parliament was created with two houses: the Lords and the Commons. The House of Lords met at the Palace of Westminster while the House of Commons did not have a *permanent* location. In 1547 the House of Commons also moved here, confirming Westminster as the central seat of government, a position it still holds today.

In 1834 a fire destroyed the Palace of Westminster. After that, Sir Charles Barry and his *assistant* Augustus Pugin created a large but balanced *complex* in neo *Gothic* style and *incorporated* the buildings that survived the fire. It includes the Clock Tower, Victoria Tower, House of Commons, House of Lords, Westminster Hall and the Lobbies.

国会大厦，又称威斯敏斯特宫，是英国两会的所在地，包括上议院和众议院。

11世纪中期，"忏悔者"爱德华国王将其宫殿移至威斯敏斯特宫，坐落于泰晤士河岸的一个中心地带。1265年，国会被分为两个议院：上议院和众议院。上议院位于威斯敏斯特宫而众议院则没有固定的所在地。1547年众议院也移至威斯敏斯特宫，这就确定了威斯敏斯特宫为中央政府所在地的位置，时至今日仍然是。

1834年一场大火烧毁了威斯敏斯特宫。大火后，查尔斯·巴里爵士和他的助手奥古斯塔斯·普金重建了一座巨大而兼具新哥特式风格的建筑，并与大火中存留下的宫殿结构相结合。威斯敏斯特宫包括钟楼、维多利亚塔、众议院、上议院、威斯敏斯特大厅以及各个会堂。

单词释义

parliamentary 议会的 Confessor 忏悔者 situate 位于……

permanent 永久的 assistant 助手 complex 复合体

Gothic 哥特式的 incorporate 合并，混合

国会大厦的构造

The Commons *Chamber*, where the House of Commons meets, was destroyed during the Second World War but rebuilt in 1950 by Sir Giles Gilbert Scott in the same neo Gothic style. The Commons Chamber's *interior* (with green colored *benches*) is rather *austere* compared to the lavishly decorated Lords Chamber (with red colored benches). Over the centuries the balance of power has moved from the *elitist* House of Lords to the more *agitated* House of Commons, where the governing party and the *opposition* are seated opposite each other with exactly two sword lengths and one foot separating the two parties.

One of several *lobbies* in the Houses of Parliament is the Central Lobby where people can meet the Members of Parliament and persuade them to defend their interests. The tower opposite the Big Ben is the Victoria Tower, built in 1860. The tower contains the records of both the House of Lords and the House of Commons since 1497. During the

下议院的议事厅是下议院的议员会见的地方，在第二次世界大战中被毁，1950年由贾尔斯·吉尔伯特·斯科特爵士以相同的新哥特风格将其重建。众议院会议厅的内部(用的是绿色座椅)要比装修华丽的上议院议事厅(用的是红色座椅)简朴一些。几个世纪以来，精英主义者的上议院和较为焦虑的众议院轮流执政，执政党和反对党互相面对面坐着，两政党的座位恰好相隔两把剑长外加一英尺的长度。

中央大厅是国会大厦的几个大厅之一，人们可以在那里会见国会议员，说服他们维护自己的权益。大本钟对面的塔是维多利亚塔，建于1860年。塔内装着上议院和众议院自1497

parliamentary year the Union Flag is hoisted on top of the 98m tall tower. The oldest part of the Houses of Parliament is Westminster Hall, dating back to 1097. The hall is one of Europe's largest *unsupported medieval* halls.

年以来的档案。议会年的时候英国国旗就会挂在98米高的塔上。国会大厦最古老的部分是威斯敏斯特大厅，该厅要追溯到1097年。威斯敏斯特大厅是欧洲最大的屋顶没有支撑的中世纪厅堂之一。

单词释义

Chamber 堂，室	interior 内部的	austere 简朴的
elitist 优秀人才	agitated 焦虑的，激动的	opposition 反对派
lobby 大厅	unsupported 没有支撑的	medieval 中世纪的

"品" 英国特色文化

特色表达One

议会中两党派有思想激进者，同样也会有stick in the mud的人，这里并不指议会人员"陷入泥潭"了，而是指代"保守派，墨守成规之人"。生活中如果你被人形容为stick in the mud那就说明别人嫌你"死板，不懂变通"了，比如Don't be a stick in the mud; let's try the other restaurant for a change.

☆ 实景链接

A：Here we are. That is the restaurant they said. 我们到了，那就是他们说的那家餐馆。

B：So many people are waiting in the line up. We might as well go home. 这么多人排队等着，咱们还是回家吧。

A：Don't be such a **stick in the mud**; let's try the other restaurant for a change. 别那么死板行不行，咱们到别的餐馆试试。

B：I am just so exhausted. 我实在太累了。

特色表达Two

在很多国家的官方机构里，都不同程度地存在着一些"形式主义"和"繁文缛节"，在英语中有个有趣的说法"red tape"，反映的就是这种官僚作风。

原来以前的英国官方文件惯例上是用red tape(红色布带)系成一扎一扎的，red tape 的象征意义就由此而来。来看一个例句：We have to cut through all of the red tape to quickly attain a goal.（我们必须跳过所有的繁文缛节，以便迅速实现目标。）

☆ 实景链接

A：What's the main purpose of this conference? 这次会议的主要目的是什么？

B：To talk about how to implement our new plan. 是为了探讨如何实施新计划。

A：We have to cut through all of the **red tape** to quickly attain our goal. 我们必须跳过所有的繁文缛节，以便迅速实现我们的目标。

B：I can't agree more. 我非常同意。

拓展特色句

1. I wanted to get to the Houses of Parliament. 我想去国会大厦看看。

2. The Houses of Parliament, as we know today, were rebuilt after the fire. 如今我们所熟知的国会大厦是在大火后重建的。

3. The Houses of Parliament were covered with a thick blanket of snow. 英国国会大厦的房顶覆盖了一层厚厚的积雪。

"聊" 英国特色文化

A：What is the Houses of Parliament? I read it everywhere.

B：It is also known as the Palace of Westminster. It is the seat of Britain's two parliamentary houses, the House of Lords and the House of Commons.

A：The House of Lords? What is that?

B：The House of Lords is the upper house of the Parliament of the United Kingdom. It has its own support services separates from the Commons. Most new members of the

A：什么是国会大厦？到处都能读到它。

B：它又称威斯敏斯特宫，是英国两会的所在地，包括上议院和众议院。

A：上议院？什么是上议院？

B：上议院是英国的上院。上议院有自己的支持服务体系，独立于众议院。上议院的大部分新成员都是被任命的。

A：那众议院呢？

B：众议院的新成员都是由选民选举产生的。

House of Lords are appointed.

A: How about the House of Commons?

B: They are voted by constituency.

A: Where are the House of Lords and the House of Commons then?

B: Well, the House of Lords meets at the Palace of Westminster while the House of Commons meets at the Commons Chamber.

A: 那上议院和众议院在哪儿?

B: 嗯,上议院在威斯敏斯特宫,下议院则在下议院议事厅。

"问" 英国特色文化

国会大厦内都有哪些规定?

威斯敏斯特宫在几个世纪以来,制定和形成了一系列规定和传统。17世纪后,在上下两院厅室内禁止吸烟。结果,议员们用鼻烟取而代之,看门人也为此保留有鼻烟匣子。同时议员们也不能在与会厅室内饮食,但或对于英国财政大臣例外。进厅必须脱帽,军装不被允许,官职证章等也不必佩戴。双手不可插兜。刀剑等利器也不在携带之列,为保管武器,每位下议院议员都在暂存处有一条缎带。动物也不在威斯敏斯特宫许可之列,导盲犬例外;嗅探犬和警用马匹则可以在外场活动。

阅读笔记

239

圣保罗大教堂

圣保罗大教堂的前世今生

The *majestic* St. Paul's Cathedral was built by Christopher Wren between 1675 and 1711. It is one of Europe's largest *cathedrals* and its dome is only *exceeded* in size by that of the St. Peter's Basilica in Rome.

St. Paul's Cathedral has had an *eventful* history. Five different churches were built at this site. The first church, dedicated to the *apostle* Paul, dates back to 604 AD, when King Ethelbert of Kent built a wooden church on the *summit* of one of London's hills for Mellitus, *Bishop* of the East Saxons. At the end of the 7th century, the church was built in stone by Erkenwald, Bishop of London. In 962 and again in 1087, the cathedral was destroyed by fire, but each time it was rebuilt and expanded. In 1669, three years after the Great Fire, Christopher Wren was tasked with the construction of a new church to replace the destroyed Gothic cathedral.

庄严的圣保罗大教堂是克里斯多夫·雷恩在1675至1711年间建造的。它是欧洲最大的教堂之一，它的穹顶大小仅次于罗马圣彼得大教堂。

圣保罗大教堂有着曲折的历史。5个不同的教堂曾在此处建立。第一个教堂是使徒保罗致力建造的，这要追溯到公元604年，那时候肯特国王艾塞尔伯特在伦敦一座小山的山顶上为东撒克逊人的主教梅里图斯用木头建了一座教堂。7世纪末期，该教堂被伦敦的主教用石头重建。962年和1087年，大教堂均遭火烧毁，每一次都被重修及扩建。1669年，大火结束3年后，克里斯多夫·雷恩接手了新教堂的建造任务，以此来取代被烧毁的哥特式教堂。

单词释义

majestic 庄严的	cathedral 大教堂	exceed 超过
eventful 多变故的	apostle 使徒，信徒	summit 顶点
Bishop 主教		

圣保罗大教堂的构造及文化

The *dome* reaches a height of 111 meters and weights about 66,000 ton. Eight *arches* support the dome. On top of the dome is a large *lantern* with a weight of 850 ton.

560 Steps lead visitors along three galleries all the way to the top of the dome. The first gallery, the Whispering Gallery, just inside the dome, is renowned for its *acoustics*. The second gallery, the Stone Gallery, is situated at a height of 53 meter on the outside of the dome, right above the *colonnade*. On top of the dome, at a height of 85 meter, is the narrow Golden Gallery, which *encircles* the lantern's base. From here you have a magnificent view over the City.

The *Baroque* interior is just as imposing as the exterior of the church. The *mosaics* on the ceiling were added in 1890 by William Richmond after Queen Victoria complained that there was not enough color in the cathedral. The *baldachin* above the *altar* was rebuilt in 1958 after it was damaged by *bombardments* during World War II. The only monument in the church that survived the fire of 1666 is the tomb of John Donne, from 1631.

The church was the site of a number of important historic events

教堂的穹顶高达111米，重达66000吨，由八座拱桥支撑。穹顶冠以一个重达850吨的巨型灯笼式天窗。

游客要登上560个台阶，穿过三个画廊才能到达穹顶顶端。第一个画廊，回音廊，就在穹顶的里面，以它的回声效果著名。第二个画廊，石廊，坐落于穹顶外面53米高处，就在柱廊的上方。在穹顶的上端，85米高处，是窄长的金廊，环绕着灯笼式天窗的底部。在那里你能看到非常壮观的伦敦市景色。

教堂巴洛克式的内部结构与其外部结构一样宏伟。1890年，维多利亚女王抱怨教堂内色彩不足，之后威廉·里士满便在天花板上添加了马赛克图案。祭坛上方的华盖是在1958年重建的，它曾被第二次世界大战的炮弹击毁。教堂内唯一躲过1666年大火的历史遗迹是约翰·邓恩的坟墓，于1631年所建。

圣保罗大教堂是很多重要历史事件

such as the funeral of Admiral Nelson in 1806 and the funeral of Winston Churchill in 1965. Prince Charles and Lady Diana Spencer married here in 1981.

发生的地方，比如1806年海军上将纳尔逊的葬礼，以及1965年温斯顿·丘吉尔的葬礼。1981年查尔斯王子和戴安娜王妃也是在这里举行的婚礼。

单词释义

dome 穹顶，圆顶

arch 拱形

lantern 灯笼式天窗

acoustics 声学效果

colonnade 柱廊

encircle 包围

Baroque 巴洛克风格

Mosaic 马赛克

baldachin 华盖

altar 祭坛

bombardment 轰炸，炮击

"品"英国特色文化

特色表达One

在西方传统婚礼上，新人在教堂各持一条绳索并将两端打结tie the knot，表示两人的生活从此结合在一起，将对方紧紧拴住，也就是我们所说的"永结同心，白头偕老"的意思，也有"结婚，举行婚礼"之意。并且，古老的迷信认为如果将两根手指交叉，就能带来好运。于是手指交叉cross one's fingers就成了祈祷、祝福的表现。

实景链接

A：When are you two going to tie the knot? 你们俩什么时候举行婚礼啊？

B：Next year. After Daisy graduates. 明年。黛西毕业后。

A：Wish you happiness all your life. We'll be **crossing our fingers** for you! 希望你们终生幸福。我们会为你祈祷的。

B：Thank you. 谢谢。

特色表达Two

在教堂参加婚礼的时候，大家看到新郎帅气有型、新娘聪明漂亮一定会感叹天生一对吧，但也会有dumb bell和dumb Dora的情况发生吧。这里的dumb bell指的可不是"哑铃"，而是"笨蛋"的意思，dumb Dora也不是"哑巴多拉"，它与Dora在俚语中都意为"傻姑娘，笨女人"。

☆ 实景链接

A： I am looking for Paul. Have any ideas where he is? 我在找保罗，知道他在哪儿吗？

B： Don't you hear that? Paul is marrying **dumb Dora** today. 你没听说吗？保罗今天跟一个傻姑娘结婚。

A： Well, he is a **dumb bell** too. They are exactly fifty-fifty. 呃，保罗也不是聪明家伙，他们正好天生一对。

B： Come on. Don't be so mean. 拜托，别那么刻薄。

拓展特色句

1. John Donne was buried at St. Paul's Cathedral. 约翰·邓恩被埋葬在圣保罗大教堂。

2. People had a parade in front of St. Paul's Cathedral. 人们在圣保罗大教堂前进行游行示威。

3. St. Paul's Cathedral is one of London's most renowned landmarks. 圣保罗大教堂是伦敦最负盛名的地标建筑之一。

"聊" 英国特色文化

A： I'm learning the history of Britain. May I ask you some questions?

B： Sure. Go ahead.

A： When was the majestic St. Paul's Cathedral built?

B： It was built by ChrisTopher Wren between 1675 and 1711.

A： Is it the biggest church in the world?

B： No. St. Peter's Basilica in Rome is the biggest. Precisely speaking it is one of Europe's largest cathedrals and its dome is only exceeded in size by that of the St. Peter's Basilica.

A： I hear that it has an eventful history,

A： 我正在学习英国历史。能问你几个问题吗？

B： 当然可以。问吧。

A： 圣保罗大教堂建于什么时候？

B： 它是克里斯多夫·雷恩在1675至1711年间建造的。

A： 它是世界上最大的教堂吗？

B： 不，罗马圣彼得大教堂才是最大的。准确地说，它是欧洲最大的教堂之一，它的穹顶大小仅次于圣彼得大教堂。

A： 我听说它的历史很曲折，是这样吗？

B： 对的，有5个不同的教堂曾在此处

is that true?

B: Yeah, five different churches were built at this site.

A: Interesting. Can you give me some detail information about it?

B: Well, I know a good website about its history. I'll send you later.

建立。

A: 挺有趣的，能告诉我一些它的详细信息吗？

B: 我知道一个不错的网址是讲它的历史的。稍后我发给你。

"问" 英国特色文化

"窃窃私语廊"是怎么回事？

英国伦敦圣保罗大教堂曾以"窃窃私语的画廊"的外号而著称。如果在画廊的某一处轻声细语的话，近的地方是听不见的，但是在远离的特定场所听得很清楚。这种神奇现象的秘诀在于椭圆形的穹顶。所有的椭圆都有两个"焦点"，而从椭圆上的任意一点到两个焦点的距离之和都是相等的。因此，如果在一个焦点位置发出声音时，利用椭圆的性质，音波反射到穹顶之后会集中到另一个焦点上。所以，如果你对着耳语廊的通孔说话，神奇回音效果在其他任一通孔都可以听到。

阅读笔记

威斯敏斯特大教堂的历史概况

Westminster Abbey, located near the Houses of Parliament, is more a historical site than a religious site. Since 1066 every royal *coronation*, with the exception of Edward V and Edward VIII has taken place in Westminster Abbey.

The abbey also serves as the burial ground for numerous politicians, *sovereigns* and artists. The abbey is *stuffed* with tombs, statues and monuments. Many coffins even stand *upright* due to the lack of space. Some of the most famous are Charles Darwin, Sir Isaac Newton and David Livingstone.

The history of the abbey starts in 1050, when King Edward The Confessor decided to build a *monastery*. Most of the present building dates from 1245 to 1272 when Henry III decided to rebuild the abbey in the Gothic style. The building was later significantly expanded: the Chapel of Henry VII was added between 1503 and 1512, while the two West Front Towers date from 1745. The youngest part of the abbey is the North entrance, completed in the 19th century.

威斯敏斯特大教堂坐落于国会大厦旁边，它更像是一座历史遗址而非宗教遗址。自1066年以来，每一次王室加冕礼，除爱德华五世和爱德华八世以外，都是在威斯敏斯特大教堂进行的。

该教堂也是众多政客、君主以及艺术家的墓地所在地。教堂内充满了坟墓、雕像和纪念碑。很多棺材因空间不足甚至直立放置。其中有些非常著名的人士，比如查尔斯·达尔文、艾萨克·牛顿公爵以及大卫·利文斯顿。

威斯敏斯特大教堂的历史要从1050年开始说起，那个"忏悔者"爱德华国王决定建一座教堂。而现今的大部分建筑要追溯到1245年至1272年间，那时亨利三世决定将该教堂建成哥特式风格的建筑。该建筑后来被大幅扩建：亨利七世小教堂在1503年和1512年被添加为教堂的一部分，教堂西部的双塔要追溯到1745年。历史最短的则是北部入口，是在19世纪修建而成。

单词释义

coronation 加冕礼   be stuffed with 充满   sovereign 君主
upright 垂直的   monastery 修道院

威斯敏斯特大教堂内景观简介

The *abbey*'s *nave* is England's highest. In the nave you find the Grave of the Unknown Warrior, a World War I soldier who died on the *battlefields* in France and was buried here in French soil. Nearby is a marble memorial stone for Winston Churchill. His body is not, like many fellow prime ministers, buried in the abbey, but in Bladon.

The Cloister was originally built in the 13th century. It was completely rebuilt after it was destroyed by a fire in 1298. The cloister was used by the *Benedictine* monks for *meditation* and exercise.

The beautiful *octagonal* Chapter house is one of the largest of its kind in England. It has an original *tile* floor dating from 1250 and 14th century *murals*.

The Henry VII *Chapel* (aka Lady Chapel), built 1503—1512, is one of the most outstanding chapels of its time, with a magnificent *vault*. The chapel has a large *stained* glass window, the Battle of Britain memorial window. The window, which dates from 1947 and replaces

威斯敏斯特大教堂的中殿是英格兰的最高点。在中殿，你能见到无名战士的坟墓，他是一名在第一次世界大战的法国战场上牺牲的士兵，用法国的土壤葬于此地。在其坟墓旁是为温斯顿·丘吉尔所建的一座大理石纪念碑。丘吉尔的尸首不像其他首相被安葬在威斯敏斯特大教堂中，而是安葬于布拉顿市。

教堂始建于13世纪。被一场大火烧毁之后于1298年彻底重建。教堂的建立是为本笃会修道士提供沉思和修炼之处。

漂亮的八角形牧师会礼堂是英格兰同类礼堂中最大的。里面有着1250年前的原始瓷砖地板以及14世纪的壁画。

亨利七世小教堂(又叫圣母堂)是在1503年至1512年建造的，有着华丽的穹顶，是当时最著名的小教堂之一。小教堂有一个很大的彩绘玻璃窗——不列颠之战纪念碑窗。该玻璃窗的修

an original window that was damaged during World War II, *commemorates fighter* pilots and crew who died during the Battle of Britain in 1940.	建要追溯到1947年，替代了原来在第二次世界大战中被毁坏的窗户，用来纪念在1940年不列颠之战中牺牲的战斗机飞行员和机组人员。

单词释义

abbey 大修道院

meditation 冥想，沉思

mural 壁画，壁饰

stained 着色的

nave 中殿

octagonal 八边形的

Chapel 小礼拜堂

commemorate 纪念

Benedictine 本笃会的

tile 瓷砖

vault 拱顶

fighter 战斗机

"器" 英国特色文化

特色表达One

到威斯敏斯特大教堂内游览，千万不要迷路，走进blind alley哦。alley这个词是"胡同"的意思，blind在本短语中则表示"(路等)走不通的"，所以该短语的含义就是"死胡同"，引申为"绝路，绝境"。多数情况下，blind alley表示的都是它的引申义。而"绝处逢生"就可以用escape from a blind alley来表示了。

实景链接

A : What do you say about Tom's present job? 你觉得汤姆现在的工作怎么样？

B : It seems to be a **blind alley**. 看起来没什么前途。

A : Yeah, and I think he is overqualified for this position. 是啊，我觉得这份工作对他来说有点大材小用了。

B : Then we should tell him about our advice as friends. 那作为朋友，我们要把我们的建议告诉他。

特色表达Two

威廉王子在威斯敏斯特大教堂迎娶新娘凯特王妃，看到那一幕一定有很多女孩梦想marry into the purple吧。传统上西方人把紫色(purple)当作高贵、贵族的颜色，所以该短语就表示"(女子)嫁入王侯显贵之家；与王子(或贵族)结婚"的含义。类似的表达还有be born in the purple，用来形容某人"出身豪门，身世显贵"。

☆ **实景链接**

A：Which is more important for Lily you think, Love or money? 你觉得爱情和金钱，哪个对丽丽来说更重要？

B：She is one of the girls who want to **marry into the purple**. So maybe money I think. 她是那种想嫁入豪门的女孩。所以，我觉得钱可能对她更重要一些。

A：What about you then? 那你呢？

B：Love, of course. 当然是爱情了。

拓展特色句

1. The nation's kings and queens are crowned in Westminster Abbey. 国王和王后都是在威斯敏斯特大教堂加冕的。

2. Their wedding ceremony took place Friday at Westminster Abbey in London. 他们的婚礼仪式周五在伦敦威斯敏斯特大教堂举行。

3. William and Kate tie the knot at London's Westminster Abbey on April 29. 威廉和凯特在4月29日于威斯敏斯特大教堂结为连理。

"聊" **英国特色文化**

A：Do you know Westminster Abbey? I always confuse it with St. Paul's Cathedral.

B：Well, just remember Westminster Abbey is more a historical site than a religious site.

A：Why do you say that?

B：Since 1066 every royal coronation, with the exception of Edward V and Edward VIII has taken place in Westminster Abbey. The abbey also serves as the burial ground for numerous politicians, sovereigns and artists.

A：Such as?

A：你知道威斯敏斯特大教堂吗？我总是把圣保罗大教堂和它混淆。

B：只要记住威斯敏斯特大教堂更倾向于是一座历史遗址而非宗教遗址就行了。

A：你为什么这么说？

B：自1066年以来，每一次王室加冕礼，除爱德华五世和爱德华八世以外，都是在威斯敏斯特大教堂进行的。该教堂也是众多政客、君主以及艺术家的墓地所在地。

A：比如说都有谁？

B：比如查尔斯·达尔文、艾萨克·牛顿公爵以及大卫·利文斯顿。

B：Charles Darwin, Sir Isaac Newton and David Livingstone.

A：What about the view in it?

B：The beautiful octagonal Chapter house is one of the largest of its kind in England, and the chapel has a large stained glass window which I like the most.

A：里面的景观怎么样？

B：它那漂亮的八角形牧师会礼堂是英格兰同类礼堂中最大的，而且小教堂有一个很大的彩绘玻璃窗，是我最喜欢的。

"问" 英国特色文化

威斯敏斯特大教堂内"圣石"的传说你知道吗？

据说圣石是《旧约》里提到的雅各梦见天梯的枕头。圣人预言，谁得到这块石头谁就将统治世界。谁都想得到它，在争夺之中，圣石先后到过埃及、西班牙、爱尔兰。公元850年，苏格兰人从爱尔兰人手里将圣石抢来，被视为君权神授的标志。1296年爱德华一世征服苏格兰，将圣石带到了伦敦，安置在威斯敏斯特大教堂的加冕宝座下，并坐在上面举行了加冕仪式。从此，"斯库恩"圣石成英国的镇国之宝和王权的象征，新国王只有坐在圣石上加冕，王权才能得到认可。这一传统从爱德华一世到现在的伊丽莎白二世，国王换了一个又一个，"龙椅"也换过多次，唯一不变的就是这块石头，它见证了英国王室700多年的历史。

阅读笔记

巨石阵

巨石阵的历史及组成

Begun as a simple *earthwork enclosure*, Stonehenge was built in several stages, with the unique *lintelled* stone circle being *erected* in Wiltshire in the late *Neolithic period* around 2500 BC. It remained important into the early Bronze Age, when many burial *mounds* were built nearby. Today Stonehenge, together with Avebury and other associated sites, forms the heart of a World Heritage Site with a unique and dense concentration of *prehistoric monuments*. Stonehenge is one of the most impressive prehistoric *megalithic* monuments in the world on account of the sheer size of its megaliths, the *sophistication* of its concentric plan and architectural design, the shaping of the stones, uniquely using both Wiltshire Sarsen sandstone and Pembroke Bluestone, and the *precision* with which it was built.

巨石阵的修建从一个简单的圆形土堤开始，分为几个阶段完成，约公元前2500年新石器时代末期一架独特的过梁石圈开始竖立于威尔特郡。鉴于其附近建有许多古坟，巨石阵对探索青铜时代依然有着重要的意义。如今巨石阵带着独特且密集的史前遗迹的身份与埃夫伯里巨石圈以及周边的相关遗址构成了世界遗产地的中心。它凭借其巨石的庞大规模、同心轴平面和结构设计的复杂性、石群的形状，以及罕见的石材——威尔特郡砂岩和彭布洛克青石，加之其建造的精密程度成为世界上最令人印象深刻的史前遗迹之一。

单词释义

earthwork 土方工程　　　enclosure 围墙　　　　　lintel 过梁
erect 竖立　　　　　　　Neolithic period 新石器时代　　mound 坟堆
prehistoric 史前的　　　megalithic 用巨石造成的　sophistication 复杂
precision 精密度

巨石阵的地标意义

Stonehenge is the most *architecturally* sophisticated prehistoric stone circle in the world. The design, position, and inter-relationship of the monuments and sites are evidence of a wealthy and highly organised prehistoric society able to *impose* its concepts on the environment. An outstanding example is the *alignment* of the Stonehenge Avenue and Stonehenge stone circle on the *axis* of the midsummer sunrise and midwinter sunset, indicating their ceremonial and *astronomical* character.

There is an *exceptional* survival of prehistoric monuments and sites within the World Heritage site including *settlements*, burial grounds, and large constructions of earth and stone. Today, together with their settings, they form landscapes without *parallel*. These complexes would have been of major significance to those who created them, as is apparent by the huge investment of time and effort they represent. They provide an insight into the *mortuary* and ceremonial practices of the period, and are evidence of prehistoric technology, architecture, and astronomy. The careful siting of monuments in

巨石阵是世界上建筑架构最复杂的史前石圈。这一文物古迹的设计、位置摆放以及结构关联度都显示出一个富足且组织性极强的史前社会能够将其观念施加于环境之上。一个最突出的例子就是，巨石阵的对齐大道和巨石阵石圈的轴线会在夏至日指出日出的方向，冬至日指出日落的方向，以暗示其仪式和天文特征。

在世界文化遗产中这一例外残存下来的史前文物古迹包括定居场所、坟场和大型土石建筑物。如今，它连同它的建造地点一起形成了无与伦比的风景。这些复合式建筑群对建造他们的人有着重大的意义，非常明显地反映出建造人所付出的巨额时间和努力。它们让我们洞悉该时代的殡葬事宜和礼仪性活动，同样也是史前科技、农业以及天文学造诣的体现。这

relation to the landscape helps us to further understand the Neolithic and Bronze Age.

一遗迹选址谨慎，与地形有关，能帮助我们更深地了解新石器时代和青铜器时代。

单词释义

architecturally 建筑上地
axis 轴线
settlement 定居点
in relation to 与……有关的

impose 强加
astronomical 天文学的
parallel 对比

alignment 队列；对齐
exceptional 例外的
mortuary 死的

英国特色文化

特色表达One

当看到巨石阵这一奇观的时候肯定有很多人被blown away了，blow是指"风吹"，难道blown away是被风吹跑的意思吗？其实该短语可以表示"留下深刻印象；深深打动"之意，而"……给我留下了深刻印象"就可以说成I am blown away by...或者..blow me away。

☆ 实景链接

A：How did you feel when you first saw the Stonehenge? I thought it was incredible. 你第一次见巨石阵是什么感觉？我觉得很不可思议。

B：I was also **blown away** by it. 它也给我留下了深刻印象。

A：The landscape is just unparalleled. 那风景真是无与伦比啊。

B：What's more, it has had more than one function. 更重要的是，它还有很多功能。

特色表达Two

巨石阵的石材非常坚硬，所以才会于千万年后依然残存了下来。石头坚硬是众所周知的，那么heart of stone大家能猜到是什么意思吗？该短语字面解释是"用石头建造的心"，常被用来形容人"铁石一样的心肠"，表达某人冷酷无情之意。have no heart也有异曲同工之妙。

☆ 实景链接

A: Have you seen the moving film? 你看那部感人的电影了吗？

B: Yeah, I can't help crying when the hero and the heroin exchanged their rings. 看了，在看到男女主角交换戒指的时候我忍不住哭了。

A: The sight would have moved a **heart of stone**. 这种情景就算是铁石心肠也会被感动的。

B: You bet. 肯定地。

拓展特色句

1. Stonehenge is one of Britain's biggest tourist draws. 巨石阵是英国吸引最多游客的景点之一。

2. Some archaeologists hold that Stonehenge was a religious site. 一些考古学家认为巨石阵曾是一个宗教遗址。

3. Can you tell me about the significance of Stonehenge? 你能给我讲讲巨石阵的重大意义吗？

"聊" 英国特色文化

A: Hey Jim, look at this building in the picture. Wasn't it fantastic?

B: Well, it is. What is that?

A: It was called Stonehenge which is erected in Wiltshire, England. Today it, together with Avebury and other associated sites, forms the heart of a World Heritage Site.

B: It seems quite strange and impressive.

A: Yes. Stonehenge is one of the most splendid prehistoric megalithic monuments in the world.

B: What does it mean for British people?

A: It is a holy place for them. The archaeologists found out at least 63 skeletons in 2013 when they studied

A: 嘿，吉姆，你看照片里这座建筑，是不是很棒？

B: 嗯，确实很棒，那是什么建筑？

A: 它叫巨石阵，竖立在英格兰的威尔特郡。如今它和埃夫伯里巨石圈以及周边的相关遗址构成了世界遗产地的中心。

B: 它看起来很奇怪，给人印象很深刻。

A: 是的。巨石阵是世界上最壮观的史前遗迹之一。

B: 它对英国人来说有什么意义呢？

A: 对于他们而言这里是个神圣的地方。考古学家2013年研究它时发现了63具人类尸骨。他们推测这里以前是墓地。

it. They inferred that there used to be a graveyard.

B: How mysterious! It must be a lot of fun there.

B: 真神秘！一定是一个好玩儿的地方。

"问" 英国特色文化

建立这么一座 "石头城" 究竟为何?

几个世纪以来，没有人知道巨石阵的真正用途，许多年以来，人们对这座巨石阵的用途做出了种种猜测。一些人通过考古发掘，发现土堤内侧有多处墓穴，便据此推测它是古代部落酋长的坟墓。而出土的大量兽骨残骸则被怀疑是祭陵用的牺牲品，于是有人判断，巨石阵是祭祖用的祭祀场所。还有结论认为这是一座古代天文台。牛津大学的霍金斯教授通过仔细观察和严密的计算认为通过巨石阵石环和土环的结构关系，可以精确了解太阳和月亮的12个方位，并观测和推算日月星辰在不同季节的起落，所以产生了如此推测。

阅读笔记

Part 8

不可不知的英国名人

童贞女王
——伊丽莎白一世

伊丽莎白一世的一生

Elizabeth I (7 September 1533—24 March 1603) was queen *regnant* of England and Ireland from 17 November 1558 until her death. Sometimes called "The Virgin Queen", "Gloriana" or "Good Queen Bess", Elizabeth was the fifth and last monarch of the Tudor dynasty. Elizabeth's *deft* political skills and strong personal character were directly responsible for putting England (at the time of her *accession* in 1558 a weak, divided *backwater* far outside the mainstream of European power and cultural development) on the road to becoming a true world economic and political power and restoring the country's lost sense of national pride. Few English monarchs enjoyed such political power, while still maintaining the devotion of the whole of English society. Although she entertained many marriage proposals and flirted *incessantly*, she never married or had children.

伊丽莎白一世(1533年9月7日—1603年3月24日)在1558年11月17日开始继任女王，统治英格兰和爱尔兰直到她去世。她有时被叫作"童贞女王"，"荣光女王"或者"英明女王"。伊丽莎白是都铎王朝第5位君主，也是最后一位。伊丽莎白凭借其机敏的政治手腕与强势的个人魅力直接将英国(在她1558年即位时，英国是一个弱小且四分五裂的闭塞之国，无法与欧洲的主流大国相媲美，文化发展也非常落后)发展成为一个世界经济与政治大国，重树了英国人民所失去的民族自豪感。很少有英国君主能享有如此的政权，同时对整个英国社会有着贡献。尽管很多人不停地向她求婚、献媚，但她从未结婚，也没有任何子嗣。

单词释义

regnant 统治的　　　　　　deft 机敏的　　　　　　accession 就职
backwater 停滞不前的状态　incessantly 不间断地

女王的情感纠葛

Succession became a pressing issue for Elizabeth once she took the throne. She showed her talents as a **diplomat**, managing a number of **suitors** and potential royal matches during her reign. Through her father and her sister, Elizabeth had seen the troubles and challenges of royal marriages. Mary had made an unpopular choice in marrying Phillip II of Spain, who shared in her devotion to the Roman Catholic faith. In the hopes of **reuniting** their two countries once more, Phillip even offered to wed Elizabeth at one time.

Other suitors for Elizabeth's hand included the king of Sweden, Archduke Charles of Austria, and the future King Henry III of France. She used her availability as a means **to political ends**, but she never agreed to marriage. She herself seemed to have some interest in a member of her court, Robert Dudley, and their relationship was the subject of much gossip and **speculation**. Both parties came **under suspicion** after the mysterious death of Dudley's wife.

Elizabeth, however, seemed to have no interest in sharing power with a spouse. Over time, she **cultivated** her image as a queen married to her job and her people.

自伊丽莎白即位以来，继承权的问题成了其面临的一个紧迫问题。她在位期间，不仅向世界展示了其出色的外交能力，还能在众多求婚者和潜在的王室适婚者中全身而退。从她父亲和姐姐的经历中，伊丽莎白看到了王室间婚姻所造成的困扰与挑战。姐姐玛丽嫁给了西班牙的腓力二世，两人均信仰罗马天主教，该婚姻并不受英国人民欢迎。腓力二世为了使西班牙和英国再度联合，甚至还一度提出与伊丽莎白结婚。

其他向伊丽莎白求婚的人还有瑞典的国王、奥地利的查尔大公，以及法国未来的国王亨利三世。她利用自己未婚待嫁的身份作为一种外交手段，但从未答应过任何人的求婚。她似乎对一个叫作罗伯特·杜德利的臣子感兴趣，且两人之间的关系一直是各种流言与猜测的话题焦点。他们的关系是在杜德利夫人神秘死亡后被人们怀疑的。

但伊丽莎白似乎不太想与配偶分享权力。久而久之，她将自己塑造成一个全心全意为她的国家和人民奉献的形象。因这一为国"献身"的精

For this dedication Elizabeth earned the nickname, the "Virgin Queen."

神，伊丽莎白获得了"童贞女王"的绰号。

单词释义

succession 继位   diplomat 外交家   suitor 求婚者

reunite 再联合   to political ends 为政治目的   speculation 猜测

under suspicion 遭怀疑   cultivate 培养

"品"英国特色文化

特色表达One

对很多新世纪诞生的人来说，谈起伊丽莎白女王就好像是before the Flood的故事一样。这里的before the Flood字面上指"在洪水之前的日子"，其实它的意思是"在远古时代，很久以前"。

☆ 实景链接

A：My little sister tells me that she admire the Elizabeth I. 我的小妹告诉我她崇拜伊丽莎白一世。

B：Ah, your sister has a lofty aspiration. 哇，你妹妹志向远大啊。

A：Yeah, for many people, they don't know Elizabeth I, some even regard her a great lady **before the food**, but my sister like her very much. 是的，对很多人来说，他们都不知道伊丽莎白一世，有的人甚至以为她是远古以前的伟大女性，但我小妹却非常喜欢她。

B：Well, she is somebody of worth. 嗯，伊丽莎白一世是一位值得尊重的重要人物。

特色表达Two

英国的孩子对伊丽莎白女王的盛名可以说很是清楚，但中国的孩子可就Know the ABC了。这里的Know the ABC字面指"知道ABC"，字母ABC指代"很简单，很基础的东西"，所以，在俚语中，英国人们常用该短语来形容"一窍不通或一知半解"。

☆ 实景链接

A：My history teacher told me that Elizabeth I is a great lady, and her beauty drew many zealous suitors. 我的历史老师告诉我，伊丽莎白一世是一位伟大的女性，她的美貌吸引了很多热情的求婚者。

B：I think her personal charisma is also a factor. 我想她的个人魅力也是一个因素。

A：Yeah, I like her very much; I wanna buy some books about her as a gift to my little sister. 是的，我很喜欢她，我想买一些有关她的书作为礼物送给我妹。

B：That's good, I guess few of today's children **know the ABC** about this great lady. 现在的孩子估计没有几个知道这位伟大的女性了。

拓展特色句

1. Under Elizabeth I England defeated Spain to dominate the time of Armada, has become a maritime power. 在伊丽莎白一世统治下，英国打败了称霸一时的西班牙无敌舰队，一跃成为海上强国。

2. The drama in England flourished under the rule of Elizabeth I. 在伊丽莎白一世时代英国戏剧繁荣兴旺。

3. Cate Blanchett plays the role of Elizabeth I in the film *Elizabeth I*. 凯特·布兰切特在电影《伊丽莎白一世》中扮演伊丽莎白一世。

"聊" 英国特色文化

A：I just watched the movie *Elizabeth I*.

B：Who is Elizabeth I.?

A：Her full name is Elizabeth Tudor. She is the last Tudor monarch in the 15th century. She became the queen of England in her 25s.

B：Was she a good monarch?

A：I think so.

B：What's the reason?

A：Elizabeth is known as "the virgin queen", kept unmarried all her life.

A：我刚刚看了电影《伊丽莎白一世》。

B：谁是伊丽莎白一世？

A：她的全名叫伊丽莎白·都铎。她是都铎王朝的最后一位君主。她25岁的时候成为了英格兰的女王。

B：她是一名好君主吗？

A：我认为是。

B：原因呢？

A：伊丽莎白被称为"童贞女王"，终身未嫁。她视人民为自己的孩子，

She regarded her people as her children and totally devoted herself to the construction and development of England.

B： That's unbelievable.

A： Yeah, besides that, her deft political skills and strong personal character were directly responsible for putting England on the road to becoming a true world economic and political power.

并且全身心投入于英格兰的建设和发展中。

B：真是令人难以置信。

A：是啊，此外，伊丽莎白机敏的政治手腕和强势的个人魅力直接将英国发展成为一个世界经济和政治大国。

"问" 英国文化特色

为什么星期五不吃鱼?

在英国伊丽莎白一世统治期间，英语中出现了一个新成语叫"eat no fish"(不吃鱼)。当时，英国的许多百姓为了表明自己的态度：站在伊丽莎白一世一边与天主教划清界限，他们的一项标志性的做法和口号是"星期五不吃鱼"。"星期五不吃鱼"又缩略成"不吃鱼"，这个短语"不吃鱼"就成了一种与政府保持一致的标志，于是在英语中，"不吃鱼"就成了表示拥戴政府的行为，"不吃鱼的人"就成了"忠于政府的人"以至于成了"诚实可信的人"的同义词。

阅读笔记

维多利亚女王

女王简介

Queen Victoria was the monarch of the United Kingdom of Great Britain and Ireland from 20 June 1837 until her death. From 1 May 1876, she used the additional title of Empress of India. She *inherited the throne* at the age of 18 and the United Kingdom was already an established *constitutional* monarchy, in which the *sovereign* held relatively little direct political power. Privately, Victoria attempted to influence government policy and *ministerial* appointments. Publicly, she became a national *icon*, and was identified with strict standards of personal morality.

Her reign of 63 years and seven months, which is longer than that of any other British monarch and the longest of any female monarch in history, is known as the Victorian era. It was a period of industrial, cultural, political, scientific, and military change within the United Kingdom, and was marked by a great expansion of the British Empire.

维多利亚从1837年6月开始担任大不列颠和爱尔兰联合王国的女王统治英国，直至去世。从1876年5月1日起，她有了印度女皇的头衔。维多利亚于18岁继承王位，当时的英国已经是君主立宪制国家，君主拥有相对较少的政权。私下里，维多利亚试图影响政府政策和内阁任命。在公开场合，她是国家的一个象征符号，以其严格的个人道德标准著名。

她在位共63年零7个月，比英国任何一位君主统治的时间都要长，是历史上女性君主在位时间最长的一个。历史上，人们将她统治的时期称为"维多利亚时代"。在这个时期内，英国的工业、文化、政治、科学和军事方面都有所改善，该时期的特点是大英帝国开始大幅扩张。

单词释义

inherit the throne 继承王位　　constitutional 宪法的　　sovereign 君主
ministerial 内阁的

金灿灿的维多利亚时期

The 19th Century was a time of *unprecedented* expansion for Britain in term of both of industry and Empire. Although Victoria's popularity *ebbed* and flowed during her reign, towards the end of her crown, she had become a symbol of British *imperialism* and pride.

The Victorian period also *witnessed* great advances in science and technology. It became known as the steam age, enabling people to easily travel throughout the UK and the World.

Queen Victoria was *emblematic* of this period. She was an enthusiastic supporter of the British Empire. She celebrated at Lord Kitchener's victory in the Sudan. She supported British involvement in the Boer War. She was also happy to preside over the expansion of the British Empire, which was to *stretch* across the globe. In 1877 Queen Victoria was made Empress of India, in a move *instigated* by the *imperialist* Disraeli. Famously, at the end of the Victorian period, people could say "the sun never set on the British Empire".

在19世纪期间，英国的工业和国土范围都被空前地扩张。尽管维多利亚在位后期不再那么受人们欢迎，但她已经成为了大英帝国与英国自傲感的象征符号。

在维多利亚时期，英国的科学与技术也有了很大的进步，被称为蒸汽时代，人们可以很容易地走遍英国与世界。

维多利亚女王是这一时期的象征。她是大英帝国热情的支持者。她在苏丹庆祝基奇纳勋爵的胜利，支持英国加入布尔战争，并且带领英国进行扩张，国土延伸至世界各地。1877年，维多利亚女王受帝国主义者迪斯雷利的唆使，成为印度女皇。在维多利亚统治后期，人们称英国为著名的"日不落帝国"。

单词释义

unprecedented 前所未有的　　ebb 衰退，减少　　imperialism 帝国主义
witness 目击，见证　　emblematic 象征的　　stretch 延伸
instigate 唆使　　imperialist 帝国主义者

"品" 英国特色文化

特色表达One

作为英国皇家代表的维多利亚女王肯定是每天wear Sunday clothes。这里的wear Sunday clothes难道是指"穿着星期天才穿的衣服"吗？其实，在俚语中，这个短语指"最漂亮的衣服"，可以理解为周日放假了，女孩们穿着最靓丽的衣服出门去玩。

☆ 实景链接

A：How great the Queen Victoria is! 维多利亚女王是多么伟大的人啊！

B：Of course, her reign of 63 years and seven months is known as the Victorian era. 当然啊，她在位的63年零7个月还被称为"维多利亚时代"呢。

A：Yeah, I want to be a lady like her, so I can **wear Sunday clothes** every day. 是啊，我想成为像她一样的女性，这样我每天都能穿最好的衣服。

B：So do I. 我也是。

特色表达Two

当时的维多利亚女王英姿飒爽，可谓风华绝代，应该有不少人carry a torch for她吧。torch是"火炬"的意思，难道这里的carry a torch for指的是"拿着一支火炬"？当然不是了，在俚语中，它的意思是"暗恋某人，单恋某人"。

☆ 实景链接

A：Queen Victoria was emblematic of the British Empire. 维多利亚女王是大英帝国的象征。

B：You're right, the Victorian Age is often boasted of as an age of progress. 你说得对，维多利亚时代常常被夸耀为进步时代。

A：She was really great! Many gentlemen must **carry a torch for** her in her age. 她太伟大了，在她统治下的时代里，肯定有很多绅士暗恋过她。

B：That's for sure. 那是肯定的。

拓展特色句

1. Queen Victoria is the longest reigning monarch in British history. 维多利亚女王是英国历史上在位时间最长的一位君主。

2. Queen Victoria wore a beautiful white wedding dress to marry her sweetheart that year. 那一年，维多利亚女王穿着白色婚纱嫁给她的挚爱。

3. He is a descendant of Queen Victoria. 他是维多利亚女王的后裔。

"聊" 英国特色文化

A: Do you know Queen Victoria?

B: I have heard of her but do not know very well about her.

A: She was the monarch of the United Kingdom of Great Britain and Ireland from 20 June 1837 until her death.

B: When did she pass away?

A: In 1901. Her reign is longer than that of any other British monarch and the longest of any female monarch in history, is known as the Victorian era.

B: What did she do for the country then?

A: She implemented many policies in industrial, cultural, political, scientific, and military change within the United Kingdom. At the end of the Victorian period, people could say "the sun never set on the British Empire".

A: 你知道维多利亚女王吗？

B: 我听说过，但不是很了解。

A: 她从1837年6月开始担任大不列颠和爱尔兰联合王国的女王统治英国，直至去世。

B: 她什么时候去世的？

A: 1901年的时候。她在位时间比英国任何一位君主统治的时间都要长，是历史上女性君主在位时间最长的一个，她统治的时期历史上称为"维多利亚时代"。

B: 那她都为这个国家做了什么？

A: 她在工业、文化、政治、科学和军事方面实施了很多政策，在维多利亚统治后期，人们称英国为著名的"日不落帝国"。

"问" 英国特色文化

维多利亚女王与鸦片战争有关吗？

1837年维多利亚女王即位时，英国已经完成了资本主义工业革命，为了满足国家寻找原料地和销售市场的要求，英国开始在世界各地建立殖民地和自治领。1840年英国占领了新西兰，这标志着英国在全世界的殖民体系形成。1839年，林则徐在虎门销烟，极大程度上打击了英国政府的倾销政策，1840年初，维多利亚女王在议会上发表了著名的演说，呼吁"为了大英帝国的利益"，向中国发动战争。第一次鸦片战争遂始。

> 阅读笔记

铁娘子——撒切尔夫人

铁娘子的一生

Margaret Hilda Thatcher was a British politician who was the Prime Minister and the Leader of the Conservative Party. She was the longest-serving British Prime Minister of the 20th century and is the only woman to have held the office. A Soviet journalist called her the "Iron Lady", a nickname that became associated with her *uncompromising* politics and leadership style. As Prime Minister, she *implemented* policies that have come to be known as Thatcherism.

Thatcher became the first woman to serve as the opposition leader in the House of Commons. As party leader, Thatcher made history in May 1979, when she was appointed Britain's first female prime minister. Margaret Thatcher died on April 8, 2013, at the age of 87. Thatcher's policies and actions continue to be debated by *detractors* and supporters alike, illustrating the *indelible* impression that she has left on Britain and nations worldwide.

玛格丽特·希尔达·撒切尔是一位英国政治家，她不仅曾问鼎英国首相，还曾领导保守党。她是20世纪任职时间最长的也是英国唯一任职的女首相。前苏联的一名记者称她为"铁娘子"，这一绰号与其坚定的政治策略和领导风格有着很大关系。作为首相，她颁布了一系列的政策，被人们称为"撒切尔主义"。

撒切尔是第一位反对众议院的女性领导人。作为党魁，撒切尔于1979年5月被任命为英国第一位女首相，这一盛事也永久地载入英国史册。玛格丽特·撒切尔逝世于2013年4月8日，享年87岁。如今，她的政策和做法仍然为其批评者和支持者所争论，证明撒切尔给英国以及全世界留下了不可磨灭的印象。

单词释义

uncompromising 不妥协的　　　implement 实施　　　detractor 批评者
indelible 难忘的，擦不掉的

铁娘子名言

1. If you just set out to be liked, you would be prepared to *compromise* on anything at any time, and you would achieve nothing.

2. I am in politics because of the conflict between good and evil, and I believe that in the end good will *triumph*.

3. If you want something said, ask a man. If you want something done, ask a woman.

4. Where there is *discord*, may we bring harmony. Where there is error, may we bring truth. Where there is doubt, may we bring faith. And where there is despair, may we bring hope.

5. Pennies don't fall from heaven—they have to be earned here on Earth.

6. We want a society where people are free to make choices, to make mistakes, to be generous and *compassionate*. This is what we mean by a moral society; not a society where the state is responsible for everything, and no one is responsible for the state.

7. Being powerful is like being a lady. If you have to tell people you are, you aren't.

8. Any woman who understands the problems of running a home will

WHERE THERE IS **DISCORD** MAY WE BRING **HARMONY** WHERE THERE IS **ERROR** MAY WE BRING **TRUTH** WHERE THERE IS **DOUBT**

1. 如果你一心为了讨喜，那你就要准备随时随地屈就，并且你会一事无成。

2. 从政是因为有正邪之争，而我坚信邪不胜正。

3. 如果你需要信口开河、会说的人，得找个男人；如果你需要会做事儿的人，一定要找个女人！

4. 凡是有不和的地方，我们要为和谐而努力；凡是有谬误的地方，我们要为真理而努力；凡是有疑虑的地方，我们要为信任而努力；凡是有绝望的地方，我们要为希望而努力。

5. 钱不会从天上掉下来，必须脚踏实地去挣。

6. 我们想要一个人民可以自由地选择、犯错、持有宽容及同情心的社会。这就是我们所谓的道德社会；而不是一个需要国家肩负全责，而无人为国家负责的社会。

7. 做大人物就像做淑女一样。如果你告诉人们你是，那就说明你不是。

be nearer to understanding the problems of running a country.

8. 了解持家难处的女性，较易明白治国之难处。

单词释义

compromise 妥协，让步   triumph 胜利   discord 不和

compassionate 富于同情心的

"品" 英国特色文化

特色表达One

各花入各眼，有的人不喜欢强势的撒切尔夫人，他们认为女人应该在家好好相夫教子，而也有人赞赏她，认为她可是easy on the eye的。这里的 easy on the eye不是说"很容易看出"哦，其实，在俚语中它的意思是"赏心悦目"。

实景链接

A: Thatcher has said "Being powerful is like being a lady". 撒切尔夫人说过"做大人物就要像做淑女一样"。

B: Yeah, I want to be a great lady like her. 是的，我想成为一位像她一样的伟大女性。

A: So do me. To us, Thatcher is **easy on the eye**; but to others, she may be too dominant. 我也是。对我们而言，撒切尔夫人相当赏心悦目，但其他人也许认为她过于强势。

B: But, I like her even though she can be dominant. 但尽管她有时盛气凌人，我还是喜欢她。

特色表达Two

面对像撒切尔夫人这样强势的政坛领袖，任何banana oil都是没用的。这里的banana oil难道是"香蕉油"吗？其实，这个短语在俚语中指的是"阿谀奉承或花言巧语"，比如被花言巧语蒙骗就能说成be deceived by the banana oil。

实景链接

A: I think Thatcher knew her own mind, and she may never be deceived by her **Banana oil**. 我想撒切尔是一位有主见的女性，她应该

不会被阿谀奉承所迷惑。

B：Of course, she is called "Iron Lady". 当然啊，她可是被称作"铁娘子"的。

A：She is such a great lady. I wish I could become like her one day. 她就是这样一位伟大的女性，我希望能有一天像她那样。

B：You can do it! I got your back. 你一定行的！我支持你。

拓展特色句

1. Lady Thatcher will not be seeing him. 撒切尔夫人是不会接见他的。

2. Meryl Streep plays Thatcher, a woman with high standards, a short temper and a taste for whiskey in *The Iron Lady*. 在影片《铁娘子》中梅丽尔·斯特里普扮演一个高标准要求自己、脾气暴躁、喜欢喝威士忌的女人。

3. He is a devoted Thatcherite. 他是撒切尔的忠实追随者。

"聊" 英国特色文化

A：Why is Margaret Hilda Thatcher called "Iron Lady"?

B：This name was from a Soviet journalist, a nickname that became associated with her uncompromising politics and leadership style.

A：I know that she is the Prime Minister and the Leader of the Conservative Party.

B：That's true. She was the longest-serving British Prime Minister of the 20th century and is the only woman to have held the office.

A：Has she passed away?

B：Yeah, Margaret Thatcher died on April 8, 2013, at the age of 87.

A：I know that she had a lot of well-known sayings. Which one do you

A：为什么人们称玛格丽特·希尔达·撒切尔为"铁娘子"？

B：这个称号来自一个前苏联的记者，与其坚定的政治策略和领导风格有着很大关系。

A：我知道她是英国的首相和保守党的领袖。

B：没错。她是20世纪任职时间最长的，也是英国唯一任职的女首相。

A：她已经去世了吗？

B：是的，玛格丽特·撒切尔逝世于2013年4月8日，享年87岁。

A：我知道她有很多名言。你最喜欢哪句？

B：钱不会从天上掉下来，必须脚踏实地去挣。我还读过她的传记《唐宁街岁月》和《通往权利之路》。

like best?

B: Pennies don't fall from heaven—they have to be earned here on Earth. I also read her biography *Downing Street Years* and *Path to power*.

"问" 英国特色文化

何为"撒切尔主义"？

撒切尔主义(Thatcherism)，即撒切尔夫人上台后在保守党内出现的一股占统治地位的"新右派"势力的意识形态，是当代西方"新自由主义"与"保守主义"的"混血儿"，在新工党执政前主宰英国政坛近20余年。它一方面坚持新自由主义的自由市场经济理论，另一方面又主张新保守主义的文化右翼纲领政策；它反对建立在凯恩斯经济学和对福利国家的支持之上的"共识政治"，是更为广泛的，从某种程度上说是国际性的反对平等主义和集体主义倾向的一部分。

阅读笔记

丘吉尔首相

丘吉尔的辉煌人生

Winston Leonard Spencer-Churchill (30 November 1874—24 January 1965) was a British *politician* who was the Prime Minister of the United Kingdom from 1940 to 1945 and again from 1951 to 1955. Widely regarded as one of the greatest wartime leaders of the 20th century, Churchill was also an officer in the British Army, a historian, a writer, and an artist. He is the only British Prime Minister in history to have received the Nobel Prize in Literature, and was also the first person to be made an *Honorary* Citizen of the United States.

Sir Winston Churchill has been recognized as one of the greatest men of the late nineteenth and of the twentieth century. He was an *extraordinary* war leader to whom the Western World must be forever *in debt*. He was a *prophet* in his own time.

温斯顿·伦纳德·斯宾塞·丘吉尔(1874年11月30日—1965年2月24日)是英国的一名政治家，在1940年至1945年期间出任英国首相，并于1951年至1955年再次担任首相。他被人们普遍认为是20世纪最伟大的战争领袖之一。另外，丘吉尔还是英国陆军的一名军官，一名历史学家，一名作家，还是一名艺术

家。他是英国历史上唯一获得诺贝尔文学奖的首相，而且是被美国授予荣誉公民的第一人。

温斯顿·丘吉尔爵士被评为19世纪后期以及20世纪最伟大的人之一。他是西方世界永远无法忘怀的杰出战争领袖。在他统治的时代，他还是一名预言家。

单词释义

politician 政治家

in debt 欠情

Honorary 荣誉的

prophet 预言家

extraordinary 非凡的

丘吉尔首相励志名言

1. Never, never, never, never give up.

2. Courage is going from failure to failure without losing enthusiasm.

3. I like a man who *grins* when he fights.

4. Courage is what it takes to stand up and speak; courage is also what it takes to sit down and listen.

5. Study history, study history. In history lies all the secrets of *statecraft*.

6. Success is going from failure to failure without losing enthusiasm.

7. Attitude is a little thing that makes a big difference.

8. We make a living by what we get, but we make a life by what we give.

9. A *pessimist* sees the difficulty in every opportunity; an optimist sees the opportunity in every difficulty.

10. I never worry about action, but only about inaction

11. I have nothing to offer but blood, toil, tears and *sweat*.

12. All the great things are simple, and many can be expressed in a single word: freedom; justice; honor; duty; mercy; hope.

13. Kites rise highest against the wind, not with it.

14. A lie gets halfway around the

1. 永远，永远，永远，永远都不要放弃。

2. 勇气就是不断失败，而不丧失热情。

3. 我喜欢微笑着战斗的人。

4. 勇气是能站起来侃侃而谈。勇气也是能坐下来静静倾听。

5. 学习历史，学习历史。历史中藏着一切治国之道。

6. 成功就是不断失败，而不丧失热情。

7. 态度决定一切。

8. 我们因获得而生存，但我们靠付出而创造人生。

9. 悲观主义者从每个机遇中看到困难，乐观主义者从每个困难中看到机遇。

10. 我从不担心行动。而只担心没有任何行动。

11. 我能奉献的，只有鲜血、苦干、眼泪和汗水。

12. 伟大的事情总是简单，最伟大的事情只有一个词：自由；正义；荣誉；责任；仁慈；希望。

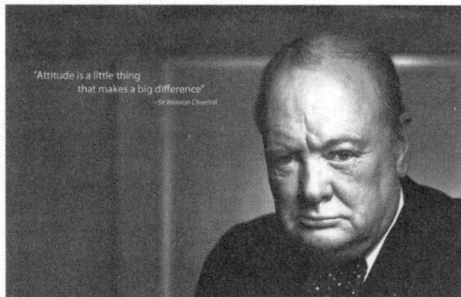

"Attitude is a little thing that makes a big difference"
—Sir Winston Churchill

world before the truth has a chance to get its pants on.

15.Success is not final, failure is not *fatal*: it is the courage to continue that counts.

16.We shall show mercy, but we shall not ask for it.

13. 风筝顶着风高飞，而不是顺着风。

14.真理还没机会穿上裤子时谎言已经满街跑了。

15.成功不要紧，失败不致命。继续前行的勇气，才最可贵。

16.我们会展示出我们的仁慈。但我们不会向别人要求仁慈。

单词释义

grin 露齿笑
sweat 汗水

statecraft 治国才能
fatal 致命的

pessimist 悲观主义者

"品" 英国特色文化

特色表达One

英国伟大的首相丘吉尔的很多名言都是告诫人们或是坚持不懈，或是put your back into某件事。有人疑问"put your back into"是指什么？其实说的就是"埋头干，全力以赴"的意思。

实景链接

A：I want to be a politician like Churchill. 我想成为一名像丘吉尔一样的政治家。

B：Really? Is that your dream? Why? 真的吗？那是你的梦想吗？为什么呢？

A：Yeah, Churchill has said "Never, never, never, never give up." I want to pattern my life upon him. 是的，丘吉尔曾说道"永远，永远，永远，永远都不要放弃。"他是我的榜样。

B：Then you need to **put your back into** being such a great man. 那你得需要全力以赴才能成为他那样的伟人了。

特色表达Two

有人认为丘吉尔不仅出身显赫，而且sitting pretty，所以才能最后当选英国首相。其实，丘吉尔的成功也离不开其个人努力、人格魅力以及军旅生涯。这里

的sitting pretty指的是"处于极有利的位置，过着舒服的生活"，通俗点将就是
"吃穿不愁"的意思。

☆ **实景链接**

A：Do you think Churchill is a great Prime Minister of the United Kingdom. 你觉得丘吉尔是大英帝国的一位伟大的首相？

B：Yeah, I have read some books about his success to be a Prime Minister , he is worthy of our praise. 是的，我曾读过他成功竞选首相的书籍，他值得人们赞许。

A：But there were some people think Churchill was **sitting pretty**, and all his success owned to his Family. 但是很多人认为丘吉尔整天游手好闲，混吃混喝，他的成功全归于他的家族势力。

B：Maybe some facts prejudiced them against him. 也许是有些事实让他们对他有偏见吧。

拓展特色句

1. He became Prime Minister and led Britain to victory in the Second World War. 他成了首相，并领导英国在第二次世界大战中取得了胜利。

2. I've listened to this Churchill's address for several times. 这段丘吉尔的演讲我已经听了好几遍了。

3. I want to take a quote often attributed to the historical figure Winston Churchill. 我想引用历史人物丘吉尔经常说的一段话。

"聊" **英国特色文化**

A：What are you busy doing these days?

B：I'm reading the book *The Unnecessary War*.

A：Who's the author?

B：Winston Leonard Spencer-Churchill.

A：The Prime Minister Churchill? The man who was made an Honorary Citizen of the United States?

A：这些天你在忙什么呢？

B：我在读《不需要的战争》这本书呢。

A：作者是谁？

B：温斯顿·伦纳德·斯宾塞·丘吉尔。

A：首相丘吉尔？被美国授予荣誉公民的那个人？

B：是的。他是美国授予荣誉公民的第一人，而且获得了1953年的诺贝尔

B： Yes. He was the first person to be made an Honorary Citizen of the United States. And he got the Nobel Prize for Literature in 1953. He is the only British Prime Minister in history to have received the Nobel Prize in Literature.

A： Wow, he is really versatile.

B： Yes. Churchill was also an officer in the British Army, and an artist.

A： I want to read this book, where can I find it?

B： I borrowed it from the library. I think you can buy it in the bookshop or online.

文学奖。他是英国历史上唯一获得诺贝尔文学奖的首相。

A： 哇，他真是多才多艺啊。

B： 是的。并且丘吉尔还是英国陆军的一名军官，还是一名艺术家。

A： 我想读这本书，在哪儿能找到呢？

B： 我是从图书馆借的。我觉得你从书店或者网上都能买到。

"问" 英国特色文化

温斯顿·丘吉尔是民族英雄吗？

英国首相温斯顿·丘吉尔是在第二次世界大战期间，带领英国人民取得伟大胜利的民族英雄，丘吉尔三度当选时代年度人物，是与斯大林、罗斯福并立的"三巨头"之一，是矗立于世界史册上的一代伟人。在第二次世界大战的关键时刻，他以一个杰出政治家的巨大勇气和高度灵活性，从英国人民的根本利益出发，完成了英国政治和他本人政治生涯中的重大历史性转折，使不同意识形态下的反法西斯力量结成了统一战线，从而保证了赢得战争的最后胜利。

摇滚王朝披头士

披头士的飞速走红

The Beatles were an English rock band that formed in Liverpool, in 1960. With John Lennon, Paul McCartney, George Harrison, and Ringo Starr, they became widely regarded as the greatest and most influential act of the rock era. Rooted in *skiffle* and 1950s rock and roll, the Beatles later *experimented* with several genres, ranging from pop ballads to *psychedelic* rock, often *incorporating* classical elements in innovative ways. In the early 1960s, their enormous popularity first emerged as "*Beatlemania*".

They gained popularity in the United Kingdom after their first *hit*, "*Love Me Do*", in late 1962. They acquired the nickname the "Fab Four" as Beatlemania grew in Britain over the following year, and by early 1964 they had become international stars, leading the "British Invasion" of the United States pop market. In 2004, Rolling Stone ranked the Beatles as the greatest artist of all time. In 2008, the group topped Billboard magazine's list of the all time most successful "Hot 100" artists; as of 2013, they hold the

披头士是一支成立于1960年英国利物浦的摇滚乐队。乐队成员有约翰·列侬、保罗·麦卡特尼、乔治·哈里森以及林戈·斯塔尔，他们被普遍认为是摇滚界最伟大最具影响力的乐队。披头士的音乐风格来自于早期爵士乐和20世纪50年代的摇滚乐，而后他们还尝试了各种曲风，从流行情歌到迷幻摇滚，常以创新的方式融入古典元素。在20世纪60年代早期，其万人追捧的人气掀起了一阵"披头士狂热"。

1962年，他们第一张热销唱片《Love Me Do》发行后，在英国受到了热烈欢迎。接下来的一年里，披头士狂热在英国迅速增长，他们获得了"披头士四人组"的绰号，并且于1964年成为国际明星，引领了美国流行音乐市场的"英伦入侵"。2004年，《滚石》将披头士列为有史以来最伟大的艺术家。2008年，该组合在《公告牌》杂志上位居有史以来最成功的"100位最热门艺术家"的榜首；在2013年，他们创造了

record for most number-one hits on the Hot 100 chart with 20.

纪录，头号热门100首歌曲排行榜中有20首是他们的歌。

experiment 尝试　　　　　psychedelic 迷幻的　　　　　skiffle 早期爵士乐
incorporate 合并　　　　　Beatlemania 披头士狂热　　　hit 唱片或表演获得成功

披头士的影响

According to the RIAA, the Beatles are the best-selling band in the United States, with 177 million certified units. They not only *sparked* the British Invasion of the US, they became a globally influential *phenomenon* as well. Their musical innovations and commercial success inspired musicians worldwide. On radio, their arrival marked the beginning of a new era. They helped to *redefine* the album as something more than just a few hits *padded out* with "filler", and they were primary innovators of the modern music video. *Emulation* of their clothing and especially their hairstyles, which became a mark of *rebellion*, had a global impact on fashion.

The Beatles changed the way people listened to popular music and experienced its role in their lives. From what began as the Beatlemania fad, the group's popularity grew into what was seen as an *embodiment*

据美国唱片工业协会表示，披头士是在美国最畅销的组合，有1.77亿的专辑销量认证。他们不只发动了"英伦入侵"，而且成为了一个在全球有着影响力的现象。他们在音乐上的创作才华和商业上的成就激励了全球所有的音乐人。对于无线广播来说，他们的到来标志着一个新时代的来临。他们帮助重新定义了专辑的意义，专辑不再只是用"填充器"将几首歌压缩在一起，他们是现代音乐视频的主要创新者。他们的服装被人模仿，尤其是发型，成为了一种叛逆的标志，对全球的时尚界产生了影响。

披头士改变了人们听流行音乐的方式，让人们开始体验自己在生活中

of sociocultural movements of the decade. As icons of the 1960s counterculture, they became a *catalyst* for *bohemianism* and activism in various social and political arenas, fuelling movements such as women's liberation, gay liberation and *environmentalism*.

所扮演的角色。从起初的披头士狂热开始，后来披头士的人气逐渐成为10年内社会与文化运动的一种体现。作为20世纪60年代反主流文化的偶像人物，他们刺激了玩世作风和不同社会及政治领域内行动主义的形成，并且促进了妇女解放运动、同性恋解放运动以及环境保护主义运动。

单词释义

- spark 发动
- padded out 用填料填满
- embodiment 体现
- environmentalism 环境保护论
- phenomenon 现象
- emulation 效仿
- catalyst 催化剂
- redefine 重新定义
- rebellion 叛逆
- bohemianism 玩世不恭的作风

"品"英国特色文化

特色表达One

在"披头士热"盛行的时代，只要商店出售该乐队的专辑或周边产品，就少有in the black的情况出现。这里的in the black指的是"亏损状态"而不是"在黑暗中"。

☆实景链接

A：Do you heard the "Beatlemania"? 你听过"披头士热"吗？

B：Uh, do you mean the "Beatlemania" first emerged in the early 1960s? 呃，你说的是20世纪60年代崛起的"披头士热"吗？

A：That's it! 就是那个！

B：Well, I heard that many people like their music, so shops which selling their CDs in that times has never been in the black. 哦，我听说当时很多人热衷他们的音乐，所以当时买披头士CD的商店都不会亏损。

特色表达Two

披头士刚出道的时候，有很多人对他们定位不清，以为他们的乐队是a real

card。这里的a real card说的是"惹人开心的、逗趣的活宝"，可不是"一张真正的卡片"。

☆ 实景链接

A：Do you know the Beatles? 你知道披头士吗？

B：Of course, I know some of them, such as John, John, Paul and George. 当然啦，我认识他们当中的几个，例如约翰、保罗和乔治。

A：Ah, I am a fan of John Lennon. 哇，我是约翰·列侬的粉丝。

B：Really? Someone think he is a real card. 真的吗？有的人认为约翰是一个活宝。

拓展特色句

1. The Beatles influenced so much of society. 披头士对社会产生了很大的影响。

2. My Dad often played The Beatles' music so loud when I was young. 在我年轻的时候我爸爸经常很大声地放披头士的音乐。

3. For some fans, it could never be an "authentic" Beatles track without Lennon's participation. 对一些粉丝来说，没有约翰·列侬的参与，就不算是"真正的"披头士歌曲。

"聊" 英国特色文化

A：What are you listening?

B：*Hey Jude* from the Beatles.

A：It's really old.

B：But it's classic.

A：Who are the members of the Beatles? Do you remember that?

B：John Lennon, Paul McCartney, George Harrison, and Ringo Starr.

A：It was such an influential band at that time, right?

B：Sure. They changed the way people

A：你在听什么呢？

B：披头士的《嘿，朱迪》。

A：真老啊。

B：但是很经典。

A：成员都有谁，你记得吗？

B：约翰·列侬、保罗·麦卡特尼、乔治·哈里森以及林戈·斯塔尔。

A：他们在当时是一支非常有影响力的乐队，对吗？

B：当然。他们改变了人们听流行音乐的方式，让人们开始体验自己在生

listened to popular music and experienced its role in their lives.

A: That's not easy. What are their achievements?

B: In 2004, Rolling Stone ranked the Beatles as the greatest artist of all time. In 2008, the group Topped Billboard magazine's list of the all time most successful "Hot 100" artists; as of 2013, they hold the record for most number-one hits on the Hot 100 chart with 20.

活中所扮演的角色。

A: 那可不容易。他们有哪些成就？

B: 2004年，滚石乐队将披头士列为有史以来最伟大的艺术家。2008年，该组合在《公告牌》杂志上位居有史以来最成功的"100位最热门艺术家"的榜首；在2013年，他们创造了纪录，头号热门100首歌曲排行榜中有20首是他们的歌。

"问" 英国特色文化

披头士对世界有什么影响？

首先，披头士继承了摇滚乐头十年的成果，并且以自己的创造和革新，丰富和发展了摇滚乐，把摇滚乐带到了一个新的历史阶段。从此，摇滚乐脱离开了单纯的娱乐音乐，它有了更多的让人思考的东西，更多的隐藏在音乐背后的东西。20世纪60年代成长起来的英美两国的年轻人，大多深受披头士的影响。可以说他们的歌声影响了一代人的艺术趣味、服装款式和发型、生活方式和人生态度。"披头士"的出现使更多的学者开始研究摇滚乐现象，以及摇滚乐的音乐和歌词，以致后来大学里也开设了摇滚乐课程。

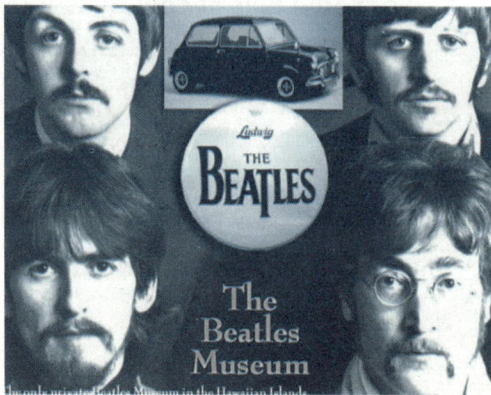

阅读笔记

文学巨匠——莎士比亚

莎士比亚概况

William Shakespeare (26 April 1564 – 23 April 1616) was an English poet and playwright, widely regarded as the greatest writer in the English language and the world's *pre-eminent* dramatist. He is often called England's national poet and the "Bard of Avon". His *extant* works, including some *collaborations*, consist of about 38 plays, 154 *sonnets*, two long narrative poems, and a few other verses. His plays have been translated into every major living language and are performed more often than those of any other playwright.

Shakespeare was a respected poet and playwright in his own day, but his reputation did not rise to its present heights until the 19th century. In the 20th century, his work was repeatedly adopted and rediscovered by new movements in scholarship and performance. His plays remain highly popular today and are constantly studied, performed, and *reinterpreted* in diverse cultural and political contexts throughout the world.

威廉·莎士比亚(1564.4.23—1616.4.23),英国诗人、剧作家,被广泛认为是最伟大的英语语言作家和世界杰出的剧作家,通常被称为英国的民族诗人和"吟游诗人"。现存作品(包括合作作品)有38部戏剧、154首十四行诗、两首长叙事诗和几首其他诗歌。他的戏剧有各种主要语言的译本,且表演次数远远超过其他任何戏剧家的作品。

莎士比亚在世时被尊为诗人和剧作家,但直到19世纪他的声望才达到今日的高度。20世纪,他的作品常常被新学术运动改编并重新发现价值。他的作品直至今日依旧广受欢迎,在全球以不同文化和政治形式演出和诠释。

单词释义

pre-eminent 杰出的 extant 现存的 collaboration 合作
sonnet 十四行诗 reinterpret 重新解释

281

莎翁对后世文学的影响

Shakespeare's work has made a lasting impression on later theatre and literature. In particular, he expanded the dramatic potential of *characterisation*, plot, language, and *genre*. Until *Romeo and Juliet*, for example, romance had not been viewed as a worthy topic for tragedy. Soliloquies had been used mainly to convey information about characters or events; but Shakespeare used them to explore characters' minds. His work heavily influenced later poetry. The Romantic poets attempted to revive Shakespearean verse drama, though with little success. Critic George Steiner described all English verse dramas from Coleridge to Tennyson as "*feeble variations* on Shakespearean themes".

Shakespeare influenced novelists such as Thomas Hardy, William Faulkner, and Charles Dickens. The American novelist Herman Melville's soliloquies owe much to Shakespeare; his Captain Ahab in *Moby-Dick* is a classic *tragic* hero, inspired by King Lear. Scholars have identified 20,000 pieces of music linked to Shakespeare's works. Shakespeare has also inspired many painters, including the Romantics

莎士比亚的著作对后来的戏剧和文学有持久的影响。实际上，他扩展了戏剧人物刻画、情节叙述、语言表达和文学体裁多个方面。例如，直到《罗密欧与朱丽叶》，爱情故事才被视作悲剧值得创作的主题。独白以前主要用于传达人物或时间的信息，但是莎士比亚用来探究人物的思想。他的作品对后来的诗歌影响重大。浪漫主义诗人试图振兴莎士比亚的诗剧，不过收效甚微。评论家乔治·斯坦纳认为从柯尔律治到丁尼生的所有英国诗剧都是"莎士比亚作品主题的微小变化"。

莎士比亚还影响了托马斯·哈代、威廉·福克纳和查尔斯·狄更斯等小说家。美国小说家赫尔曼·梅尔维尔的独白很大程度上得益于莎士比亚，他的著作《白鲸》里的亚哈船长是一个经典的悲剧英雄，含有李尔王的影子。学者们鉴定出2万首与莎士比亚的作品相关的音乐。莎士比亚对很多画家也有影响，包括浪漫主义和前拉斐尔派。精神分析学家西格蒙德·弗洛伊德在他的人性理论中引用了莎士比亚作品的心理分析，尤其是哈姆雷特。在莎士比亚时期，英语语法和拼写没有现在标准化，他对语言的运用影响了现代英语。塞缪尔·约翰逊在《约翰逊字典》中引用莎士比

and the Pre-Raphaelites. The psychoanalyst Sigmund Freud drew on Shakespearean psychology, in particular that of Hamlet, for his theories of human nature.In Shakespeare's day, English grammar, spelling and *pronunciation* were less *standardised* than they are now, and his use of language helped shape modern English. Samuel Johnson quoted him more often than any other author in his *A Dictionary of the English Language*, the first serious work of its type.

亚之处比任何其他作家都多，该字典是这个领域的第一本专著。

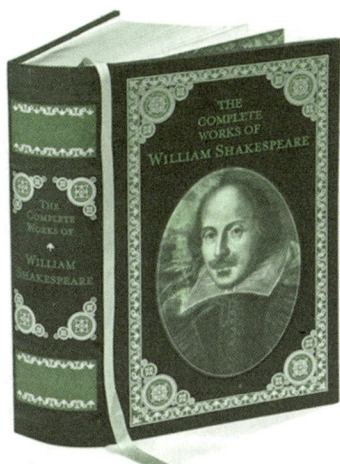

单词释义

characterization 描述
variation 变化
standardized 标准的

genre 类型
tragic 悲剧

feeble 微弱的
pronunciation 发音

"品" 英国特色文化

特色表达One

　　莎翁，多么伟大的文学家，他在写作的时候会有苦思冥想的时候吗？他也会ants in one's pants吗？或许这是个未知的谜了。ants in one's pants字面意思是"蚂蚁进到裤子里了"，想象一下，蚂蚁在裤子里乱爬的心情吧，一定是让人焦虑极了，所以引申为"紧张焦虑的心情"。

☆ 实景链接

A：Sarah has **ants in her pants**. 莎拉有点魂不守舍的。

B：What's wrong with her? 她怎么了？

A：She has been trouble in how to write some attractive and interesting compositions like Shakespeare. 她纠结于如何像莎翁一样

写一些既动人又有趣的文章。

B: This is a good idea, and is also a very big challenge. 这是一个好想法，也是一个很大的挑战。

特色表达Two

莎士比亚的戏剧若是go by the numbers，还会有人观赏吗？这里的number虽然是数字，但go by the numbers可不是说按照数字一个一个来，在俚语中，这个短语指的是"按照一定的形式，循规蹈矩地"。

☆ 实景链接

A: What's wrong with you? 你怎么了？

B: I wanna to quote a few verses from Shakespeare in my paper. 我想在论文中引用一些莎翁的诗句。

A: I like your ideas, but you'd better **go by the numbers** and follow our standard procedure. 你的点子很好，但我劝你还是按标准格式来吧。

B: Hmm. Maybe you're right. 嗯，也许你是对的。

拓展特色句

1. Shakespeare belongs to the 16th century. 莎士比亚是16世纪的人物。
2. He was reading the plays of Shakespeare. 他在读莎士比亚的戏剧。
3. *Romeo and Juliet* is a love story and a tragedy. 《罗密欧与朱丽叶》是一部爱情悲剧。

"聊" 英国特色文化

A: Do you have any plan this evening?

B: I am going to watch the play with my boyfriend.

A: What's it about?

B: Shakespeare's *Romeo and Juliet*.

A: It's really classical. Do you like Shakespeare?

B: Yes. I read a lot of his works when I was at school. Some of them are shot

A: 今晚有什么计划吗？

B: 我打算和男朋友去看话剧。

A: 关于什么的？

B: 莎士比亚的《罗密欧与朱丽叶》。

A: 真经典啊。你喜欢莎士比亚吗？

B: 喜欢。我上学的时候读过他的很多作品。有一些还被拍成了电影。

into movies.

A: But I think the vocabulary in his works is hard to understand. It's not easy to read.

B: That's because his living age is far from us.

A: 但是我觉得他作品中的词汇很难理解，读起来不容易。

B: 那是因为他的生活年代离我们太远了。

"问"英国特色文化

莎士比亚的作品为什么至今仍广受欢迎？

莎士比亚的戏剧基本取材于小说或民间传说，并在改写中注入了自己的情感与想法，给旧题材赋予更加新颖与深刻的内容。据说，莎士比亚用词高达2万个以上，其中不乏民谣、俚语、古谚语、外来词汇，还不断穿插比喻、隐喻、双关语，可见他的作品是文笔华丽又内涵丰富的。另外，剧中许多语句已融入到现代人的生活中，有的成了英语中的成语和格言，有的成了脍炙人口的口头禅，所以莎士比亚的作品依旧广受欢迎。

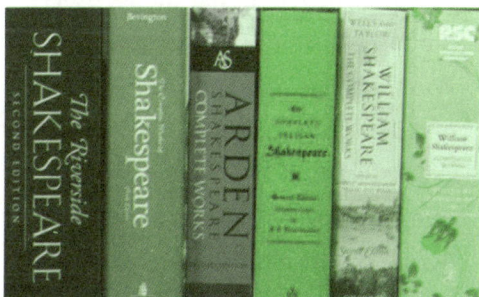

阅读笔记

文坛勃朗特三姐妹

三姐妹概况

Charlotte Bronte (1816—1855) and her sisters Emily Bronte (1818—1848) and Anne Bronte (1820—1849) have charmed, inspired, and even shocked readers from the Victorian age to the present. Raised in Haworth, Yorkshire, the three sisters produced such classics as *Jane Eyre*, *Wuthering Heights*, and *The Tenant* of Wildfell Hall.

Influenced by British Romantic poets like Wordsworth, Scott, and Byron, the Brontes produced a *cast* of unforgettable characters such as the *devoted governess*, Jane Eyre, and the lovers, Heathcliff, Cathy, and Hareton.

Their fame was due as much to their own tragic destinies as to their *precociousness*. Since their early deaths they were subject of a following that did not cease to grow. Their home, the parsonage at Haworth in Yorkshire, now the Bronte Parsonage Museum, has become a place of *pilgrimage* for hundreds of thousands of visitors each year.

夏洛蒂·勃朗特(1816—1855)、艾米莉·勃朗特(1818—1848)和安妮·勃朗特(1820—1849)三姐妹生于英国北部约克郡的霍沃斯山区，创作了如《简·爱》《呼啸山庄》和《荒野庄园的房客》这类经典的文学著作，吸引、启发并震惊了从维多利亚时代到现代的读者。

受英国浪漫主义诗人华兹华斯、斯科特和拜伦的影响，勃朗特三姐妹创作了令人难忘的人物，如忠实的家庭教师简·爱和情侣希斯克利夫、凯西和哈里顿。

她们的成功，很大程度上源于自身悲剧命运带来的早熟。因为英年早逝，勃朗特三姐妹成了日益增长的支持者讨论的对象。她们在约克郡霍沃斯的牧师住所，也就是现在的勃朗特故居博物馆，已经成为每年吸引成千上万游客的圣地。

单词释义

cast 阵容	devoted 投入的	governess 女教师
precociousness 早熟	pilgrimage 漫游	

三姐妹的文学之路

The Brontes were a nineteenth-century literary family associated with the village of Haworth in the West Riding of Yorkshire, England. The sisters, Charlotte (born 21 April 1816), Emily (born 30 July 1818), and Anne (born 17 January 1820), are well known as poets and novelists. They originally published their poems and novels under *masculine pseudonyms*, following the custom of the times practised by female writers. Their stories immediately attracted attention, although not always the best, for their passion and originality. Charlotte's *Jane Eyre* was the first to know success, while Emily's *Wuthering Heights*, Anne's *The Tenant of Wildfell Hall* and other works were later to be accepted as masterpieces of literature.

The three sisters and their brother, Branwell, were very close and during childhood developed their *imaginations* through the *collaborative* writing of increasingly *complex* stories. The effect of the deaths of first their mother, and then of their two older sisters marked them *profoundly* and influenced their writing.

勃朗特家庭是19世纪英国约克郡西部的霍沃斯村的书香门第，三姐妹夏洛蒂(生于1816年4月21日)、艾米莉(生于1818年7月30日)和安妮(生于1820年1月17日)，是著名的诗人和小说家。最初，她们用自己的男性假名发表诗歌和小说，和同时代的女性作家一样。尽管也许不是最好的作品，但是她们的小说还是以题材新颖和感情真挚迅速地引起了人们的关注。夏洛蒂的《简·爱》最先取得成功，而艾米莉的《呼啸山庄》、安妮的《荒野庄园的房客》以及其他小说后来也成了公认的文学名著。

勃朗特三姐妹和弟弟布兰威尔在儿童时代就非常亲密，经常通过想象共同创作复杂的小说。母亲和两个姐姐的早逝，深深地影响了他们和他们的作品。

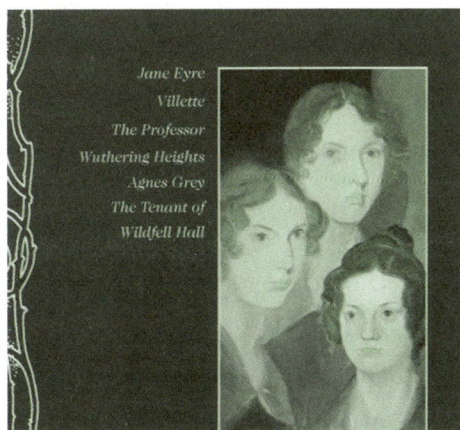

Jane Eyre
Villette
The Professor
Wuthering Heights
Agnes Grey
The Tenant of
Wildfell Hall

单词释义

masculine 男性　　　　pseudonym 笔名　　　　imagination 想象

collaborative 合作的　　complex 复杂　　　　　profoundly 深刻地

"品" 英国特色文化

特色表达One

　　勃朗特三姐妹最初以笔名写作时，应该没少受过crack the whip。这个短语的原意是"打响鞭"，据说最早源于19世纪移居美国的人们前往西部开拓新天地的时候。后来人们用它来形容"管教或者提出口头警告"。

实景链接

A: What did your son do during the summer vacation? 你的儿子在假期都干什么了？

B: Unless I **cracked the whip** he didn't do anything, even had meals these days. 他什么也不做，要是我不管教他的话，甚至连饭也不吃。

A: Well, you should **crack the whip**. 那你应该好好管教一下。

B: Yeah, or he was getting more and more out of hand. 嗯，要不然就会越来越不听话。

特色表达Two

　　每个文学作品中大概都有那么一个jerkwater town。jerk的意思是"仓促抽取"，那么jerkwater的字面就是"匆促取水"。这个俚语来自铁路用语，当时的铁路工作人员常在清冷的小镇装满火车水箱，一上完水就赶路，后来人们就用jerkwater town形容这种纯供水的偏远小镇。

实景链接

A: Did you even read Emily's Wuthering Heights? 你读过艾米莉的《呼啸山庄》吗？

B: Of course, I have read it. 当然读过。

A: Are there some **jerkwater towns** in this book? 这书里描写过偏远小镇吗？

B: I just can't recall it. 这个我还真记不清了。

拓展特色句

1. I remember this passage; it is taken from Wuthering Heights. 我记得这段话，摘录自《呼啸山庄》。

2. The author of *Jane Eyre* is Charlotte Bronte. 《简·爱》的作者是夏洛蒂·勃朗特。

3. The works of the Bronte sisters remain important to the modern literature. 勃朗特三姐妹的作品对现代文学仍然有着很重要的作用。

"聊" 英国特色文化

A: The Brontes was really a literary family.

B: Why did you say that?

A: The sisters, Charlotte, Emily and Anne, are all well known as poets and novelists.

B: I just know Charlotte, *Jane Eyre* is my favorite.

A: *Jane Eyre* was the first to know success, while Emily's *Wuthering Heights*, Anne's *The Tenant of Wildfell Hall* and other works were later to be accepted as masterpieces of literature.

B: I heard that Charlotte passed away very early.

A: All of the three sisters passed away early. It is said that their fame was due as much to their own tragic destinies as to their precociousness.

B: Where did they live?

A: The parsonage at Haworth in Yorkshire. Now the Bronte Parsonage Museum, has become a place of

A: 勃朗特家庭真是书香门第啊。

B: 为什么这么说?

A: 三姐妹夏洛蒂、艾米莉和安妮都是著名的诗人和小说家。

B: 我只知道夏洛蒂，她的《简·爱》是我最喜欢的。

A: 《简·爱》最先取得成功，而艾米莉的《呼啸山庄》、安妮的《荒野庄园的房客》以及其他小说后来也成了公认的文学名著。

B: 我听说夏洛蒂去世很早。

A: 三姐妹都很早就去世了。人们都说她们的成功，很大程度上源于自身悲剧命运带来的早熟。

B: 她们住在哪儿?

A: 在约克郡霍沃斯的牧师住所，也就是现在的勃朗特故居博物馆，已经成为每年吸引成千上万游客的圣地。

pilgrimage for hundreds of thousands
of visitors each year.

"问" 英国特色文化

夏洛蒂是如何写出《简·爱》这部书的?

《简·爱》是一部带有自传色彩的长篇小说，主要描述了主人公坚强不屈和不懈奋斗的精神，以及对人间自由幸福的渴望。夏洛蒂创作《简·爱》的时候，英国作为全球头号工业大国风头正劲。而英国妇女的地位依旧低下不受重视，她们必须从属或附庸于丈夫而生存，所以很多女子当时的生存目标就是要嫁给贵族，找一个长期饭票。而《简·爱》就是在这种社会形态下写成的。

阅读笔记

为文学奉献一生的简·奥斯汀

代表作《傲慢与偏见》

Pride and Prejudice is a novel of manners by Jane Austen, first published in 1813. The story follows the main character Elizabeth Bennet as she deals with issues of manners, *upbringing*, *morality*, education, and marriage in the society of the landed gentry of early 19th-century England. Elizabeth is the second of five daughters of a country gentleman living near the fictional town of Meryton in Hertfordshire, near London.

Though the story is set at the turn of the 19th century, it *retains* a *fascination* for modern readers, continuing near the top of lists of "most loved books" such as The Big Read. It has become one of the most popular novels in English literature and receives *considerable* attention from literary scholars. Modern interest in the book has resulted in a number of dramatic *adaptations* and an *abundance* of novels and stories *imitating* Austen's memorable characters or themes. To date, the book has sold some 20 million copies worldwide.

《傲慢与偏见》出版于1813年，是一部由简·奥斯汀创作的社会风俗小说。小说讲述了伊丽莎白·班纳特的爱情故事，反映了19世纪英国乡绅阶层的礼节、成长、教育、道德、婚姻的情态。伊丽莎白在五个姐妹中排行第二，是居住在伦敦附近的赫特福德郡麦里屯镇(虚构)的乡绅之女。

虽然小说的背景是18、19世纪之交，但是《傲慢与偏见》仍然吸引了大批现代读者，在类似于大阅读"最喜爱书籍"这类票选中持续名列前茅，已经成为英语文学中最受欢迎的小说之一，受到文学研究者的广泛关注。现在这部小说已经被改编为多部影视作品，并且小说中的人物或主题也被许多其他小说的借鉴。迄今为止，《傲慢与偏见》在全球已售出约2000万本。

单词释义

upbringing 养育	morality 道德	retain 保持
fascination 魅力	considerable 相当大的	adaptation 适应
abundance 充裕	imitate 模仿	

简·奥斯汀的一生

Jane Austen (16 December 1775—18 July 1817) was an English novelist whose works of romantic fiction, set among the landed *gentry*, earned her a place as one of the most widely read writers in English literature. Her realism, *biting* irony and social *commentary* have gained her historical importance among scholars and critics.

Austen lived her entire life as part of a *close-knit* family located on the lower *fringes* of the English landed gentry. She was educated primarily by her father and older brothers as well as through her own reading. The *steadfast* support of her family was critical to her development as a professional writer. Her artistic *apprenticeship* lasted from her teenage years into her thirties.

During this period, she experimented with various literary forms, including the *epistolary* novel which she then abandoned, and wrote and extensively revised three major novels and began a

简·奥斯汀(1775年12月16日—1817年7月18日)，英国小说家，她创作的关于乡绅的浪漫主义小说使她成为英国文学中读者最多的作家之一。同时其作品中的现实主义、辛辣讽刺和社会评论获得了学者和评论家历史性的赞誉。

奥斯汀一生都生活在英国等级较低的乡绅之家，家庭关系融洽和睦。她受到的教育主要来源于她父亲和哥哥，以及自己自学。家人给予她的坚定支持对她成为职业作家起到了至关重要的作用。她对文学的学习从十几岁一直持续到三十多岁。

在此期间，她尝试了各种文学形式，包括她后来放弃的书信体小说，创作和大量修改三部主要的小说，并准备创作第四部小说。从1811年到1816年，在陆续出版了《理智与情感》《傲慢与偏见》《曼斯菲尔德庄园》和《爱玛》后，作为已经有出版作品的作家，奥斯汀取得了成功。1818年，她死后出版社又出版了她的另外两部小说《诺桑觉寺》和《劝导》，第三部后来命名为《桑迪顿》，在她死前已经完成。

fourth. From 1811 until 1816, with the release of *Sense and Sensibility*, *Pride and Prejudice*, *Mansfield Park* and *Emma*, she achieved success as a published writer. She wrote two *additional* novels, *Northanger Abbey* and *Persuasion*, both published *posthumously* in 1818, and began a third, which was eventually titled *Sanditon*, but died before completing it.

Austen's works *critique* the novels of sensibility of the second half of the 18th century and are part of the transition to 19th-century realism. Her plots, though fundamentally comic, *highlight* the dependence of women on marriage to secure social standing and economic security.

奥斯丁的作品批评了从18世纪下半叶的情感小说，是向19世纪现实主义过渡的作品之一。她的小说情节安排，虽然从根本上看都具有喜剧特色，但突出地表现了女性依赖婚姻获得社会地位和经济安全的事实。

单词释义

gentry 绅士
close-knit 紧密的
apprenticeship 学徒期
posthumously 死后地

biting 辛辣的
fringe 边缘
epistolary 书信的
critique 批评

commentary 评论
steadfast 坚定的
additional 附加的
highlight 突出

英国特色文化

特色表达One

很多时候，作者在写作的时候经常会遇到dead end，也就是"死胡同"，这时就需要重新整理思路了。同时，dead end也可以指"路的尽头"。

⭐ 实景链接

A：Do you still write the book now? 你现在还写书吗？

B：No, because I'm at a **dead end**. 没有，最近我的思维陷入"死胡同"了。

A：You can do it slowly and pace yourself. 慢慢来，按着你自己的节奏走。

B：Well, it is just my own idea. 嗯，我也是这么想的。

💬 特色表达Two

每部小说中都有主人翁与陌生人，一般而言，主角们与陌生人的对话是比较people voice。这里的people voice可不是说"人的声音"，在俚语中，人们用它来表达"比较客气的说话声"。

⭐ 实景链接

A：Did you heard her voice? 你听过她的声音吗？

B：Wow! Her voice is so sweet. 她的声音很甜。

A：But, she just uses her **people voice** to talk with people. 但她只在与陌生人说话的时候才客气。

B：No! I do not believe it! 不会吧！我不信！

拓展特色句

1. Jane Austen completed six novels in her lifetime. 简·奥斯汀一生共创作6部小说。

2. Have you ever read Jane Austin's classic novel *Pride and Prejudice*? 你有没有读过简·奥斯汀的经典小说《傲慢与偏见》？

3. Keira Knightley starred in the film *Pride and Prejudice* which was produced by MGM. 凯拉·奈特莉曾在米高梅公司制作的《傲慢与偏见》电影中担任女主角。

"聊" 英国特色文化

A：Have you ever watches the movie *Pride and Prejudice*? It won the Oscar for best art direction in 1941.

B：Yes. It's and old movie. But compared with the movie I like the book better.

A：你看过电影《傲慢与偏见》吗？它荣获了1941年的奥斯卡最佳艺术指导奖。

B：看过。那是一部老电影。但是和电

A：I think it's a waste of time to read such a long story.

B：It's a good way to enjoy the words and imagine the scenes. To date, the book has sold some 20 million copies worldwide.

A：Is the author Jane Austen?

B：Yeah, an English novelist whose works of romantic fiction, set among the landed gentry, earned her a place as one of the most widely read writers in English literature.

A：Is there any other works to recommend me to read?

B：You can read *Sense and Sensibility*.

影相比我更喜欢看书。

A：我觉得读这么长的故事浪费时间。

B：这是一种欣赏文字，想象场景的好方法。迄今为止，《傲慢与偏见》在全球已售出约2000万本。

A：作者是简·奥斯汀吗？

B：是的，英国小说家，她创作的关于乡绅的浪漫主义小说使她成为英国文学中读者最多的作家之一。

A：有什么其他作品建议我阅读的吗？

B：你可以读读《理智与情感》。

"问" 英国特色文化

简·奥斯汀的影响力有多大？

简·奥斯汀创作小说时正值"哥特小说"风靡英国文坛。她的小说如同一股清流，生动地描写了英国乡村中产阶级的日常生活和田园风光。简·奥斯汀的作品强烈清扫了当时小说创作中的庸俗风气，在英国小说的发展史上有承上启下的意义，她因此被誉为地位"可与莎士比亚平起平坐"的作家。2013年是她的名著《傲慢与偏见》出版200周年，继英国皇家邮政专门发行邮票纪念之后，英国中央银行将她的头像印制在新版10英镑纸币上，以此纪念这位伟大的女作家。

现代喜剧电影的奠基者 ——卓别林

卓别林大师概况

Charles Spencer Chaplin was a British *comic* actor, filmmaker, and composer who rose to fame in the silent era. Chaplin became a worldwide icon through his screen *persona* "the Tramp" and is considered one of the most important figures of the film industry. His career *spanned* more than 75 years, from childhood in the Victorian era until a year before his death at age 88, and encompassed both adulation and controversy.

Chaplin wrote, directed, produced, edited, composed the music, and starred in most of his films. His films are characterised by *slapstick* combined with pathos, *typified* in the Tramp's struggles against *adversity*. Many contain social and political themes, as well as *autobiographical* elements. In 1972, as part of a renewed appreciation for his work, the Academy of Motion Picture Arts and Sciences gave Chaplin an Honorary Award for his outstanding contribution to the film industry. He continues to be held in high regard, with *The Gold Rush, City Lights, Modern Times,* and *The Great*

查理·斯宾塞·卓别林，英国喜剧演员、导演、作曲家，在默片时代闻名于世。通过对屏幕角色"流浪汉"的演绎，他成为全球偶像，被认为是电影行业最重要的人物之一。从维多利亚时代的童年开始直到88岁去世，他从业超过75年。卓别林饱受世人的崇拜，但同时也存在争议。

在他的大多数电影中，卓别林都亲自参与创作、导演、制片、剪辑和创作音乐，并饰演片中角色。他的电影以令人感伤的滑稽戏为特色，典型人物为在逆境中挣扎的流浪汉；其中许多包含社会和政治主题，同时也不乏自传因素。1972年，为再次感谢卓别林对电影行业做出的突出贡献，电影艺术与科学学院授予他荣誉奖。他一直备受赞誉，《淘金记》《城市之光》《摩登时代》和《大独裁者》也

Dictator often ranked among industry lists of the greatest films of all time.

总是在有史以来最伟大的电影中榜上有名。

单词释义

comic 连环漫画　　persona 人物角色　　span 跨度
slapstick 趣剧　　typify 作为……的典型　　adversity 逆境
autobiographical 自传的

卓别林大师装扮的故事

Charlie Chaplin's costume as "the Tramp'' is a bundle of *contradictions*: the jacket is *buttoned* too tightly, the trousers are too *baggy*, the *bowler* hat too small and the size 14 shoes much too big, as well as being worn on the wrong feet. These disparate elements combined to help *define* his screen personality and its place in the world, including his social *pretensions*. Chaplin designed the costume himself. It lasted on the screen, in numerous shorts and features, for 22 years.

There are several versions of how the Tramp costume came to be invented. One, put out by the Keystone Comedy Studio, where Chaplin worked from December 1913, was that he was passing the time one afternoon in the male dressing room—while waiting for the rain to stop—by trying on various articles belonging to other *contracted*

查理·卓别林的"流浪汉"服饰充满了矛盾的元素：夹克系得太紧，裤子太宽松，圆顶高帽太小，14码的鞋子太大而且穿错了脚。这些不同的元素结合起来有助于研究他的屏幕个性及世界地位，包括社会抱负。这些服饰都是卓别林亲自设计的，在各种专题片和短片中出现了22年。

关于流浪汉服饰的发明有几个版本的说法。启斯东电影公司的一个版本是，卓别林从1913年12月开始就在该公司工作，一天下午，他在男更衣室里等待雨停，打发时间时就试穿了其他喜剧演员的东西，"胖子"阿巴寇的裤子，明星演员福特·斯特林的鞋等。易粘胡须本来是饰演恶棍用的，他却把它剪下来做成牙刷。似乎都说得通。

他在自传中这样描述选择的过程：

"我希望一切都充满矛盾：宽松的裤子，绷紧的外套，偏小的帽子和偏大的鞋子……我添加了小胡子，我觉得，这会在不影响我表情的情况

comedians: Fatty Arbuckle's trousers, star performer Ford Sterling's shoes and so on. The stick-on moustache was intended for a villain, but he cut it down to the *dimensions* of a toothbrush. And it all seemed to work.

He described the selection process in his autobiography:

"I wanted everything to be a *contradiction*: the pants baggy, the coat tight, the hat small and the shoes large ... I added a small moustache, which, I reasoned, would add age without hiding my expression. I had no idea of the character. But the moment I was dressed, the clothes and the makeup made me feel the person he was. I began to know him, and by the time I walked on stage he was fully born."

下，使我显得更老。对于人物角色我还不清楚。但一装扮完毕，看到服饰和化妆我就知道了他是什么样的。我开始了解他，当我在台上表演的时候，他就真的诞生了。"

单词释义

contradiction 矛盾	buttoned 扣紧的	baggy 袋装的
bowler 圆顶礼帽	define 定义	pretension 自负
contracted 契约的	dimension 规格的	contradiction 矛盾

"品" 英国特色文化

特色表达One

若是每个学生都像查理·卓别林饰演的"流浪汉"一样，那老师可就麻烦了，很多老师还是喜欢teacher's pet。这个短语可不是指"教师的宠物"，而是说"老师喜爱的学生"。

实景链接

A: Lily is the **teacher's pet**. She always gets special treatment. 丽丽是老师很喜欢的学生，她总是受到特殊照顾。

B: I'm not surprised; they always give her good marks. 我并不惊讶，老师总是给她高分儿。

A: And she is a whiz at math. 而且她在数学方面很优秀。

B: Yeah, she is also beautiful. 是的，她还长得漂亮。

特色表达Two

伟大的喜剧大师查理·卓别林饰演的"流浪汉"形象在当时深入人心，作为黑白电视上的流浪汉，他有时无厘头搞笑，有时take a powder。take a powder可不是拿着香粉或炸药逃跑的意思，在俚语中它指"逃之夭夭"。

实景链接

A: Chaplin was at his best playing the little tramp. 卓别林扮演小流浪汉已达登峰造极的境界。

B: He usually played some practical jokes and **took a powder**. 他经常搞点恶作剧然后逃之夭夭。

A: Yeah, he was so funny. 是的，他太搞笑了。

B: He was, in fine, a great actor. 总而言之，他是一个伟大的演员。

拓展特色句

1. He always turned his toes out like Chaplin. 他经常像卓别林那样把脚尖向外撇。

2. Charlie Chaplin had created the great comic character of "The Tramp". 卓别林塑造了一个了不起的喜剧角色"流浪者"。

3. Modern Time by Chaplin is a silent film. 卓别林演的《摩登时代》是一部无声影片。

"聊"英国特色文化

A: This movie is really funny. By the way, what do you think is humor?

A: 这部电影真好笑。顺便问一句，你认为什么是幽默？

B：I think it's a kind of feeling. Different people have different definitions for it.

A：Sometimes it is the perfect solution for all the problems.

B：And sometimes it can be used to satirize.

A：Like Charles Spencer Chaplin?

B：Yes. He's really the most important movie star in the silent era.

A：His masterpiece should be *the Tramp*. Have you ever watched it?

B：Yes. I still remember that the jacket is buttoned too tightly, the trousers are too baggy, the bowler hat too small and the size 14 shoes much too big.

A：Haha... that's so interesting. No one can compare with him now.

B：I agree with you. It's hard to surpass.

B：我认为这是一种感觉。不同的人有不同的定义。

A：有时它是解决所有问题的方式。

B：而且有时还可以用幽默来讽刺。

A：就像查理·斯宾塞·卓别林?

B：是啊。他真是默片时代最重要的电影明星。

A：他的代表作要数《流浪汉》了。你看过吗?

B：看过。我仍然记得夹克系得太紧，裤子太宽松，圆顶高帽太小，14码的鞋子太大而且穿错了脚。

A：哈哈……太有趣了。现在没有人能和他比了。

B：我同意你的观点。很难超越了。

"问" 英国特色文化

卓别林为何能成功出演流浪汉?

卓别林最出色的角色非流浪汉莫属，而他之所以能出演这个角色离不开他的童年经历。1889年，卓别林出生于英国一个演艺家庭，从他很小的时候就开始与他的同母异父的哥哥雪尼·卓别林随他们的母亲生活。之后，他的母亲患病，他被反复送入一个收养孤儿的学校。7年后，他成了一名流浪儿。为了生存，他当过报童、玩具小贩、吹玻璃的小工人，甚至在游艺场扫过地。这些早年的贫困生活启发了他后来创造流浪汉的灵感，所以他能成功出演一个流浪汉。

人间天使
——奥黛丽·赫本

天使成名作——《罗马假日》

Roman Holiday is a 1953 romantic comedy directed and produced by William Wyler. It stars Gregory Peck as a reporter and Audrey Hepburn as a royal princess out to see Rome on her own. Hepburn won an Academy Award for Best Actress for her performance; the *screenplay* and costume design also won. Audrey played Princess Anne, weary of *protocol* and *anxious* to have some fun before she is *mummified* by "affairs of state." On a diplomatic visit to Rome, Anne escapes her royal retainers and *scampers incognito* through the Eternal City. She happens to meet American journalist Joe Bradley (Gregory Peck), who, recognizing a hot news story, pretends that he doesn't recognize her and offers to give her a guided tour of Rome. And just as naturally, Joe falls in love with her. Hepburn was the first actress to win an Oscar, a Golden Globe and a BAFTA Award for this single performance.

《罗马假日》是1953年由导演威廉·惠勒创作和执导的浪漫喜剧片，片中格里高利·派克饰演一个记者，奥黛丽·赫本饰演一位单独去罗马的皇家公主。赫本凭借出色的演出获得了奥斯卡最佳女演员奖，同时剧本和服装设计也赢得了奥斯卡奖。奥黛丽扮演的安妮公主讨厌复杂的礼仪，渴望在被"国事"累垮前出去找点乐子。于是在外交访问罗马的时候，安妮拜托了随从，隐瞒身份逃跑到达罗马城，碰巧遇到美国记者乔·布拉德雷(格里高利·派克饰)。乔立即看出这是一次热点新闻的机会，就假装没认出她，并乐意为她游玩罗马充当向导。不经意间，乔发现自己爱上了她。奥黛丽·赫本是第一个凭借一部电影就获得奥斯卡奖、金球奖和英国电影和电视学院奖的女演员。

单词释义

screenplay 剧本	protocol 协议	anxious 焦急的
mummify 成木乃伊	scamper 蹦跳	incognito 匿名者

赫本的辉煌一生

Audrey Hepburn (4 May 1929—20 January 1993) was a British actress and *humanitarian*. Recognised as both a film and fashion icon, Hepburn was active during Hollywood's Golden Age. She was ranked by the American Film Institute as the third greatest female screen legend in the history of American cinema and has been placed in the International Best Dressed List Hall of Fame. She is regarded by many to be the most naturally beautiful woman of all time.

After appearing in several British films and starring in the 1951 Broadway play Gigi, Hepburn played the Academy Award-winning lead role in *Roman Holiday*. Later performing in successful films like *Breakfast at Tiffany's, Charade, My Fair Lady*, Hepburn received Academy Award, Golden Globe and BAFTA nominations and accrued a Tony Award for her *theatrical* performance in the 1954 Broadway play *Ondine*.

She appeared in fewer films as her life went on, devoting much of her later life to UNICEF. Although contributing to the organization since 1954, she worked in some of the most profoundly *disadvantaged* communities of Africa, South America and Asia between 1988 and 1992.

奥黛丽·赫本（1929年5月4日—1993年1月20日），英国电影演员和慈善家。作为电影和时尚界的偶像，赫本一直活跃在好莱坞的黄金时代。她被美国电影学会选为百年来最伟大的女演员第3名，并成功入选国际最佳着装名人堂。许多人认为她是史上最自然美丽的女性之一。

在几部英国电影中露脸后，赫本在1951年的百老汇音乐剧中饰演女主角，其后在《罗马假日》中的表演使她获得了奥斯卡奖。后来陆续出演的成功电影有《蒂芙尼早餐》《谜中谜》《窈窕淑女》，赫本因此获得了奥斯卡奖、金球奖和英国电影和电视学院奖的提名，并凭借在1954年百老汇音乐剧《水中仙》中的表演赢得了托尼奖。

随着年龄的增长，赫本出演的电影越来越少，将更多晚年的精力投入到联合国儿童基金会中。从1954年开始她一直对该机构进行捐赠，在1988

She was awarded the Presidential Medal of Freedom in *recognition* of her work as a UNICEF Goodwill Ambassador in late 1992. A month later, Hepburn died of *appendiceal* cancer at her home in Switzerland in early 1993 at the age of 63.

年和1992年间，她甚至亲自奋战在非洲、南美洲和亚洲最不发达的地区。1992年年底，她被授予总统自由勋章，以表彰她在担任联合国儿童基金会亲善大使时所做的工作。1个月后，即1993年年初，赫本因阑尾癌死于瑞士的家中，享年63岁。

单词释义

humanitarian 人道主义者　　theatrical 戏剧性的　　disadvantaged 处于不利地位的

recognition 承认　　appendiceal 阑尾的

"品"英国特色文化

特色表达One

奥黛丽·赫本的画像是她的电影粉丝与收藏家哄抢的对象，很多人因beat us to the draw而深深遗憾不已。beat sb. to the draw可不是指把某人打倒再摁在树上，在俚语中，它的意思是"比某人抢先一步"。

实景链接

A: Audrey Hepburn is my goddess. I worship her. 奥黛丽·赫本是我的女神，我崇拜她。

B: I loved her in *Roman Holiday*, one of my favorite movies. 我爱《罗马假日》里的她，那是我最喜欢的电影之一。

A: Her painting is the jewel of my collection. 她的画是我所收藏的画中最珍贵的一幅。

B: I also wanted to buy her painting in her twenties, but another millionaire **beat me to the draw**. 我还想买她20岁时的肖像，不过另一个百万富翁捷足先登了。

特色表达Two

很多人深深迷恋奥黛丽·赫本精致的容貌，有的人甚至愿意整容成赫本的样子，如此的行为在很多人眼里都是 "whacked out"。这个短语的意思是 "疯掉了，疯疯癫癫的"，常用来形容某人疯狂不被认可的行为。

⭐ 实景链接

A： That girl is **whacked out**. 那女孩一定是疯掉了。

B： Why do you think so? 为什么呢？

A： She wants to have cosmetic surgery to fix her nose, so she may look like Audrey Hepburn. 她想去做整容手术来修正她的鼻子，这样她看起来就像奥黛丽·赫本。

B： She is haywire to think that. 她那样想真是疯了。

拓展特色句

1. The movie *Roman Holiday* made Hepburn a superstar. 电影《罗马假日》使赫本成为超级巨星。

2. Audrey played the role of a young princess in the Hollywood *film Roman Holiday.* 奥黛丽在好莱坞电影《罗马假日》中扮演了一个年轻的公主。

3. I have seen the film "My Fair Lady" twice. 电影《窈窕淑女》我已经看过2次了。

"聊" 英国特色文化

A： I'm choosing the clothes for the party. Do you have any advice?

B： Is there a theme? I don't know what kind of dress is suitable.

A： Everyone should wear like a movie star.

B： It's hard. Who do you want to play?

A： Of course Audrey Hepburn. Don't you know that I'm her super fan?

B： It's harder. Audrey Hepburn is such an elegant woman that no one can imitate her.

A： 我正在选派对穿的衣服。有什么建议吗？

B： 有主题吗？我不知道什么样的衣服合适。

A： 每个人都得穿得像一个电影明星。

B： 太难了。你想扮演谁啊？

A： 当然是奥黛丽·赫本啊。你不知道我是她的超级粉丝吗？

B： 那更难了。奥黛丽·赫本那么优雅，很难有人能模仿。

A： 我只想模仿她的穿着。就像《罗马

A： I just want to imitate her dressing. Like Princess Anne in *Roman Holiday*.

B： I think you'd better choose a white dress and high-heeled shoes.

A： Like this? There is something wrong with my waist.

B： Put on a belt. It would be better.

A： I should pay attention to my gesture.

假日》中的安妮公主一样。

B： 我觉得你最好选择白裙子和高跟鞋。

A： 像这样？我觉得腰有点问题。

B： 系个腰带吧。能好点。

A： 我得注意姿势。

"问" 英国特色文化

奥黛丽·赫本为什么被赞"人间的天使"？

奥黛丽·赫本的容貌清纯秀丽，五官深邃立体，她的身材小巧玲珑，她的气质高雅端庄。在很多人眼中，她是优雅与时尚集于一身的完美女性，她是上帝最完美的杰作，是坠入凡间的精灵。加上她热衷表演，演技精湛，她的影片受到很多人的追捧。作为一名演员，她有艺德，还时时关注儿童奉献爱心，她频频走访非洲关怀受困受难的非洲儿童，被人们赞为"人间的天使"。

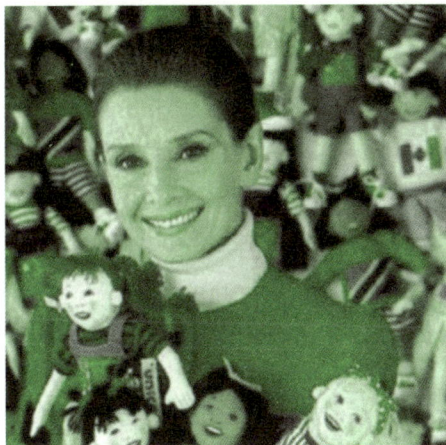

阅读笔记

足球王子——贝克汉姆

小贝的足球生涯

David Robert Joseph Beckham, OBE (born 2 May 1975) is an English former footballer. He was the first English player to win *league* titles in four countries. He announced his intention to retire at the end of the 2012–2013 Ligue 1 season on 16 May 2013 and, on 18 May 2013, played his final game of his storied 20-year career.

In international football, Beckham made his England debut on 1 September 1996, at the age of 21. He was captain for six years during which he played 58 times. Beckham has twice been runner-up for FIFA World Player of the Year, and in 2004 he was named as one of the Top 125 greatest living footballers as part of FIFA's 100th anniversary *celebration*. In 2004 he was the world's highest-paid footballer when taking into account salary and advertising deals. He has been married to Victoria Beckham since 1999, and they have four children.

大卫·罗伯特·约瑟夫·贝克汉姆 (生于1975年5月2日)，退役英格兰足球运动员，第一个在四个国家都获得联赛冠军的英国球员。2013年5月16日，在法甲联赛2012—2013赛季结束后，他宣布退役；2013年5月18日，他踢完了最后一场比赛，结束了20年富有传奇色彩的职业生涯。

1996年9月1日，贝克汉姆首次代表英格兰的国际足球比赛中出战，那年他21岁。在担任队长的6年间，他参加了58次国际大赛。贝克汉姆曾2次获得世界足球先生亚军，在2004年的国际足联100周年庆祝活动中，他被选为125位足球巨星之一。2004年，他是世界上收入最高的足球运动员，包括工资和广告代言费在内。1999年，他与维多利亚·贝克汉姆结婚，现在已有4个孩子。

单词释义

league 联盟

celebration 庆祝

小贝的时尚生涯

Beckham's fame extends beyond the *pitch*; in much of the world his name is "as instantly *recognisable* as that of *multinational* companies like Coca-Cola and IBM." Beckham's relationship and marriage to Victoria, who has been famous in her own right as part of the musical group Spice Girls, contributed to David's celebrity beyond football. So *gilded* has been the career of Beckham that Victoria revealed her nickname for her husband to be "Golden Balls".

Beckham became known as a fashion icon, and together with Victoria, the couple became *lucrative* spokespeople sought after by clothing designers, health and fitness specialists, fashion magazines, perfume and cosmetics manufacturers, hair stylists, exercise promoters, and spa and recreation companies. One recent example is a new line of *aftershave* and *fragrance*s called David Beckham Instinct. In 2002 Beckham was hailed as the ultimate "metrosexual" by the man who invented the term and has been described as such by numerous other articles since. In the world of fashion, David has already appeared on the covers of many magazines.

贝克汉姆的名声也体现在球场外。在世界上许多地方，他的名字"就像可口可乐和IBM这样的跨国公司一样，很容易就能被人认出来。"维多利亚是辣妹组合的成员，她在自己的圈子里很有名气；她与贝克汉姆的关系和婚姻更是帮助后者将名声扩大到足球以外。贝克汉姆的职业生涯无疑是镀金的，也难怪维多利亚透露她给丈夫起的昵称是"黄金球"。

贝克汉姆是有名的时尚偶像，与维多利亚一起，夫妇两人成为服装设计者、健康和健身专家、时尚杂志、香水和化妆品制造商、发型师、比赛举办人、按摩理疗公司追逐的投入不菲的代言人。最近的一个例子是，一个新款的须后水和香水名字叫做"贝克汉姆本能男士香水"。2002年，贝克汉姆被誉为终极"都市美男"，并在以后的许多文章中也获得了这样的美称。在时尚界，贝克汉姆已经出现在许多杂志的封面上。

单词释义

pitch 球场
gild 镀金
fragrance 香味

recognizable 可辨认的
lucrative 有利可图的

multinational 跨国公司的
aftershave 修脸润肤露

"品"英国特色文化

特色表达One

在英国，很多小孩子都以小贝为目标努力练习踢球，教导他们的老师会告诉他们"keep your eyes peeled."这里可不是说削掉你的眼睛，在英国口语中常指"睁大眼睛，仔细观察"。

☆ 实景链接

A：Dad took us to the museum last Friday. 上星期五爸爸带我们去博物馆。

B：Was it fun? 好玩吗？

A：Yeah, and my dad told us **keep our eyes peeled**. 好玩，父亲还要求我们仔细观看。

B：I'll go with you next time. 我下次跟你一起去。

特色表达Two

英国人尤其喜欢现场观看足球比赛，他们是如何表达比赛双方的结果呢？很多英国人常用kill这个词，因为kill除了表示"杀死"以外，还可引申指"赢了、超过某人某队"。

☆ 实景链接

A：Will you play football with us? 和我们一起去踢球，好吗？

B：OK. Let's go and ball. 好啊！走吧！

A：Let's call David. We will go together. 叫上大卫，我们一起去。

B：I also love playing football with David, because I want to **kill** him every time. 我也喜欢和大卫踢足球，因为每次都能赢他。

拓展特色句

1. Victoria got married to famous soccer player David Beckham. 维多利亚嫁给了著名足球明星大卫·贝克汉姆。

2. Of course my favorite soccer player is Beckham. 我最喜欢的足球队员当然是贝克汉姆了。

3. David Beckham is the idol of many youngsters. 大卫·贝克汉姆是很多年轻人崇拜的偶像。

"聊" 英国特色文化

A：Victoria hit the headlines again.

B：What a different woman!

A：I admire that she has such a handsome husband.

B：They are a legendary couple.

A：Yes. Beckham has twice been runner-up for FIFA World Player of the Year, he was born for football.

B：And Victoria is not a halfpenny the worse. She has been famous in her own right as part of the musical group Spice Girls.

A：It's the association between strong enterprises.

B：How can she be so thin? You know that she's the mother of four children.

A：She also has a good taste of dressing. She helps Beckham choose the proper suit every time he attends public accessions.

B：No wonder that Beckham is so crazy about her.

A：维多利亚又上头条了。

B：真是一个与众不同的女人啊。

A：真羡慕她有个这么帅的老公。

B：他们真是传奇的一对。

A：是啊。贝克汉姆曾2次获得世界足球先生亚军，他是为足球而生的。

B：维多利亚也毫不逊色。她是辣妹组合的成员，在自己的圈子里很有名气。

A：这叫强强联合。

B：她怎么能这么瘦呢？要知道，她可是4个孩子的妈妈啊。

A：她也很有品味。每次贝克汉姆出席公开场合她都帮他选择合适的衣服。

B：难怪贝克汉姆对她这么痴迷呢。

"问" 英国特色文化

小贝为什么如此让球迷痴迷?

大卫·贝克汉姆,凭借其英俊的外表和精湛的球技曾被媒体评为英国最帅球员。早在1999年时,小贝获得由英国足球杂志《世界足球》评选的世界最佳球员、世界足球先生、欧洲金球奖、欧洲最佳球员。他曾效力于曼联、皇马、AC米兰等豪门俱乐部,当时风靡世界足球界,在全球各地都有极高的影响力与知名度,人称"万人迷"。如今,小贝退役,陪着妻子,带着几个儿子和七公主过着幸福的家庭生活,但仍是很多球迷心中最帅的7号战将。

阅读笔记

唱出心碎的阿黛尔

阿黛尔的音乐成就

Adele Laurie Blue Adkins (born 5 May 1988), is an English singer, songwriter, musician, and multi-instrumentalist. Adele was offered a recording contract from XL Recordings after a friend posted her demo on Myspace in 2006. The next year she received the Brit Awards "Critics' Choice" award and won the BBC *Sound of 2008*. Her *debut* album, 19, was released in 2008 to much *commercial* and *critical* success. It *certified* four times *platinum* in the UK, and double platinum in the US. Her career in the US was boosted by a *Saturday Night Live* appearance in late 2008.

At the 2009 Grammy Awards, Adele received the awards for Best New Artist and Best Female Pop Vocal Performance. In 2011 and 2012, Billboard named Adele Artist of the Year. In 2012, Adele was listed at number five on VH1's 100 Greatest Women in Music, and the American magazine *Time* named Adele one of the most *influential* people in the world. In 2013, she received an Academy Award as well as the Golden Globe Award for Best Original Song for her song "Skyfall".

阿黛尔·劳丽·布鲁·阿德金斯（生于1988年5月5日），英国歌手、歌曲作家、音乐人及多重乐器演奏者。2006年，阿黛尔的朋友把她的音乐小样上传到Myspace后，阿黛尔获得XL唱片公司的唱片合约。翌年她得到全英音乐奖的"乐评人选择奖"，及BBC的《2008年度之声》的大奖。她的首张专辑《19》于2008年发行，取得了巨大的商业成功和评论家的好评，唱片于英国得到4次白金唱片及在美国得到双白金的成绩。阿黛尔在2008年末参与了《周末夜演唱》的演出，这个节目让更多人认识她，有助推动她的事业于美国发展。

在2009年的美国第51届格莱美奖，她夺得格莱美最佳新人及最佳流行女歌手奖。2011及2012年，阿黛尔被"公告牌排行榜"命名为年度艺人。2012年，阿黛尔跻身"VH1乐坛最伟大的女性"中，排名第五，并且美国杂志《时代周刊》命名她为"世界上最有影响力的人"之一。2013年，她凭借电影《007之天幕杀机》主题曲获得奥斯卡奖和金球奖"最佳原创歌曲奖"。

单词释义

debut 初次登台	commercial 商业广告	critical 关键的
certify 证明	platinum 白金唱片	influential 有影响的

阿黛尔的个人生活

It was reported in January 2012 that Adele was dating *charity* entrepreneur and Old Etonian Simon Konecki. In June 2012, Adele announced that she and Konecki were expecting a baby. Adele gave birth to the couple's son, Angelo, on 19 October 2012. The child is the first for Adele and the second for Konecki, who also has a daughter with his ex-wife.

Adele has been criticized by *celebrities* such as Karl Lagerfeld and Joan Rivers for her weight, but has gained the support of many others, including Lady Gaga, by stating that she is happy with her weight and would only change if it affected her health or sex life. Adele is also strongly opposed to the *sexualized* music industry and has made reference to *stunts* performed by Katy Perry, Lady Gaga, and Madonna.

Politically, Adele is a supporter of the Labour Party, despite in May 2011 having reportedly expressed views on *taxation* counter to those of the party. In April 2013, it was reported Adele had a £30 million

据2012年1月的报道，阿黛尔在和慈善企业家、老伊顿人西蒙·科内基约会。2012年6月，阿黛尔宣布，她和科内基很快要有一个宝宝了。2012年10月19日，阿黛尔产下了他们的儿子安吉洛。这是阿黛尔的第一个孩子，科内基的第二个孩子；科内基和前妻育有一女。

阿黛尔因体重问题受到名人如卡尔·拉格斐和琼·里弗斯的批评；但她声称，她对自己的体重很满意，只有当体重影响到健康或性生活的时候才会考虑减肥，此举也获得其他名人如嘎嘎小姐的支持。阿黛尔也强烈反对带有性内容的音乐产业，并特别提及了凯蒂·佩里、嘎嘎小姐和麦当娜的演出。

政治上，阿黛尔是工党的支持者，尽管2011年5月有报道显示，她表达了对工党税收政策的反对。2013年4

fortune, £10 million of it made in the previous 12 months. In June 2013, Adele was awarded an MBE in the Queen's Birthday Honours list.

月，据报道，阿黛尔有3000万英镑的财富，其中1000万是在之前的12个月里挣得的。2013年6月，阿黛尔入围女王寿辰授勋名单，并被授予帝国勋章。

单词释义

charity 慈善

celebrity 名人

sexualized 使有性特征的

stunt 噱头

taxation 征税

"品" 英国特色文化

特色表达One

阿黛尔在英国的盛名不逊于嘎嘎小姐，但也有人认为阿黛尔音乐平平而且 no great shakes。no great shakes这个短语的字面意思就是"没有太大的动摇"，在俚语中，常用它来表示"好不出色，相当平庸"。

☆ 实景链接

A：Do you know Adele? 你知道阿黛尔吗？

B：You mean the English singer? 你说的是那个英国歌手吗？

A：Yes, does her music appeal to you? 是的，你喜欢她的音乐吗？

B：Well, I like. Although some people say it was **no great shakes**. 嗯，我喜欢，虽然有些人说她的音乐毫不出色。

特色表达Two

如今，阿黛尔能功成名就，甚至斩获6项格莱美大奖，与她个人拥有an eagle eye是离不开的。an eagle eye的字面意思是"一双鹰眼"，而鹰眼一般都是很锐利的，所以人们用这个短语来形容"某人的目光很敏锐"。

☆ 实景链接

A：Adele is a great singer. 阿黛尔是个伟大的歌手。

B：Yeah, her music and performances always have breakthrough and improvements. 是的，她的音乐和表演总会有突破和进步。

A: And she is someone with **an eagle eye** watches things closely and carefully. 而且她目光敏锐，能仔细观察事物。

B: I believe she is and her musical talent is quite exceptional. 我想也是，所以她的音乐才能出类拔萃。

拓展特色句

1. I've been listening to Adele a lot recently. 我最近听了很多阿黛尔的音乐。

2. *Rolling In The Deep* was the debut single from Adele's second album. 《爱恨交织》是阿黛尔第二张专辑中的首张单曲。

3. Adele is one of the greatest soul singers in Britain. 阿黛尔是英国最伟大的灵魂歌手之一。

"聊" 英国特色文化

A: I had a good time this afternoon.

B: I can judge it from your face. What did you do?

A: I listened to the music and read my favorite magazine. It's a good way to take a break.

B: What kind of music do you like best?

A: I usually listen to soft music. It can make me relax. What about you?

B: I like pop music better. It makes me feel young.

A: There are so many singers. Who is your favorite?

B: Adele.

A: The American singer?

B: No, she's an English singer, songwriter, musician, and multi-instrumentalist.

A: 今天下午我过得很开心。

B: 从你的脸上就能看出来。你干什么了？

A: 我听音乐，看最喜欢的杂志。这是一种很好的放松的方式。

B: 你最喜欢哪种音乐？

A: 我经常听轻音乐。它可以使我放松。你呢？

B: 我更喜欢流行音乐。它让我觉得自己年轻。

A: 那么多歌手你最喜欢哪个？

B: 阿黛尔。

A: 那个美国歌手？

B: 不是，她是一名英国歌手、歌曲作家、音乐人及多重乐器演奏者。

"问" 英国特色文化

阿黛尔是一位怎样的歌手？

阿黛尔因其出色的音色与创意才能被誉为实力派歌手，她曾赢得6项格莱美大奖，她的音乐是英国灵魂歌曲的代表，也是一个完全独特的存在。很多业界人士都觉得阿黛尔充满的魔力，她做出的音乐无与伦比，比如美国著名女歌手碧昂丝·诺利斯认为阿黛尔对她的一些音乐也有积极的影响；喷火战机乐队的主唱戴夫·格罗尔认为阿黛尔的专辑《21》"具有空前的影响力，是一盘难得的好专辑，它值得拥有一切它得到的赞美"。总之，阿黛尔是个值得尊敬的优秀歌手。

阅读笔记

Part 9

英国人生活面面观

在英国，一日三餐在于"晨"

英式早餐

A full breakfast is the traditional breakfast in Britain and Ireland. It is regarded as a *staple* of traditional British and Irish *cuisine*. The term full comes from the fact the breakfast is, well, full of different food stuffs. It is also popular in British-influenced countries including the United States, Australia, New Zealand, Canada and South Africa. It is sometimes referred to as an English breakfast or a "full English breakfast".

Breakfast may begin with orange juice, *cereals*, *stewed* or fresh fruits but the heart of the Full breakfast is bacon and eggs. They are variously *accompanied* by *sausages*, *grilled* tomato, mushrooms, tea, toast and marmalade. Each country in the UK and Ireland also have their own choice of accompaniments, it is up to the individual just how much they want on their plate and their preferences.

英式早餐是英国和爱尔兰的传统早餐，是传统英国和爱尔兰菜的主食。这个词语完全来源于这样的事实，即早餐是由不同的菜肴食品组成的。英式早餐在受英联邦影响的国家也很流行，包括美国、澳大利亚、新西兰、加拿大和南非。它有时被称为英式早餐或"全英式早餐"。

早餐可以以橙汁、麦片、烩制或新鲜水果开始，但英式早餐的核心是熏肉和鸡蛋，同时搭配食物有香肠、烤番茄、蘑菇、茶、烤面包和果酱。英国和爱尔兰各自有自己的搭配食物，取决于个人的食量和偏好。

单词释义

staple 主要产品	cuisine 烹饪	cereal 谷类
stewed 焦虑不安的	accompanied 陪伴	sausage 香肠
grilled 烤的		

健康食早餐

US researchers asked men to complete *questionnaires* about what they ate and when they ate it, then tracked their health for 16 years. Those who said skipping breakfast may lead to one or more risk factors, including *obesity*, high blood pressure, high cholesterol and diabetes, which may in turn lead to a heart attack over time. And at a conference in 2012, UK scientists presented a study that explained why people who skip breakfast tend to find high calorie food more appealing later in the day: their brain *circuits* may be primed toward seeking it when fasting.

So the next time you rush out the door in the morning without something to eat, consider this: a healthy a.m. meal can give you energy, satisfy your *appetite*, and set the stage for smart decisions all day long. Researcher advises to *incorporate* many types of healthy foods into your breakfast, as this is an easy way to ensure your meal provides *adequate* energy and a healthy balance of *nutrient*s, such as protein, *carbohydrates*, vitamins and minerals. Adding nuts and chopped fruit to cereal is great way to start the day. If eating a bowl of cereal,

美国研究人员让一些人完成有关吃什么和什么时候吃的调查问卷，并用了16年的时间跟踪了这些人的健康情况。那些说不吃早餐的人可能会有一个或多个风险因素，包括肥胖、高血压、高胆固醇和糖尿病，随着时间的推移可能会导致心脏病发作。在2012年的一次会议上，英国科学家提出了一项研究，解释了为什么不吃早餐的人往往会在一天当中的某个时间段觉得高热量食物更有吸引力：在禁食时，他们的大脑回路可能会更加倾向于寻找高热量食物。

所以，下次你早上没有吃东西就匆忙出门时，想想看：健康早餐可以提供能量，满足食欲，为全天明智的决定创造条件。研究人员建议早餐最好包含多种类型的健康食物，这样就能够用简单的办法来确保早餐中含有足够的能量和健康平衡的营养，如蛋白质、碳水化合物、维生素和矿物质。在谷物中添加坚果和切碎的水果是开始一天的很好的方法。如果吃过

| try adding nuts and chopped fruit, or steel-cut *oatmeal*. | 一碗麦片，不妨再试试坚果和切碎的水果，或刀切燕麦。 |

questionnaire 问卷   obesity 肥胖   circuit 巡回

appetite 食欲   incorporate 包含   adequate 充足的

nutrient 营养物   carbohydrate 碳水化合物   oatmeal 燕麦粥

"品" 英国特色文化

特色表达One

若是发短信请朋友去吃英式早餐，对方却支支吾吾地敲了几个"Yeah"，你会不会很崩溃？这位朋友就是俚语中所指的text-killer，它的意思是"叫人无言以对的发短信人"，就是说这位朋友让你郁闷到无话可说。

☆ 实景链接

A：Would you like breakfast now? 你想要现在吃早餐吗？

B：No, I've got work to do. 不行啊，我还有事。

A：Haha, ok. 哈哈，好吧。

B：I don't know the way to use a **text-killer**... 我不知道该如何回复了……

特色表达Two

马上就要到早点时间了，你期待已久的全麦汉堡已飘荡在脑海里，可你的小伙伴却磨磨蹭蹭还没刷完牙，这时你就得shake a leg。这个短语可不是让你给他一脚，而是让你"催催他"。

☆ 实景链接

A：I am extremely hungry, can you hurry? 我太饿了，你能快点吗？

B：Take it easy. We still have ten minutes before the breakfast begins. 着什么急呀，早饭还有10分钟才开始呢。

A：Please **shake a leg**! 你就快点吧。

B：Wait one more minute. I'm almost ready! 再等我1分钟，我马上就好啦!

拓展特色句

1. I usually skip breakfast in the morning. 我早上通常不吃早餐。

2. No having breakfast will make you weak. 不吃早餐你会没精神的。

3. I can't take my time when I am having breakfast. 我没时间慢慢吃早餐。

"聊" 英国特色文化

A: Breakfast is the most important dinner. What do you usually have for breakfast?

B: It's up to my mood.

A: How about having a traditional British breakfast today?

B: What does a traditional British breakfast mean?

A: A British breakfast is the traditional breakfast in Britain and Ireland.

B: Who else eats British breakfast? Just people in Britain and Ireland?

A: It is popular in British-influenced countries including the United States, Australia, New Zealand, Canada and South Africa.

B: So many countries? What does British breakfast include?

A: The heart of the Full breakfast is bacon and eggs. They are variously accompanied by sausages, grilled tomato, mushrooms, tea, toast and marmalade.

B: It seems healthy.

A: 早餐是最重要的。你早餐通常吃什么？

B: 这取决于我的心情。

A: 今天来顿传统的英式早餐怎么样？

B: 传统的英式早餐是什么？

A: 英式早餐就是英国和爱尔兰的传统早餐。

B: 还有谁吃英式早餐？只有英国和爱尔兰吗？

A: 英式早餐在受英联邦影响的国家都很流行，包括美国、澳大利亚、新西兰、加拿大和南非。

B: 这么多？英式早餐包括什么？

A: 全套英式早餐的核心是熏肉和鸡蛋，同时搭配食物为香肠、烤番茄、蘑菇、茶、烤面包和果酱。

B: 似乎很健康。

"问" 英国特色文化

英国人还在吃传统早餐吗?

以前的英国人认为传统的英式早餐是他们的骄傲，是世界上最棒的早餐之一。但是，随着健康饮食的普及，英国人渐渐不再以英式早餐为自豪。与法式早餐相比，英国人意识到英式早餐所含的热量太高，因为早餐里含有许多油煎食品，比如熏肉和肉肠，而长期吃这种早餐将会导致高血压等疾病。因此，英式早餐在英国家庭中已经不再像以前那样受欢迎。

阅读笔记

精致的英式下午茶

下午茶的起源

Afternoon tea is the most *quintessential* English customs. However, drinking tea is a relatively new tradition which was popularized in England during the 1660s. It was not until the mid-19th century that the concept of "afternoon tea" first appeared. Afternoon tea was introduced in England by the seventh *Duchess* of Bedford Anna in 1840. At that time, the dinner was served late at 8 o'clock in the evening. It was a long period between lunch and dinner and the Duchess felt hungry around 4 o'clock in the afternoon. So she asked the maid to bring her tea and *pastries* to her room in the late afternoon. This became a habit of hers and she also invited her friends to join the tea party. The afternoon tea became fashionable in English society and in the 1880s, British upper-class started to enjoy the afternoon tea with friends between 4 and 5 o'clock.

英国习俗最精髓的部分就是下午茶。然而，喝茶是17世纪60年代才在英国流行开来的，是个相对较新的传统。直到19世纪中叶，"下午茶"这个概念才首次出现。1840年，下午茶由第七任贝德福德公爵夫人安娜引进到英国。当时，晚餐设在晚上8点。因此午餐和晚餐之间时间间隔比较长，公爵夫人在下午4点左右就饿了。于是她吩咐女仆临近傍晚时将茶和点心送到她的房间。这逐渐成为了她的一个习惯，而且她还邀请了朋友参加她的茶会。下午茶在英语国家逐渐流行起来。到19世纪80年代，英国上层社会的人也开始在下午4点到5点之间与好友一起享受下午茶。

单词释义

quintessential 精髓的，精粹的　　　　Duchess 公爵夫人　　　　pastry 面粉糕点

去伦敦品下午茶

Traditional afternoon tea consists of a selection of *dainty* sandwiches, scones served with *clotted* cream. Cakes and pastries are also served. Tea grown in India or Ceylon is poured from silver tea pots into delicate bone china cups. Nowadays however, in the average suburban home, afternoon tea is likely to be just a biscuit or small cake and a mug of tea, usually produced using a teabag.

To experience the best of the afternoon tea tradition, *indulge* yourself with a trip to one of London's finest hotels or visit a *quaint* tearoom in the west country. The Devonshire Cream Tea is famous world wide and consists of scones, strawberry jam and the vital ingredient, Devon clotted cream, as well as cups of hot sweet tea served in china teacups. Many of the other counties in England's west country also *claim* the best cream teas: Dorset, Cornwall and Somerset. There are a wide selection of hotels in London offering the quintessential afternoon tea experience. Hotels offering traditional afternoon tea include Claridges, the Dorchester, the Ritz and the Savoy, as well as Harrods and Fortnum and Mason.

传统的下午茶包括精选三明治、英式奶油松饼，还有蛋糕和其他甜点。选用印度或锡兰出产的茶叶放入银质茶壶内泡茶，再将茶水倒在精致的骨瓷茶杯中饮用。但是如今，普通的郊区人家喝下午茶的时候，可能只有一块饼干或一小块蛋糕，外加一大杯茶，而且通常喝的都是袋泡茶。

如果想体验最棒的下午茶传统，就放纵自己1次，去伦敦最豪华的酒店享受一番吧，或者去西南部各郡的古雅茶室也能体验到。德文郡的奶油茶点是世界闻名的，茶点包括司康饼、草莓果酱，还有至关重要的配料，德文郡的奶油块，还有几杯陶瓷茶杯盛装的热甜茶。英格兰西南部的其他许多郡县也称他们有着最好的奶油茶点：比如多塞特郡、康沃尔郡，还有萨默塞特郡。伦敦有很多可供选择的酒店能为你提供精致的下午茶体验。提供传统式下午茶的酒店有克拉瑞芝、多切斯特、丽兹酒店、沙威酒店，还有哈罗兹酒店、福特纳姆和梅森酒店。

单词释义

dainty 美味的　　　　clotted 成块状的　　　　indulge oneself 放纵自己

quaint 古雅的　　　　claim 声称

"品" 英国特色文化

特色表达One

　　每一天都是一个新的开始，若是精神状况不好，一整天mondaze可是会浪费了美好的一天，赶紧来点下午茶振作起来吧！mondaze这个词在俚语里的意思是某个人处在"恍惚的状态"。

☆ 实景链接

A：Lily, good heavens, what's come over you? 天哪，莉莉，你怎么了？

B：I got chewed out by the boss, because I was in a total **mondaze**. 因为一天恍惚，所以被老板骂了。

A：Well, let's go over for afternoon tea. It's on me. 好了，我们去那儿喝下午茶吧，我请客。

B：OK. I want to relax. 好，我正好也想放松一下。

特色表达Two

　　下午茶被誉为英国人的传承文化，但你若对某些工作狂说享受一下下午茶，放松一下吧，他可能会告诉你"You wastin my minutes." 我们知道waste是浪费的意思，wastin是wasting的口语用法，这句话的意思是"你在浪费我的时间。"

☆ 实景链接

A：Don't you go outside and do things in the sun? 你不想出去走走，晒晒太阳吗？

B：I haven't time. I'm too busy. 我没空，我太忙了。

A：How about having some tea with me? 那和我一起去喝下午茶怎么样啊？

B：Come on, **you wastin my minutes**. 算了吧，你这是在浪费我的时间。

拓展特色句

1. Drinking afternoon tea is a british tradition. 喝下午茶是英国人的一项传统习惯。

2. My guidebook recommends afternoon tea at the Ritz. 我的导游书推荐去丽兹酒店喝下午茶。

3. Do you know how comes the afternoon tea? 你知道下午茶的由来吗?

"聊" 英国特色文化

A: I'm exhausted after so much work. How about having afternoon tea with me?

B: No problem.

A: Do you know English afternoon tea?

B: Not very well. I want to listen respectfully.

A: Well, let me tell you something. Afternoon tea is the most quintessential English customs.

B: When did they begin this custom?

A: Drinking tea was popularized in England during the 1660s. It was not until the mid-19th century that the concept of "afternoon tea" first appeared.

B: What do they have for afternoon tea?

A: Traditional afternoon tea consists of a selection of dainty sandwiches, scones served with clotted cream.

B: How about today?

A: Nowadays afternoon tea is likely to be just a biscuit or small cake and a mug of tea, usually produced using a teabag.

A: 干了这么多工作真是累死了。去喝杯下午茶怎么样?

B: 没问题。

A: 你了解英式下午茶吗?

B: 不是很了解。我愿意洗耳恭听。

A: 好吧，我来给你讲讲。英国习俗的最精髓的部分就是下午茶。

B: 他们什么时候开始这项传统的?

A: 喝茶是17世纪60年代才在英国流行开来的。直到19世纪中叶，"下午茶"这个概念才首次出现。

B: 下午茶他们吃些什么呢?

A: 传统的下午茶包括精选三明治、英式奶油松饼，还有蛋糕和其他甜点。

B: 那现在呢?

A: 如今，下午茶可能只有一块饼干或一小块蛋糕，外加一大杯茶，而且通常喝的都是袋泡茶。

"问" 英国特色文化

英国下午茶有几部分?

英国的下午茶通常有三部分,首先是亲朋好友或自娱自乐享用美味点心,通常是享用三层塔的点心,会有一些三明治、草莓塔、泡芙、英式松饼等。其次就是品赏精致的茶器,早期维多利亚下午茶华丽独特又清新自然,好的茶品、瓷器、音乐、甚至好心情是英式下午茶必备的环节。最后就是重中之重的品茶,一般是大吉岭与伯爵茶、锡兰茶等几种,有时会配置甜美的玫瑰花茶或奶茶。

阅读笔记

不可不提的 fish and chips

炸鱼薯条的历史

Fish and chips is a hot meal of English origin. It consists of *battered* fish, commonly Atlantic cod or haddock, and deep-fried chips. A common side dish is *mushy* peas.

Fish and chips became a stock meal among the working classes in the United Kingdom as a consequence of the rapid development of *trawl* fishing in the North Sea, and the development of railways which connected the *ports* to major industrial cities during the second half of the 19th century, which meant that fresh fish could be rapidly transported to the heavily populated areas. Deep-fried fish was first introduced into Britain during the 17th century by Jewish *refugees* from Portugal and Spain, and is derived from pescado frito. In 1860, the first fish and chip shop was opened in London by Joseph Malin.

炸鱼和薯条起源于英国的热饭，包括炸鱼块（以大西洋鳕鱼或黑线鳕最为常见）和油炸薯片，常见的配菜是豌豆糊。

随着拖网渔业在北海的快速发展和在19世纪下半叶连接港口到主要工业城市的铁路的发展，新鲜的鱼可以迅速运至人口密集地区，鱼和薯条成为英国工人阶级常见的食物。油炸鱼源于酥炸鱼，在17世纪由葡萄牙和西班牙的犹太难民首次引入英国。1860年，约瑟夫·马林在伦敦开了第一家炸鱼薯条店。

单词释义

battered 磨损的　　　　mushy 糊状的　　　　trawl 拖网
port 港口　　　　　　　refugee 难民

英国人是快餐控

More than half of all meals eaten out in Britain are from fast food restaurants, alarming figures reveal. Burgers, fried chicken, pizzas, *kebabs* and take-out curry account for 50.4 per cent of meals bought outside the home.

The fast food *boom* may worry health experts who will see it as likely to fuel the national obesity *epidemic* across all age groups. The growth comes from all sections of society, including families, pupils skipping school meals and workers who do not have access to a workplace canteen. Low prices, with burgers available for as little as 99p each, are a particular appeal in the current economic climate. At the same time, fast food chains such as McDonald's and smaller rivals including GBK and Byron Burger have made a major effort to appeal to middle-class families. Families are opting to go to fast food chains like this McDonalds Restaurant, in Oldbury, West Midlands, instead of sit down "full service" eateries.

令人担忧的数据显示，在英国，吃饭超过一半在快餐店进行；汉堡、炸鸡、比萨、烤肉串和外卖咖喱占外买食物的50.4%。

快餐业的急速发展使专家担心，这可能会导致全国各个年龄段肥胖症的流行。数据的增长来自于社会各个阶层，包括家庭、不吃学校食物的学生和没有工作食堂的工人。价格低廉，例如汉堡每个99便士，在当前经济环境下极具独特的吸引力。同时，快餐连锁店如麦当劳和规模较小的竞争对手GBK和拜伦汉堡已做出巨大努力，去吸引中产阶级的家庭。他们都愿意选择去这样的快餐连锁店，如西米德兰兹郡奥尔德伯里的麦当劳餐厅，而不是去"全套服务"餐馆里坐下来吃饭。

单词释义

kebab 烤肉串	boom 繁荣	epidemic 传染病

"品" 英国特色文化

特色表达One

如今英国人开始注意营养均衡，不再一味追求快餐的速度，他们开始cold feet快餐是否影响身体健康。这里的cold feet意为"担心，退缩，发慌"，常用在口语中，表示有的人一开始对一件事情很有信心和把握，可关键时刻就怯场了。

☆ 实景链接

A：Smith started a fast food chain. 史密斯开了一家快餐连锁店。

B：Now many people likes fast food. 现在很多人都喜欢吃快餐。

A：Yeah, the fast food is tasty to eat. 是啊，而且快餐尝起来不错。

B：But I had **cold feet**, because I fear that may make me fat. 但我不敢吃，害怕自己会变胖。

特色表达Two

英国人是实实在在的快餐控，有的人甚至一边开车一边吃快餐，开车的人还乐在其中，但若是intexticated，那就别尝试了，这是很危险的行为。intexticated指的是"一边开车一边发短信"。

☆ 实景链接

A：I heard that Ben got in a car accident. 我听说本出车祸了。

B：He is always eating as he drove. 他总是一边开车，一边吃东西。

A：But this time he was **intexticated**. 但是这次他是一边开车，一边发短信。

B：He usually drives carelessly like this. 他开车总是那么不小心。

拓展特色句

1. What do you want on your sandwich? 你的三明治上想加点什么？

2. I'll have one cheese pizza, please. 请给我来个芝士比萨。

3. For here or to go? 在这儿吃还是带走？

"聊" 英国特色文化

A: It's lunch time. Let's stop working and have lunch. What do you have for lunch?

B: I usually choose fast food. I just have half an hour and don't have enough time to wait.

A: There are lots of people just like you. It is invested that more than half of all meals eaten out in Britain are from fast food restaurants.

B: Yeah, but I have no choice.

A: Don't you worry about your health?

B: I do know it's bad for my health and I'm getting fatter and fatter.

A: It's time for you to slow down and enjoy some real food. How about tonight? Let's go to some real restaurant and forget about your rubbish food.

B: That's a good idea. I will wait for you at the gate.

A: 该吃午饭了。我们停下手里的工作去吃饭吧。你午饭吃什么？

B: 我通常吃快餐。我只有半个小时的时间，所以没时间等。

A: 有许多人像你一样。调查显示，在英国，超过一半的人在快餐店吃饭。

B: 是啊，但是我也没办法。

A: 你不担心自己的健康吗？

B: 我知道这的确会伤害我的身体，而且我变得越来越胖。

A: 你该放慢节奏好好享受一顿真正的食物了。今晚怎么样？我们去一家真正的餐馆，忘记你的垃圾食品吧。

B: 好主意。我在门口等你。

"问" 英国特色文化

英国人爱快餐，那法国人呢？

有调查表示，将近一半的英国人选择快餐，因为他们太喜欢快餐的滋味了，要是让他们放弃快餐，简直是要了他们的命。然而，隔海相望的法国人却难以认同这一点，法国人崇尚精致美食，他们讲究食材，讲究烹饪技巧，讲究进食的情调环境。调查显示，81%的法国人拒绝快餐，因为快餐含有太多的热量，而很多法国人认为苗条的身材是法国浪漫文化的一部分，也是一种骄傲。

英国人排队变得易抓狂

排队曾是英国特色风景

The English are famous for being very polite. They have this passion for queuing and appear to *outsiders* to have endless patience—as you would expect from a nation that can endure a five-day cricket match. The British queue everywhere for everything, including football tickets, buses, fast food, post offices, government offices, cafeterias, doctors' and dentists' waiting rooms, supermarkets, banks, *payphones* and so on. Queuing isn't always a *necessity*, but simply a *herd instinct* that *compels* people to *huddle together*. So join the back of the queue! If there is any confusion about whether there is one queue or more for several different cashiers, you should still wait your turn and stay behind everyone who arrived before you. English people do not try to get to the front first; they are very fair.

英国人是以礼貌闻名的。他们喜欢排队，喜欢向外来者展现出非常有耐心的样子——比如你能想象英国能忍受长达5天的板球比赛吗。英国人做什么事情都会排队，包括买足球票，乘坐公交车，买快餐食品，去邮局寄信，到政府机关办事，去自助餐厅就餐，等待医生或牙医就诊，超市买东西，银行办业务，打付费电话等。有

些情况是不用排队的，就是英国人的一种从众心理，让他们都聚在一起排队。所以，去队尾排队吧！就算你不知道出纳员前面是不是有一队，或者几个不同的出纳员前面有好几队，你都应该排队等着，站在比你先到的人的后面。英国人是不会设法到最前面去的，他们是很公平的。

单词释义

outsider 外来者
herd instinct 群体心理

payphone 付费电话
compel 迫使

necessity 必要
huddle together 聚在一起

越来越不满排队了

A nation *renowned* for the art of queuing may be losing its patience, a survey has shown, with the average British adult able to stand in line for only 10 minutes and 42 seconds before *tempers* start to fray. The most *loathed* lines were in supermarkets, followed by the Post Office and airport check-in and security. Older *respondents* over 55 became *restless* in a queue nearly three minutes before younger people but those aged under 35 were more likely to take their frustration out on those around them. Two thirds of respondents said "faffing", or dawdling, by those in front of them was the thing they hated most.

Most Brits would rather avoid queues entirely, with eight in 10 adults instead choosing to pay their bills online, according to the survey by the Payments Council, the body for setting payment strategy in Britain. The online poll of 2,006 adults found that one in five people do their shopping at night to avoid the lines. "Our research shows that more of us are waking up to the fact that you can skip the queue altogether, saving time and money, by using 'queue *dodging tactics*' like

一项调查显示，向来以喜欢排队著称的英国人可能正在失去耐性：英国成人平均能忍受的排队时间仅为10分42秒，超过这个时间，他们的脾气就变得暴躁起来。英国人最讨厌排队的地方是超市，其次是邮局和在机场办理登机手续及安检。55岁以上的被调查者在排队时，比年轻一些的人要早3分钟失去耐性。但是35岁以下的人更容易把情绪发泄到周围的人身上。2/3的被调查者称他们最讨厌的事情就是前面的人磨蹭或拖拉。

根据英国付款委员会开展的这项调查，大多数英国人会尽量避免排队，80%的成人会选择在网上付费。该委员会负责英国付款政策的制定。这项涵盖了2006名成年人的在线调查发现，1/5的人在夜间购物，以避免排队。该委员会的一位女发言人说，"调查表明，我们当中越来越多的人正在意识到一个事实，也就是我们其

internet shopping, online banking and paying bills *electronically*," said a council spokeswoman.

实可以通过像网上购物、网上银行和电子支付等使用'排队逃避策略'，避免排队，节省时间和金钱。"

单词释义

renowned 有声望的
respondent 回应者
tactic 战略

temper 脾气
restless 焦躁不安的
electronically 电子地

loathe 厌恶
dodge 躲避

"品"英国特色文化

特色表达One

若前往英国留学，可得遵守英国社会的Dos And Don'ts，比如排队。Dos And Don'ts的意思是"该做的事情与不该做的事情"，还可以指"行为准则，注意事项"。

实景链接

A：It's difficult to travel to new countries. 去一个陌生的国家旅行是一件很累的事。

B：Why do you think so? 为什么你那样认为？

A：It takes a while to learn all their cultural **dos and don'ts**. 要花好多时间了解他们的风俗习惯。

B：That's the way it must be. 但那是必须要做的。

特色表达Two

在国内过马路时，常常是凑够一拨人就走，心里想着这么多人，反正司机不敢动。若去了英国可得lick the habit。lick一般指"舔"，但lick the habit可不是"舔习惯"，在俚语中，人们用它形容"克服坏习惯"。

实景链接

A：Don't jump the queue, or other people will not be pleased. 别插队，否则别人会不高兴的。

B: I am in a great hurry. 我很着急。

A: This is not the reason for you to jump the queue. 这可不是你插队的理由。

B: Ok, I'll **lick the habit**. 好吧，我会改的。

拓展特色句

1. They queued to get into the cinema. 他们排队等候进入电影院。

2. He queues patiently at the bus stop everyday. 他每天都耐心地在公共汽车站排队。

3. They all complied with the public order to queue up. 他们都很遵守社会秩序去排队了。

"聊" 英国特色文化

A: There is a man trying to jump the queue over there.

B: Someone should stop him. It's not fair. We have waited for such a long time.

A: No one likes to wait but we should obey the rules and be polite.

B: Yes. You know what even the most polite English men don't like queuing.

A: Really?

B: Yes. A survey has shown that the average British adult is able to stand in line for only 10 minutes and 42 seconds before tempers start to fray.

A: That sounds interesting. It will lose a lot of time to stand in line.

B: So, nowadays, most Brits would rather avoid queues entirely. About 90% of them are choosing to pay their bills online.

A: 那儿有一个人想插队。

B: 应该有人制止他。这不公平。我们都等了这么长时间了。

A: 没人喜欢等待，但是我们得遵守规则并且表现出礼貌。

B: 是啊。即使是最有礼貌的英国人都不喜欢排队。

A: 是吗？

B: 对啊。一项调查显示，英国成人平均能忍受的排队时间仅为10分42秒，超过这个时间，他们的脾气就变得暴躁起来。

A: 听起来挺有意思。排队会浪费很多时间的。

B: 所以，现在，多数英国人会尽量避免排队。80%的成人会选择在网上付费。

"问" 英国特色文化

为什么英国人爱排队?

在英国,排队似乎是绅士行为。其实,英国人之所以养成爱排队这种社会秩序,主要还是一种传统和大环境使然。无论什么学历、背景,在这种氛围下,都会自觉遵守已有的规则。如果插队,即使没人特意指责你,众人的眼神也会令你心慌慌。英国这种大环境是各种因素的交织下应运而生的,比如教育、道德约束,还有历史的沉淀。可以说,排队和遵守规则,已经成为英国人的与生俱来的生活习惯。

阅读笔记

英国男人的骑士精神

骑士精神的起源

Chivalry, or the *chivalric* code, is the traditional code of conduct associated with the *medieval* institution of knighthood. Chivalry arose from an *idealized* German custom. It was originally *conceived* of as an *aristocratic* warrior code. Over time its meaning has been refined to emphasise more ideals such as the knightly *virtue*s of honour, courtly love, *courtesy*, and less *martial* aspects of the tradition.

Knights vowed to be loyal, generous, and "of noble bearing". Knights were required to tell the truth at all times and always respect the honour of women. Knights not only vowed to protect the weak but also *vowed* to guard the honor of all fellow knights. They always had to obey those who were placed in *authority* and were never allowed to refuse a challenge from an equal. Knights lived by honor and for glory. Knights were to fear God and maintain His Church. Knights always kept their faith and never turned their back on a foe. Knights despised *pecuniary* reward. They persevered to the end in any enterprise begun.

骑士精神，或骑士准则，是与中世纪的骑士制度相关的传统行为准则。骑士精神源自理想化的德国风俗，原本被看作是贵族战士的行为准则。随着时间的推移，它的意义已经细化为强调更多的理想，如骑士的美德荣誉感、宫廷式恋爱、讲礼貌以及减少传统的武力应用。

骑士要宣誓忠诚，慷慨和"举止高贵"；要一直说实话，并总是尊重妇女的荣誉；要发誓保护弱者，维护所有骑士的荣誉；必须服从权威，不得拒绝公平的挑战。骑士靠荣誉而活，为荣耀而战；敬畏上帝，维护教会；保持信仰，从不拒绝帮助敌人；鄙视金钱奖励；对任何坚持的事业从一而终。

单词释义

chivalric 骑士的   medieval 中世纪的   idealized 理想化的

conceive 构思   aristocratic 贵族   virtue 美德

courtesy 礼貌   martial 军事的   vow 发誓

authority 主权   pecuniary 金钱

与时俱进的现代骑士精神

Historically, chivalry was seen as an integral, and *indispensable*, feature of the British "gentleman". Throughout history and literature, *flawless* manners and polite *masculinity* were the defining characteristics of the British gent. Today, however, men face the tricky challenge of adapting traditional gestures to fit in with modern Britain's more relaxed ways. Chivalry may be the *courteous* behaviour of a man towards a woman, but when is it out-dated and patronising, and when is it appropriate and well-mannered? New Chivalry is all about the natural *gesture*, striking a balance between treating a woman like a lady, but respecting her independence.

Men holding doors open for women is still a chivalrous gesture, even in our less-gallant times. If, however, a woman arrives at the door first and starts to open it, a man shouldn't awkwardly rush in front of her with grand *exclamations*

从历史上看，骑士精神被视为英国"绅士"不可或缺或必不可少的特征。纵观历史和文学，有着完美礼仪和礼貌的男子气概是英国绅士的显著特点。然而，今天的男性面临的棘手挑战是调整传统的姿态以适应现代英国更放松的生活方式。骑士精神可能是男人对女人的礼貌行为，但是当它显得过时和需要屈尊的时候还需要这样吗，什么时候才是适宜的，才算有礼貌的？新骑士精神是强调自然的姿态，在尊重女性和尊重她的独立之间找到平衡点。

男人帮女人开门仍然是骑士的姿态，即使是在很少讲骑士精神的现代社会。然而，如果女人走到门前准备开门，那么男人就不该笨拙地冲到她面前，大声喊道"我来开门！"从传统上看，男人走在路边是礼貌的行为。但是，如果女人不经意间走到路边，并未觉得不自在，男人再试图避开她，走在路边就显得太笨拙了。女人第一次进入房间时男人应该站起来迎接她。然而，每次女人去洗手间，去找东西喝，诸如此类，男人就没有

of "I'll get that!." Traditionally, it was considered polite for a man to walk on the *kerbside* of the street. If, however, a woman naturally falls in step on the kerbside and seems comfortable with it, then it would be clumsy for him to start *dodging* around her to try and walk on the outside. A man should stand up to greet a woman when she enters the room for the first time. There is no need, however, for him to be like a jack-in-the-box every time she goes to the loo, goes to get a drink and so on.

必要像盒子里的玩偶一样，随时准备蹦出来。

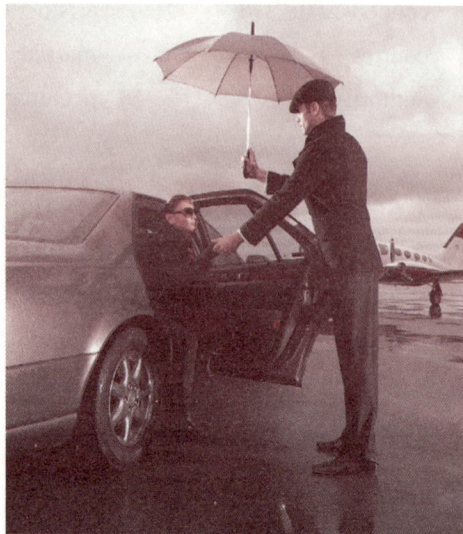

单词释义

indispensable 不可缺少的

courteous 谦卑的

kerbside 街边

flawless 完美的

gesture 姿态

dodging 避开

masculinity 男性

exclamation 欢呼

"品" 英国特色文化

特色表达One

在英国，骑士精神很重要的一点就是尊重女性。崇尚骑士精神的男士会关心照顾女士，他们认为女士call dibs on一些事情，他们更有义务帮助她们。call dibs在英国俚语中指的是"有权利要求做某事"。

☆ 实景链接

A: It's said that the legend of King Arthur represents the apotheosis of chivalry. 据说，亚瑟王的传说代表骑士精神的顶峰。

B: Yeah, and many people drunk on their own chivalry, some even thought the ladies could **call dibs on** them. 是的，而且很多人沉醉于自己的骑士精神，有的人甚至认为女士们可以使唤他们。

A: Oh, is it true? 哦，真的吗？

B: Yeah, but it may be exaggerated. 是啊，但是可能有些夸张的成分。

特色表达Two

骑士精神很重要的一点内涵就是乐于助人，他们乐意pitch in。这个短语在俚语中的意思是"一起来帮忙，做出贡献"。

☆ 实景链接

A: Bob, if you **pitches in**, we'll soon get the job done. 鲍勃，如果你加入的话，我们就能很快完成了。

B: But, I feel very sluggish. 但是，我一点也不想动。

A: Well, you are chivalrous! 拜托，你不是有骑士精神的人嘛！

B: Please wait just a few minutes. 请多等几分钟。

拓展特色句

1. Don't say chivalry is dead, ladies. 女士们，请不要说骑士精神消失了。

2. A knight would fight for his lady under such a circumstance. 在这种情况下，一位骑士会为他心爱的女人而战。

3. I was kinda impressed by his chivalry. 我有点被他的骑士精神所感动。

"聊" 英国特色文化

A: Our new boss is really a gentleman. I almost fall in love with him.

B: He comes from Britain, right?

A: How do you know?

B: It's the characteristic of British men. Have you heard of chivalry?

A: Yes. Because of that British men are so gentle.

B: It's a way for them to show politeness respect. For instance, each time a woman stands up they should stand

A: 我们的新老板真是一个绅士。我几乎要爱上他了。

B: 他是不是来自英国？

A: 你怎么知道的？

B: 这是英国男人的特点。听说过骑士精神吗？

A: 听说过。正是因为那样英国男人才这么温文尔雅。

B: 这是他们表达礼貌和尊重的方式。比如每次一个女人起身时他们都要站起来。

up.

A： If my boyfriend can be so gentle I will marry him.

B： Except he is a gentleman, you must think about some other factors, such as his character.

A： OK. I will.

A： 如果我的男朋友这么绅士，我就嫁给他。

B： 除了绅士外，也还有一些其他的因素要考虑，比如性格。

A： 好的。我会的。

"问" 英国特色文化

如今的英国还热衷于骑士精神吗？

英国历史悠久，文化底蕴深厚，其骑士精神是英国文化的重要象征。据调查显示，如今很多英国人依然热衷于骑士精神，他们认为男士应该继承并且将这种精神发扬下去。比如说男人要主动帮女士拿包或提行李箱；在火车或者汽车上男士应主动把座位让给女士，即使是年轻且没有怀孕的女性。另外，在英国，骑士精神也体现出一种尊重女士的绅士风度。

阅读笔记

英国帽子文化

帽子礼仪的起源

When a gentleman "dons" his hat to leave or "*doffs*" his hat to a lady, his actions are being described by two British *colloquialisms* that come from contractions of the phrases "do on" meaning "to do", and the Middle English "doffen", which became "don off" meaning "to do off"! Hats are tipped, (or doffed) slightly lifting the hat off your forehead, when meeting a lady (remove your hat if you stop to talk), or to "say" to anyone, male or female – thank you, excuse me, hello, goodbye, you're welcome or how do you do.

Tipping of the hat is a *conventional gesture* of politeness. This hat tipping custom has the same origin as military saluting, which came from the raising of *medieval* Knights face visors to show *friendliness*. Hats are worn less now, but at the turn of the 20th century, all adults wore hats whenever they left the house. It was a matter of good personal *hygiene*, since hats were a protection from industrial dirt.

当一位绅士戴上(dons)帽子离开，或向一位女士脱(doffs)帽，他的行为可以用两句英国口语形容来说明："dons"是"do on"的缩写，意思是要去做，"doffs"是中古英语"doffen"的缩写，意思是去做完。见到女士时，稍稍举帽，(或)将帽轻微脱离前额(如果没有讲话就要摘去帽)，或向任何男性或女性"说"谢谢你、对不起、嗨、再见、欢迎你或你好。

稍稍举帽是传统的表达礼貌的姿态，这个风俗和军人敬礼一样来自中世纪，骑士将护面提高，以表示友好。现在很少人戴帽了，但在19、20世纪之交，无论何时离开屋子，所有的成年人都戴帽。这表示绅士讲究良好的个人卫生，因为帽可以隐藏个人的污垢。

单词释义

doff 脱(衣、帽)　　　colloquialism 白话　　　conventional 符合习俗的

gesture 姿态　　　　　medieval 中世纪的　　　friendliness 友好

hygiene 卫生

帽子礼仪

Hats are *compulsory* at a *diminishing* number of British social occasions. Women should wear a hat to Royal Ascot race meetings; hats are traditional, but by no means compulsory, at British weddings, and a matter of personal choice for *christenings* or *funerals*. It is *notoriously* difficult to socially kiss while wearing a wide-brimmed hat. There is a knack to tilting the head at a suitable angle, but two ladies both in wide *brimmed* hats should avoid such an 'intimate' greeting. Nowadays in Britain, gentlemen rarely wear hats except for morning dress, when grey felt top hats are de rigueur. They should be worn on the front of the head or carried under the arm, but should not be worn indoors or in the formal photographs.

For the Royal Enclosure at Royal Ascot, however, they are *obligatory* and must be worn at all times. It's also important to perfect 'doffing' a top hat - raising it above the head to greet guests with real panache.

在人数较少的英国社交场合，戴帽是必须的。女人去皇家爱斯科赛马会应戴帽；帽子是传统装饰，但在英国婚礼上不是必须的，在洗礼和葬礼上取决于个人的选择。戴宽边帽社交性地亲吻是很不方便的。诀窍就是将帽倾斜一定的角度，但两位戴宽边帽的女士应该尽量避免这种"亲密"的问候。如今在英国，男士很少戴帽子，除非穿常礼服时，灰色毡制大礼帽是必不可少的。这时帽子应戴在前额，或携在臂下，但在室内或正式照片中不要戴帽子。

然而，在皇家爱斯科赛马会的围场内，必须时时戴帽子。同样重要的

Baseball caps are, first and *foremost*, a "youth" fashion. They should only be worn with extremely casual clothes, or for sport. They should never be worn back to front.

是，神气十足地与客人打招呼时，最好"脱"帽——将帽子轻轻提高至头顶。棒球帽，一种"年轻的"时尚，它们只能与便服搭配，或在运动时才戴。但是他们从不把棒球帽反过来戴。

单词释义

compulsory 义务的
funeral 葬礼
obligatory 必须的

diminish 减少
notoriously 臭名昭著地
foremost 最重要的

christening 洗礼
brimmed 满到边际的

"品" 英国特色文化

特色表达One

很多人都疑问，英国人遵守所谓的"帽子礼仪"不累吗？其实有些人还是会觉得knock them up。这里的knock someone up可不是说"使某人怀孕"，在英国口语中，它常指"累坏了"。

实景链接

A: Why are you always busy at work? You need to have a rest. 你为什么一直工作啊？你需要休息一会儿了。

B: I have much work to do. 我还有很多工作要做。

A: But nothing is more important than your health. 但是没有什么比你的身体健康更重要。

B: Yeah, it really **knocks me up**. I'll rest when the current rush is over. 是，这份工作真把我累垮了。忙完这段时间后我会休息的。

特色表达Two

每当提到英国人，很多人的第一反应就是"绅士"。在生活中英国人确实是绅士，即使你问他们不喜欢回答的问题，他们也少有直接拒绝，而是先说"That's a good question."这句话的意思是"这是个好问题。"通常用在不知如何回答时，用来拖延时间。

343

☆ 实景链接

A：Can I ask you a question? 我能问你个问题吗？

B：Sure. 当然可以。

A：What did you talk to Sam when we had the meeting yesterday? 昨天我们开会的时候你和山姆说了什么？

B：Well, **that's a good question**... 呃，这是个好问题……

拓展特色句

1. Why do the British like to wear hats? 为什么英国人那么喜欢戴帽子？

2. That gentleman raised his cap in token of respect to us. 那位绅士举帽向我们表示敬意。

3. Kate wore a black Top-hat on her head. 凯特的头上戴着一顶黑色的高顶礼帽。

"聊" 英国特色文化

A：Recently I watched some British movies. I find that they usually wear a hat. Why do British people like hats so much?

B：It must due to their culture. Sometimes they use hats to say hello, sometimes to show politeness, sometimes to decorate.

A：A hat can play such an important role. What kind of occasions should they wear a hat?

B：Hats are traditional, but by no means compulsory, at British weddings, and a matter of personal choice for christenings or funerals.

A：How does a woman wear a hat?

B：They always tilt the head at a suitable angle.

A：最近我看了一些英国电影。我发现他们经常戴帽子。为什么英国人这么喜欢帽子？

B：这是因为他们的文化。有时他们用帽子打招呼，有时表示礼貌，有时用来装饰。

A：帽子扮演这么重要的角色。什么样的场合要戴帽子呢？

B：帽子是传统装饰，但在英国婚礼上不是必须的，在洗礼和葬礼上取决于个人的选择。

A：那女人们怎么戴帽子呢？

B：她们总是将帽倾斜一定的角度。

A：What about the baseball cap? Do they like wearing?

B：Of course. They should only be worn with extremely casual clothes, or for sport.

A：I got it.

A：那棒球帽呢？他们喜欢戴吗？

B：当然，但是它们只能与便服搭配，或在运动时才戴。

A：哦，了解了。

"问" 英国特色文化

英国人有多爱戴帽子？

在英国的大街小巷，经常能看到戴着帽子的人，有爱美的靓妹，有时髦的男青年，有刻板的老学究，甚至学生的校服也包含帽子。据说哈罗公学有传统规定，在这里上学的贵族子弟上学时需要人人戴一顶硬草帽。在伦敦的各大商场里，卖帽子的柜台也是生意兴隆，这里有各种各样的帽子，罩着轻纱的，插着羽毛的，就像演出道具一样。帽子已深入英国人生活的方方面面，英国人参加婚礼、葬礼、生日聚会，甚至包括听歌剧、听演讲和看划船比赛，都要戴帽子。

阅读笔记

英式婚姻文化

威廉王子与凯特王妃的童话婚礼

Prince William and Kate Middleton met in 2001. Their *engagement* on 20 October 2010 was announced on 16 November 2010. The build-up to the wedding and the occasion itself attracted much media attention. The occasion was a public holiday in the United Kingdom and featured many *ceremonial* aspects, including use of the state *carriages* and roles for the Foot Guards and Household Cavalry.

Events were held around the Commonwealth to mark the wedding; organisations and hotels held events across Canada, over 5,000 street parties were held throughout the United Kingdom, and one million people *lined* the route between Westminster Abbey and Buckingham Palace. The ceremony was viewed live by tens of millions more around the world, including 72 million on the YouTube Royal Channel. In the United Kingdom, television audiences *peaked* at 26.3 million viewers, with a total of 36.7 million watching part of the *coverage*.

威廉王子和凯特·米德尔顿相识于2001年。他们于2010年11月16日对外宣布他们已于10月20日举办订婚仪式。婚礼的筹备及婚礼本身吸引了媒体的广泛关注。婚礼当天也成了英国的公共假日，整个仪式极具礼仪特色，包括贵宾车的使用以及近卫步兵和骑兵护卫。

英联邦国家都举行活动来庆祝这场婚礼。加拿大的各机构和酒店组织了庆祝活动；英国举行了超过5000场街头派对，还有100万人列队聚集在威斯敏斯特大教堂和白金汉宫之间的路上。世界各地成千上万的人们观看了这场婚礼仪式的直播，其中有7200万人是通过YouTube皇家频道收看的。在英国，有2630万名观众收看了电视直播，且一共有3670万收看了部分报道。

单词释义

engagement 婚约	ceremonial 一时的	carriage 运输
line 排成一行	peak 达到最高点	coverage 覆盖

英式婚礼小迷信

There are some interesting *superstitions* in the U.K. that are still believed to this day.

1. A bride should wear white, and so should her bridesmaids

Queen Victoria popularized the white wedding dress when she wed in 1840. Before, brides just wore their best dress for the ceremony. In the U.S., women are told never to wear white out of respect to the bride and to not *detract* attention from her on her big day, but the tradition is different in the U.K. An old superstition advises bridesmaids and *groomsmen* to dress similarly to the bride and groom to *ward off* evil spirits.

2. Spiders aren't scary

If you find one in your wedding dress it is said to be good luck! Bad luck would be encountering a *funeral* on your way to the wedding.

3. Invite a *chimney* sweep

Their *attendance* at a wedding is also considered good luck! Apparently King George III was riding his horse in a royal *procession* when a dog bit the horse's legs and made the king completely lose control of his ride. A man rushed out to help and then disappeared into the crowd. When the king later went back to

如今，英国仍然有人相信一些有趣的迷信。

1. 新娘要穿白色，伴娘也要穿白色

1840年，维多利亚女王在结婚时穿着了白色的婚纱，带来了白色婚纱的潮流。在此之前，新娘会直接穿着她们最好的衣服来参加典礼。在美国，出于对新娘的尊重和避免在大喜之日抢走她的风头，女性被告知不要穿白色衣服，但英国的风俗不是这样。古老的迷信要求伴娘和伴郎的着装要与新娘新郎相同，以达到辟邪的目的。

2. 蜘蛛不可怕

如果在婚纱上发现了蜘蛛，据说你要交好运了！但在参加婚礼的路上碰到葬礼是不吉利的。

3. 邀请烟囱清洁工

烟囱清洁工来参加婚礼也被认为是可以带来好运的！据说，国王乔治三世在骑马巡游时，一条狗咬伤了马腿，于是国王完全失去对马的控制。

thank the man for saving his life, all he found out was that he was a chimney sweep.

这时一个人冲上来帮忙，然后迅速消失在人群中。国王后来感谢他的救命恩人时发现，这个人是一名烟囱清洁工。

单词释义

superstition 迷信　　detract 贬低　　groomsmen 男傧相

ward off 避开　　funeral 葬礼　　chimney 烟囱

attendance 出席　　procession 进程

"品"英国特色文化

特色表达One

在婚礼上，男方回忆他的新娘不但是最好的伴侣，还是个懂得他的知心朋友，于是会这样形容：She is my ace. 这句话是说新娘是纸牌里的"A"吗？其实，在俚语中，ace可以指"知心的朋友"。

实景链接

A: Look, Jack saluted his new wife with a gentle kiss. 看，杰克用温柔一吻赞赏了他的新娘。

B: Jack is a wonderful guy and he loves his wife. 杰克是个好男人，他爱他的妻子。

A: I agree. Do you know something about his wife? 我同意。你了解他的新娘吗？

B: I heard that she is his **ace**. 我听说她是他的知己。

特色表达Two

虽然女朋友总是walk all over him，但其实这也是一种爱的方式，因此他们仍然办了一场浪漫的婚礼。这里的walk all over sb.可不是说从某人身边走过，在俚语里，它的意思是"任意欺负某人"的意思，可以说，这是野蛮女友常有的表现。

☆ **实景链接**

A：Do you know Bert's girlfriend always **walk all over him**? 你知道吗，伯特的女朋友总是欺负他？

B：Bert is so nice to his girlfriend. 伯特对他的女朋友太好了。

A：But his girlfriend was still dissatisfied with him. 但是她的女朋友仍然对他不满意。

B：I think quarrels of lovers are a kind of renewal of love. 我想，情侣间的争吵对爱情来说是一种新生。

拓展特色句

1. All the wedding invitations have been sent out. 所有的结婚请帖都发出去了。

2. The two young lovers decide to marry in secret. 这对年轻的恋人决定秘密结婚。

3. The couple always holds a celebration on their wedding anniversary. 这对夫妇每年都要庆祝结婚纪念日。

"聊" 英国特色文化

A：Hey, Helen, long time no see. What are you busy with?

B：I'm preparing for the wedding. I'm scrambling now.

A：Congratulations! What can I do for you?

B：You are so sweet. I called you out to look for a wedding dress with me.

A：No problem. I'm good at it. I'm the right person.

B：Look. I like this one. Don't you think it is amazing?

A：It's similar to the one that Princess Kate wears.

B：Do I look beautiful wearing this one?

A：嘿，海伦，好久不见了。你忙什么呢？

B：我在准备婚礼呢。现在都忙得四脚朝天了。

A：恭喜啦！我能帮你做些什么？

B：你真好。我打电话叫你出来是为了找一件婚纱。

A：没问题。我擅长这个。你算找对人了。

B：看。我喜欢这件。你不觉得很惊艳吗？

A：像凯特王妃穿的那件。

B：我穿这件漂亮吗？

A：漂亮。你穿上挺好看的。但是我觉

A: Yes. You look good in it. But I think it's a little longer.

B: Never mind. I can deal with it. Are there any superstitions for the wedding?

A: I just know that a bride should wear white, and so should her bridesmaids.

B: OK. So I also need to choose a white dress for my bridesmaid.

得有点长。

B: 没关系。我能处理。关于婚礼有什么迷信吗？

A: 我只知道新娘要穿白色礼服，伴娘也要穿白色。

B: 好的。所以我还要给伴娘选一件白色礼服。

"问" 英国特色文化

英式婚礼偏爱哪些道具？

英国人爱花，英式婚礼少不了鲜花的点缀，所以英国人喜欢在花园里举办婚礼。其实，一场典型的英式花园婚礼中还少不了精致的骨瓷。骨瓷最早产生于英国，是英国贵族极其青睐的精致器皿，非常适用于婚礼装扮，尤其是户外花园婚礼。然后是甜美可口的cupcake，即"纸杯蛋糕"。因为英国人非常喜爱cupcake，甚至称其为仙女蛋糕，因为cupcake既小巧又可爱，就像童话中的仙女。

阅读笔记

英国浩大的音乐盛典

格拉斯顿伯里音乐节——英国摇滚范儿

Music festivals are a big part of British youth culture. Glastonbury Festival is the biggest and most widely known of these festivals, and all the most popular music artists will play here. Tickets for the festival always sell out within an hour or 2 of going on sale each year. The festival takes place in south west England at Worthy Farm. The size and nature of the festival—held over three or four days in the open air, with performers, *crew* and paying festival goers staying in tents, *caravans* and *motorhomes*—has meant that the weather is significant.

The festival is held in a huge field. People can sleep in tents, or tipi's which are a special kind of round tent, and some will barely sleep for 3 days so they can listen to all their favourite/or new bands! The festival is quite funny because often in England it is very rainy, and sometimes thousands of people will wear wellington boots and even dance in the rain!

音乐节是英国年轻人文化的重要组成部分。其中，格拉斯顿伯里音乐节是英国最大也是最有名的音乐节，所有最受欢迎的音乐人都前来演出。每年音乐节的门票都能在1~2小时之内被抢购一空。格拉斯顿伯里音乐节一般在英国西南部的沃西农场举行。由于音乐节的规模和性质是为期3~4天的户外演出，表演者、工作人员和观众都必须住在帐篷、旅行车或者野营车里，因此这就意味着天气好坏尤为重要。

音乐节是在开阔的场地举行。人们可以睡在帐篷或一种叫做tipi's的特殊圆形帷帐里。有些人在这3天里几乎不怎么睡觉，这样就可以听到所有他们喜欢的乐队或新乐队的表演！整个音乐节非常有趣，因为英国本身多雨，因此经常可以看见上千人穿着惠灵顿长靴在雨中跳舞！

单词释义

crew 全体人员　　　　caravan 大篷车　　　　motorhome 野营车

351

逍遥音乐会——英国古典范儿

The Proms, more formally known as The BBC Proms, or The Henry Wood Promenade Concerts presented by the BBC, is an eight-week summer season of daily *orchestral* classical music concerts and other events held annually, *predominantly* in the Royal Albert Hall in London. Founded in 1895, each season currently consists of more than 70 concerts in the Albert Hall, a series of chamber concerts at Cadogan Hall, additional Proms in the Park events across the United Kingdom on the last night, and associated educational and children's events.

Prom is short for *promenade* concert, a term which originally referred to outdoor concerts in London's pleasure gardens, where the audience was free to stroll around while the orchestra was playing. In fact this tradition has been *revived* in parks and stately homes around the UK at promenade concerts such as the Battle Proms. In the context of the BBC Proms Promming now refers to the use of the standing areas inside the hall for which ticket prices are much lower than for the reserved seating. Single-concert standing Promming tickets for either the Arena

逍遥音乐会的正式名称更广为人知，叫做BBC逍遥音乐节，或者BBC亨利·伍德逍遥音乐会。这个音乐节在夏季举办，历时8个星期，每天都有管弦乐古典音乐会以及其他每年一度的节目，通常在皇家阿尔伯特音乐厅演出。音乐会于1895年首次举行，每季度的活动包括在阿尔伯特音乐厅举行的超过70场演唱会、在卡多岗音乐厅举行的系列室内乐演奏会、音乐节最后一夜在英国各地公园举行的额外音乐会以及相关的教育和儿童活动。

音乐会(Prom)是逍遥音乐会(promenade concert)的缩写，这个词的原意是指在伦敦休闲公园举行的露天音乐会，当管弦乐队演奏时，观众可以自由走动。事实上这个传统已经在英国公园和豪华住宅的逍遥音乐会上再次出现，例如巴特尔音乐会。而在BBC逍遥音乐节上，这个传统现在指的

or Gallery can be bought only on the day of the concert, which can give rise to long queues for well-known artists or works. Proms concert-goers, particularly those who stand, are most **commonly** referred to as "Prommers".

是在大厅内划分可自由站立的区域，该区域的票价远远低于预订的座位。单场逍遥音乐会的表演场地或走廊站票只在音乐会当天售出，这让许多人不惜排队观看著名的艺术家或作品。参加逍遥音乐会的人，尤其是那些站着观看节目的观众通常被叫做"逍遥人"。

单词释义

orchestral 管弦乐的
revived 复活的

predominantly 显著地
commonly 通常地

promenade 舞会

"品"英国特色文化

特色表达One

成功举办音乐会后岂能不庆祝一回呢？英国人在观赏完音乐会后，有的人会呼朋引伴去booze。这里的booze作名词就是"酒"的意思，但这个词作动词更常见，表示"狂饮，暴饮"的意思。

☆ 实景链接

A: Let's go out and **booze** up! 走，咱们出去喝个痛快！

B: Em, I have been off the booze for a month now. 呃，我已经1个月不喝酒了。

A: Come on, this party would be more fun if we had some **booze**. 这个派对要是有酒就更好玩了。

B: Sorry, I don't want to break my rule against drinking. 抱歉，我不想打破不喝酒的规定。

特色表达Two

只要热爱音乐的人就能参加音乐会吗？那也得有钱呀，因为很多高档的音乐会的门票还是很贵的，那些音乐会是deep pocket的特享。deep pocket的字面意思是指"深口袋"，在俚语中被引申用来指"富有的人"，因为富人钱多，才需要深口袋多装钱。

☆ 实景链接

A：I'd like to go to that concert. 我想去听那个音乐会。

B：Well, you have to pay 30 pounds admission. 好吧，你得付30英镑入场费。

A：Do you know it's Ellie's first concert? 你知道吗，那是埃利的首场音乐会?

B：But, the concert is for the **deep pockets**. 但是，这场音乐会是为富人们准备的。

拓展特色句

1. Music festivals are often presented with a certain theme. 音乐节通常都是以特定的主题呈现的。

2. Music from the baroque, classical, and romantic period is performed during the festival. 音乐节上表演了巴洛克式的、古典的和浪漫时期的传统音乐。

3. At the festival, the singer was welcomed by the huge crowd of fans. 在音乐节上，这位歌手受到了大量粉丝的欢迎。

"聊" 英国特色文化

A：You seem excited. What happened?

B：I get the ticket of Maksim's concert.

A：That's great. By the way, do you know the Glastonbury Festival?

B：Glastonbury Festival is one of the biggest and most widely-known festivals.

A：I hope I can go there.

B：You know that Glastonbury Festival is really good but it's far from us. So I'm satisfied that I can go to Maksim's concert. Maksim is a genius, he has been invited to play *Olympic Dream* for the Athens Olympics, and the chance that he comes to China is

A：你看起来很兴奋。发生什么了?

B：我搞到了马克西姆音乐会的票。

A：太好了。顺便问一下，你知道格拉斯顿伯里音乐节吗?

B：格拉斯顿伯里音乐节是最大也是最受关注的音乐节之一。

A：我希望我可以去。

B：你知道，格拉斯顿伯里音乐节确实不错，但是离我们太远了。所以能去马克西姆的音乐会我也很满足。马克西姆是个天才，他曾被邀请为雅典奥运会弹奏《奥林匹克梦想》，他来中国的机会也很少。

A：谁和你一起去?

rare.

A：Who will go there with you?

B：My girl friend. She's also his fan.

A：Then, have a good time.

B：我女朋友。她也是他的粉丝。

A：那么，祝你们玩儿得愉快。

"问" 英国特色文化

英国人有多爱音乐节？

毋庸置疑，英国人在狂热的夏季会举办各种各样的夏季音乐节，参加音乐节的不仅有刚出道的新星，更多的是大红大紫的著名歌星，盛大的音乐节吸引了来自世界各地的音乐迷，不管你是古典音乐迷、摇滚乐迷、电子乐迷，还是爵士乐迷，都可以在英国找到属于你的音乐节。

阅读笔记

英式葬礼

英式葬礼仪式——逝者身体护理

In Britain, *funerary* practices begin with the lay or official declaration of death, and consist of small attentions to the body itself, such as closing the eyes and covering the face. The 'laying-out' of the body—or '*rendering* the last offices' was in the past a job traditionally done by women, often the local midwife. It involved undressing and washing the body, *plugging* its *orifices*, if necessary placing coins (traditionally pennies) on the *eyelids*, and a *bandage* under the chin, to hold these parts closed, dressing the body in its grave clothes, and holding limbs straight (with bandages or ribbons around the body at the elbows, wrists, and ankles, and sometimes a thread around the big toes) ready for placing in the *coffin*. Today the female tradition is continued to some extent *inasmuch* as most hospital, hospice, and district nurses who do the job are women. However, in cases of death at home undertakers are now generally swiftly called to remove the body, and the process of laying-out is done by available staff—male or female—away from the location of death or mourning.

在英国，丧葬仪式首先会正式宣布死亡，对尸体进行轻微处理，如闭眼和遮面。"陈殓"尸体——或进行"最后安葬祈祷"，在过去按照传统是由女人，通常是当地的产婆来完成。这包括脱衣清洗尸体，堵塞鼻口(如有必要眼睑放置硬币(传统便士)，颌部裹以绷带，以确保这些部位闭合)，给尸体穿寿衣，使四肢保持平直(在尸体的肘、腕和脚踝处裹以绷带或丝带，在大脚趾缠以细线)，为陈尸棺木做好准备。今天，这一传统在某种程度上仍得到了传承，因为大多数医院、收容所和巡回服务护士的工作都是由女人进行的。但是，如果死者是寿终正寝，死者家属被要求立即将尸体运离死亡地或哀悼场所，可使用的人员，无论男女，都可以马上陈殓尸体。

单词释义

funerary 葬礼的　　　　render 致使　　　　plug 插入

orifice 孔板　　　　　　eyelid 眼皮　　　　bandage 绷带

coffin 棺材　　　　　　inasmuch 因……的原因

英国人为什么如此注重葬礼仪式

In the past, each aspect of lay funerary *ritual* had *multiple* levels of practical *justification* and traditional meaning. The eyelids are generally the first part of the body to set in *rigor mortis*, just before the jaw, hours after death. A corpse whose eyes refused to close was traditionally believed to *presage* further deaths, so closing the eyes was *imperative* to forestall the *omen*, and to prevent survivors' unease.

The dead body is an object of great *potency*, with a powerful presence of its own. Part of this effect derives from its *embodiment* of the power of death, part from the strangeness death works upon it. British funeral practices reveal that there existed a conception of a transitional period between death and burial in which the body was regarded as 'neither alive nor fully dead'.

In a physical sense, of course, we are all familiar with this *notion*—in the currently continuing difficulty in defining the precise moment of death, the possibility of *resuscitation*,

在过去，丧葬仪式的所有流程都具有多层面的实际理由和传统意义。人死数小时后，眼睑通常是最先僵直的，然后是颌部。传统上认为，尸体不闭眼预示着新的死亡，故而死者必须闭眼，预先阻止凶兆和生者的不安。

尸体蕴含伟大的力量，其形体依然存在。这种效应部分源于死亡力量的形象化，部分源于死亡的肃穆。英国的丧葬仪式表明，在死亡和下葬之间存在一个过渡时期的概念，在此期

and in the phenomenon of organs, which, though *extracted* from corpses, are yet sufficiently alive to support life again in the body of another. Old British customs and beliefs—such as the belief that a signature taken while the corpse is still warm had the same status as in life, that a corpse could indicate *displeasure* if a will read before it was false, or that it would bleed if a murderer came into its *vicinity*—seem to attribute sentience to the dead body.

间，尸体"非生亦非死"。

从形体意义上说，当然，我们都熟悉这一概念——现在依然难以准确确定死亡时、复活的可能性；从尸体可以提取器官，它们并未死亡并足以拯救其他人的生命。旧的英国风俗和迷信——比如在尸体温度尚存时署名就和人没死效果是一样的，在尸体前宣读假的遗嘱它会表达不满，如果凶手前来尸体会流血——似乎是赋予尸体以知觉。

单词释义

ritual 仪式	multiple 多样的	justification 辩护
rigor 严厉	mortis 尸斑	presage 预感
imperative 必要的	omen 预兆	potency 效能
embodiment 体现	notion 概念	resuscitation 复苏
extracted 提取的	displeasure 不愉快	vicinity 邻近

"品"英国特色文化

特色表达One

若是周边的人遇上了不幸的事，或做事过于冲动时，可以适当劝一下"You must hold your horses."这句话可不是叫你抓稳你的马匹，在俚语中，人们用其引申意义指"你一定要镇静。"

☆实景链接

A: John had been knocked down by a car. 约翰出事了，他被一辆小汽车撞倒了。

B: Oh, no! This is horrible. How's he doing now? What shall I do? 哦不，太可怕了，现在他怎么样了？我要做点什么呢？

A: **You must hold your horses.** John is currently in hospital, he'll soon pull through. 你要冷静，约翰现在医院，他会很快好起来的。

B: God bless you, John. It's out of my hands now. 愿上帝保佑你，约翰，我现在是无能为力了。

特色表达Two

同世界很多国家一样，在英式葬礼上，该忌讳的要注意，不在别人伤心的日子说大喜事，如果有人缺心眼提到了，你可以用"Can we get around this issue?"来提醒他，显而易见，这句话的意思是"我们能避开这个话题吗？"get around 指"避开"。

实景链接

A: Hi, Zack, today is a real red letter day. 嘿，扎克，今天真是个大喜的日子。

B: Come on, Tom, it was Admiral William's funeral. 汤姆，正经点，这是威廉将军的葬礼。

A: I'm sorry to obtrude on you at such a time, but I really wanna to tell you … 我很抱歉在这个时候打扰你，但我真的想告诉你……

B: **Can we get around this issue?** It is not a proper time. 我们能避开这个话题吗？这不是合适的时机。

拓展特色句

1. Her funeral will be performed according to church rites. 她的葬礼将会按照教堂的仪式来举行。

2. Laughing and joking are improper at such a funeral. 在这种葬礼场合，大笑和开玩笑是不合适的。

3. His funeral was scheduled for this afternoon in London. 他的葬礼安排在今天下午伦敦举行。

"聊" 英国特色文化

A: I have to ask one day off. One of my English friends passed away. I will attend her funeral.

A: 我得请一天假。我的一个英国朋友去世了。我要去参加她的葬礼。

B: 我很抱歉。我能为你做些什么？

B： I'm sorry to hear that. What can I do for you?

A： This is my first time to attend an English funeral. What should I pay attention to?

B： OK, let me tell you something about it.

A： Thanks.

B： In Britain, funerary practices begin with the lay or official declaration of death, and consist of small attentions to the body itself. Then they can do the following things. English people care a lot about the funerals.

A： So I'd better wear formal suit.

B： Black is safe. You can wear a hat and take a handkerchief.

A： OK. I know what to prepare. Thank you again.

A： 这是我第一次参加英式葬礼。有什么需要注意的吗？

B： 那我就给你讲讲英国葬礼吧。

A： 谢谢啊。

B： 在英国，丧葬仪式首先是正式宣布死亡，对尸体进行轻微处理。接下来才能做其他的事。英国人很注重葬礼。

A： 所以我最好穿正装。

B： 黑色是最安全的。你可以戴顶帽子再带条手帕。

A： 好的。我知道要准备什么了。再次谢谢。

"问" 英国特色文化

在英国，丧葬费也飞涨吗？

曾有报道说，如今，丧葬费用高涨，英国人"死不起了"。据英国《每日邮报》报道，巴思大学政策研究所的调查显示，过去一年，丧葬费用平均上涨7%，达到7622英镑。而2004年至2013年，丧葬费上涨达到80%，预计今后5年将继续涨价。在英国，最普通的葬礼、埋葬或火化费的平均需要就达到几千英镑，其他更体面的葬礼则更加昂贵。总之，很多英国人开始流行海葬。

英式足球的起源

The modern soccer game in Britain was originated as a war game. For a long time, the game of soccer was played between rival towns and villages in which hundreds of people are allowed to take part, including rights of kicking, *punching* and every other violent activity. King Edward 3rd and Queen Elizabeth 1 were against the *savage* nature of soccer and even enacted strict laws against soccer player.

After thousands of year the same game was *re-invented* by the English. Soccer begin to take shape in England in 1863 when association soccer and rugby soccer *split off* on their *unlike* path. After that the first soccer association was founded at the land of England. The first soccer match was played between England and Scotland in 1872, at that time soccer was *rarely* played outside the UK.

现代英式足球比赛在英国最开始是一种军事演习。很长时间以来，足球比赛都是在对手城镇和村庄之间展开的，数百人获准参加，选手有权利踢打对手，用拳猛击对手，或者实施其他暴力行为。国王爱德华三世和女王伊丽莎白一世都反对这种野蛮的足球运动，甚至针对足球运动员制定了严格的法律。

经过几千年的演变，英国人已重新将这一游戏进行了改造。1863年，随着英式足球与橄榄球在不同的发展道路上逐渐分离，足球运动开始规范成形。在那之后，第一个足球协会在英格兰成立。第一次足球比赛是在1872年英格兰和苏格兰之间展开的，在那个时候，英国之外的国家还很少玩足球。

单词释义

punch 用拳猛击　　savage 野蛮的　　re-invent 重新发明创造
split off 分离　　unlike 不同的　　rarely 很少地

这些体育项目都起源于英国

Many international sports were introduced by the British who take their *leisure* time very seriously. There is widespread *participation* in sport in Britain.

Football (or "soccer" as it is *colloquially* called), the most popular sport in England as well as in Europe, has its traditional home in England where it was developed in the 19th century.

The game "Rugby" was invented at Rugby School in Warwich shire in the early 19th century.

Cricket, the most typically English of sports, has been in existence since the16th century. On an international level, 5-day Cornhill Test Matches.

Although tennis has been played for centuries, the modern game originated in England in late 19th. The main *tournament* is the annual Wimbledon *fortnight*, one of the 4 tennis "Grand Slam" tournaments.

There is a considerable following and participation of *athletics* in Britain. For example, the London Marathon, which takes place every spring.

The home of golf is Scotland where the game has been played since the 17th century and naturally

许多国际体育项目是由严谨对待休闲时间的英国人引进的，在英国，人们广泛参与体育运动。

足球（口语叫"英式足球"），在英格兰和欧洲是最受欢迎的运动，其传统老家在英格兰，出现于19世纪。

英式橄榄球比赛19世纪初创立于沃尔威克郡的拉格比学校，因此而得名。

板球，英国人最典型的体育运动，自从16世纪以来已存在。国际比赛是5天的康希尔决赛。

尽管网球已打了好几个世纪，但现代比赛却起源于19世纪末的英格兰。主要比赛是一年一度的温布尔登两周赛，这是四大满贯网球锦标赛之一。

英国参加田径的人很多，例如伦敦的马拉松赛，每年春季举行。

高尔夫球的故里是苏格兰，自从17世纪以来这项运动就在那儿盛行。

the oldest golf club in the world is there: The Honourable Company of Edinburgh Golfers. The Walker Cup for *amateurs* and the Ryder Cup for professionals.	全世界最古老的高尔夫俱乐部也在那里——爱丁堡高尔夫球会员荣誉公司。业余球员参加沃克杯，职业球员参加莱德杯。

单词释义

participation 参与　　　　colloquially 口语地　　　　tournament 联赛
fortnight 两星期　　　　　athletic 运动的　　　　　　amateur 业余爱好者

"品" 英国特色文化

特色表达One

　　小贝是外貌与实力兼备的优秀球员，但Good lenses, bad frames。足球界还有很多实力选手。这里的Good lenses, bad frames可不是字面的"好的镜腿，坏的镜框"，在俚语中人们常用这个短语指"人不可貌相"。

☆ 实景链接

A： Beckham is widely regarded as the sport's greatest player. 贝克汉姆被普遍认为是球坛最了不起的球员。

B： Yeah, I think he is the most attractive player in England. 是的，我认为他是全英最帅的球员。

A： And there are still many other good players in England. 英国还有很多其他优秀的球员。

B： Yeah, you wouldn't know it by looking at him...**good lenses, bad frames**. 是的，光看外表是看不出什么的，人不可貌相。

特色表达Two

　　足球是一项需要团队合作竞技的综合运动，尤其考量运动员的意志与信心，要是有谁是errorist，就会影响整个团队的和谐与成绩。我们知道error是错误，那么这个errorist的意思是睁眼说瞎话的人，犯错不承认还自以为是的人。

☆ 实景链接

A：I dislike Bob. 我讨厌鲍勃。

B：Why? 为什么呢?

A：Bob is such an **errorist**. 鲍勃就是个瞪眼说瞎话的人。

B：It seems that he really makes you angry. 看来他真的让你很生气。

拓展特色句

1. Which team do you support? 你支持哪个队?

2. He shot five baskets during the game. 他在比赛中投中了五球。

3. They scored a three pointer before the clock was stopped. 他们在比赛结束前投进了一个三分球。

"聊" 英国特色文化

A：You watched the sports channel all the time. It's boring.

B：I love sports. Can you believe that British people can endure a five-day cricket match?

A：They must be insane.

B：You know what, they are crazy about sports.

A：What kind of sports are there in Britain?

B：Soccer, rugby, cricket, tennis, athletics and golf.

A：Golf is really a kind of elegant sports. Do you know the origin of it?

B：You can't baffle me with that! The home of golf is Scotland where the game has been played since the 17th century.

A：OK. I think I'd better do some sports

A：你总是看体育频道。太无聊了。

B：我喜欢运动。你能相信英国人能忍受长达5天的板球比赛吗?

A：他们一定是疯了。

B：要知道,他们痴迷于体育运动。

A：那他们都有什么体育运动?

B：英式足球、橄榄球、板球、网球、田径和高尔夫球。

A：高尔夫球确实是一项优雅的运动。你知道它的起源吗?

B：这可难不倒我。高尔夫球的故里是苏格兰,自从17世纪以来这项运动就在那儿盛行。

A：好吧。我想我最好也得多做运动了。整天坐在办公室里,这对我的身体不好。

B：这周末打高尔夫球怎么样?

A：是个好主意。

now. I sit in the office the whole day; it's bad for my health.

B：How about playing golf this weekend?

A：That's a good idea.

"问" 英国特色文化

英国人有足球情结吗?

英国人爱踢足球，足球文化早已渗透他们生活中的方方面面。首先，伦敦是英国的政治、经济、文化中心，也是英国著名的足球之城，有很多支职业足球俱乐部。英国小孩从小就爱踢足球，也讲究踢球技术，追求团队合作。英国人往往对足球比赛全力以赴，他们尊重规则，讲究公平竞赛。另外，足球类的书籍在英国可是畅销书的头牌，也是体育类书籍大热门。据说，无论在什么时候，只要有足球比赛，英国人一定欣然前往。

阅读笔记

阅读笔记

Part 10

穿越回去看看英国历史

玫瑰战争

王朝争夺战

The Wars of the Roses were a series of dynastic wars fought between supporters of two *rival branches* of the royal House of Plantagenet: the houses of Lancaster and York for the *throne* of England. They were fought in several *sporadic episodes* between 1455 and 1485, although there was related fighting both before and after this period. They resulted from the social and financial troubles following the Hundred Years' War, combined with the *minority* and weak rule of Henry VI, which revived interest in the alternative claim to the throne of Richard, Duke of York. The final victory went to a relatively remote Lancastrian claimant, Henry Tudor, who *defeated* the last Yorkist king Richard III and married Edward IV's daughter Elizabeth of York to unite the two houses. The House of Tudor *subsequently* ruled England and Wales until 1603.

玫瑰战争是金雀花王室的两支后裔的支持者兰开斯特家族和约克家族为争夺英格兰王位而展开的王朝战争。1455年至1485年，内战断断续续地发生，尽管在此前后也有此类争斗发生。造成战争的原因是百年战争带来的社会和金融危机，以及亨利六世的年幼和治国不力，这再次激起了贵族们觊觎着更改约克公爵理查德的王位继承权。战争最终的结局是相对较远的兰开斯特家族的亨利·都铎打败了上一任的约克国王理查德三世，并与约克的爱德华四世的女儿伊丽莎白结婚，将两个家族联合了起来。都铎王朝后来统治英格兰和威尔士，直到1603年。

单词释义

rival 竞争对手　　　　branch 分支　　　　throne 王权
sporadic 零星的　　　　episode 插曲，一段情节　minority 未成年
defeat 打败　　　　　　subsequently 随后

为什么叫"玫瑰战争"

The name "Wars of the Roses" refers to the Heraldic badges associated with the two royal houses, the White Rose of York and the Red Rose of Lancaster. It came into common use in the nineteenth century after the *publication* of Anne of Geierstein by Sir Walter Scott. Scott based the name on a scene in William Shakespeare's play *Henry VI* Part 1, set in the gardens of the Temple Church, where a number of noblemen and a lawyer pick red or white roses to show their loyalty to the Lancastrian or Yorkist faction *respectively*. The Yorkist faction used the symbol of the white rose from early in the conflict, but the Lancastrian red rose was apparently introduced only after the victory of Henry Tudor at the Battle of Bosworth, when it was combined with the Yorkist white rose to form the Tudor rose, which symbolised the *union* of the two houses.

Most of the *participants* in the wars wore *livery badges* associated with their immediate lords or patrons under the prevailing system of so-called "bastard *feudalism*". For example, Henry Tudor's forces at Bosworth fought under the banner of a red dragon, while the Yorkist army

"玫瑰战争"这一名称源自两个王室家族的徽标，即约克的白玫瑰和兰开斯特的红玫瑰。沃尔特·司各特爵士的小说《盖厄斯坦的安妮》于19世纪出版后，玫瑰战争的说法才开始广泛使用。司各特根据威廉·莎士比亚的历史剧《亨利六世》第一部分在圣殿教堂花园的场景创造了这个名称，在这个场景中，许多贵族和律师分别选择红色或白色玫瑰来表达他们对兰开斯特或约克家族的忠诚。在战争初期，约克家族使用白玫瑰作为象征；但兰开斯特家族似乎是在亨利·都铎赢得了博斯沃思原野战役后才选用红玫瑰作为象征，与约克家族的白玫瑰一起构成了都铎的玫瑰，象征着两个家族的联合。

大部分参战的人都根据所谓的"变态封建主义"流行体系佩戴他们的直接领主或庇护人的专有徽章。例如亨利·都铎的军队在博斯沃思战役

used Richard III's personal device of a white *boar*.

中以红龙为战旗，而约克军队的旗帜则是理查德三世的白野猪。

单词释义

publication 出版	respectively 各自地	union 联盟
participant 参与者	livery 专有的	badge 徽章
feudalism 封建制度	boar 野猪	

"品" 英国特色文化

特色表达One

　　玫瑰战争期间，英国社会混乱不堪，不通晓点儿street smart是难以生存下来的。这里的street smart字面意思是"街道的智慧"，在俚语中常用它的引申意义指"在城市生存的必要手段"，比如如何保护自己。

☆ 实景链接

A：There was a great deal of suffering during the war. 战争期间，人们饱受痛苦。

B：And in troubled times, keeping calm is no guarantee of security. 而且在乱世，镇定并不能保障安全。

A：I think the local people had to learn some **street smart** to protect themselves. 我想那些当地人民得学一些手段来保护自己。

B：Yes. So many heroes sprang at that time. 是的。所以那个时代出现了很多英雄。

特色表达Two

　　战争就如同big gun手中的棋子，不是普通小市民们可以操控的。big gun在这里可不是指"大枪"，在俚语中，它的意思是"大人物，重要的人"，可以指那些对全局有重要影响的人。

☆ 实景链接

A：It's said that the wars are actually run by the **big gun**. 据说，这些战争实际上是由大人物操纵的。

B: That's too cruel. War necessarily causes misery and waste. 这太残酷了。战争必然造成痛苦和破坏。

A: And the war caused great sufferings and losses to the local people. 战争也会给当地人民造成巨大的痛苦和损失。

B: Yeah, it soon came to the people that the war was bloody. 人们不久就痛苦地意识到战争是血腥的。

拓展特色句

1. The key to the recovery of England from the Wars of the Roses had been Henry VII's concentration upon domestic stability. 玫瑰战争以后，英国恢复的关键是亨利七世着力于国内的稳定。

2. The slaughter of the nobility in the Wars of the Roses left the way ready for the establishment of the Tudor dominion. 玫瑰战争屠杀了贵族，为都铎王朝的统治扫清了障碍。

3. The Tudor Dynasty was founded after the Hundred Years War and the Rose War. 都铎王朝是在英法百年战争和红白玫瑰战争结束之后建立的。

"聊" 英国特色文化

A: It's not peaceful in some countries. We'd better stay at home.

B: Don't worry. We are in the age of peace.

A: No one likes war. But there were plenty of wars in the history.

B: It sounds that you know a lot about the wars and history.

A: Not really. I just know some when I learned British history.

B: Do you know why they arouse wars?

A: There were different reasons. Some of these were for the throne.

B: Like The Wars of the Roses?

A: 有些国家真的不安全。我们最好在家待着。

B: 别担心。我们现在是处于和平年代。

A: 没有人喜欢战争。可是历史上曾有那么多战争。

B: 听起来你很了解战争和历史啊。

A: 不是很了解。我只是在学英国历史时了解过一些。

B: 你知道他们为什么发动战争吗？

A: 原因都不相同。有的是为王位。

B: 就像玫瑰战争？

A：Yes. And there are other wars, some for the land, some for petroleum and some for women.

B：I think all of the wars are because of desire.

A：It's an incisive conclusion.

A：没错。还有其他的战争，有的为土地，有的为石油，还有的为女人。

B：我认为所有的战争都是因为欲望。

A：这是一个精辟的总结。

"问" 英国特色文化

玫瑰战争的意义是什么？

在玫瑰战争中，战争的双方兰开斯特家族和约克家族同归于尽，大批封建旧贵族在互相残杀中或阵亡或被处决，直接导致了新兴贵族和资产阶级的力量不断增长，并成为都铎王朝新建立的君主专制政体的支柱。从这个意义上说，玫瑰战争是英国专制政体确立之前封建无政府状态的最后一次战争。而在经济上，这次战争促使封建农业开始向资本主义农业转变，使得英国工业、手工业迅速发展起来。

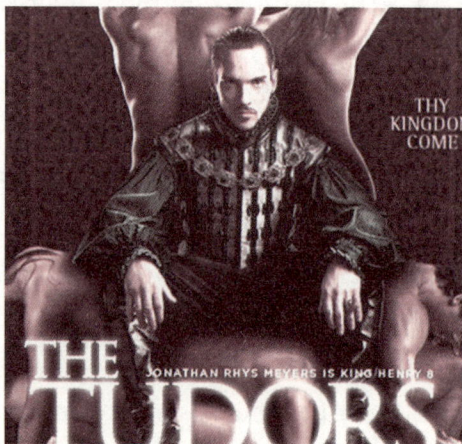

阅读笔记

玫瑰战争后的英国

The English Bourgeois Revolution broke out in the 17th century. The Wars of the Roses had greatly weakened the *feudal* noble class. The Enclosures had *dispossessed* many peasants of their lands and driven them to cities. The Reformation had criticized those religious *doctrines* which served feudal relations and deprived the church of its lands and wealth, weakening one of the *mainstays* of the feudal order. Meanwhile, *ideology* and morality had also witnessed big changes. A new class was rising in England. The *bourgeois* revolution was just around the corner.

During the last years of Elizabeth's reign, relations between the Monarchy and the bourgeoisie were *strained*. Elizabeth died in 1603 without a successor and James VI of Scotland was welcomed to the English throne as James I. This was the beginning of the *unification* of the two countries and it gave birth to the name Great Britain.

17世纪，英国的资产阶级革命爆发。玫瑰战争已经大大削弱了封建贵族阶级。圈地运动使许多农民失去了土地，并被赶到城市。宗教改革批判了那些服务于封建关系和剥夺教会土地和财富的宗教教义，削弱了封建秩序的支柱之一。与此同时，意识形态和道德领域也发生了巨大变化。一个新兴的阶级在英格兰迅速发展，资产阶级革命一触即发。

在伊丽莎白统治的最后几年，王室和资产阶级之间的关系已趋于紧张。1603年，伊丽莎白去世，在没有继任者的情况下，苏格兰国王詹姆斯六世被推为英格兰国王，即詹姆斯一世。这是两国统一的开始，使得一个新的名字"大不列颠"诞生了。

单词释义

feudal 封建制度的　　　dispossess 剥夺　　　doctrine 教条
mainstay 支柱　　　　　ideology 意识形态　　bourgeois 资本家
strain 拉紧　　　　　　unification 统一

英国资产阶级革命

Upon James I's death, his son succeeded him as Charles I who behaved like a *dictator* and showed no respect to Parliament. Charles I was in favor of Catholicism and showed his *readiness* to restore the old ceremonies of the Roman Catholic Church. He persecuted the Protestants, especially the Puritans. This caused great *uneasiness* among the people who had benefited from the Reformation. The war between Parliamentarians and Royalists *namely* the English Civil War lasted from 1642—1651. The War led to the Commonwealth of England (1649—1653), and then with a Protectorate (1653—1659), under Oliver Cromwell's personal rule.

A new Parliament, composed of both Houses, was again assembled after Cromwell's son abdicated. The new Parliament began to negotiate with Charles I's son who later became Charles II. Charles II was welcomed back to the restored English throne and the Republic came to an end.

Upon Charles II's death, his successor, James II(his brother), attempted to be an absolute monarch, to ignore Parliament, and to *revive* Catholicism in England. A Bill of Rights was drawn up, which clearly spelled out the powers of the people through Parliament and *prohibited absolutism* on the part of

詹姆斯一世死后，他的儿子查尔斯一世继位，他表现得像个独裁者，完全不把议会放在眼里。查尔斯一世支持天主教，表达了自己恢复旧的罗马天主教教会的愿望。他迫害新教徒，尤其是清教徒，引起了从宗教改革中受益的人的极大不安。议会党人和保皇派之间的战争即英国内战从1642年持续到1651年。战争产生了英格兰联邦(1649—1653)和护国公奥利弗·克伦威尔(1653—1659)的个人统治。

克伦威尔的儿子下台后，由两院组成的新议会再次召开。新议会与查尔斯一世的儿子，即后来的查尔斯二世展开谈判。查理二世受拥戴重新继承英格兰王位，共和国宣告结束。

查尔斯二世死后，继承人他的弟弟詹姆斯二世完全推行封建专制，他

future monarchs, declared that in the future all kings and queens of England would be members of the Church of England. James II was dethroned, and the Dutch-born William III and his wife, Mary(James II's daughter), were invited by Parliament to become king and queen of England. It was called Glorious Revolution of 1688 or White Revolution, because it caused no bloodshed. The English king, instead of controlling Parliament, had to receive his crown from Parliament. This marked the real beginning of the constitutional monarchy in England.

无视议会，企图恢复天主教在英国的地位。议会起草了《权利法案》，清晰地阐明人们通过议会行使权力，禁止未来的君主实行专制，并宣布未来所有的英格兰国王和女王必须是英国国教的成员。詹姆斯二世被废黜，荷兰人威廉三世和他的妻子玛丽(詹姆斯二世的女儿)受议会邀请成为英格兰的国王和王后。这就是1688年的光荣革命或者叫做白色革命，因为没有发生流血事件。英格兰国王不但无法控制议会，还必须接受议会的拥戴。这标志着英国的君主立宪制真正开始了。

单词释义

dictator 独裁者　　　　readiness 敏捷　　　　uneasiness 不安
namely 也就是　　　　prohibit 阻止　　　　absolutism 绝对论

"品" 英国特色文化

特色表达One

英国虽然实行君主立宪制，但还是保留王室的，所以当今存在很多名人be born to the purple。在这里的be born to the purple可不是出生于紫色，历史上很多王室都崇尚紫色，认为紫色最为高贵和优雅，所以这个短语是"出身贵族"之意。

☆实景链接

A: Do you know which rapper she worked for? 那你知道她宣传的是哪位艺人吗？

B: Catherine? Maybe. 可能是凯瑟琳吧？

A: Who is Catherine? 凯瑟琳是谁啊？

B: Not very clear. But I've heard that she was **born to the purple**. 不太清楚，但我听说她出身皇家。

📃 特色表达Two

　　参加过战争的老一辈人谈起过去的辉煌革命时，常常不忘提起某个eye candy。这个eye candy是糖果做的眼睛吗？那也太恐怖了，其实这个短语的意思是"绝代美人"，毕竟乱世出英雄，而美人衬英雄。

☆ 实景链接

A：Andrea is an **eye candy** at that time. 安德莉亚在当时可是个绝世美人。

B：She was beloved of all who knew her. 凡是认识她的人都喜欢她。

A：And Simon is a hero known in the time of misfortune. 还有西蒙，他可是乱世英雄。

B：Yeah, I admire him. 是啊，我很敬佩他。

拓展特色句

1. Constitutional monarchy began after the Glorious Revolution in 1688. 君主立宪制从1688年的光荣革命后开始。

2. England had experienced great changes after the English Bourgeois Revolution. 英国在英国资产阶级革命后经历了很大的变化。

3. The constitutional monarchy is a fruit of English Bourgeois Revolution. 君主立宪制是英国资产阶级革命的结果。

"聊" 英国特色文化

A：In today's history lesson I learned a new word "constitutional monarchy". But I don't quite understand it.

B：Briefly speaking, there is a monarch as the head of the state under constitutional system.

A：Can you give me an example?

B：The United Kingdom is a typical example.

A：That is to say they have both constitutional system and a queen.

A：今天的历史课上我学到了一个新词，"君主立宪制"。但是，我不太明白它是什么意思。

B：简短来说，就是在宪制体制下有一个君主作为国家元首。

A：能给我举个例子吗？

B：英国就是一个典型的例子。

A：也就是说他们既有宪制体制也有女王。

B：可以这么说。

B：You can say so.

A：Can you tell me something more?

B：Sure. The queen identity is lifelong and her status is higher than any other civilians.

A：Then how did constitutional monarchy come from in the UK?

B：Glorious Revolution was the basis and *Bill of Rights* marked the real establishment of the constitutional monarchy in the United Kingdom.

A：能再给我多讲点吗？

B：当然，女王是终身的。她的地位要高于普通百姓。

A：那么英国的君主立宪制是怎么来的呢？

B：光荣革命是基础，《权利法案》则标志着英国君主立宪制的确立。

"io" 英国特色文化

为什么《权利法案》象征着君主立宪制的开始？

起初，1688年的"光荣革命"推翻了复辟的斯图亚特王朝，迎立信奉新教的荷兰执政威廉和玛丽同时登位。后来，威廉三世和玛丽二世于1689年召集议会，通过《权利法案》。之后又通过《王位继承法》，从法律上确认"议会主权"原则，极大地限制了王权，主要是未经议会同意，国王不得擅自批准法律、废除法律或中止法律之实施。从此，专制君主为受宪法约束的立宪君主所取代，英国议会制君主立宪政体初步确立。

阅读笔记

工业革命解放全世界

工业革命概况

The Industrial Revolution was the transition to new *manufacturing* processes in the period from about 1760 to sometime between 1820 and 1840. This transition included going from hand production methods to machines, new chemical manufacturing and iron production processes, improved *efficiency* of water power, the increasing use of *steam* power and the development of machine tools. It also included the change from wood and other bio-fuels to coal. It began in Great Britain and within a few decades had spread to Western Europe and the United States.

The Industrial Revolution marks a major turning point in history; almost every aspect of daily life was influenced in some way. In particular, average income and population began to *exhibit unprecedented sustained* growth. For the first time in history, the living standards of the masses of ordinary people have begun to *undergo* sustained growth.

工业革命发生在大约1760年到1820年至1840年间，是向新制造工艺转变的过渡，包括从手工生产过渡到机器生产，新的化学制造和炼铁工艺、水力效率的提高，增加蒸汽动力的使用以及机械工具的发展。此外，也包括从使用木材和其他生物燃料向燃煤的过渡。工业革命始于英国，并在随后的几十年内扩展到西欧和美国。

工业革命标志着历史上一个重大的转折点；日常生活的方方面面几乎都受到了某种程度上的影响。特别是人均收入和人口开始出现前所未有的快速增长。广大普通民众的生活水平也开始经历持续的发展，这在历史上还是第一次。

单词释义

manufacturing 制造业　　efficiency 效率　　steam 蒸汽
exhibit 展览　　unprecedented 空前的　　sustained 持续的
undergo 经历

工业革命对人类的意义

The Watt steam engine, fuelled primarily by coal, propelled the Industrial Revolution in Great Britain and the world. GDP per *capita* was broadly stable before the Industrial Revolution and the *emergence* of the modern capitalist economy. The Industrial Revolution began an era of per-capita economic growth in capitalist economies. Economic historians are in agreement that the *onset* of the Industrial Revolution is the most important event in the history of *humanity* since the *domestication* of animals and plants.

The era was a period in which fundamental changes occurred in agriculture, *textile* and metal manufacture, transportation, economic policies and the social structure in England. This period is appropriately labeled revolution, for it thoroughly destroyed the old manner of doing things; yet the term is simultaneously *inappropriate*, for it *connotes abrupt* change. The changes that occurred during this period (1760—1850), in fact, occurred gradually. The year 1760 is generally accepted as the eve of the Industrial Revolution. In reality, this eve began more than two centuries before this date. The late 18th century and the

瓦特蒸汽机最初用煤作燃料，它推动了工业革命在英国乃至整个世界的发展。在工业革命和现代资本主义经济兴起之前，人均国内生产总值一直比较稳定，而工业革命在资本主义经济体中开启了人均经济增长的新时代。经济历史学家一致认为，工业革命的开始在人类历史中是从驯化动物和种植植物以来最重要的事件。

工业革命时期是英国的农业、纺织、金属加工、交通、经济政策和社会结构都发生根本性变化的一个时期。恰当地说，这一时期的特点就是革命，因为它彻底摧毁了过去的生产方式；但同时这个词也并不恰当，因为革命意味着突然的变革。事实上，在此期间(1760—1850)变化是逐渐发生的。1760年被认为是工业革命即将开始的前夕。但事实上工业革命的前夕

early l9th century brought to *fruition* the ideas and discoveries of those who had long passed on, such as, Galileo, Bacon, Descartes and others.

在两个世纪以前就已经开始。在18世纪末、19世纪初，伽利略、培根、笛卡尔和其他那些去世已久的人们的想法和发现终于成为了现实。

单词释义

capita 资本

humanity 人道

inappropriate 不适当的

fruition 完成

emergence 出现

domestication 驯养

connote 意味

onset 开始

textile 纺织

abrupt 突然的

"品"英国特色文化

特色表达One

英国工业革命后，人们的生活水平提高了，很多人开始注重穿着打扮，因为没人想被人认为cheesy。我们知道cheese是"奶酪"的意思，但cheesy可不是指像奶酪一样的人，在俚语中，它的意思是"很土的，庸俗的"。

☆ 实景链接

A：Vera has smartened up since I met her last. 自我上次见到维拉之后，她变得漂亮了。

B：Yeah, she looks **cheesy** before. 是的，她之前看起来很土。

A：I want to ask her how to get skinny and pretty. 我想问问她如何变瘦变漂亮。

B：Come on, you are pretty enough. 拜托，你已经很漂亮了。

特色表达Two

工业革命后，英国的贵族阶层过着纸醉金迷的奢华生活，有的烟鬼见面就是一句："You got a cig?"这里的cig是cigarette的缩写，所以这句话的意思就是"你带烟了没？"后来常用于寒暄语。

⭐ **实景链接**

A：What a magnificent day! 今天天气好极了！

B：Yeah, the weather is nice today. 是的，今天天气很好。

A：**You got a cig**? 你有烟吗？

B：No, I am no smoking. 不，我不抽烟。

拓展特色句

1. The industrial revolution changed the structure of English society. 工业革命改变了英国社会的结构。

2. What was happening in Britain during the Industrial Revolution was not an isolated phenomenon. 工业革命期间英国发生的一切并不是孤立的现象。

3. There is an increase in carbon emission since the beginning of the Industrial Revolution. 自工业革命开始，碳排放量有所上升。

"聊" 英国特色文化

A：Look at my achievement.

B：Have you washes a thousand dresses and shirts?

A：Don't make a fun of me. Not that much, just dozens of.

B：You must be very exhausted.

A：Not really. The new washing machine helps me a lot.

B：It seems that you should thank Watt.

A：Why did you say that?

B：It was Watt's steam engine that propelled the Industrial Revolution in Great Britain and the world.

A：OK. I got it. You mean the Industrial Revolution.

B：Do you agree?

A：看看我的成果。

B：你洗了1000件裙子和衬衣吗？

A：别拿我开玩笑了。没那么多，也就几十件吧。

B：你一定累了吧。

A：也没有。新的洗衣机帮了我大忙。

B：看来你得感谢瓦特了。

A：怎么这么说？

B：是瓦特的蒸汽机推动了工业革命在英国和世界的发展。

A：好吧，我懂了。你说的是工业革命啊。

B：你同意吗？

A: Of course. Or I am washing the dirty clothes by hands.

B: Yes. The Industrial Revolution totally changed our lives.

A: 当然。否则我现在还在用手洗脏衣服呢。

B: 是啊。工业革命彻底地改变了我们的生活。

"问" 英国特色文化

英国的工业革命改变了什么？

在工业革命早期，英国人被迫适应着新的生活，他们从农庄搬到城市，全家大半生都在工厂工作，这种突然的变化导致很多问题，比如说关于卫生、福利及养老的问题一举爆发，还有清洁、住房、警察及犯罪等问题。但工业化及其随同的变化提高了英国人的生活标准，人们开始享受与以前不同的娱乐精神世界。而且工业化也改变了政府，促进了英国的民主化进程。

阅读笔记

第一次世界大战

英国在第一次世界大战中扮演的角色

The United Kingdom was one of the Allied Powers during the First World War of 1914—1918, fighting against the Central Powers (the German Empire, the Austro-Hungarian Empire, the Ottoman Empire and the Kingdom of Bulgaria). The country's armed forces were reorganized—the war marked the creation of the Royal Air Force, for example—and increased in size because of the introduction, in January 1916, of forced *conscription* for the first time in the country's history as well as the raising of the largest all-volunteer army in history, known as Kitchener's Army, of more than two million men. The *outbreak* of war has generally been regarded as a socially *unifying* event, though this view has been challenged by more recent *scholarship*. In any case, responses in the United Kingdom in 1914 were similar to those amongst populations across Europe.

英国是1914至1918年发生的第一次世界大战的同盟国成员之一，与德国及其同盟国(德意志帝国、奥匈帝国、奥斯曼帝国和保加利亚王国)形成对抗。英国武装部队进行了重组——比如第一次世界大战标志着英国空军的成立，此外，1916年1月首次采用了强制征兵制，同时建立了历史上规模最大的志愿军——超过200万人的基钦纳军队，使军队的规模大大增加。第一次世界大战的爆发一般被看作是统一了社会的事件，尽管这个观点在近来遭到了学者的挑战。不论如何，英国1914年的反应与其他欧洲大陆的人们是没有什么差别的。

单词释义

conscription 征兵　　　　outbreak 爆发　　　　unify 统一
scholarship 学识

第一次世界大战给英国带来的巨大创伤

In the post war publication *Statistics of the Military Effort of the British Empire During the Great War 1914—1920*, the official report lists 908,371 "soldiers" as being either killed in action, dying of wounds, dying as prisoners of war or missing in action in the World War. Listed separately were the Royal Navy war dead and missing of 32,287 and the Merchant Navy war dead of 14,661. The figures for the Royal Flying Corps and the nascent Royal Air Force were not given in the War Office report.

The war was a major economic *catastrophe* as Britain went from being the world's largest overseas investor to being its biggest debtor, with interest payments *consuming* around 40 percent of the national *budget*. Inflation more than doubled between 1914 and its peak in 1920, while the value of the Pound Sterling fell by 61.2 percent. Reparations in the form of free German coal depressed the local industry, *precipitating* the 1926 General Strike. The military historian Correlli Barnett has argued that "in objective truth the Great War in no way *inflicted crippling* economic damage on Britain" but that the war only "crippled the British psychologically".

第一次世界大后出版的《大英帝国在1914—1920年世界大战中的军事行动的统计数据》显示，在第一次世界大战中，官方报告有908371名士兵在战场上丧生，死于重伤、作为俘虏被处决和失踪。分开列出的有皇家海军的阵亡和失踪军人人数为32287人，商船舰队军人死亡人数为14661人。陆军航空队和新建的皇家空军在第一次世界大战中的统计数据未列入陆军部的报告中。

第一次世界大战使给英国带来了巨大的经济灾难，因为它使英国从世界上最大的海外投资国变成世界上最大的债务国，仅支付债务的利息就耗去了40%的国家预算。通货膨胀在1914年增长了1倍，到1920年达到顶峰，当时英镑的价值下跌了61.2%。以免费的德国煤充当战争赔偿不利于英国工业的发展，导致了1926年的大罢工。军事历史学家康瑞利·巴奈特认为，"从客观事实上说，第一次世界大战绝没有给英国造成严重的经济损失"，但是第一次世界大战"给英国带来了心理创伤"。

单词释义

catastrophe 大灾难   consume 消耗   budget 预算
precipitate 沉淀物   inflicted 强加   crippling 造成严重后果的

"品" 英国特色文化

特色表达One

第一次世界大战中，很多男子离家，留守在家的妇女不得不承担家庭的重担，为了bread而操心。我们知道bread一般意思是"面包"，因为大多数英国人的一日三餐离不开面包，后来就用bread指代"养家糊口的钱"。

☆ 实景链接

A：It's said that women belong to home, while men belong to the fields during the Great War. 据说第一次世界大战期间，女人留在家里，而男人则要走上战场。

B：And the women had to see young men off to the war. 那么妇女们不得不送年轻男人上战场。

A：So women had to take care of the household but also bring home the **bread**. 这样妇女们不仅要料理家务，而且还得养家。

B：Yeah, they have grubbed for a living. 她们为了生活而辛苦工作着。

特色表达Two

在第一次世界大战期间，有的小伙子宁愿被女友dump也要义无反顾地去参军，因为不想因为自己出了意外而让女友伤心一生。这里的dump是指"被甩"，而不是常见的"丢下，扔弃"。

☆ 实景链接

A：Do you know Martin is **dumped** by Kelly? 你知道吗，马丁被凯丽甩了。

B：I heard that Martin tried to join the army. 我听说马丁想要参军。

A：But Kelly didn't approve. 但是凯丽不同意。

B：So they had a quarrel, and they do not speak to each other. 所以他们吵架了，谁也不理谁。

拓展特色句

1. Millions of people were immolated in World War I. 数百万的人们在第一次世界大战中被杀死。

2. As World War I drew to a close in 1918, millions of American veterans returned home. 在1918年第一次世界大战结束之际，几百万美国兵回到家乡。

3. Many people believe that the First World War in Europe had been a terrible mistake. 许多人认为欧洲发生的第一次世界大战是一个可怕的错误。

"聊"英国特色文化

A： You are unhappy. What happened? Tell me.

B： Nothing. I just read the book and the war makes me sad. Why did they have to war? Did they really get what they want from the war?

A： The war was a major economic catastrophe which made Britain went from being the world's largest overseas investor to the biggest debtor.

B： Besides that, the war crippled the countries psychologically.

A： Yes. The citizens had a bad life at that time. The family members were forced to separate from each other.

B： Peace is the most important thing for a country.

A： Fortunately, we had gone over it. Cheer up.

B： OK. Let's listen to some music and soothe our mood.

A： 你不开心了。发生什么事了？告诉我。

B： 没什么。我只是在看书，战争让我感到伤心。他们为什么要发动战争呢？他们从战争中得到想要的东西了吗？

A： 我不这么认为，比如，第一次世界大战给英国带来了巨大的经济灾难，使英国从世界上最大的海外投资国变成了最大的债务国。

B： 此外，战争给国家带来了巨大的心理创伤。

A： 是的。在那个时候人们过着糟糕的生活。家庭成员被迫分离。

B： 对一个国家来说，和平是最重要的。

A： 还好我们都经历过来了。振作起来。

B： 好吧。我们听些音乐舒缓一下心情。

"问" 英国特色文化

第一次世界大战对英国社会有哪些影响？

首先，第一次世界大战使大量英国男子背井离乡参战，而留在家里的妇女不得不接替男子，参与大量战时工作，于是妇女作为家庭支柱，开始承担稳定社会的重任。这一方面促进了英国妇女的广泛就业，为英国取得第一次世界大战的最后胜利做出了不可磨灭的贡献；另一方面在很大程度上改善了英国妇女的社会经济地位，加速了女权运动的发展。在第一次世界大战后，英国妇女终于获得了选举权。可以说，第一次世界大战推动了英国妇女解放运动的发展。

阅读笔记

第二次世界大战

英国在第二次世界大战中的主要表现

When Britain *declared* war on Nazi Germany at the *outset* of World War II, it was in possession of a large empire of territories that had achieved varying degrees of independence. The assistance provided by the British Empire to Britain in terms of *manpower* and *material* was critical to the war effort, but it proved impossible to defend itself against *simultaneous* attacks by the Axis Powers. Britain turned to the United States for support in *prosecuting* the war and defence of the Empire. Although Britain and the Empire emerged from the war as victors, and captured territories were returned to British rule, the costs of the war and the nationalist fervour that it had stoked meant that it was a *catalyst* for the rapid *decolonization* which took place in the following decades.

第二次世界大战爆发后，当英国向纳粹德国宣战时，仍然是拥有广阔领土的大英帝国，尽管帝国的领土都取得了一定程度的独立。帝国给英国在人力和物力方面的支持对战争所起的作用是至关重要的，但是事实也证明，帝国很难抵挡轴心国同时发起的多方攻击。于是，英国转向美国，希望在战争进程和帝国防御上寻求支持。尽管从表面上看，大英帝国是战胜国，被占领的领土也归还了英帝国，但是战争耗费的代价和战争激起的民族主义狂热情绪证明了，第二次世界大战是快速非殖民化的催化剂，殖民地在接下来的几十年里纷纷借机取得了独立。

单词释义

declare 宣布　　　　　outset 开端　　　　　manpower 人力
material 材料　　　　　simultaneous 同时的　prosecute 迫害
decolonization 非殖民地化　catalyst 催化剂

第二次世界大战后英国势力范围的削弱

World War II confirmed that Britain was no longer the great power it had once been, and that it had been *surpassed* by the United States on the world stage. It *sealed* the fate of the British Empire, though the United Kingdom had begun loosening control over its empire earlier. In 1931, the United Kingdom granted independence within the empire to Australia, Canada, the Irish Free State, New Zealand, Newfoundland, and South Africa. The countries became the first members of the Commonwealth of Nations, an association of countries and dependencies (now called overseas territories) that succeeded the empire.

After World War II, the peoples of Africa and Asia increased their demands for independence. The United Kingdom could no longer keep control of its colonies. In 1947, India and Pakistan became independent nations within the Commonwealth. In 1948, Ceylon became an independent Commonwealth country. That same year, Burma achieved independence and left the Commonwealth. In 1949, the Irish Free State declared itself the independent Republic of Ireland and also left the Commonwealth. That same year, Newfoundland became a

第二次世界大战再次证实，英国已经不再是曾经的强国，在世界舞台上已被美国超过了。第二次世界大战封锁了大英帝国的命运，尽管英国对帝国的控制在更早的时候就减弱了。1931年，英国在帝国内授权澳大利亚、加拿大、爱尔兰自由邦、新西兰、纽芬兰和南非获得独立。这些国家后来成为英联邦最早的成员国，英联邦是继承帝国的国家和托管地(现在叫做海外领地)联盟。

第二次世界大战后，非洲和亚洲人们要求独立的呼声更加强烈了。英国再也无法控制它的殖民地。1947年，印度和巴基斯坦成为英联邦内的独立国家。1948年，锡兰成为独立的联邦国家。同年，缅甸独立，离开

province of Canada. South Africa was not a member of the Commonwealth from 1961 to 1994 because the United Kingdom had *criticized* its racial policies. Blacks made up a majority of the population in South Africa, but whites controlled the government.

了英联邦。1949年，爱尔兰自由邦宣布独立为爱尔兰共和国并脱离了英联邦。同年，纽芬兰成为加拿大的一个省。南非从1961年到1994年不是英联邦的成员国，因为英国批评其种族政策。黑人在南非人口中占绝大多数，但是白人控制了政府。

单词释义

surpass 超过   seal 密封   criticize 批评

"品" 英国特色文化

💬 特色表达One

战争是残酷的，很多英国将士bought the farm in the World War II。这里可不是说英国将士在第二次世界大战中买下了农场，在俚语中，buy the farm这个短语可以暗示"死亡，埋葬"的意思，所以这个短语指"在第二次世界大战中阵亡。"

☆ 实景链接

A：War always brings death and famine. 战争总是导致死亡和饥荒。

B：Especially the Second World War, many people were killed. 尤其是第二次世界大战，导致许多人死亡。

A：I heard that Warren's grandpa **bought the farm** in the World War II. 我听说沃伦的祖父死于第二次世界大战。

B：Yes, we all feel sad about the death of his grandpa. 是的，我们都为他的祖父感到悲伤。

💬 特色表达Two

第二次世界大战期间，妻离子散，多少年后再次团聚时却是两眼泪汪汪，不识眼前人，徒留一句"I don't know you from Adam."这句话的字面意思是我从亚当开始就不认识你了，那么可以引申解释为"我压根儿不认识你"。

⭐ **实景链接**

A：Your face reminds me of Thomas. 你的脸使我想起了托马斯。

B：Who is Thomas? 谁是托马斯？

A：Don't you remember? 你不记得了吗？

B：Come on, **I don't know him from Adam**. 拜托，我和他素不相识。

拓展特色句

1. The Second World War burst out in 1939. 第二次世界大战于1939年爆发了。

2. Japan was in alliance with Germany and Italy during the Second World War. 第二次世界大战时，日本和德国、意大利结盟。

3. They destroyed a large amount of cultural relics during the period of the Second World War. 在第二次世界大战期间，他们摧毁了大量的文物。

"聊" 英国特色文化

A：You are reading all the time. It seems that you like reading.

B：Yes. And I prefer historical books.

A：Don't you think they are boring? I think it's hard to understand.

B：They are a little complicated but I can have some fun to read them.

A：What is this book about?

B：It's about World War II.

A：A famous theme.

B：Yes. No one likes wars.

A：Do you think Britain got profits from it?

B：I don't think so. World War II confirmed that Britain was no longer the great power. And after World

A：你总是在看书。似乎你喜欢阅读。

B：是的。而且我喜欢这些历史书。

A：你不认为无聊吗？我觉得很难读懂。

B：是有一点复杂。但我读的时候会有一些乐趣。

A：这本书是关于什么的？

B：关于第二次世界大战。

A：是个著名的题材。

B：是啊。没有人喜欢战争。

A：你认为英国从中获利了吗？

B：我认为没有。第二次世界大战证实了英国已经不再是曾经的强国。而且第二次世界大战后，英国再也无法控制它的殖民地了。

A：嗯，我也是这么认为的。

War II, the United Kingdom could no longer keep control of its colonies.

A： Well, I have the same idea.

"问" 英国特色文化

第二次世界大战中英国的作用？

首先，英国海军对纳粹德国的全面封锁，利用其驱逐舰和巡洋舰巡航以及遍布世界的殖民地构成了一个严密的封锁网。其次，英国军队是地面进攻主力之一，虽然英国陆军的兵力动员不如前苏联和美国，但就其兵力来说仍是盟军老四。然后，英国的海军打击纳粹海上力量。还有英国对第二次世界大战的物资支援、保护航运线等。

阅读笔记

阅读笔记

图书在版编目（CIP）数据

每天聊点英国文化：一本书读懂英国 / 金利主
编.北京：化学工业出版社，2014.6（2025.10重印）
ISBN 978-7-122-20379-3

Ⅰ.①每… Ⅱ.①金… Ⅲ.①英语-口语 ②文化-概
况-英国 Ⅳ.①H319.9 ②G156.1

中国版本图书馆CIP数据核字（2014）第072324号

责任编辑：马　骄　　　　　　　　　装帧设计：尹琳琳
责任校对：陈　静

出版发行：化学工业出版社（北京市东城区青年湖南街13号　邮政编码
100011）印　　装：盛大（天津）印刷有限公司
710mm×1000mm　1/16　印张25　字数400千字
2025年10月北京第1版第9次印刷

购书咨询：010-64518888
售后服务：010-64518899
网　　　址：http://www.cip.com.cn
凡购买本书，如有缺损质量问题，本社销售中心负责调换。

定　　价：58.00元　　　　　　　　　版权所有　违者必究